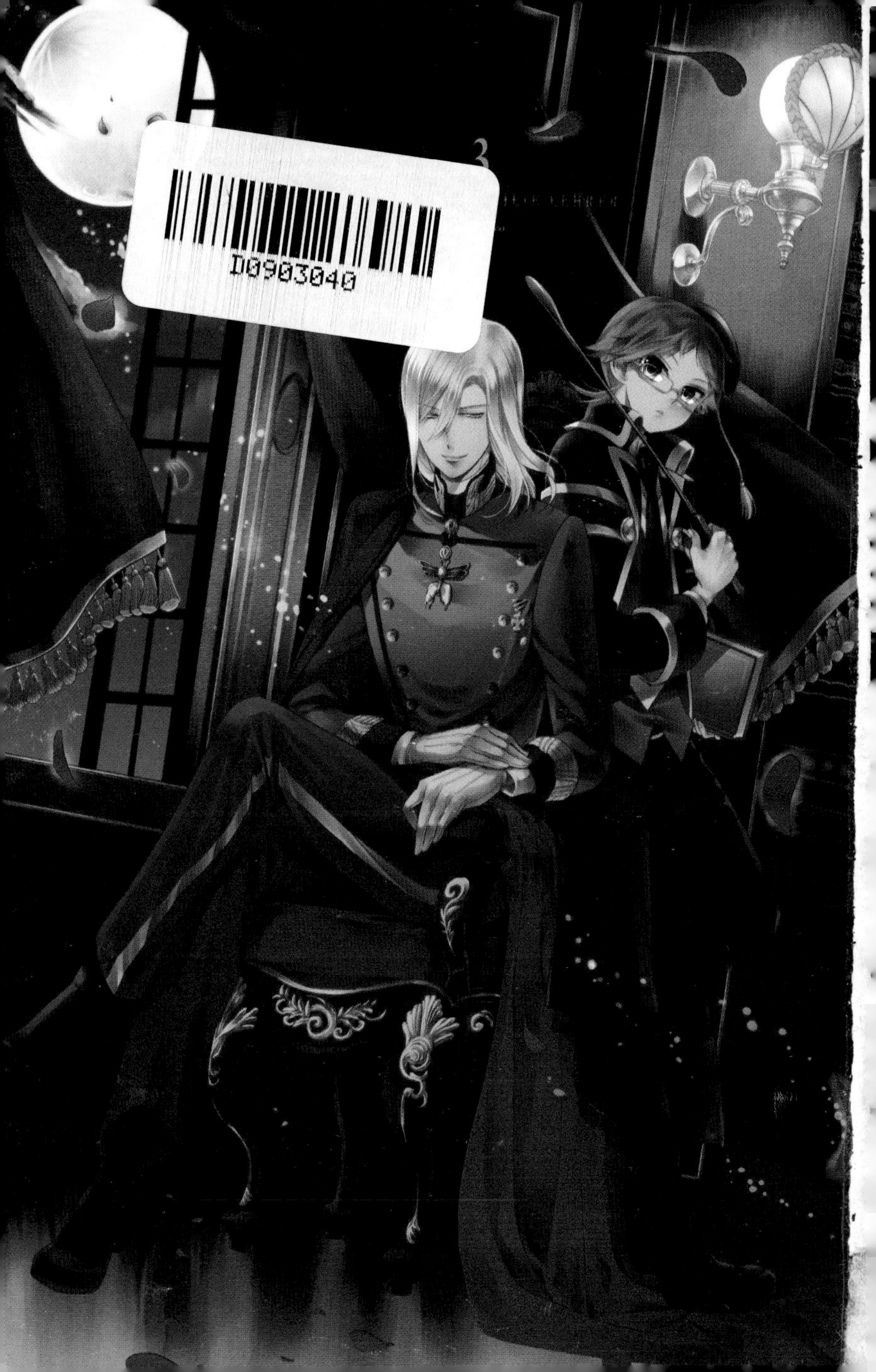

KÖNIGLICHE FAMILIENLEHRER

CONTENTS

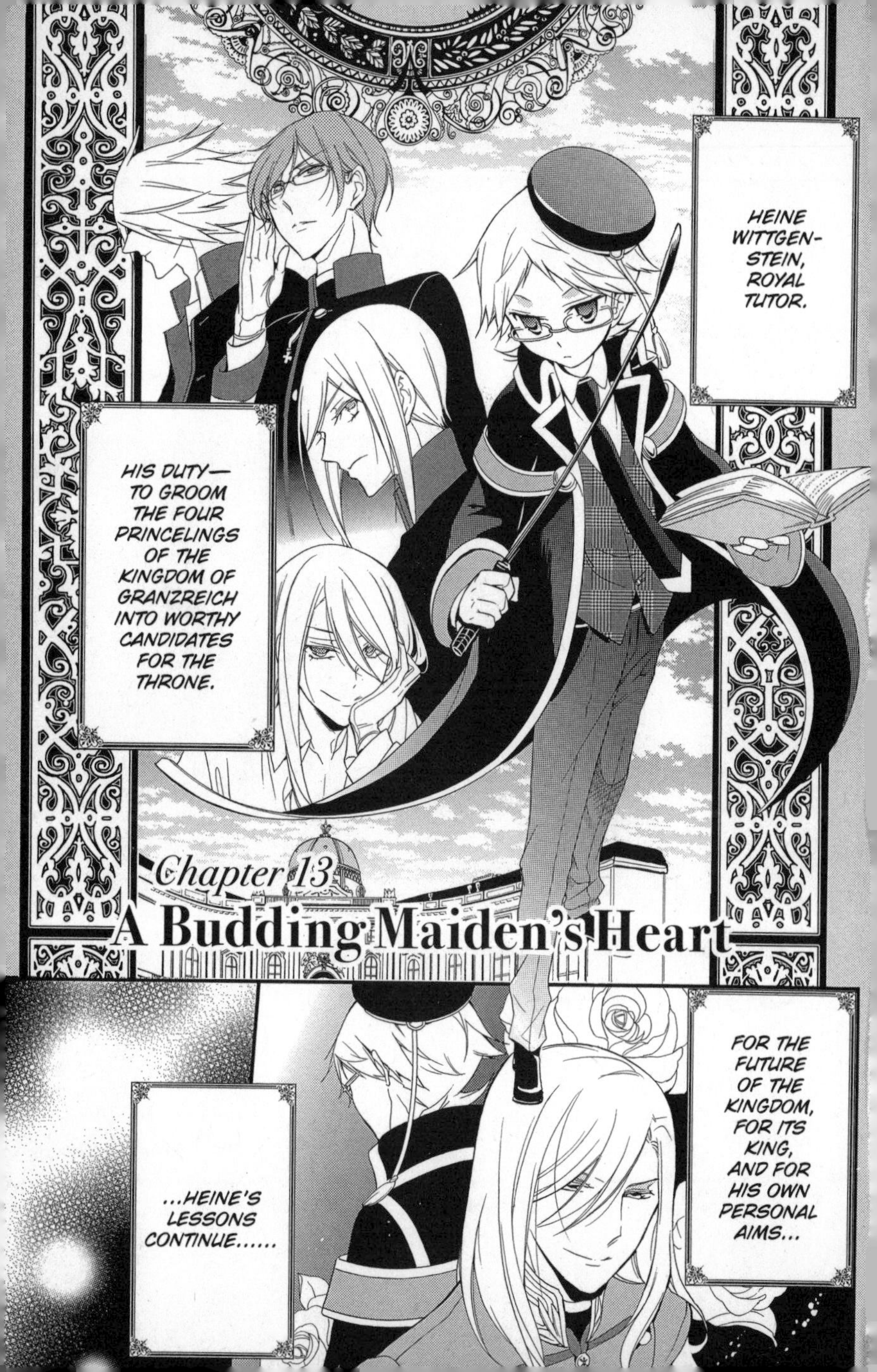
HEINE WITTGENSTEIN, ROYAL TUTOR.
HIS DUTY—TO GROOM THE FOUR PRINCELINGS OF THE KINGDOM OF GRANZREICH INTO WORTHY CANDIDATES FOR THE THRONE.
Chapter 13
A Budding Maiden's Heart
FOR THE FUTURE OF THE KINGDOM, FOR ITS KING, AND FOR HIS OWN PERSONAL AIMS...
...HEINE'S LESSONS CONTINUE......

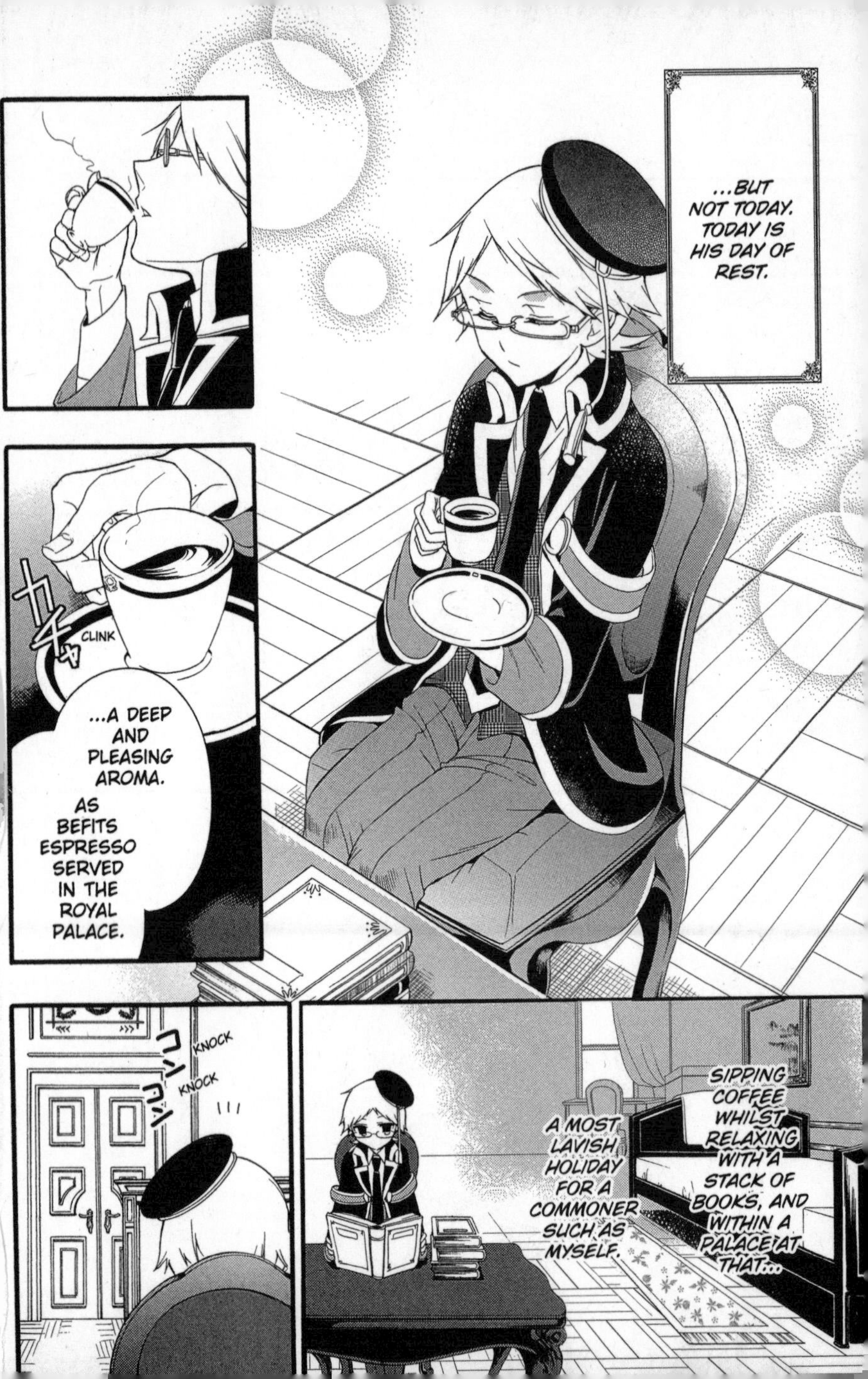
...BUT NOT TODAY. TODAY IS HIS DAY OF REST.
CLINK
...A DEEP AND PLEASING AROMA.
AS BEFITS ESPRESSO SERVED IN THE ROYAL PALACE.
SIPPING COFFEE WHILST RELAXING WITH A STACK OF BOOKS, AND WITHIN A PALACE AT THAT...
A MOST LAVISH HOLIDAY FOR A COMMONER SUCH AS MYSELF.
KNOCK
KNOCK

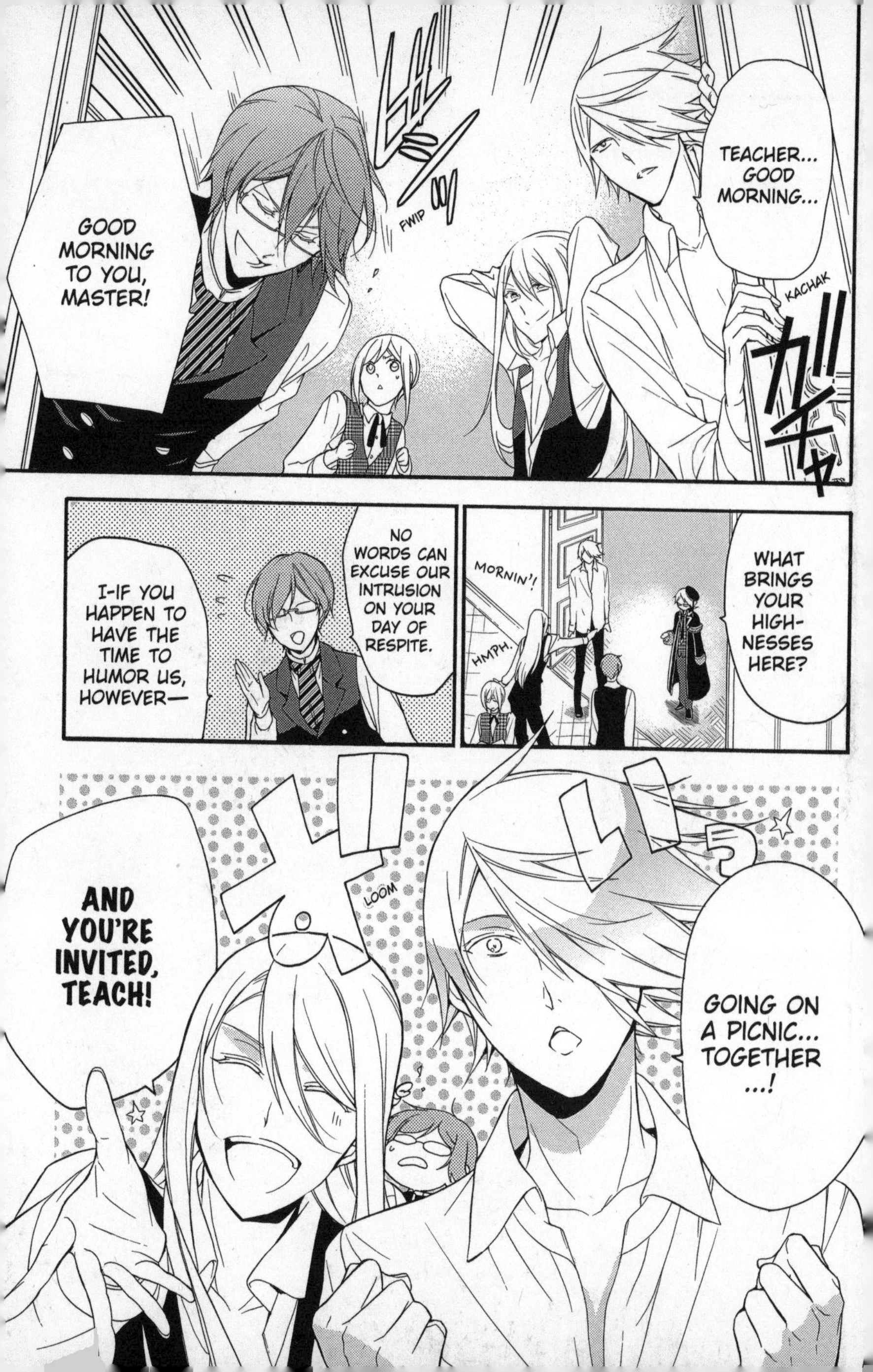
TEACHER... GOOD MORNING...
KACHAK
ガチャ
FWIP
GOOD MORNING TO YOU, MASTER!
WHAT BRINGS YOUR HIGHNESSES HERE?
MORNIN'!
HMPH.
NO WORDS CAN EXCUSE OUR INTRUSION ON YOUR DAY OF RESPITE.
I-IF YOU HAPPEN TO HAVE THE TIME TO HUMOR US, HOWEVER—
GOING ON A PICNIC... TOGETHER ...!
LOOM
AND YOU'RE INVITED, TEACH!

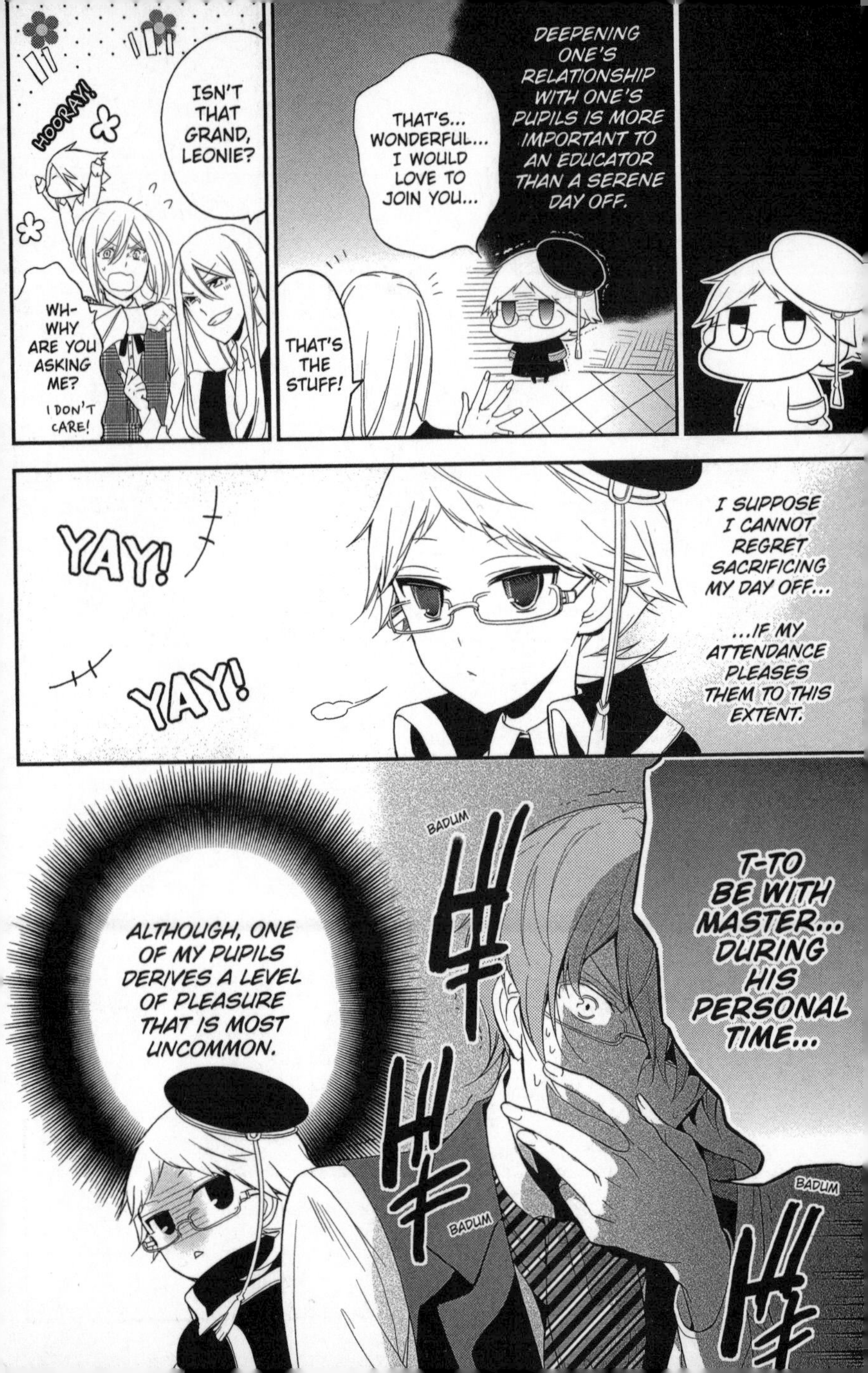
DEEPENING ONE'S RELATIONSHIP WITH ONE'S PUPILS IS MORE IMPORTANT TO AN EDUCATOR THAN A SERENE DAY OFF.
THAT'S... WONDERFUL... I WOULD LOVE TO JOIN YOU...
THAT'S THE STUFF!
ISN'T THAT GRAND, LEONIE?
HOORAY!
WH-WHY ARE YOU ASKING ME?
I DON'T CARE!
I SUPPOSE I CANNOT REGRET SACRIFICING MY DAY OFF...
...IF MY ATTENDANCE PLEASES THEM TO THIS EXTENT.
YAY!
YAY!
T-TO BE WITH MASTER... DURING HIS PERSONAL TIME...
BADUM
BADUM
BADUM
ALTHOUGH, ONE OF MY PUPILS DERIVES A LEVEL OF PLEASURE THAT IS MOST UNCOMMON.

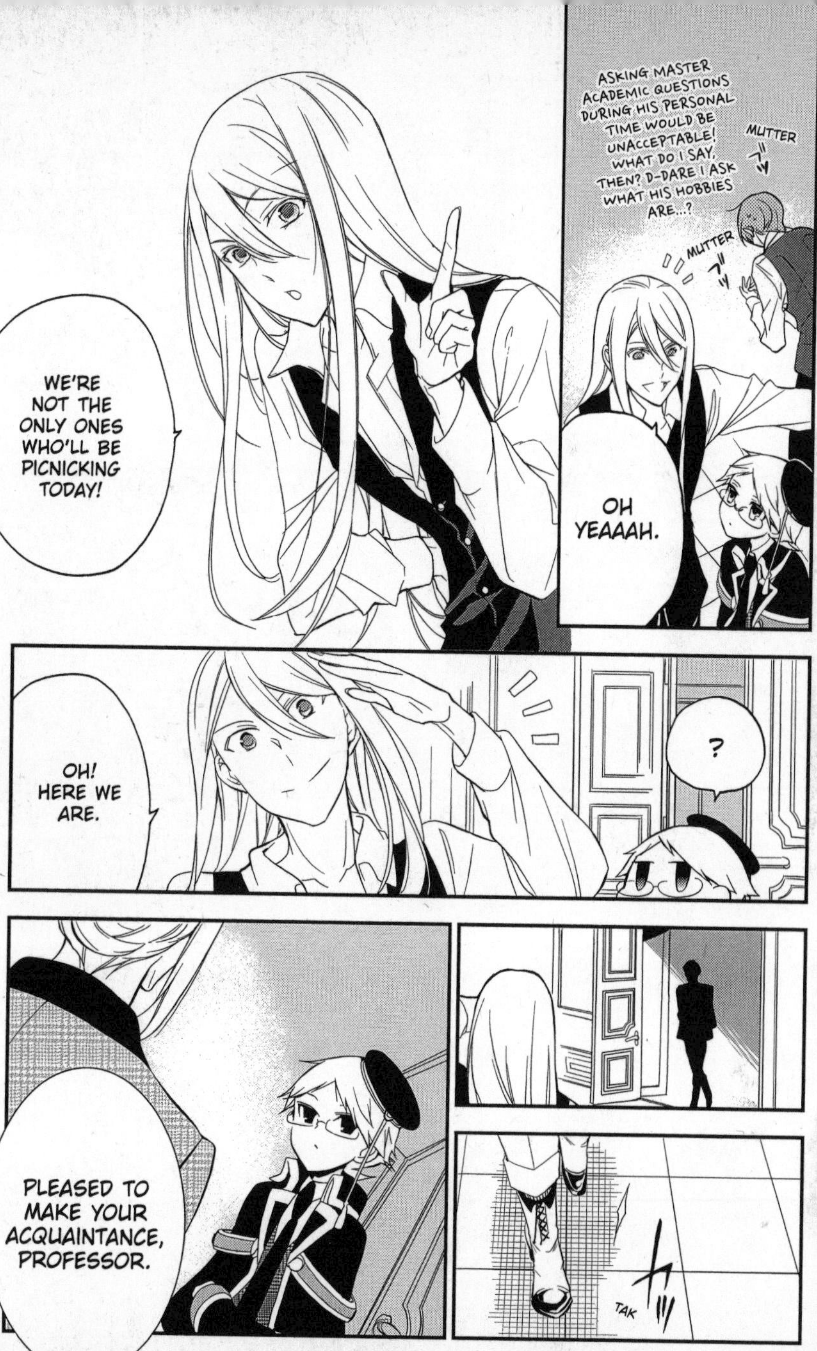
ASKING MASTER ACADEMIC QUESTIONS DURING HIS PERSONAL TIME WOULD BE UNACCEPTABLE! WHAT DO I SAY, THEN? D-DARE I ASK WHAT HIS HOBBIES ARE...?
MUTTER
MUTTER
OH YEAAAH.
WE'RE NOT THE ONLY ONES WHO'LL BE PICNICKING TODAY!
?
OH! HERE WE ARE.
TAK
PLEASED TO MAKE YOUR ACQUAINTANCE, PROFESSOR.

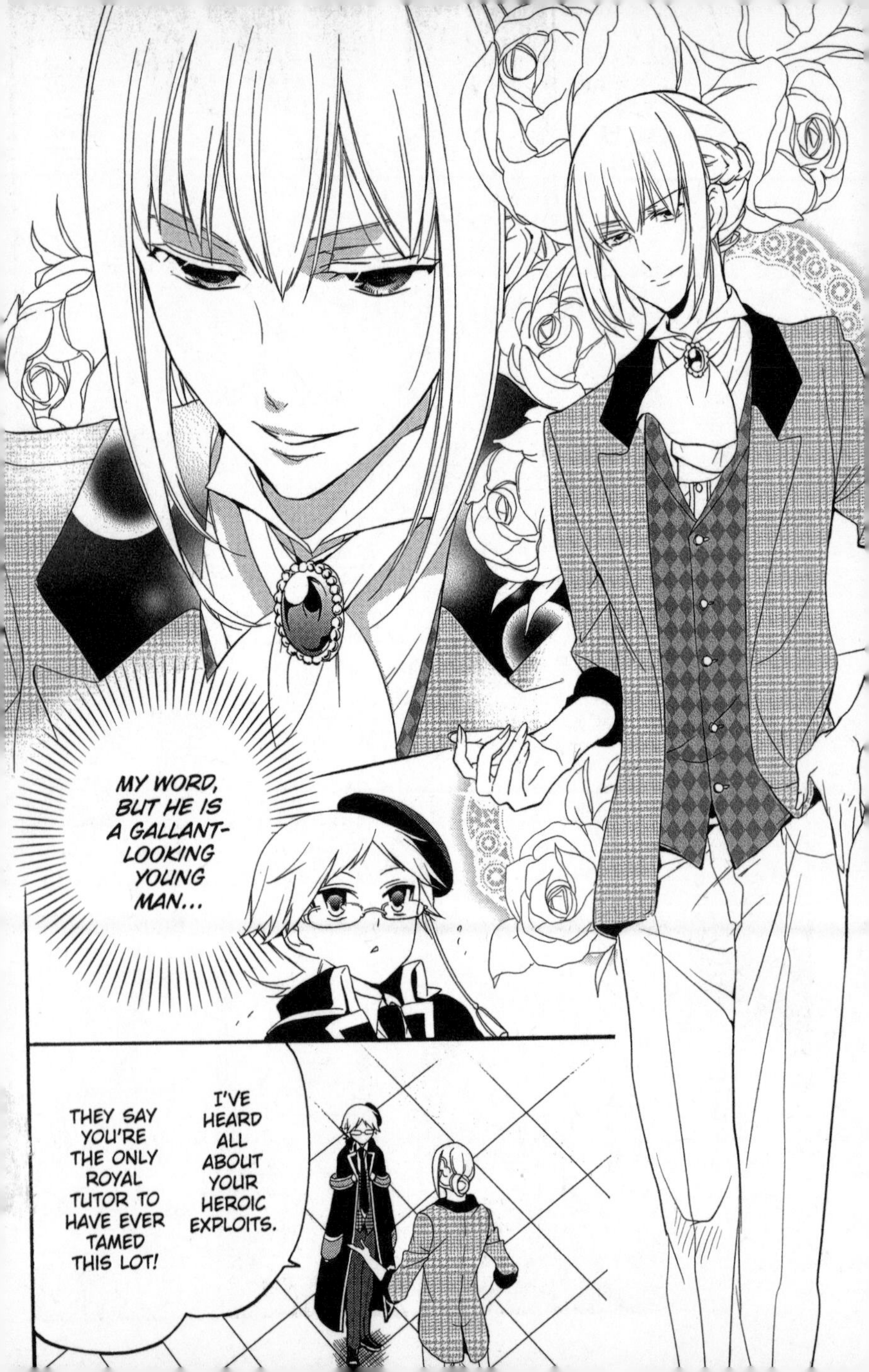
MY WORD, BUT HE IS A GALLANT-LOOKING YOUNG MAN...
I'VE HEARD ALL ABOUT YOUR HEROIC EXPLOITS.
THEY SAY YOU'RE THE ONLY ROYAL TUTOR TO HAVE EVER TAMED THIS LOT!

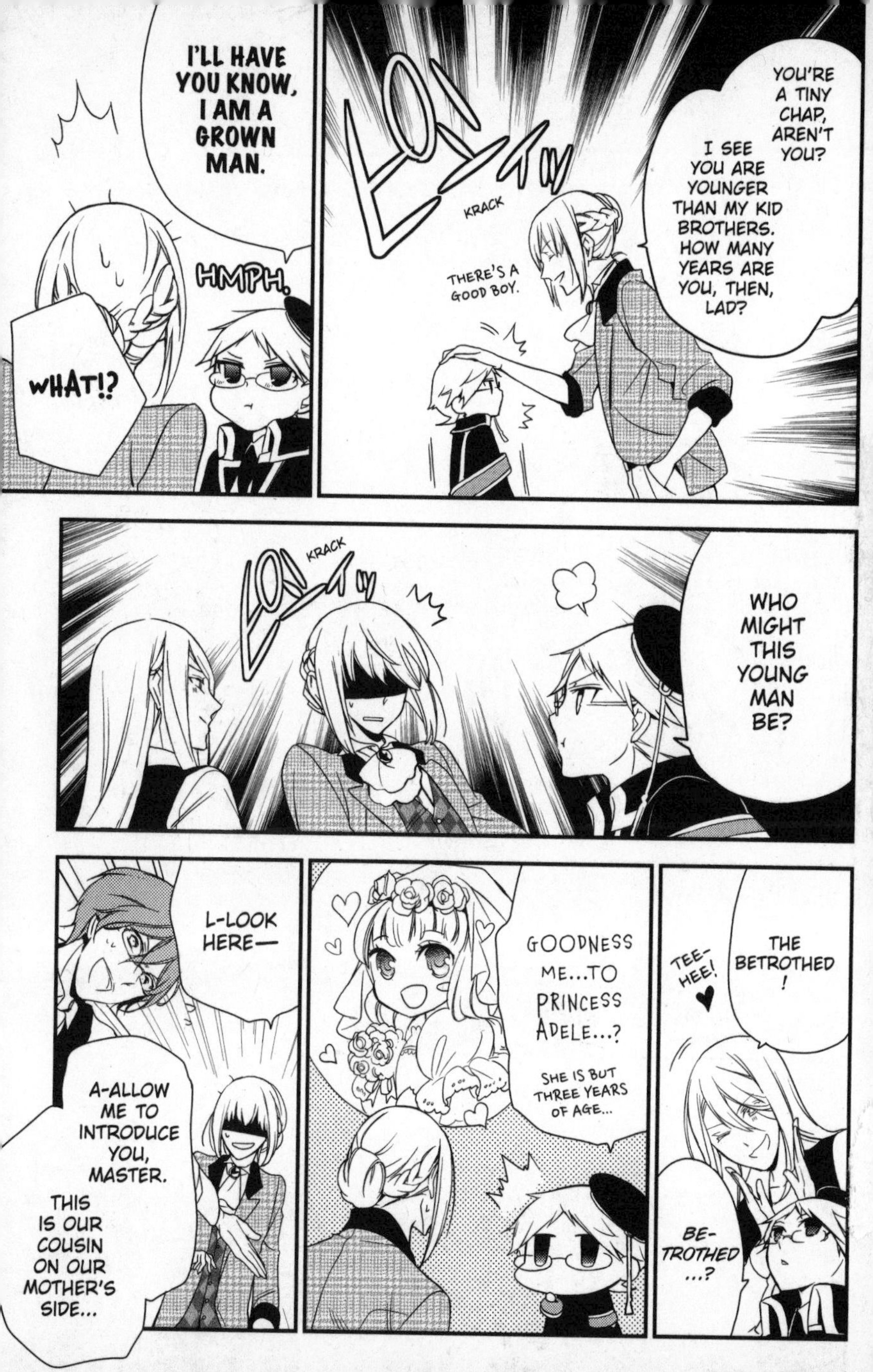
YOU'RE A TINY CHAP, AREN'T YOU?
I SEE YOU ARE YOUNGER THAN MY KID BROTHERS. HOW MANY YEARS ARE YOU, THEN, LAD?
KRACK
THERE'S A GOOD BOY.
I'LL HAVE YOU KNOW, I AM A GROWN MAN.
HMPH.
WHAT!?
WHO MIGHT THIS YOUNG MAN BE?
KRACK
THE BETROTHED!
TEE-HEE!
BE-TROTHED...?
GOODNESS ME...TO PRINCESS ADELE...?
SHE IS BUT THREE YEARS OF AGE...
L-LOOK HERE—
A-ALLOW ME TO INTRODUCE YOU, MASTER.
THIS IS OUR COUSIN ON OUR MOTHER'S SIDE...

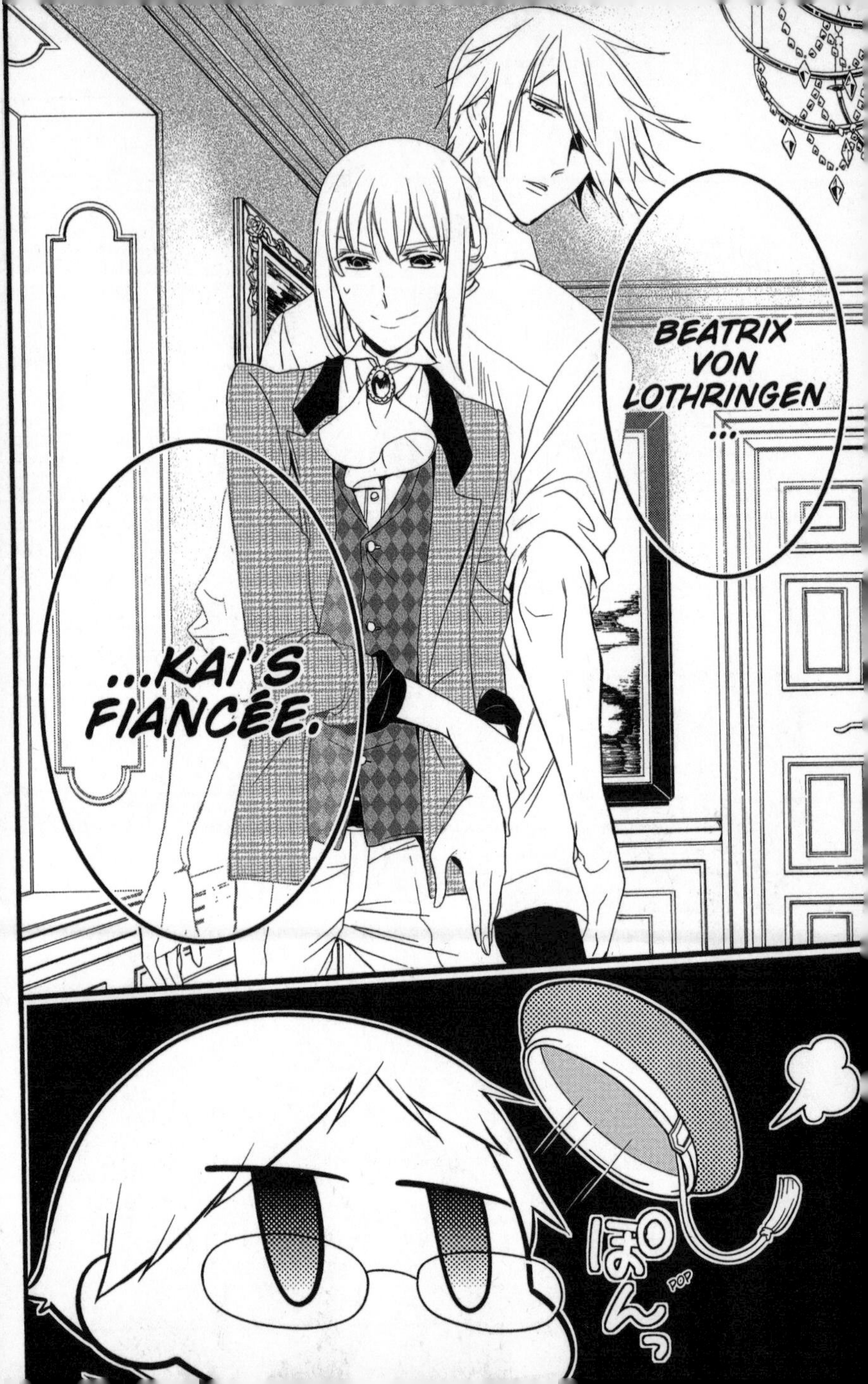
BEATRIX VON LOTHRINGEN ...
...KAI'S FIANCÉE.
ぽんっ
POP

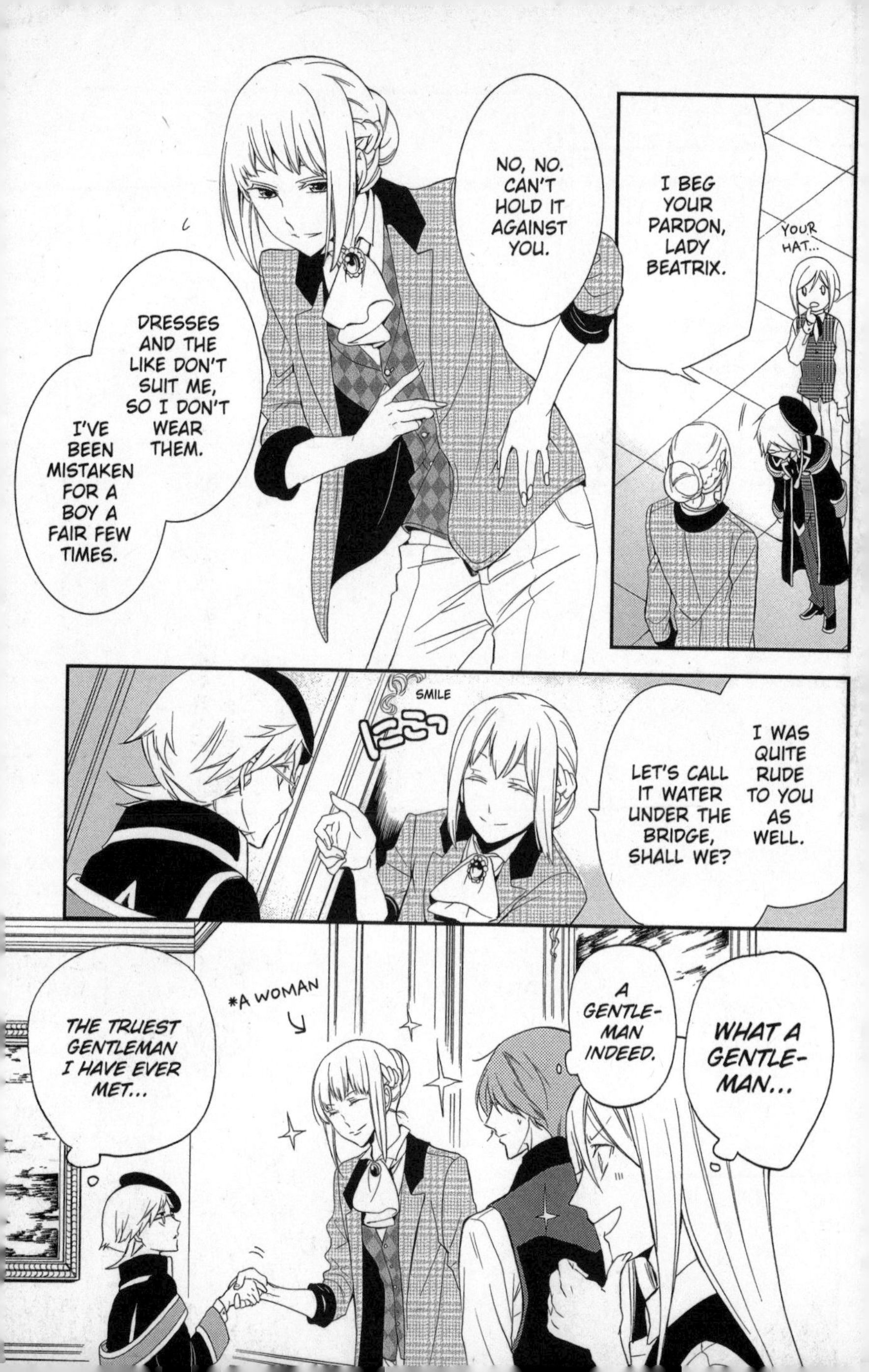
I BEG YOUR PARDON, LADY BEATRIX.
YOUR HAT...
NO, NO. CAN'T HOLD IT AGAINST YOU.
DRESSES AND THE LIKE DON'T SUIT ME, SO I DON'T WEAR THEM.
I'VE BEEN MISTAKEN FOR A BOY A FAIR FEW TIMES.
I WAS QUITE RUDE TO YOU AS WELL.
LET'S CALL IT WATER UNDER THE BRIDGE, SHALL WE?
にこっ
SMILE
WHAT A GENTLEMAN...
A GENTLEMAN INDEED.
*A WOMAN
THE TRUEST GENTLEMAN I HAVE EVER MET...

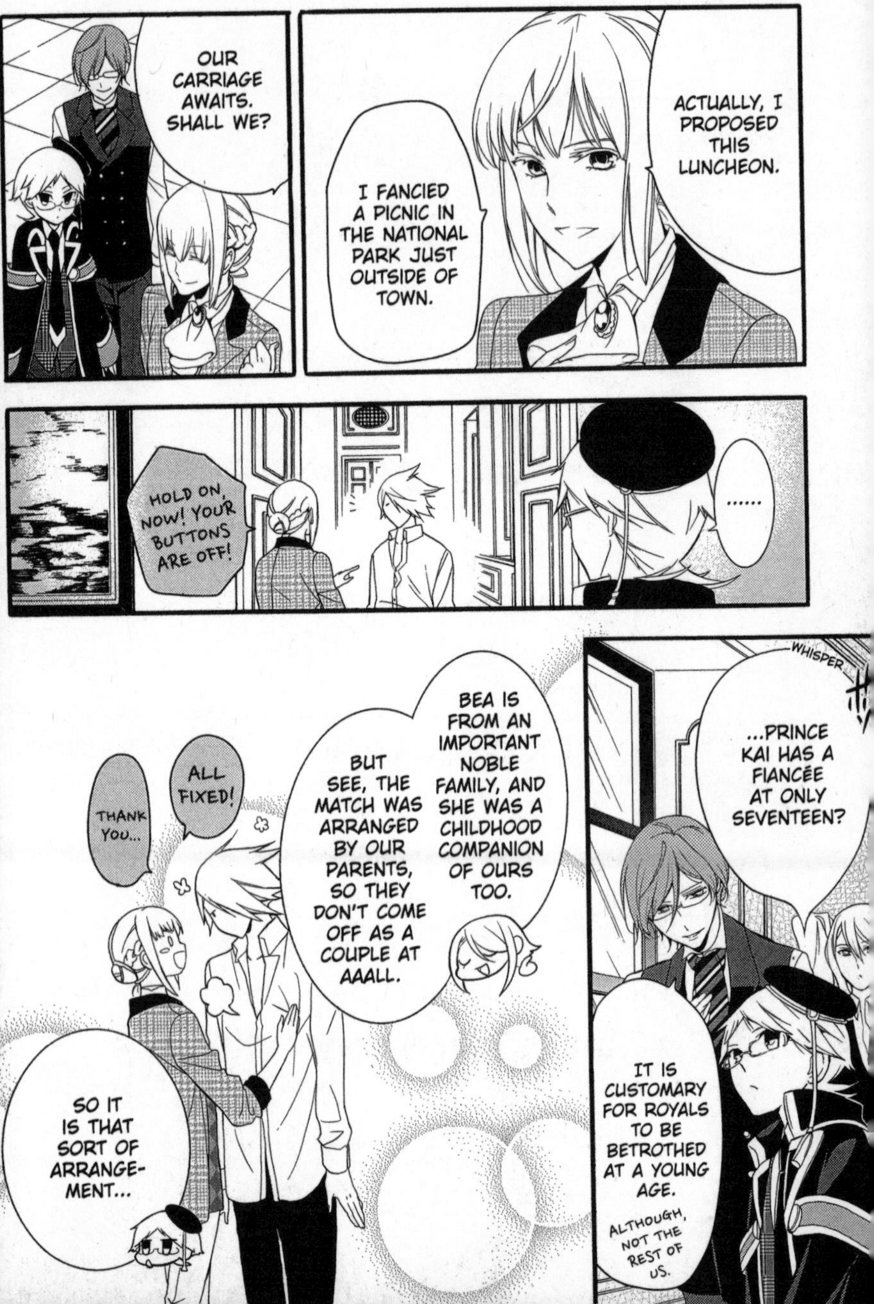
ACTUALLY, I PROPOSED THIS LUNCHEON.
I FANCIED A PICNIC IN THE NATIONAL PARK JUST OUTSIDE OF TOWN.
OUR CARRIAGE AWAITS. SHALL WE?
......
HOLD ON, NOW! YOUR BUTTONS ARE OFF!
WHISPER
...PRINCE KAI HAS A FIANCÉE AT ONLY SEVENTEEN?
IT IS CUSTOMARY FOR ROYALS TO BE BETROTHED AT A YOUNG AGE.
ALTHOUGH, NOT THE REST OF US.
BEA IS FROM AN IMPORTANT NOBLE FAMILY, AND SHE WAS A CHILDHOOD COMPANION OF OURS TOO.
BUT SEE, THE MATCH WAS ARRANGED BY OUR PARENTS, SO THEY DON'T COME OFF AS A COUPLE AT AAALL.
ALL FIXED!
THANK YOU...
SO IT IS THAT SORT OF ARRANGE-MENT...

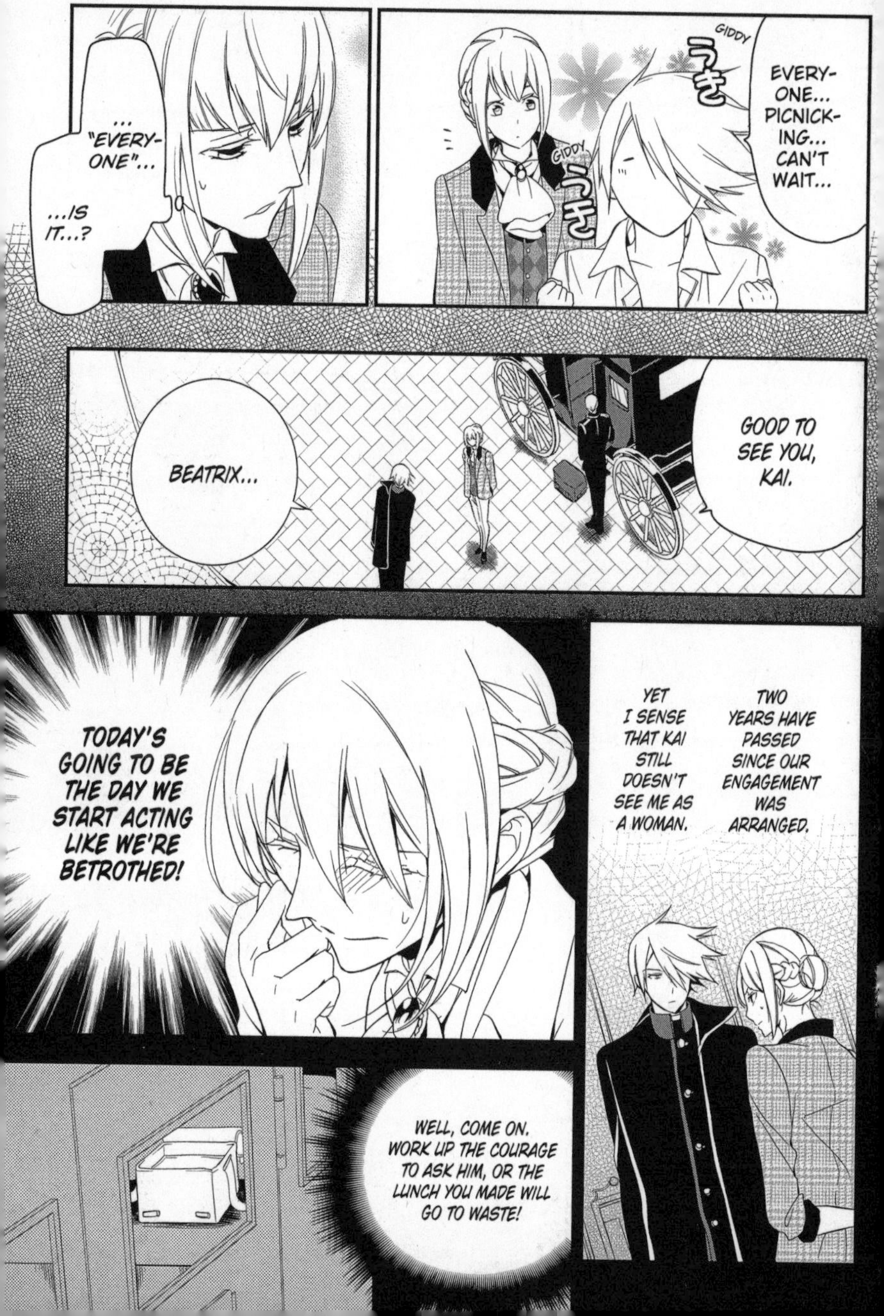
GIDDY
うき
EVERY-ONE... PICNICK-ING... CAN'T WAIT...
GIDDY
うき
... "EVERY-ONE"...
...IS IT...?
GOOD TO SEE YOU, KAI.
BEATRIX...
TWO YEARS HAVE PASSED SINCE OUR ENGAGEMENT WAS ARRANGED.
YET I SENSE THAT KAI STILL DOESN'T SEE ME AS A WOMAN.
TODAY'S GOING TO BE THE DAY WE START ACTING LIKE WE'RE BETROTHED!
WELL, COME ON. WORK UP THE COURAGE TO ASK HIM, OR THE LUNCH YOU MADE WILL GO TO WASTE!

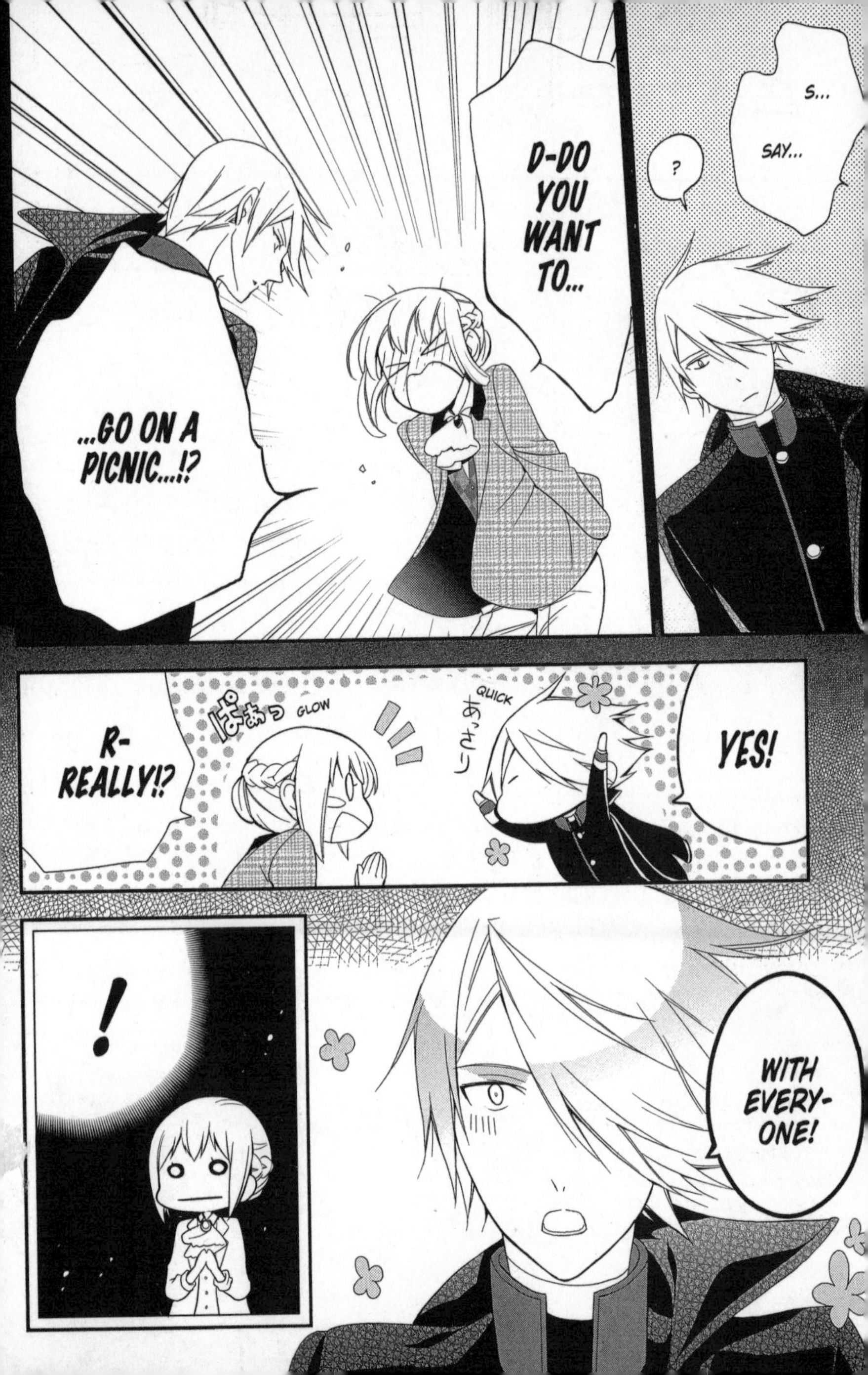
S...
SAY...
?
D-DO YOU WANT TO...
...GO ON A PICNIC...!?
YES!
あっさり QUICK
ぱあっ GLOW
R-REALLY!?
WITH EVERY-ONE!
!

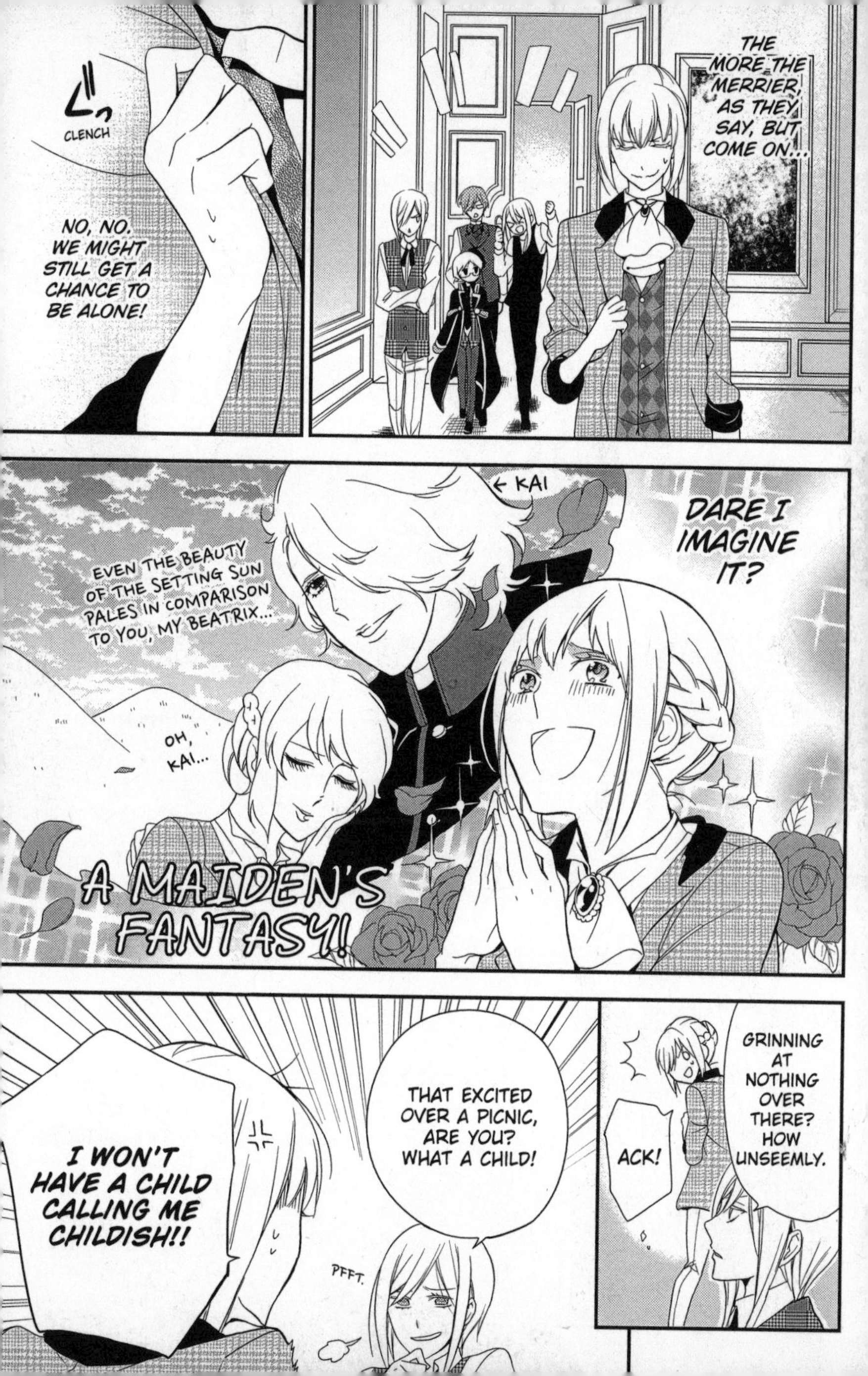
THE MORE THE MERRIER, AS THEY SAY, BUT COME ON...
CLENCH
NO, NO. WE MIGHT STILL GET A CHANCE TO BE ALONE!
DARE I IMAGINE IT?
← KAI
EVEN THE BEAUTY OF THE SETTING SUN PALES IN COMPARISON TO YOU, MY BEATRIX...
OH, KAI...
A MAIDEN'S FANTASY!
GRINNING AT NOTHING OVER THERE? HOW UNSEEMLY.
ACK!
THAT EXCITED OVER A PICNIC, ARE YOU? WHAT A CHILD!
PFFT.
I WON'T HAVE A CHILD CALLING ME CHILDISH!!

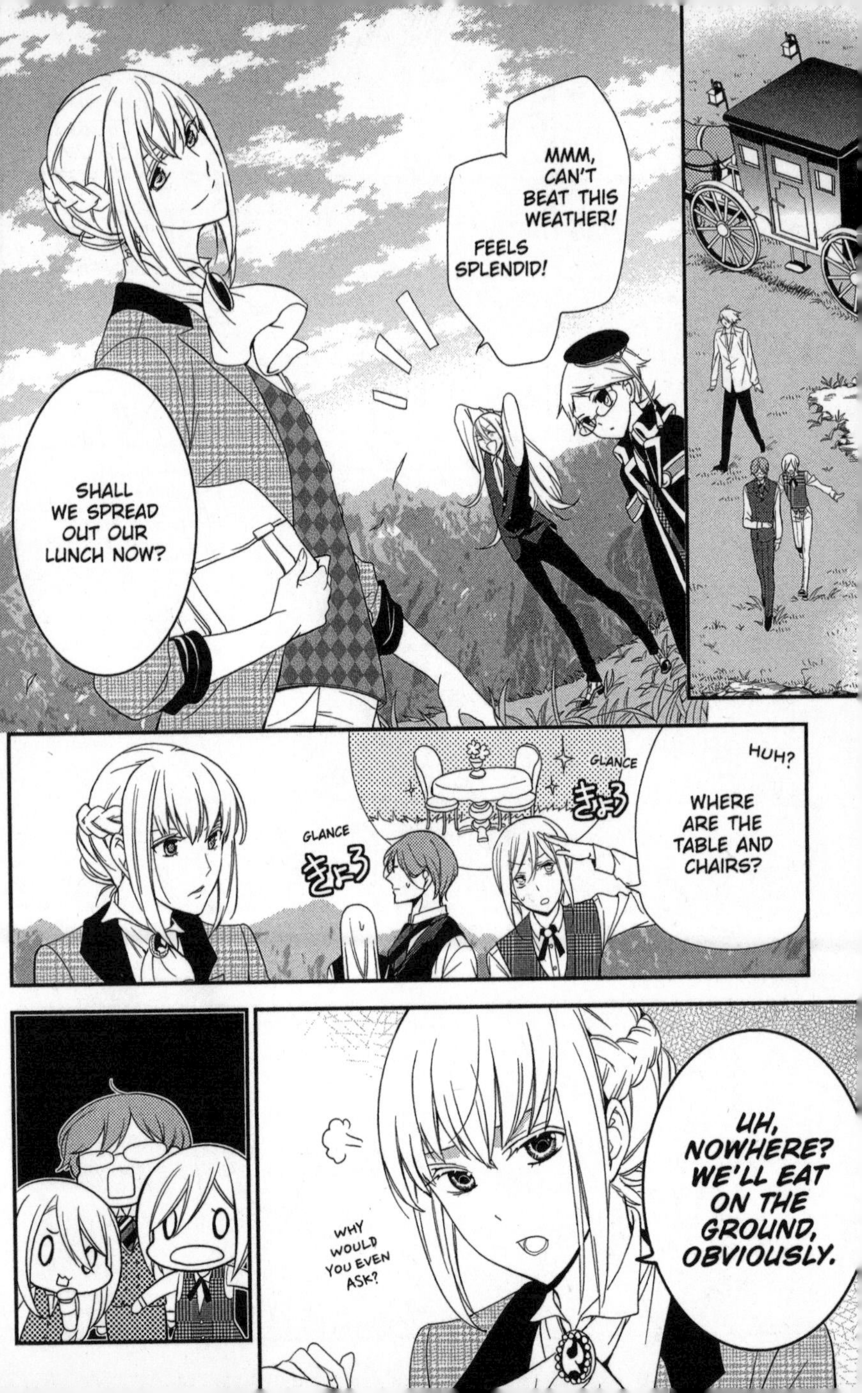
MMM, CAN'T BEAT THIS WEATHER!
FEELS SPLENDID!
SHALL WE SPREAD OUT OUR LUNCH NOW?
HUH?
WHERE ARE THE TABLE AND CHAIRS?
GLANCE
きょろ
GLANCE
きょろ
UH, NOWHERE? WE'LL EAT ON THE GROUND, OBVIOUSLY.
WHY WOULD YOU EVEN ASK?

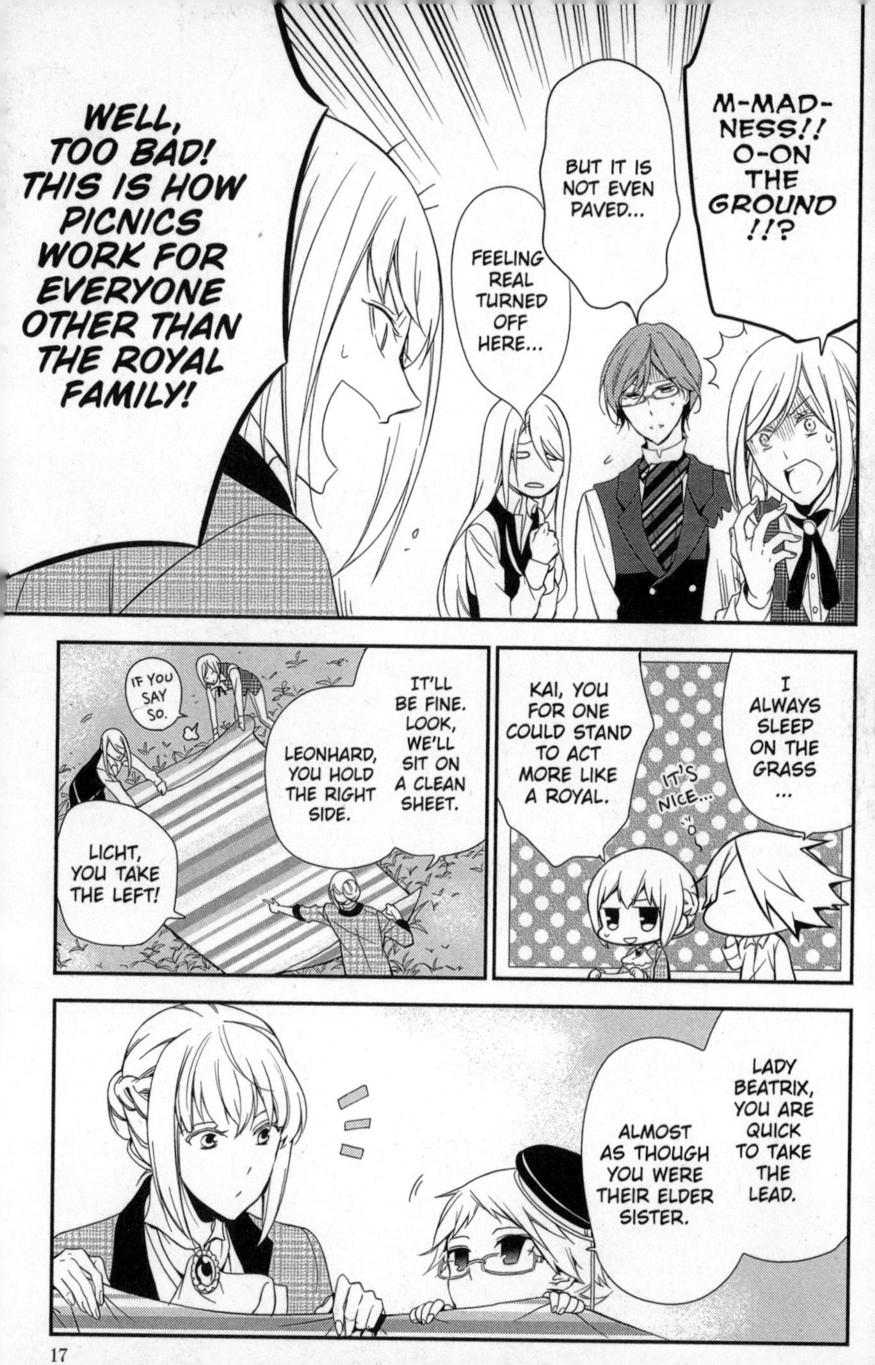
M-MADNESS!! O-ON THE GROUND!!?
BUT IT IS NOT EVEN PAVED...
FEELING REAL TURNED OFF HERE...
WELL, TOO BAD! THIS IS HOW PICNICS WORK FOR EVERYONE OTHER THAN THE ROYAL FAMILY!
I ALWAYS SLEEP ON THE GRASS ...
IT'S NICE...
KAI, YOU FOR ONE COULD STAND TO ACT MORE LIKE A ROYAL.
IT'LL BE FINE. LOOK, WE'LL SIT ON A CLEAN SHEET.
LEONHARD, YOU HOLD THE RIGHT SIDE.
IF YOU SAY SO.
LICHT, YOU TAKE THE LEFT!
LADY BEATRIX, YOU ARE QUICK TO TAKE THE LEAD.
ALMOST AS THOUGH YOU WERE THEIR ELDER SISTER.

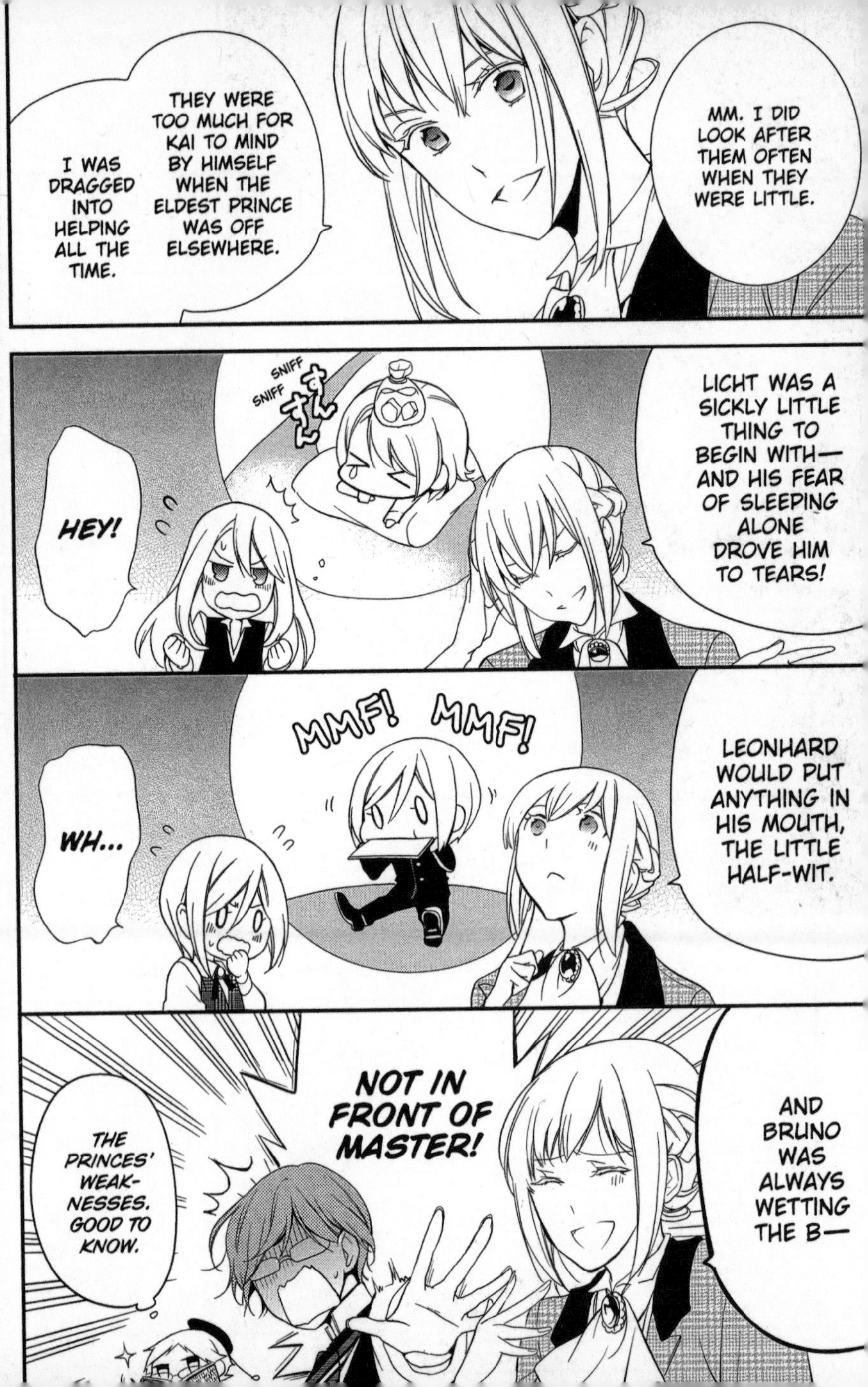
MM. I DID LOOK AFTER THEM OFTEN WHEN THEY WERE LITTLE.
THEY WERE TOO MUCH FOR KAI TO MIND BY HIMSELF WHEN THE ELDEST PRINCE WAS OFF ELSEWHERE.
I WAS DRAGGED INTO HELPING ALL THE TIME.
LICHT WAS A SICKLY LITTLE THING TO BEGIN WITH— AND HIS FEAR OF SLEEPING ALONE DROVE HIM TO TEARS!
すんすん
SNIFF SNIFF
HEY!
LEONHARD WOULD PUT ANYTHING IN HIS MOUTH, THE LITTLE HALF-WIT.
MMF! MMF!
WH...
AND BRUNO WAS ALWAYS WETTING THE B—
NOT IN FRONT OF MASTER!
THE PRINCES' WEAK-NESSES. GOOD TO KNOW.

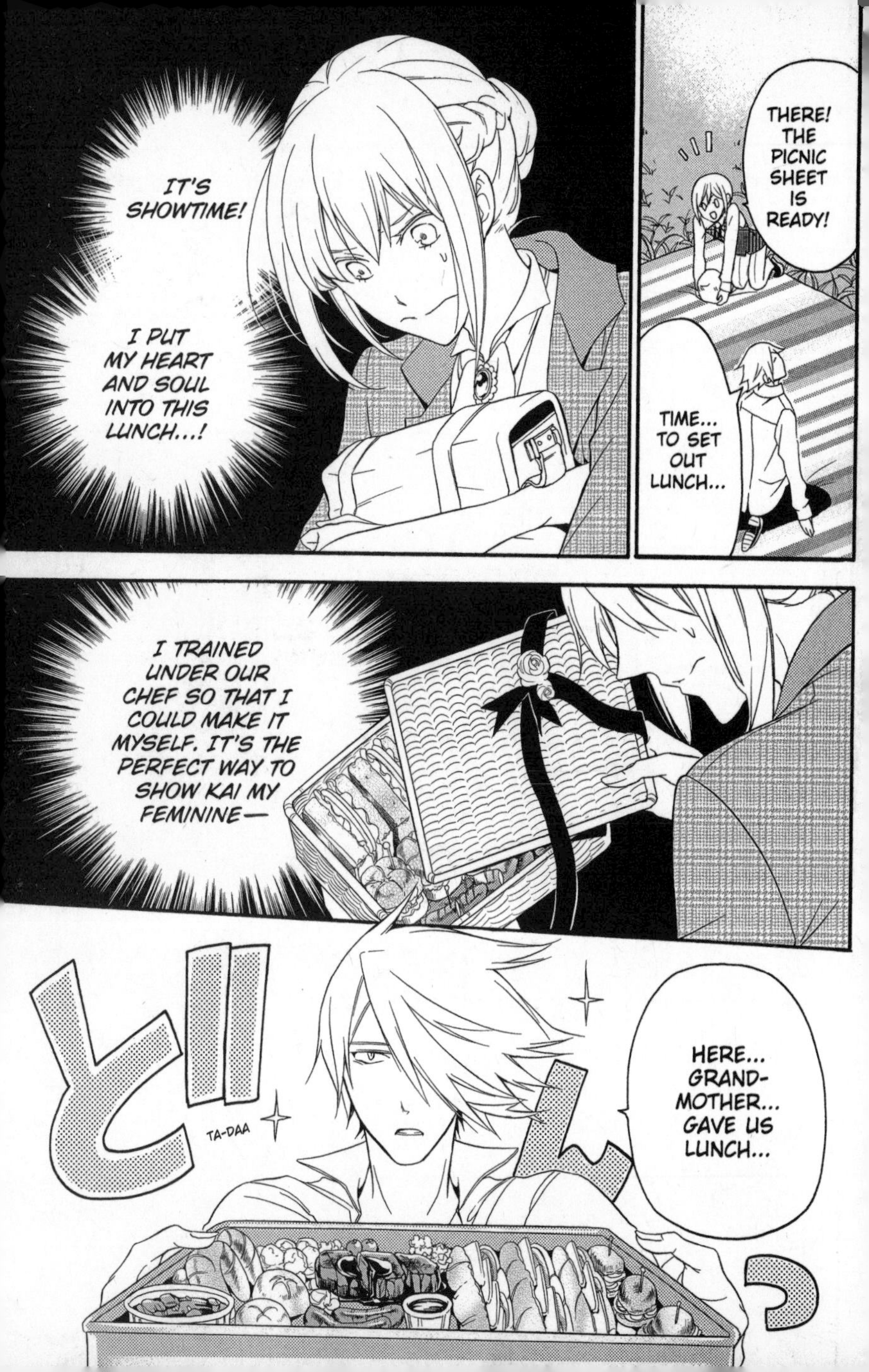
THERE! THE PICNIC SHEET IS READY!
TIME... TO SET OUT LUNCH...
IT'S SHOWTIME!
I PUT MY HEART AND SOUL INTO THIS LUNCH...!
I TRAINED UNDER OUR CHEF SO THAT I COULD MAKE IT MYSELF. IT'S THE PERFECT WAY TO SHOW KAI MY FEMININE—
HERE... GRANDMOTHER... GAVE US LUNCH...
TA-DAA

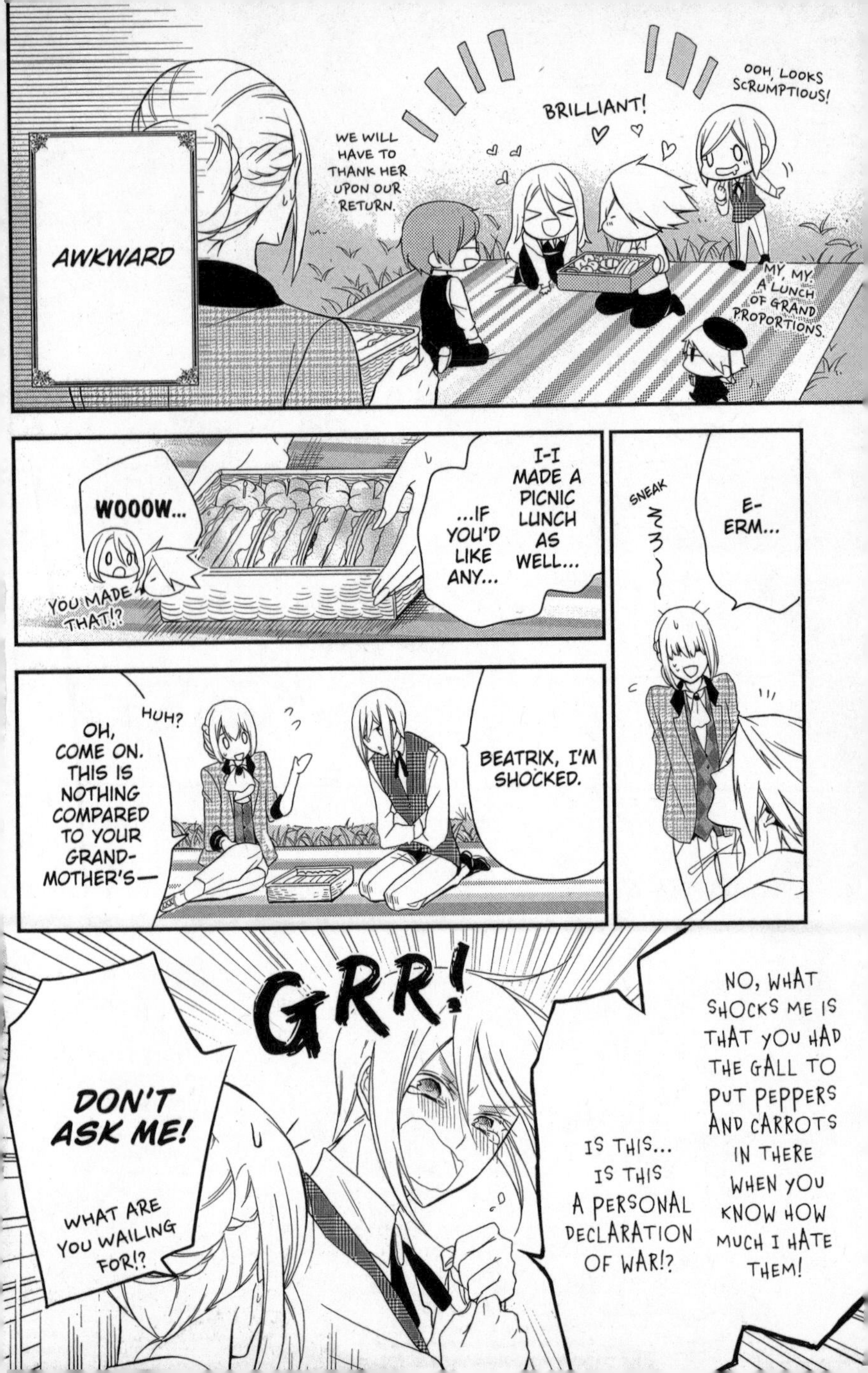
OOH, LOOKS SCRUMPTIOUS!
BRILLIANT!
MY, MY. A LUNCH OF GRAND PROPORTIONS.
WE WILL HAVE TO THANK HER UPON OUR RETURN.
AWKWARD
E-ERM...
SNEAK
I-I MADE A PICNIC LUNCH AS WELL...
...IF YOU'D LIKE ANY...
WOOOW...
YOU MADE THAT!?
BEATRIX, I'M SHOCKED.
HUH?
OH, COME ON. THIS IS NOTHING COMPARED TO YOUR GRANDMOTHER'S—
NO, WHAT SHOCKS ME IS THAT YOU HAD THE GALL TO PUT PEPPERS AND CARROTS IN THERE WHEN YOU KNOW HOW MUCH I HATE THEM!
GRR!
IS THIS... IS THIS A PERSONAL DECLARATION OF WAR!?
DON'T ASK ME!
WHAT ARE YOU WAILING FOR!?

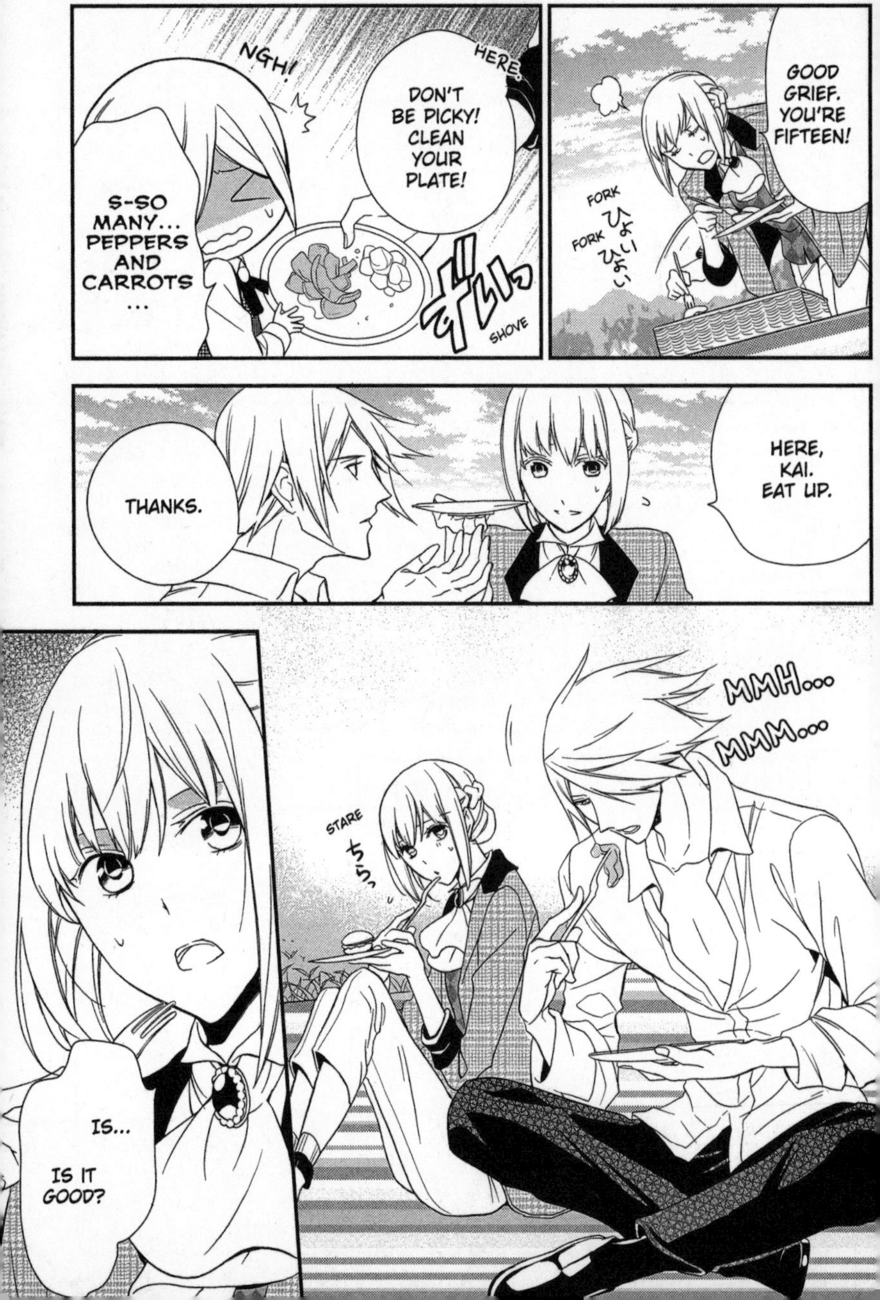
GOOD GRIEF. YOU'RE FIFTEEN!
FORK ひょい
FORK ひょい
HERE.
DON'T BE PICKY! CLEAN YOUR PLATE!
NGH!
S-SO MANY... PEPPERS AND CARROTS...
ずいっ
SHOVE
HERE, KAI. EAT UP.
THANKS.
MMH...
MMM...
STARE ちらっ
IS...
IS IT GOOD?

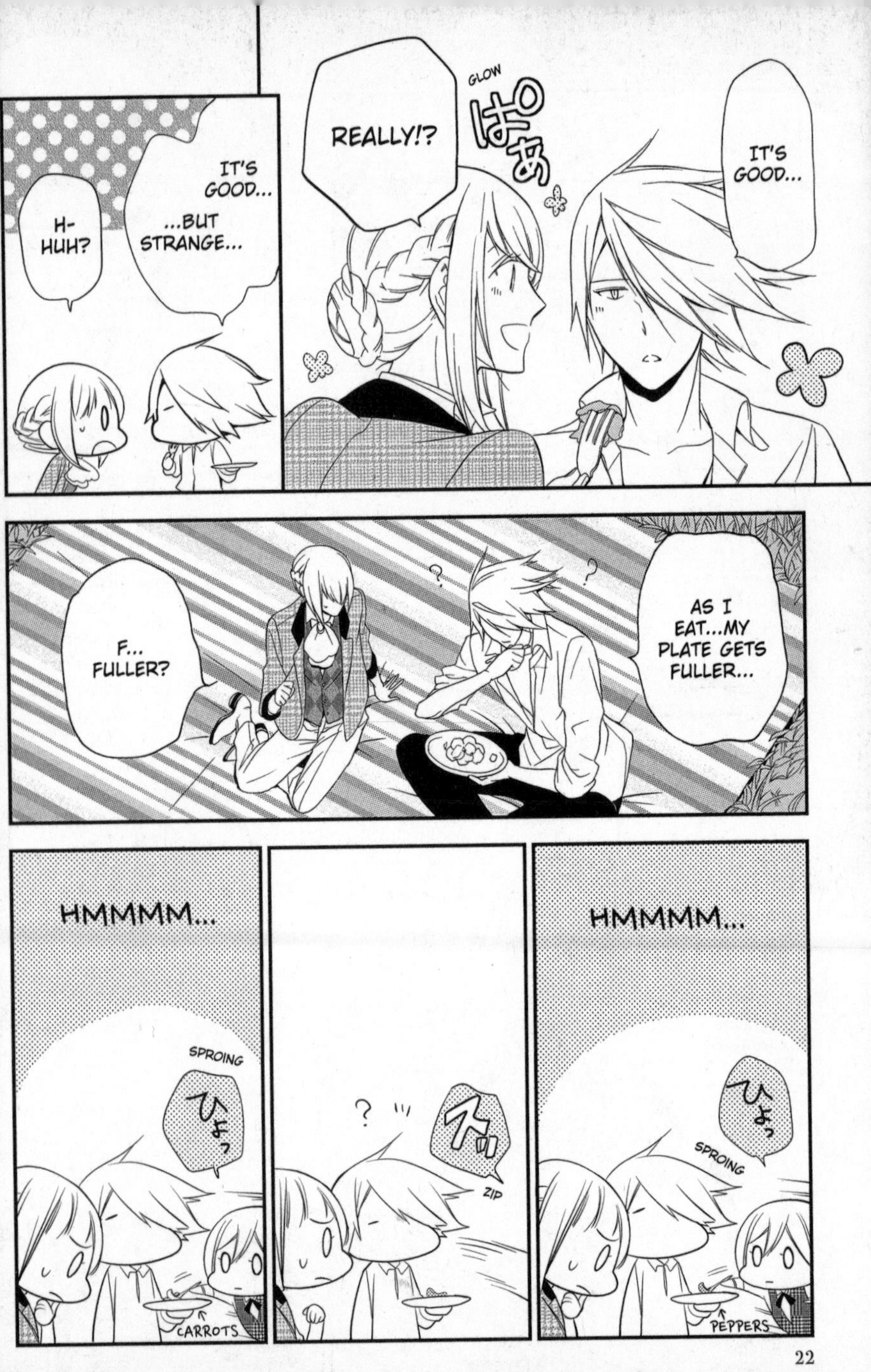
IT'S GOOD...
GLOW
ぱあ
REALLY!?
IT'S GOOD...
...BUT STRANGE...
H-HUH?
AS I EAT...MY PLATE GETS FULLER...
F... FULLER?
HMMMM...
ひょっ
SPROING
PEPPERS
ZIP
HMMMM...
SPROING
ひょっ
CARROTS

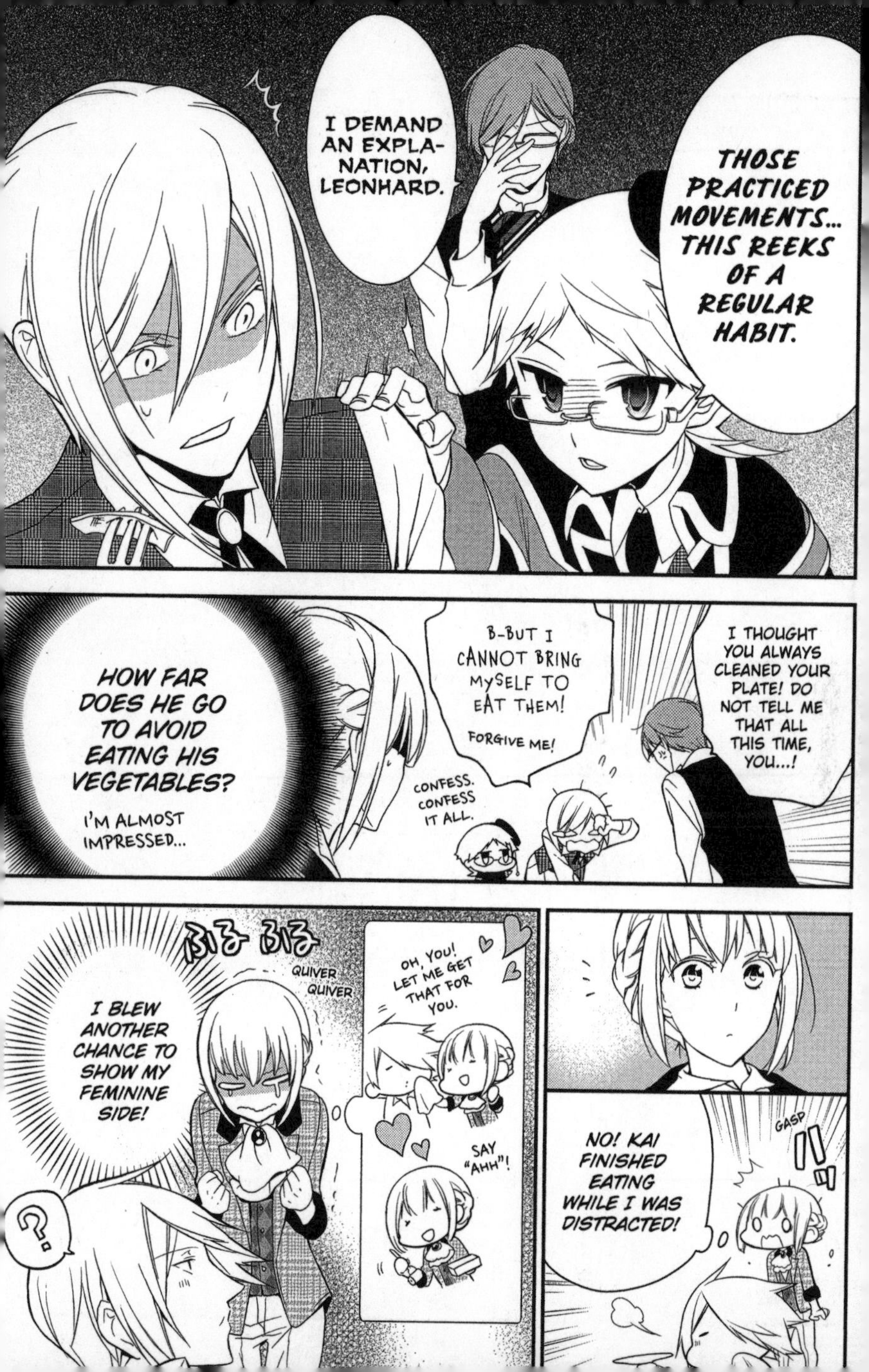
THOSE PRACTICED MOVEMENTS... THIS REEKS OF A REGULAR HABIT.
I DEMAND AN EXPLA-NATION, LEONHARD.
I THOUGHT YOU ALWAYS CLEANED YOUR PLATE! DO NOT TELL ME THAT ALL THIS TIME, YOU...!
B-BUT I CANNOT BRING MYSELF TO EAT THEM!
FORGIVE ME!
CONFESS. CONFESS IT ALL.
HOW FAR DOES HE GO TO AVOID EATING HIS VEGETABLES?
I'M ALMOST IMPRESSED...
GASP
NO! KAI FINISHED EATING WHILE I WAS DISTRACTED!
OH, YOU! LET ME GET THAT FOR YOU.
SAY "AHH"!
ふる ふる
QUIVER QUIVER
I BLEW ANOTHER CHANCE TO SHOW MY FEMININE SIDE!
?

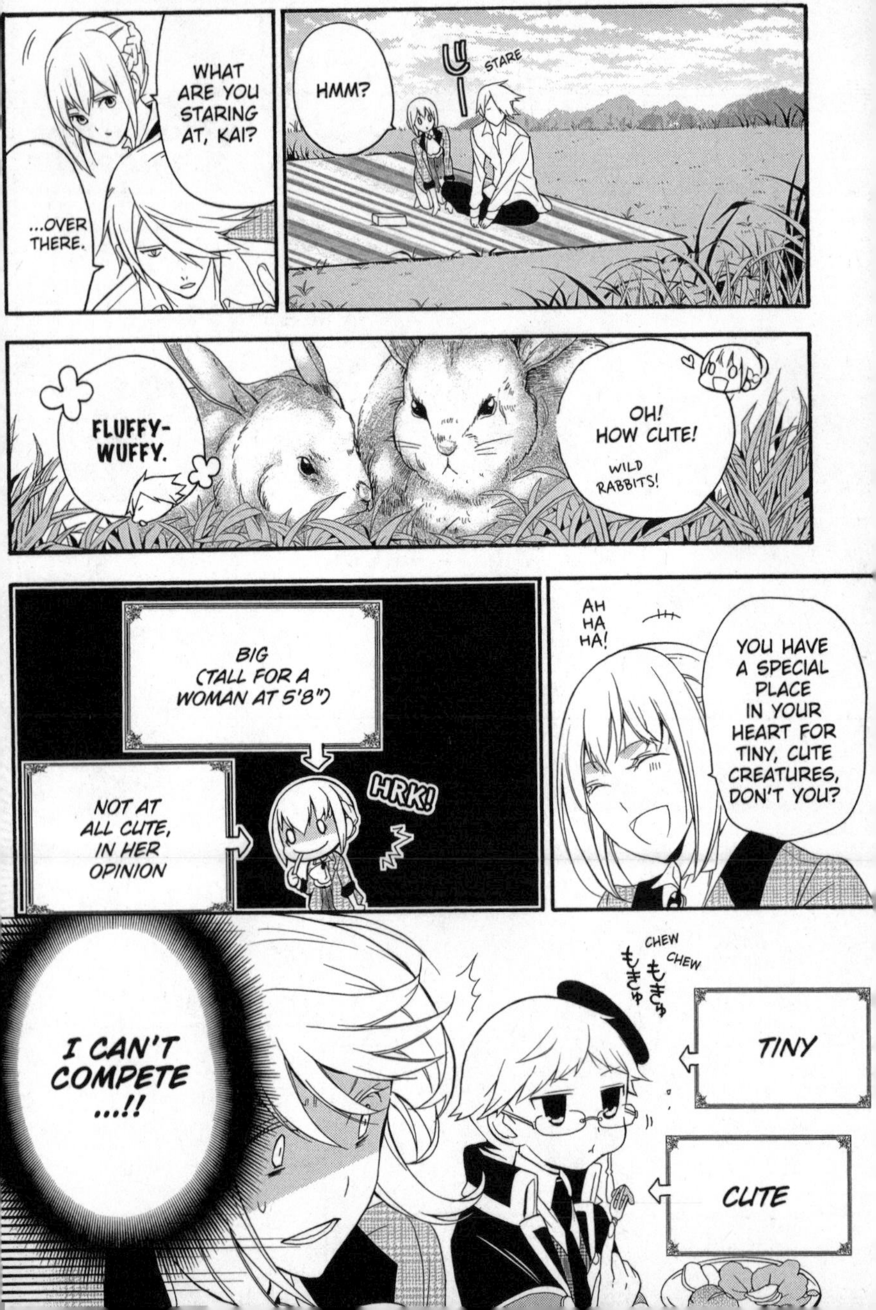
HMM?
STARE
WHAT ARE YOU STARING AT, KAI?
...OVER THERE.
OH! HOW CUTE!
WILD RABBITS!
FLUFFY-WUFFY.
AH HA HA!
YOU HAVE A SPECIAL PLACE IN YOUR HEART FOR TINY, CUTE CREATURES, DON'T YOU?
BIG (TALL FOR A WOMAN AT 5'8")
HRK!
NOT AT ALL CUTE, IN HER OPINION
CHEW CHEW
もきゅ もきゅ
TINY
CUTE
I CAN'T COMPETE ...!!

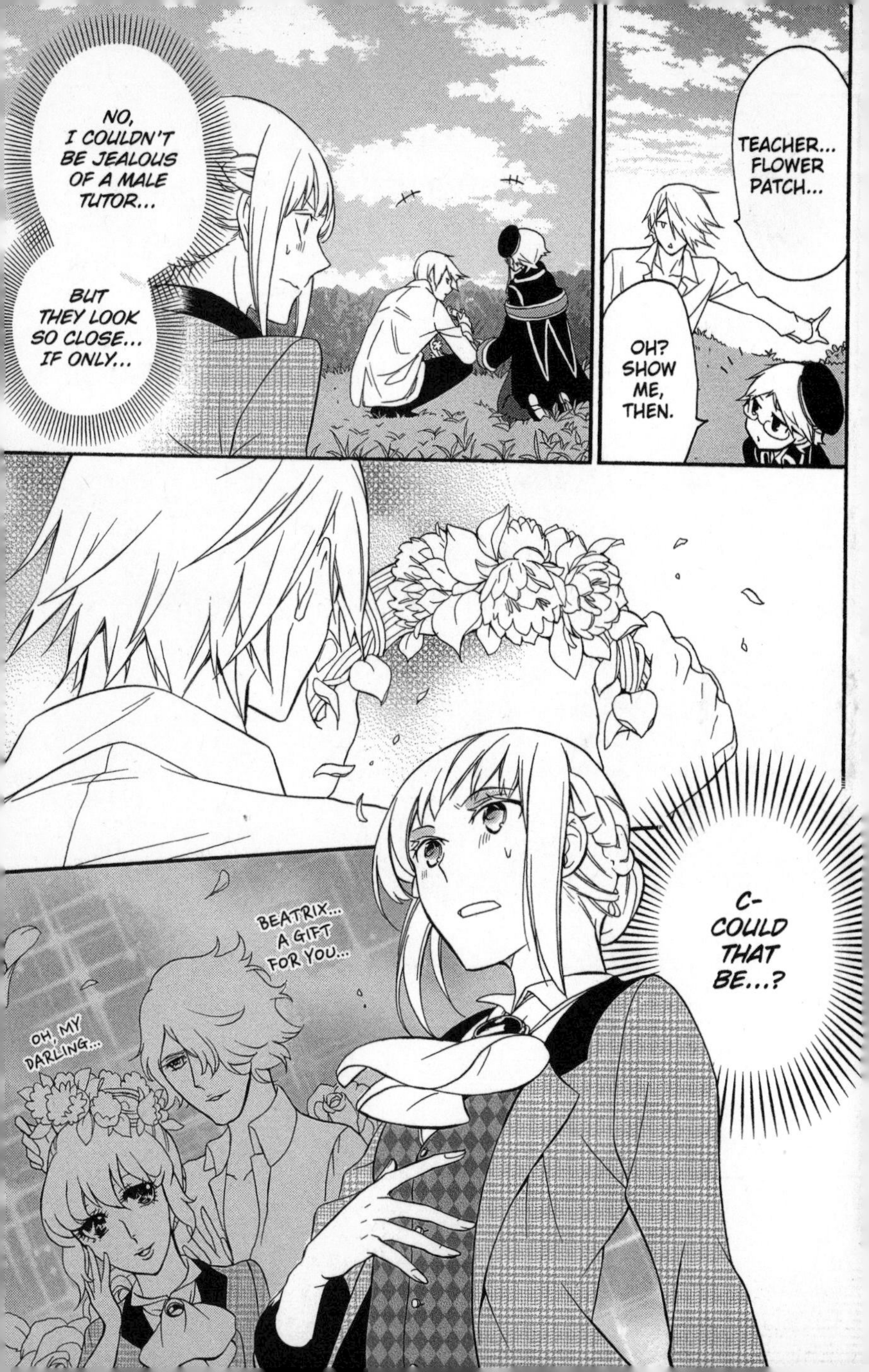
TEACHER... FLOWER PATCH...
OH? SHOW ME, THEN.
NO, I COULDN'T BE JEALOUS OF A MALE TUTOR...
BUT THEY LOOK SO CLOSE... IF ONLY...
C-COULD THAT BE...?
BEATRIX... A GIFT FOR YOU...
OH, MY DARLING...

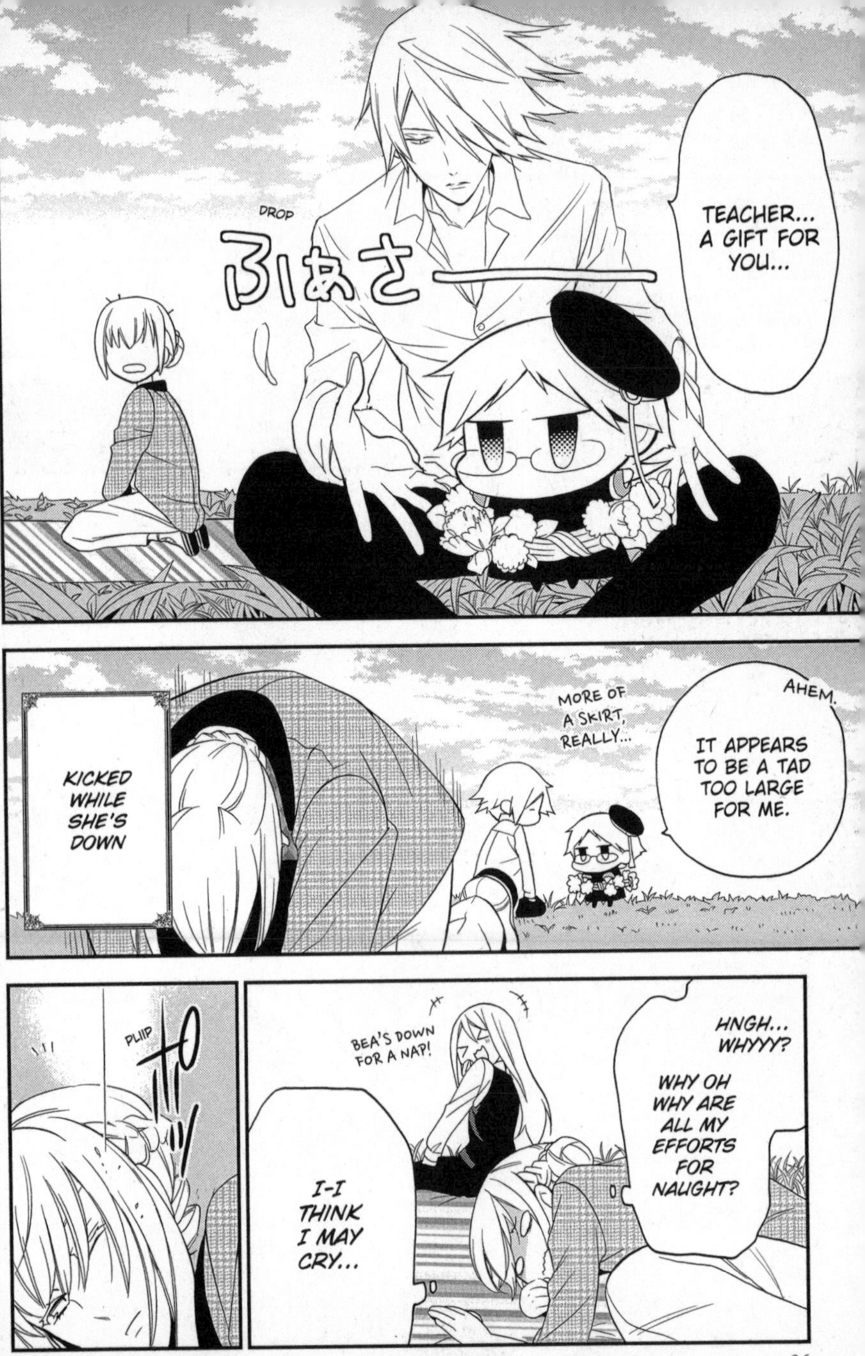
TEACHER... A GIFT FOR YOU...
DROP
ふぁさー
AHEM.
IT APPEARS TO BE A TAD TOO LARGE FOR ME.
MORE OF A SKIRT, REALLY...
KICKED WHILE SHE'S DOWN
HNGH... WHYYY?
WHY OH WHY ARE ALL MY EFFORTS FOR NAUGHT?
BEA'S DOWN FOR A NAP!
I-I THINK I MAY CRY...
PLIIP

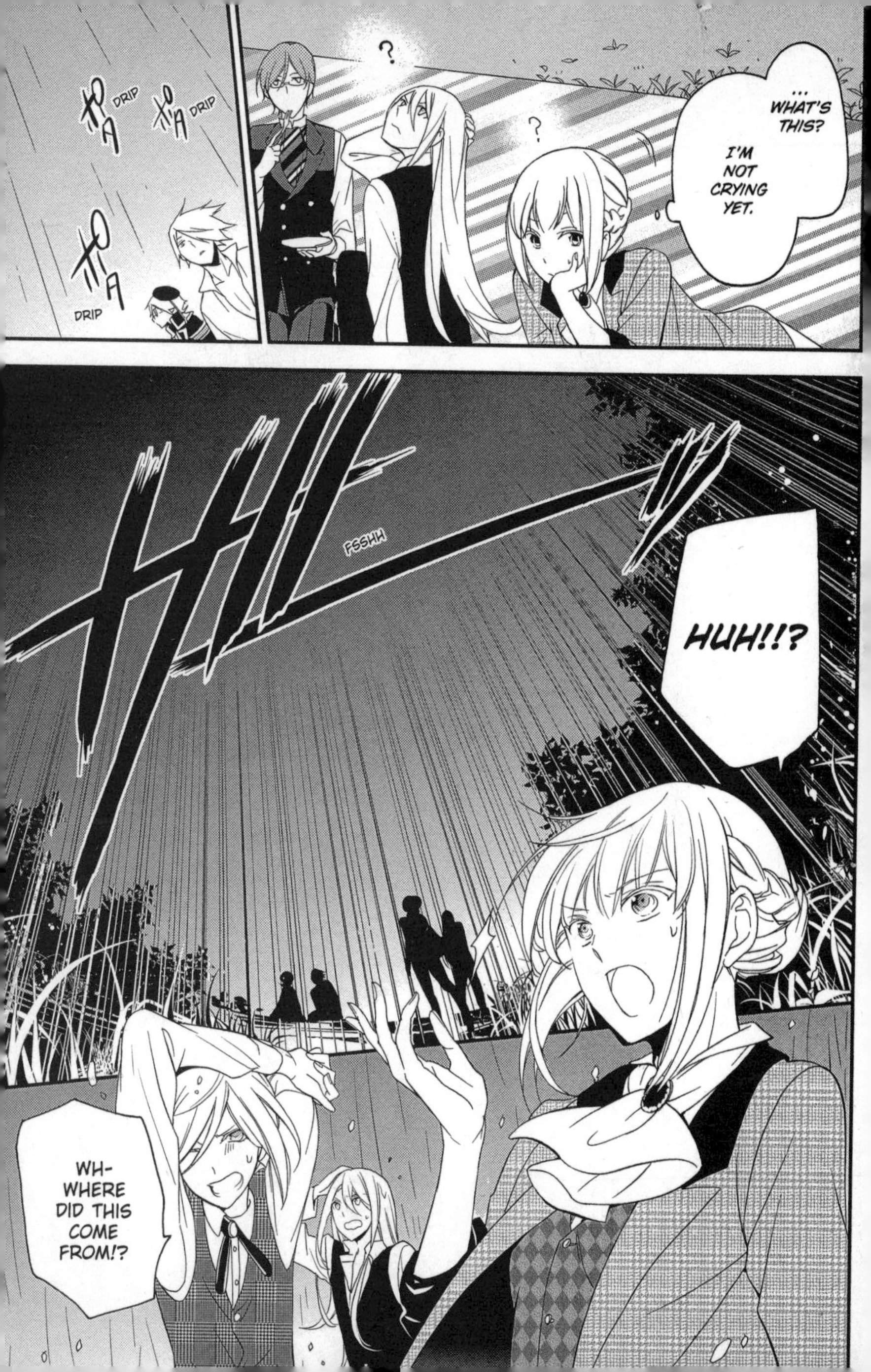
?
?
... WHAT'S THIS?
I'M NOT CRYING YET.
DRIP
DRIP
DRIP
HUH!!?
FSSHH
WH- WHERE DID THIS COME FROM!?

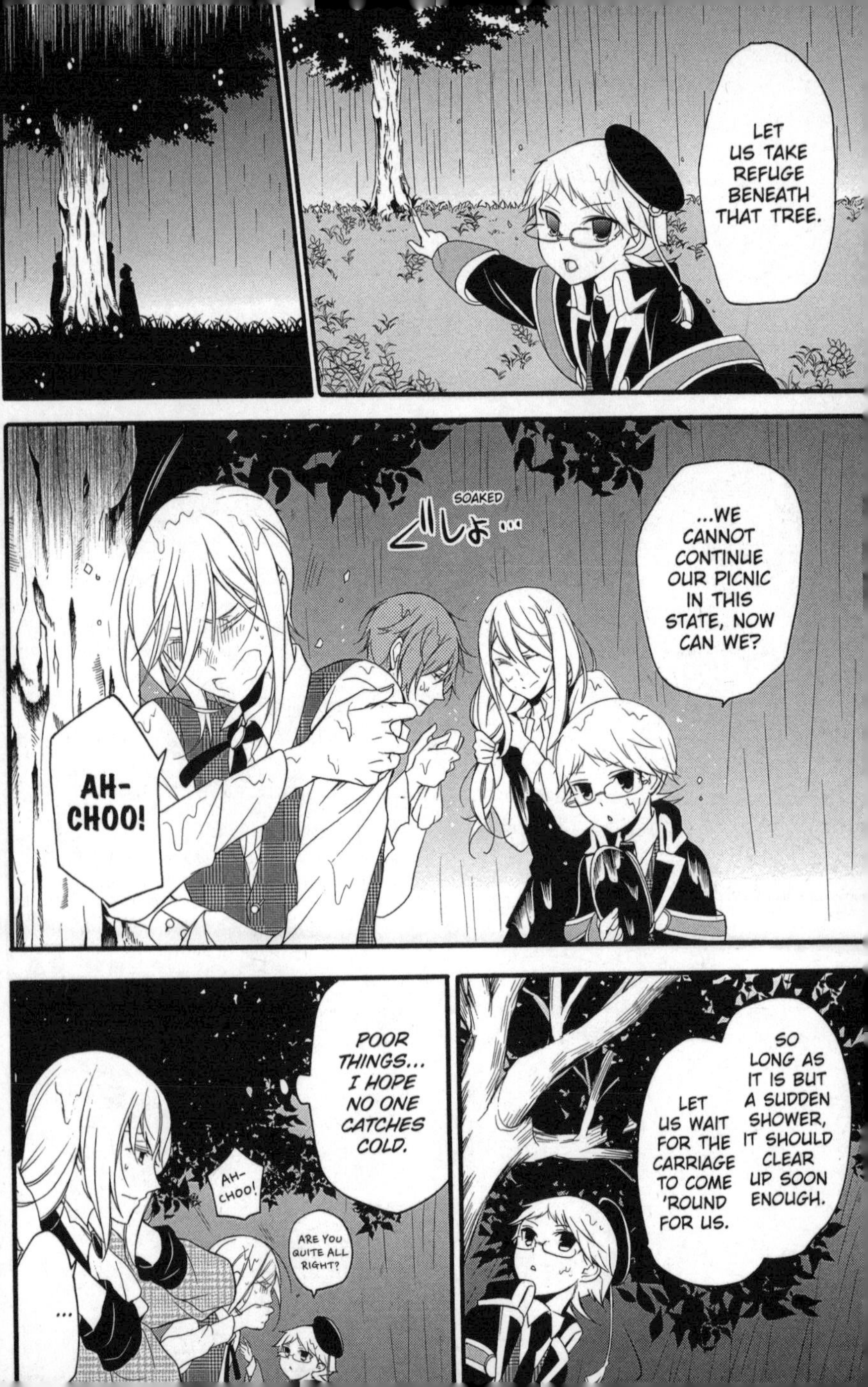
LET US TAKE REFUGE BENEATH THAT TREE.
...WE CANNOT CONTINUE OUR PICNIC IN THIS STATE, NOW CAN WE?
SOAKED
ぐしょ…
AH-CHOO!
SO LONG AS IT IS BUT A SUDDEN SHOWER, IT SHOULD CLEAR UP SOON ENOUGH.
LET US WAIT FOR THE CARRIAGE TO COME 'ROUND FOR US.
POOR THINGS... I HOPE NO ONE CATCHES COLD.
AH-CHOO!
ARE YOU QUITE ALL RIGHT?
...

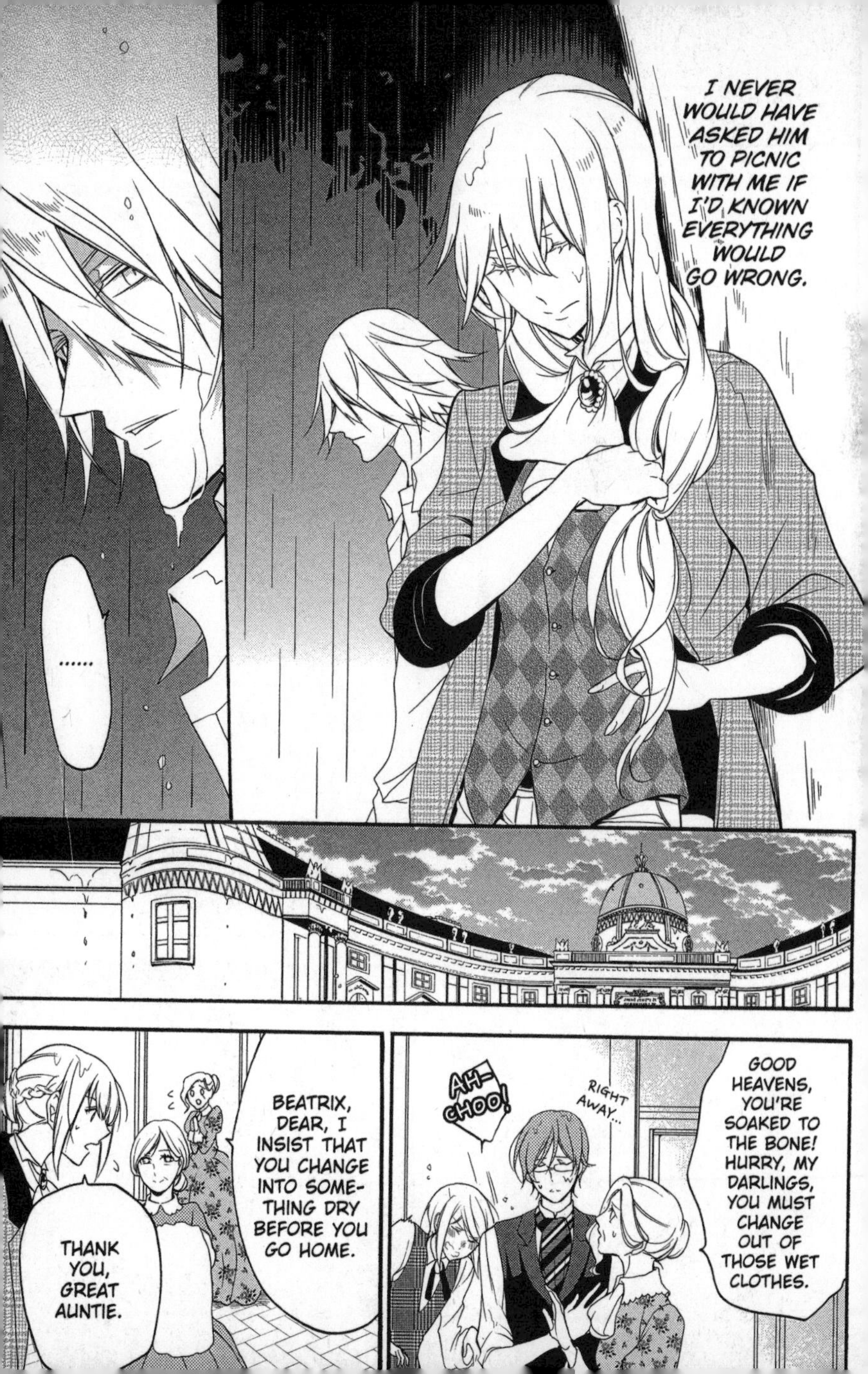
I NEVER WOULD HAVE ASKED HIM TO PICNIC WITH ME IF I'D KNOWN EVERYTHING WOULD GO WRONG.
......
GOOD HEAVENS, YOU'RE SOAKED TO THE BONE! HURRY, MY DARLINGS, YOU MUST CHANGE OUT OF THOSE WET CLOTHES.
RIGHT AWAY...
AH-CHOO!
BEATRIX, DEAR, I INSIST THAT YOU CHANGE INTO SOMETHING DRY BEFORE YOU GO HOME.
THANK YOU, GREAT AUNTIE.

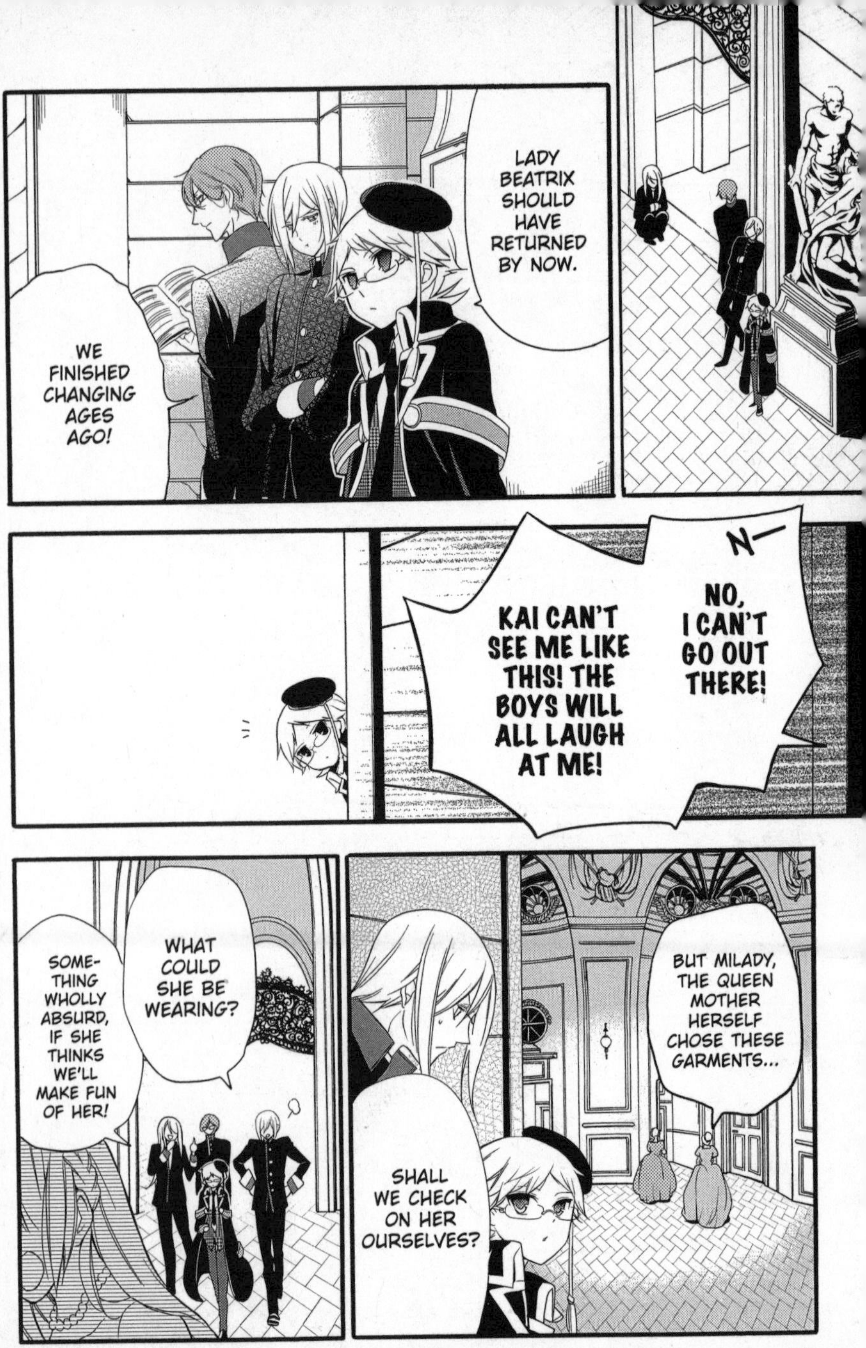
LADY BEATRIX SHOULD HAVE RETURNED BY NOW.
WE FINISHED CHANGING AGES AGO!
N—
NO, I CAN'T GO OUT THERE!
KAI CAN'T SEE ME LIKE THIS! THE BOYS WILL ALL LAUGH AT ME!
BUT MILADY, THE QUEEN MOTHER HERSELF CHOSE THESE GARMENTS...
SHALL WE CHECK ON HER OURSELVES?
WHAT COULD SHE BE WEARING?
SOME-THING WHOLLY ABSURD, IF SHE THINKS WE'LL MAKE FUN OF HER!

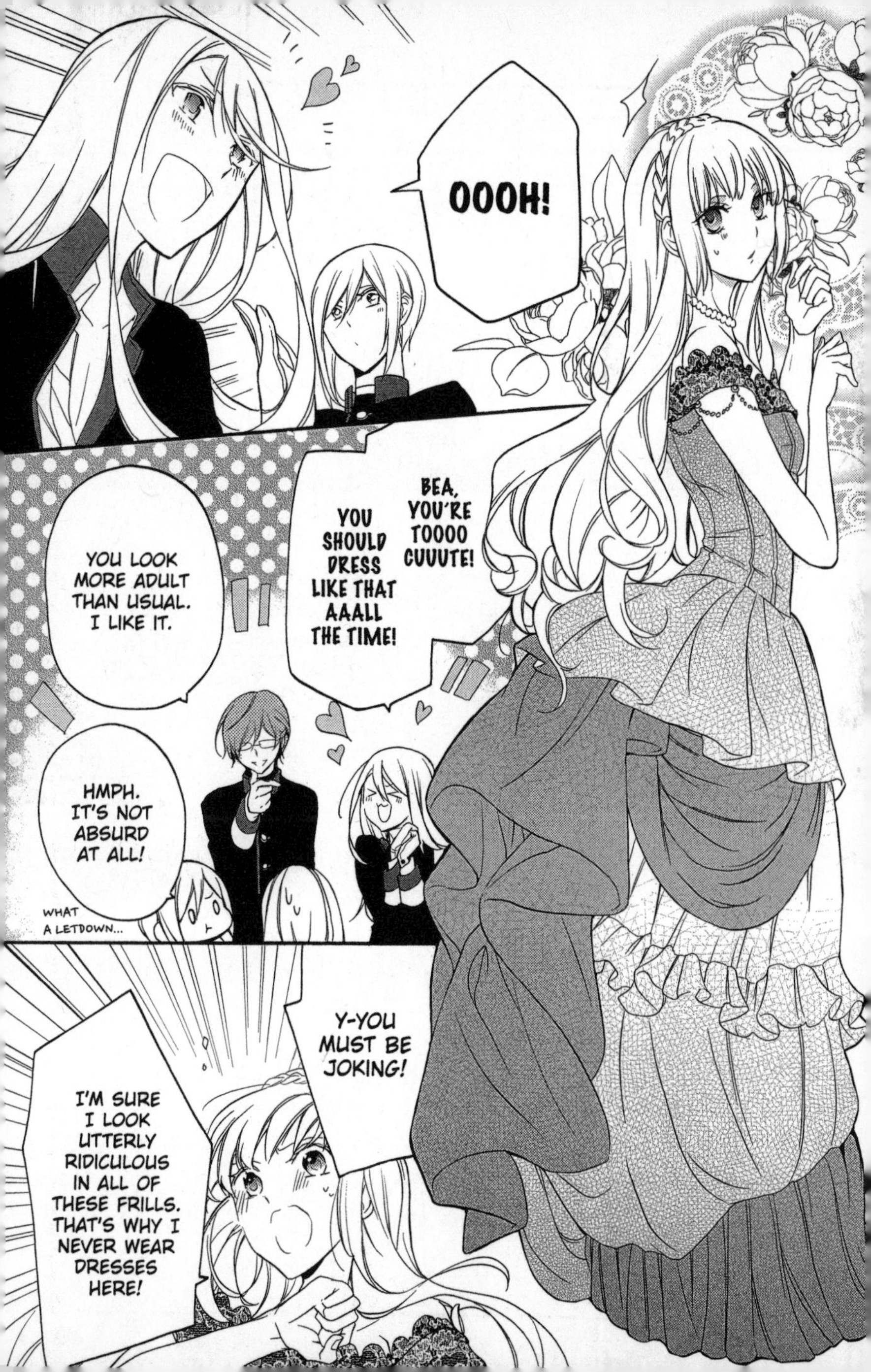
OOOH!
BEA, YOU'RE TOOOO CUUUTE!
YOU SHOULD DRESS LIKE THAT AAALL THE TIME!
YOU LOOK MORE ADULT THAN USUAL. I LIKE IT.
HMPH. IT'S NOT ABSURD AT ALL!
WHAT A LETDOWN...
Y-YOU MUST BE JOKING!
I'M SURE I LOOK UTTERLY RIDICULOUS IN ALL OF THESE FRILLS. THAT'S WHY I NEVER WEAR DRESSES HERE!

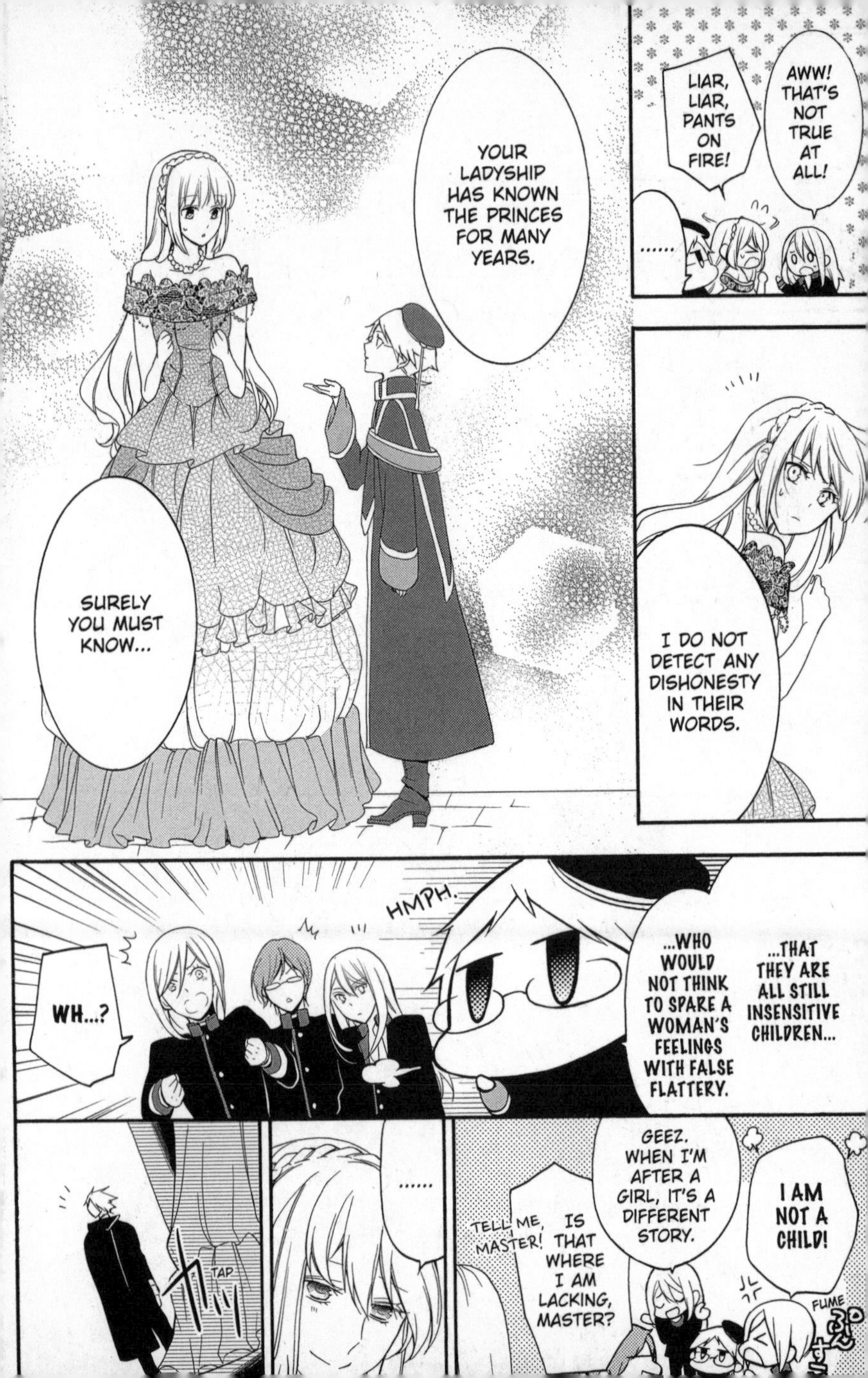
AWW! THAT'S NOT TRUE AT ALL!
LIAR, LIAR, PANTS ON FIRE!
......
I DO NOT DETECT ANY DISHONESTY IN THEIR WORDS.
YOUR LADYSHIP HAS KNOWN THE PRINCES FOR MANY YEARS.
SURELY YOU MUST KNOW...
...THAT THEY ARE ALL STILL INSENSITIVE CHILDREN...
...WHO WOULD NOT THINK TO SPARE A WOMAN'S FEELINGS WITH FALSE FLATTERY.
HMPH.
WH...?
I AM NOT A CHILD!
FUME
GEEZ. WHEN I'M AFTER A GIRL, IT'S A DIFFERENT STORY.
IS THAT WHERE I AM LACKING, MASTER?
TELL ME, MASTER!
......
TAP

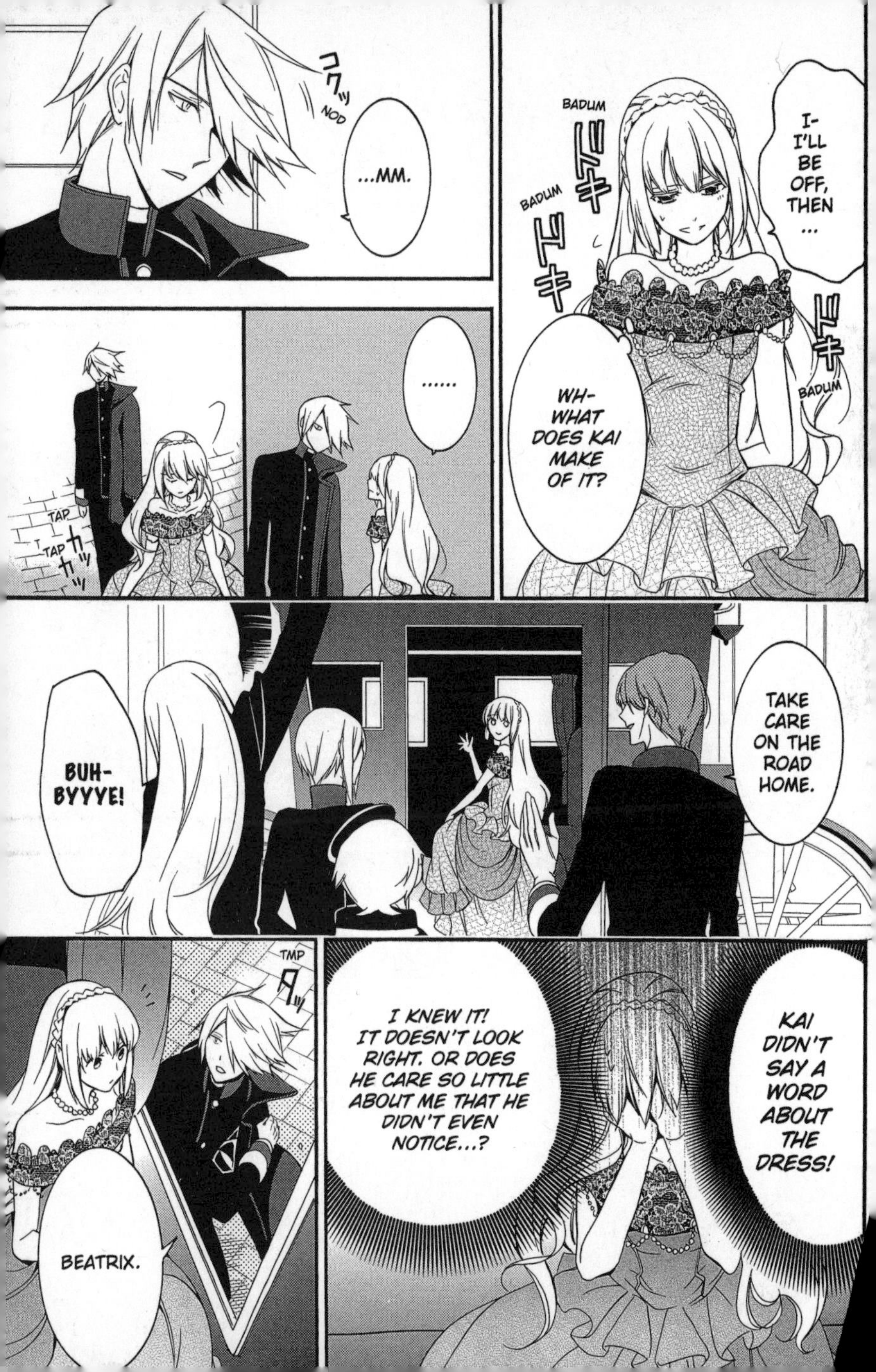
I- I'LL BE OFF, THEN...
BADUM
BADUM
WH- WHAT DOES KAI MAKE OF IT?
BADUM
NOD
...MM.
......
TAP
TAP
TAKE CARE ON THE ROAD HOME.
BUH-BYYYE!
KAI DIDN'T SAY A WORD ABOUT THE DRESS!
I KNEW IT! IT DOESN'T LOOK RIGHT. OR DOES HE CARE SO LITTLE ABOUT ME THAT HE DIDN'T EVEN NOTICE...?
TMP
BEATRIX.

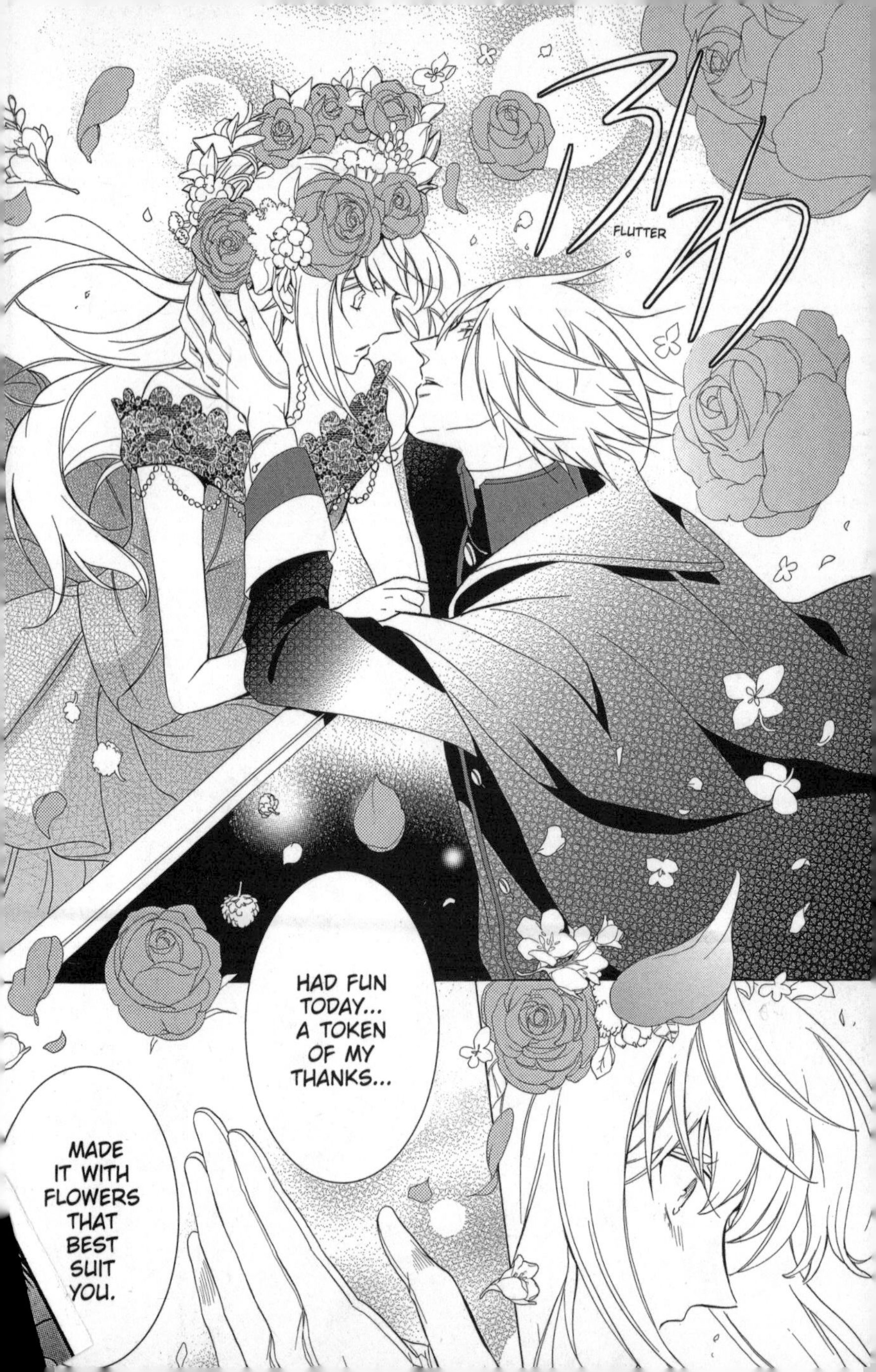
FLUTTER
HAD FUN TODAY... A TOKEN OF MY THANKS...
MADE IT WITH FLOWERS THAT BEST SUIT YOU.

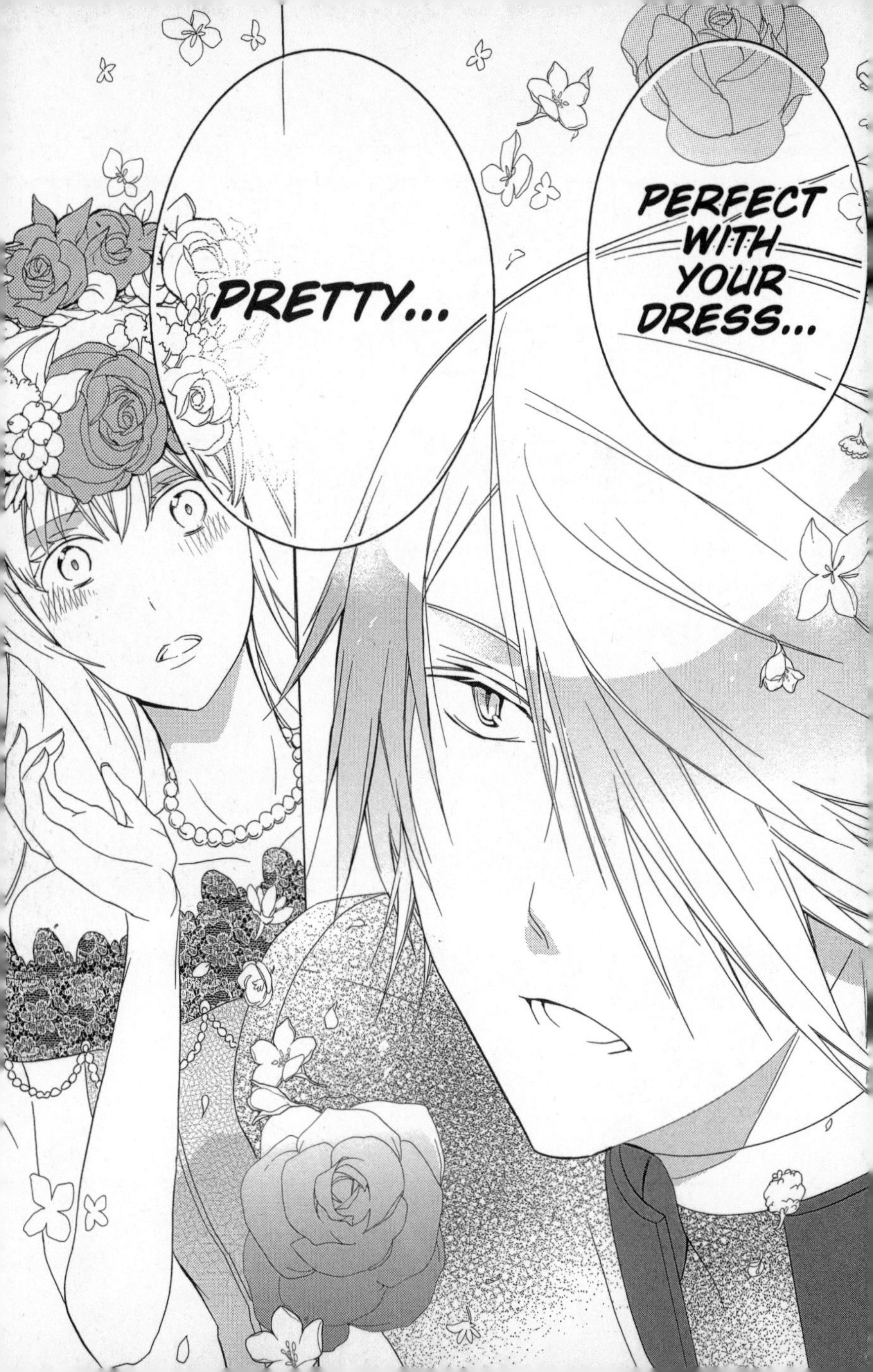
PERFECT WITH YOUR DRESS...
PRETTY...

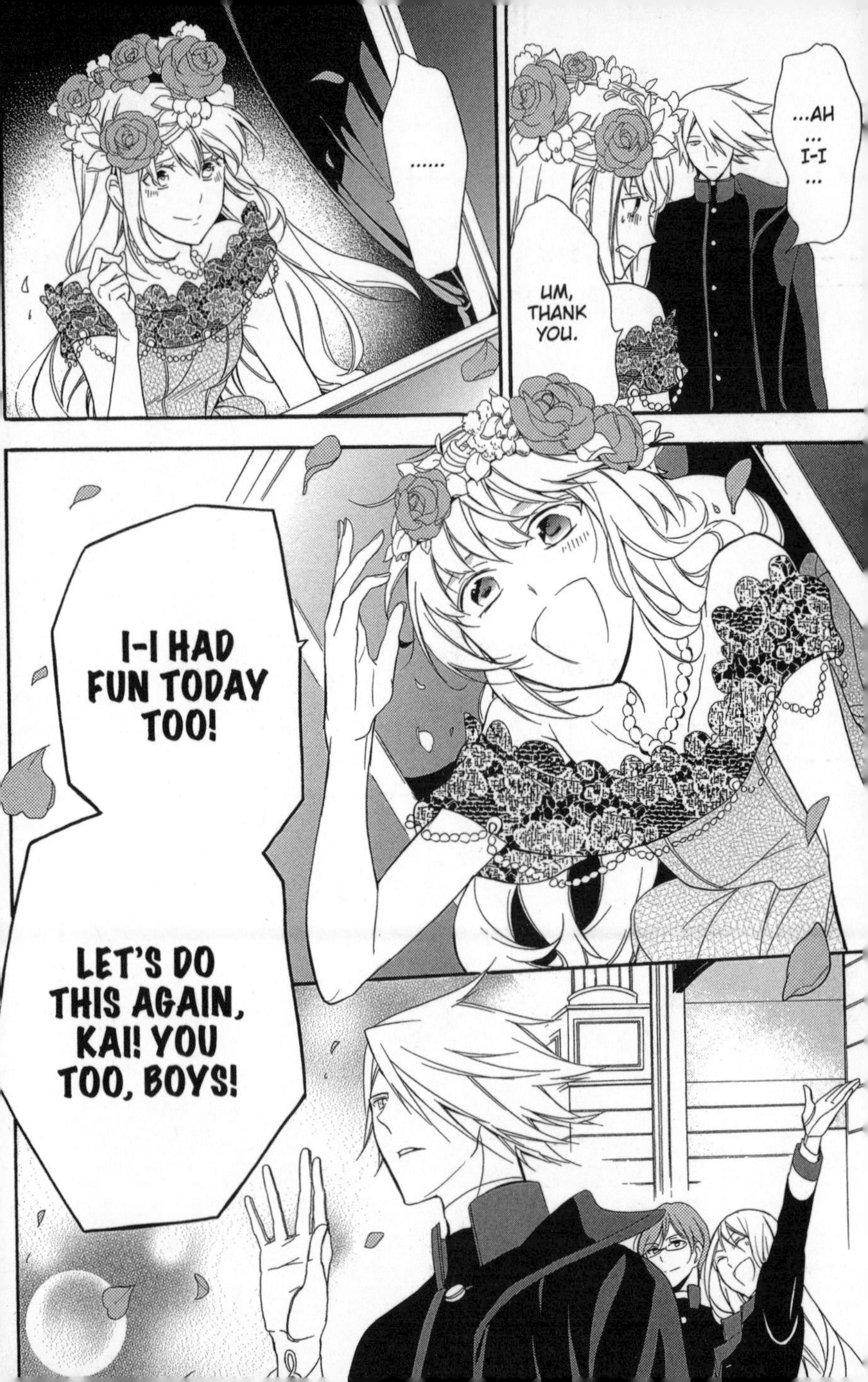
...AH ... I-I ...
UM, THANK YOU.
......
I-I HAD FUN TODAY TOO!
LET'S DO THIS AGAIN, KAI! YOU TOO, BOYS!

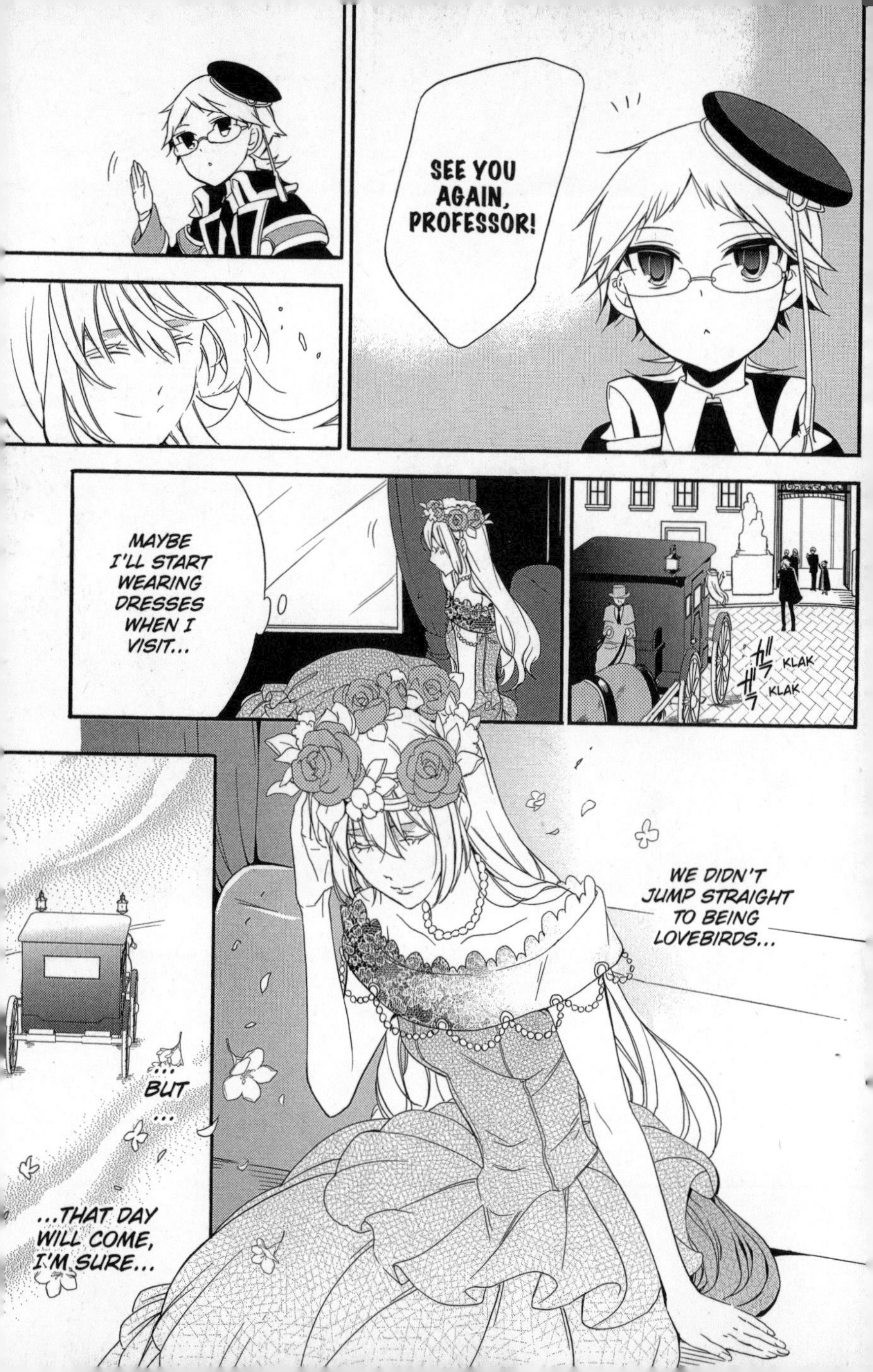
SEE YOU AGAIN, PROFESSOR!
ガラ KLAK
ガラ KLAK
MAYBE I'LL START WEARING DRESSES WHEN I VISIT...
WE DIDN'T JUMP STRAIGHT TO BEING LOVEBIRDS...
...BUT...
...THAT DAY WILL COME, I'M SURE...

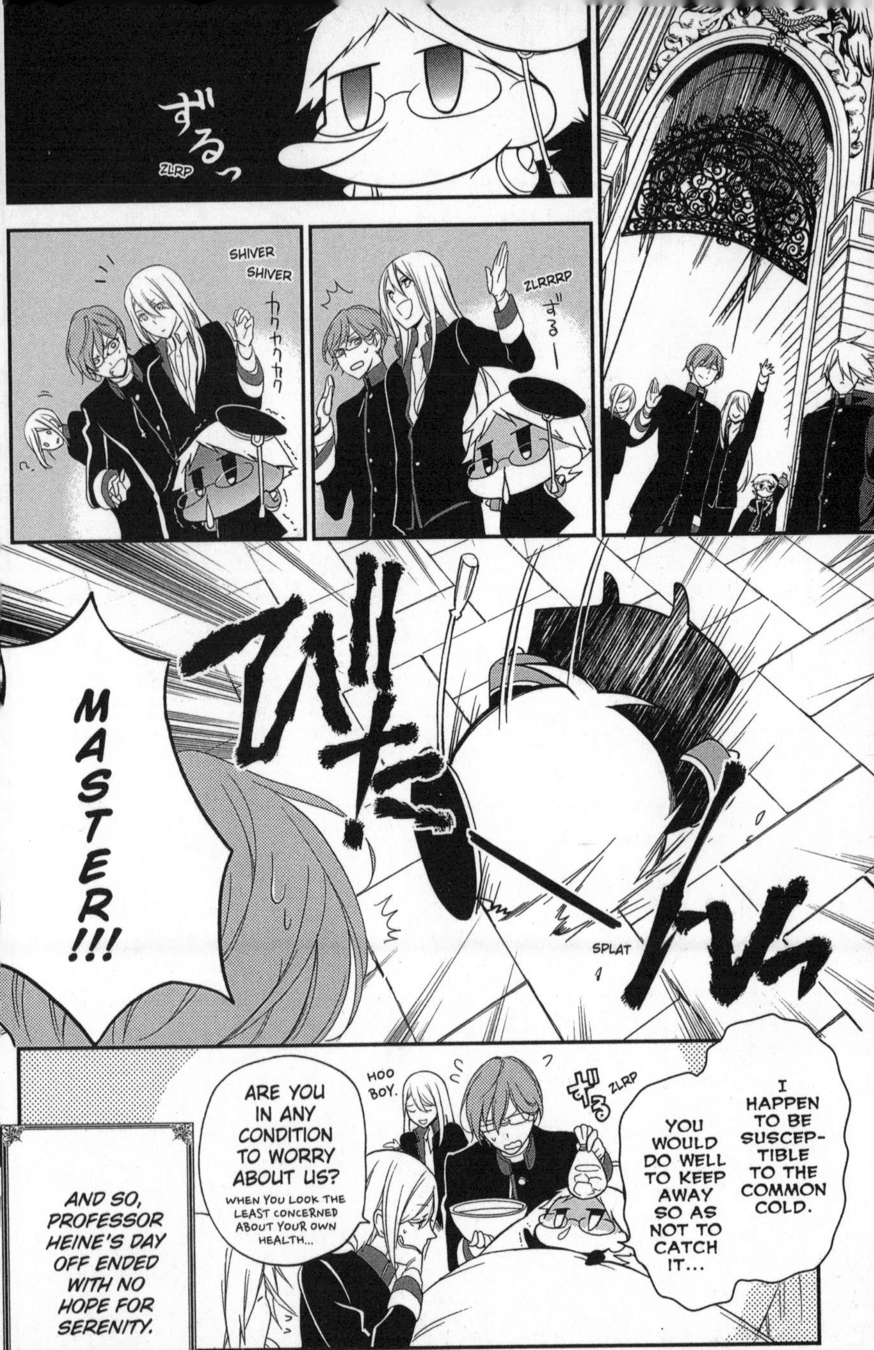
ずるっ
ZLRP
ZLRRRP
ずるー
SHIVER SHIVER
カクカクカク
MASTER!!!
SPLAT
I HAPPEN TO BE SUSCEP-TIBLE TO THE COMMON COLD.
YOU WOULD DO WELL TO KEEP AWAY SO AS NOT TO CATCH IT...
ずる
ZLRP
HOO BOY.
ARE YOU IN ANY CONDITION TO WORRY ABOUT US?
WHEN YOU LOOK THE LEAST CONCERNED ABOUT YOUR OWN HEALTH...
AND SO, PROFESSOR HEINE'S DAY OFF ENDED WITH NO HOPE FOR SERENITY.

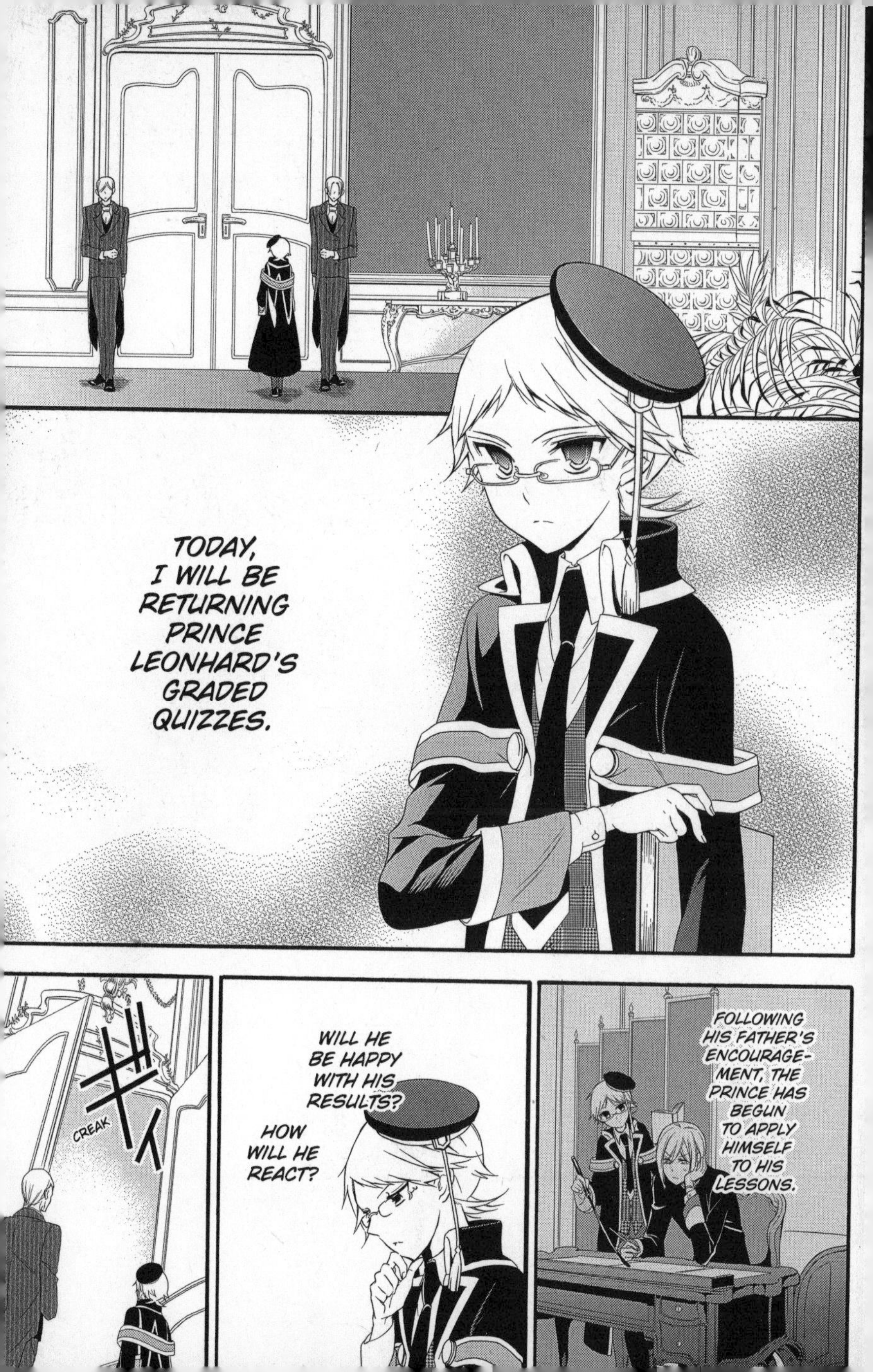
TODAY, I WILL BE RETURNING PRINCE LEONHARD'S GRADED QUIZZES.
FOLLOWING HIS FATHER'S ENCOURAGE-MENT, THE PRINCE HAS BEGUN TO APPLY HIMSELF TO HIS LESSONS.
WILL HE BE HAPPY WITH HIS RESULTS?
HOW WILL HE REACT?
CREAK

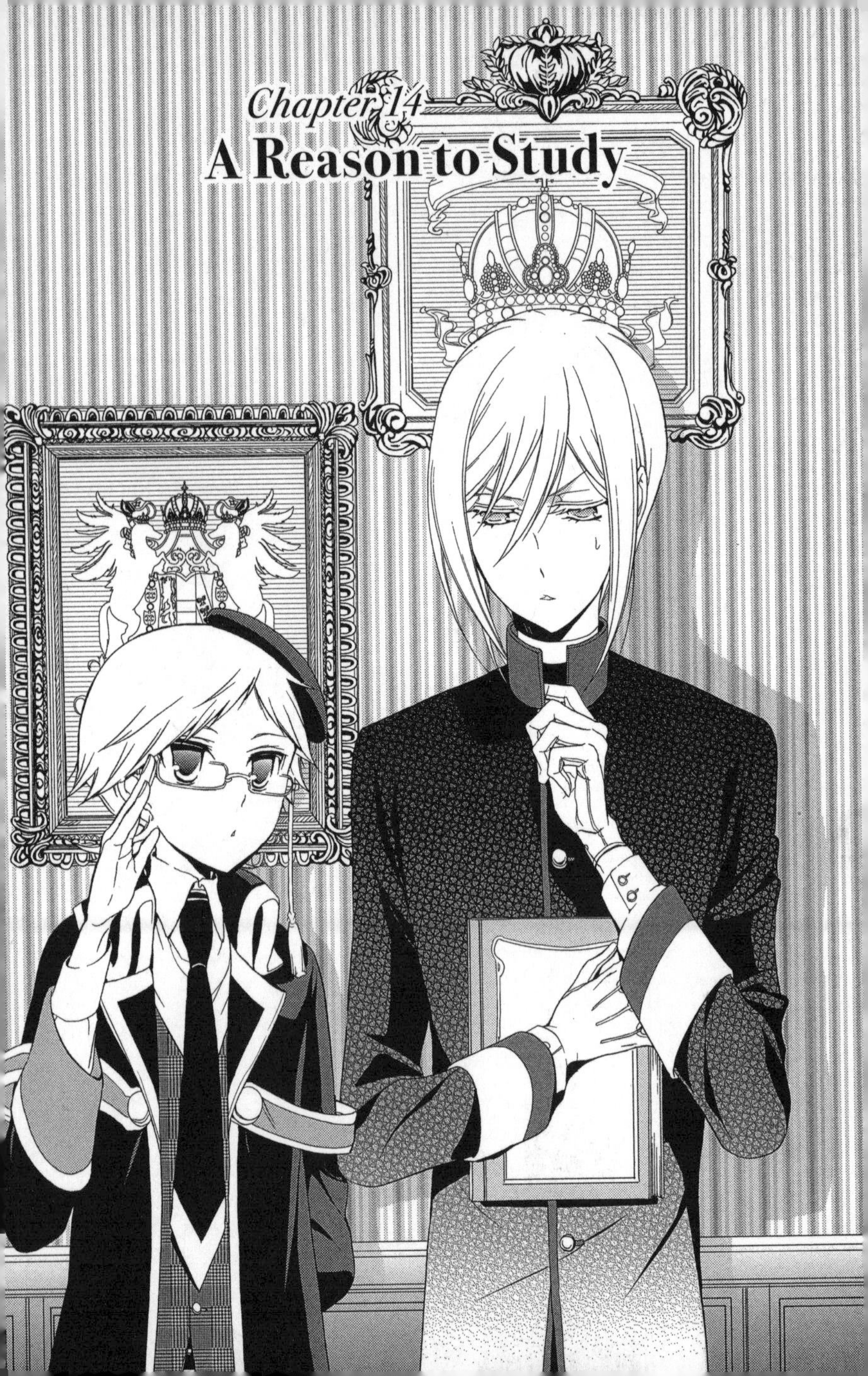
Chapter 14
A Reason to Study

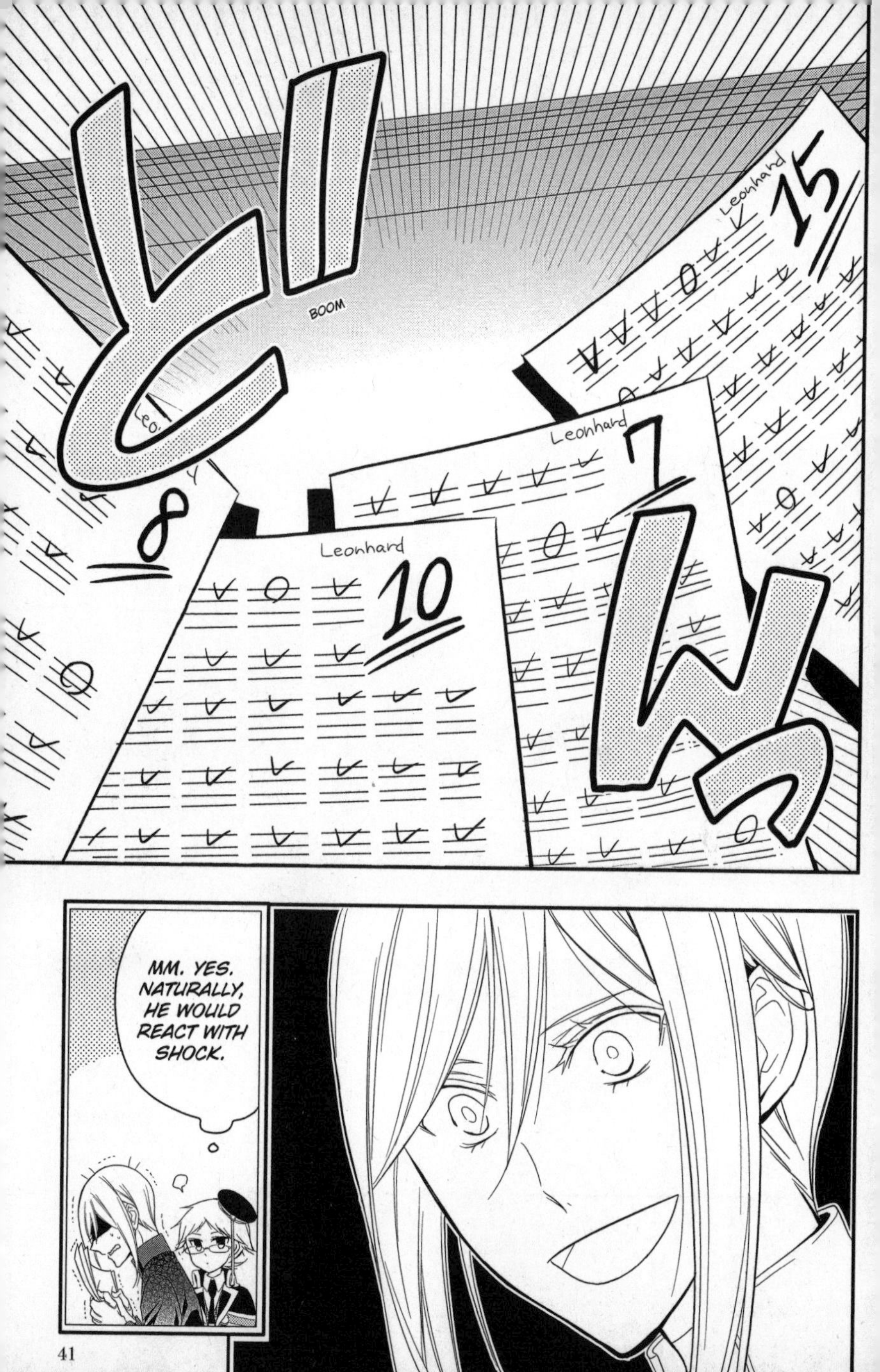
BOOM
Leonhard
15
Leonhard
7
Leonhard
10
8
MM. YES. NATURALLY, HE WOULD REACT WITH SHOCK.

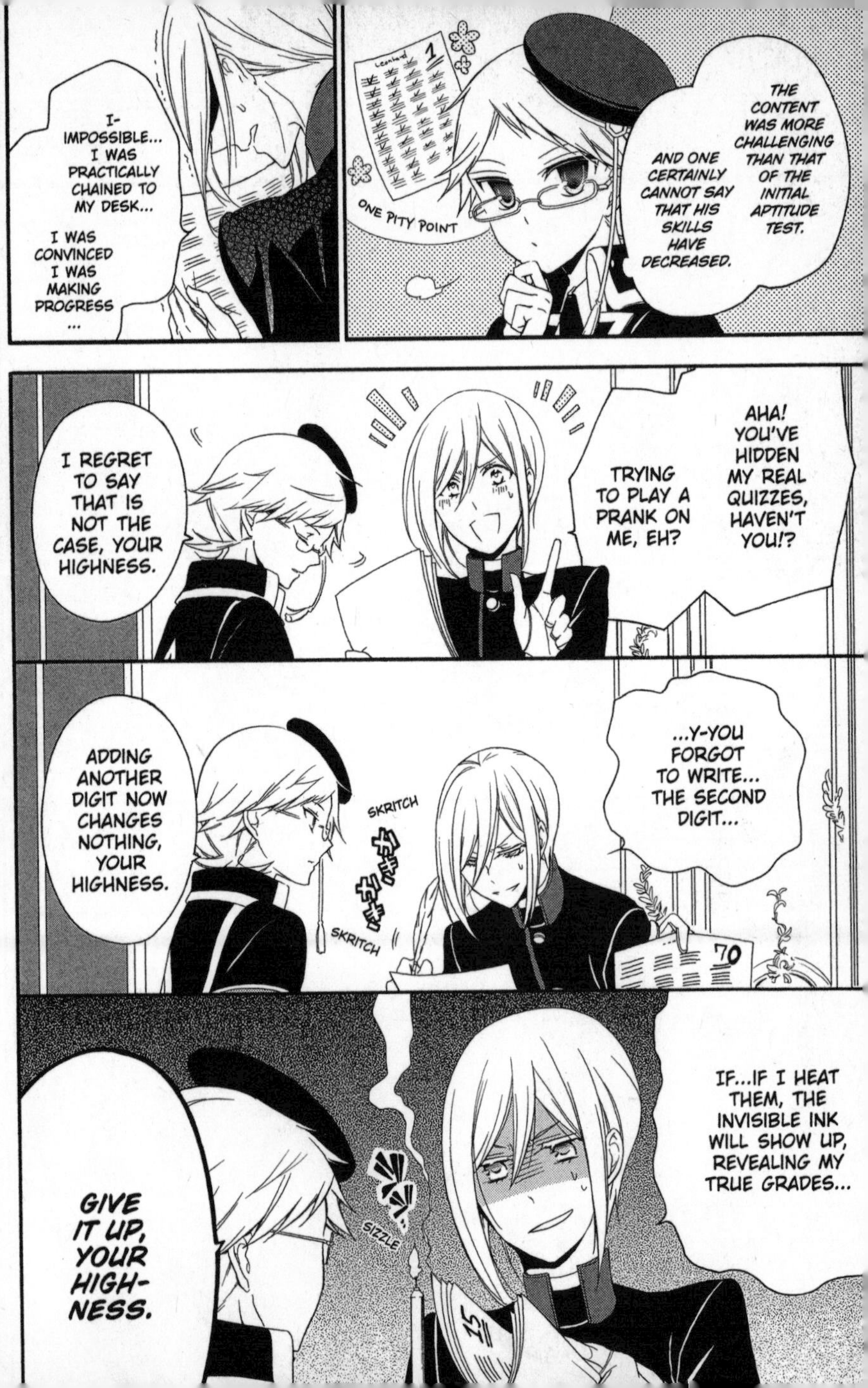
THE CONTENT WAS MORE CHALLENGING THAN THAT OF THE INITIAL APTITUDE TEST.
AND ONE CERTAINLY CANNOT SAY THAT HIS SKILLS HAVE DECREASED.
1
ONE PITY POINT
I- IMPOSSIBLE... I WAS PRACTICALLY CHAINED TO MY DESK...
I WAS CONVINCED I WAS MAKING PROGRESS ...
AHA! YOU'VE HIDDEN MY REAL QUIZZES, HAVEN'T YOU!?
TRYING TO PLAY A PRANK ON ME, EH?
I REGRET TO SAY THAT IS NOT THE CASE, YOUR HIGHNESS.
...Y-YOU FORGOT TO WRITE... THE SECOND DIGIT...
70
SKRITCH
SKRITCH
ADDING ANOTHER DIGIT NOW CHANGES NOTHING, YOUR HIGHNESS.
IF...IF I HEAT THEM, THE INVISIBLE INK WILL SHOW UP, REVEALING MY TRUE GRADES...
15
SIZZLE
GIVE IT UP, YOUR HIGH-NESS.

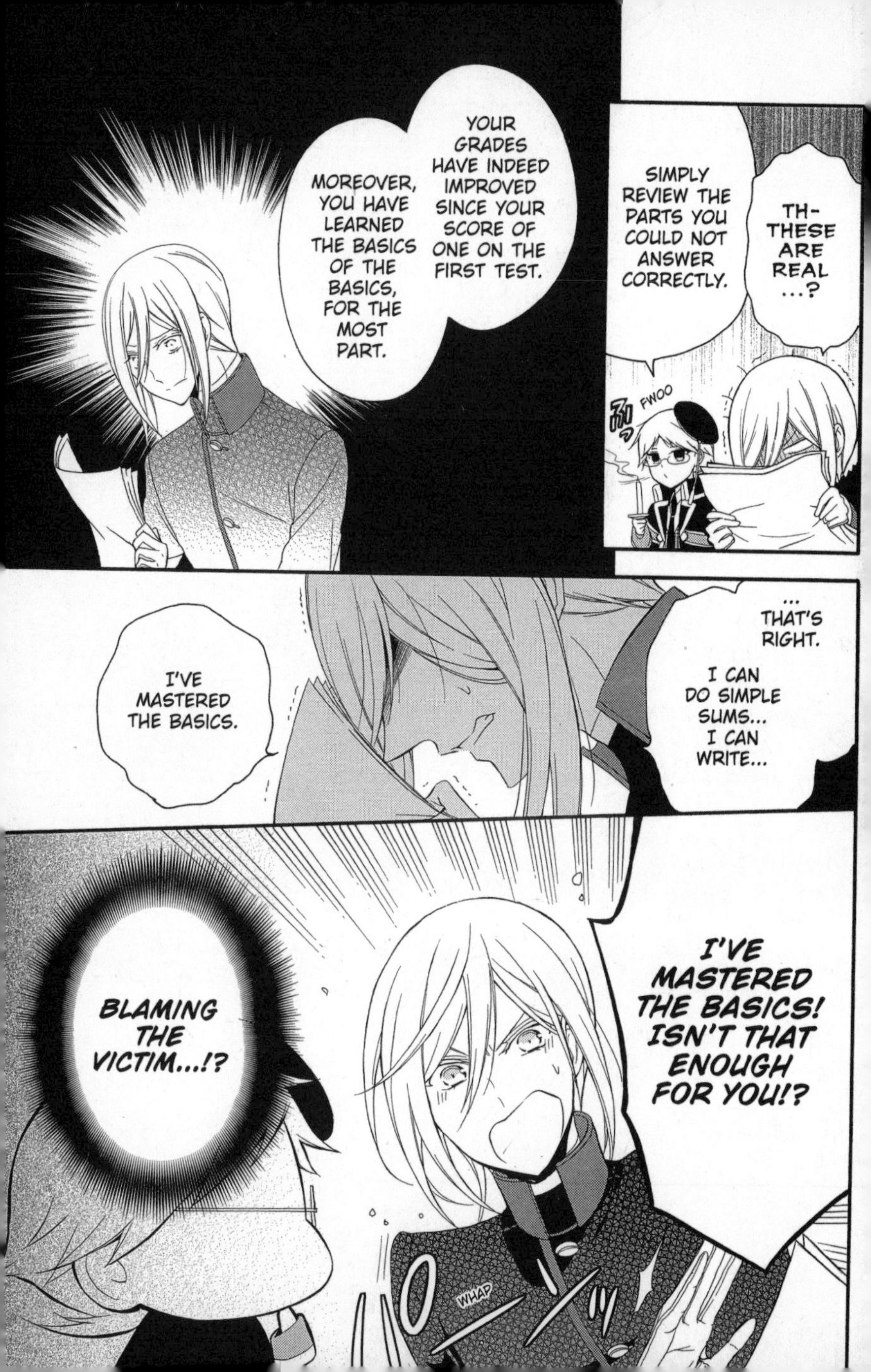
TH-THESE ARE REAL...?
SIMPLY REVIEW THE PARTS YOU COULD NOT ANSWER CORRECTLY.
FWOO
YOUR GRADES HAVE INDEED IMPROVED SINCE YOUR SCORE OF ONE ON THE FIRST TEST.
MOREOVER, YOU HAVE LEARNED THE BASICS OF THE BASICS, FOR THE MOST PART.
... THAT'S RIGHT.
I CAN DO SIMPLE SUMS... I CAN WRITE...
I'VE MASTERED THE BASICS.
I'VE MASTERED THE BASICS! ISN'T THAT ENOUGH FOR YOU!?
BLAMING THE VICTIM...!?
WHAP

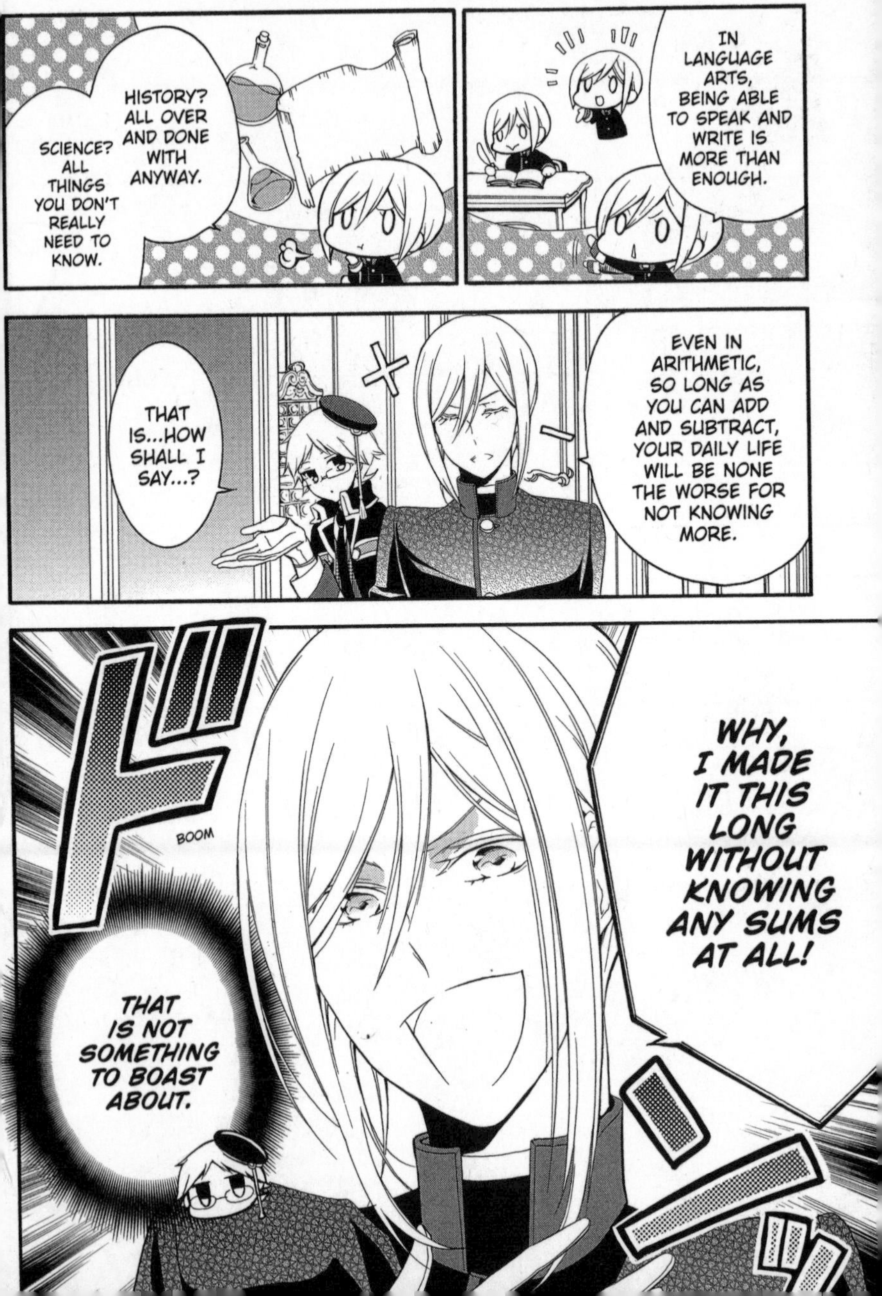
IN LANGUAGE ARTS, BEING ABLE TO SPEAK AND WRITE IS MORE THAN ENOUGH.
HISTORY? ALL OVER AND DONE WITH ANYWAY.
SCIENCE? ALL THINGS YOU DON'T REALLY NEED TO KNOW.
EVEN IN ARITHMETIC, SO LONG AS YOU CAN ADD AND SUBTRACT, YOUR DAILY LIFE WILL BE NONE THE WORSE FOR NOT KNOWING MORE.
THAT IS...HOW SHALL I SAY...?
WHY, I MADE IT THIS LONG WITHOUT KNOWING ANY SUMS AT ALL!
BOOM
THAT IS NOT SOMETHING TO BOAST ABOUT.

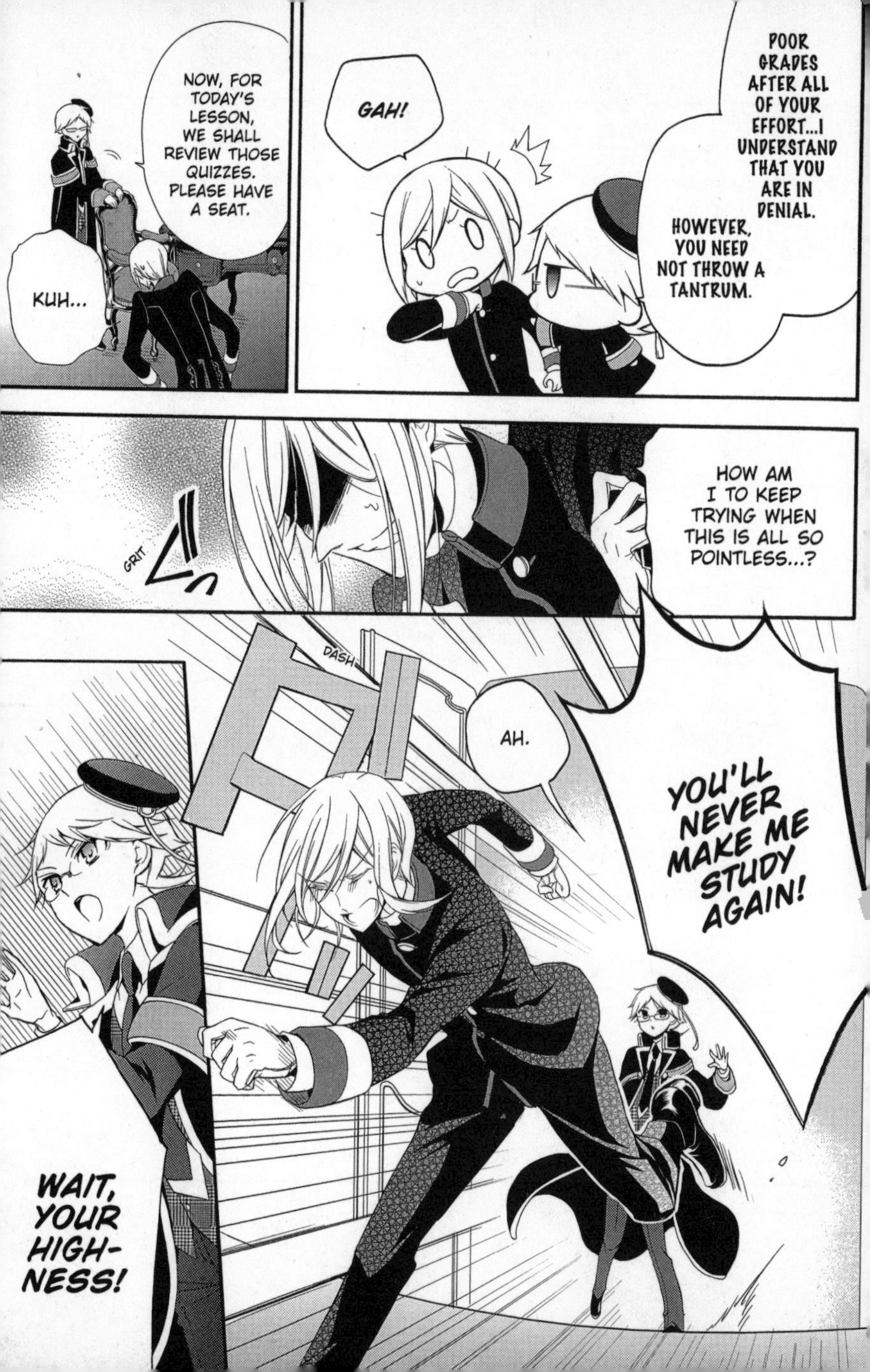
POOR GRADES AFTER ALL OF YOUR EFFORT...I UNDERSTAND THAT YOU ARE IN DENIAL.
HOWEVER, YOU NEED NOT THROW A TANTRUM.
GAH!
NOW, FOR TODAY'S LESSON, WE SHALL REVIEW THOSE QUIZZES. PLEASE HAVE A SEAT.
KUH...
HOW AM I TO KEEP TRYING WHEN THIS IS ALL SO POINTLESS...?
GRIT
YOU'LL NEVER MAKE ME STUDY AGAIN!
DASH
AH.
WAIT, YOUR HIGH-NESS!

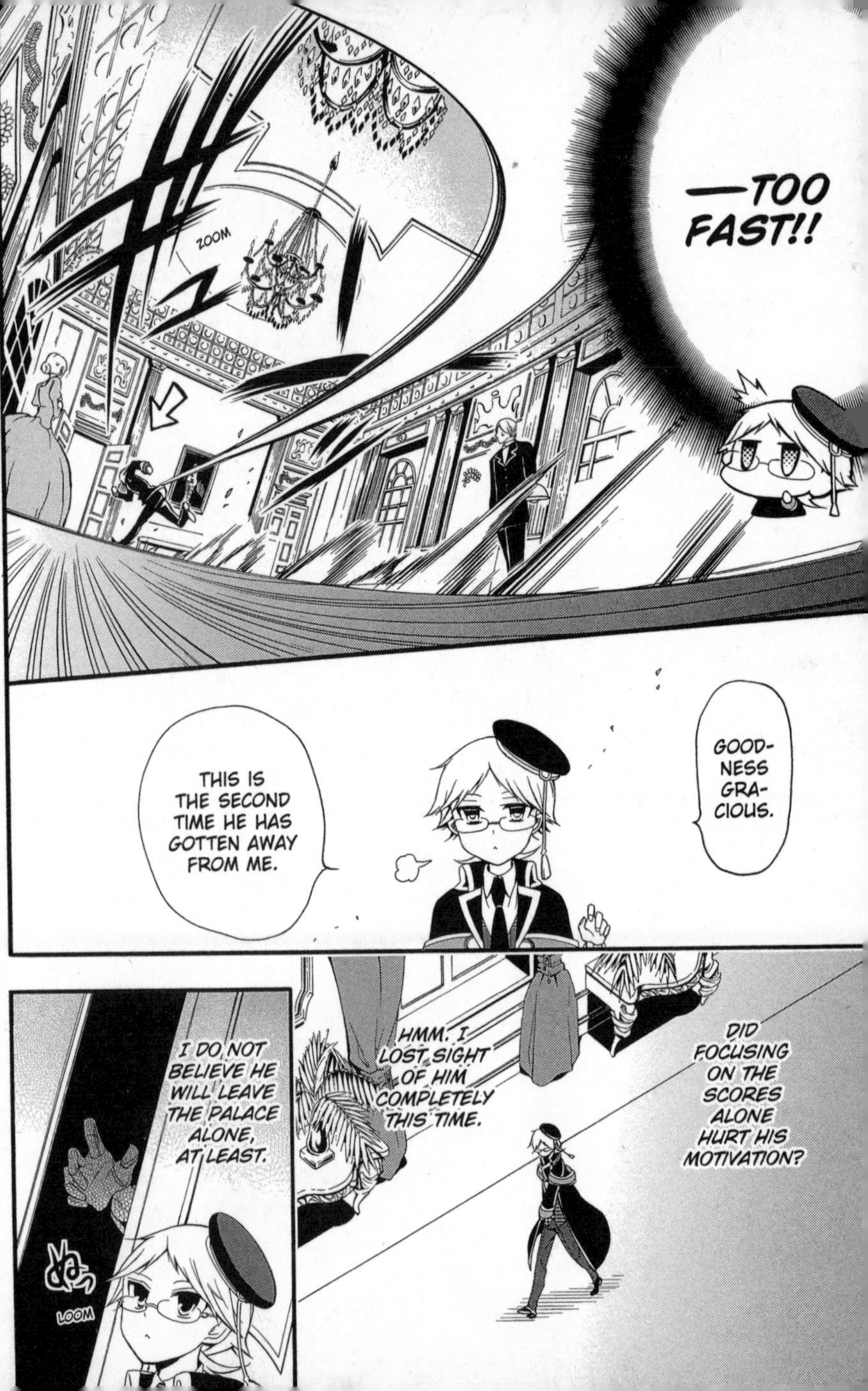
—TOO FAST!!
ZOOM
GOOD-NESS GRA-CIOUS.
THIS IS THE SECOND TIME HE HAS GOTTEN AWAY FROM ME.
DID FOCUSING ON THE SCORES ALONE HURT HIS MOTIVATION?
HMM. I LOST SIGHT OF HIM COMPLETELY THIS TIME.
I DO NOT BELIEVE HE WILL LEAVE THE PALACE ALONE, AT LEAST.
LOOM

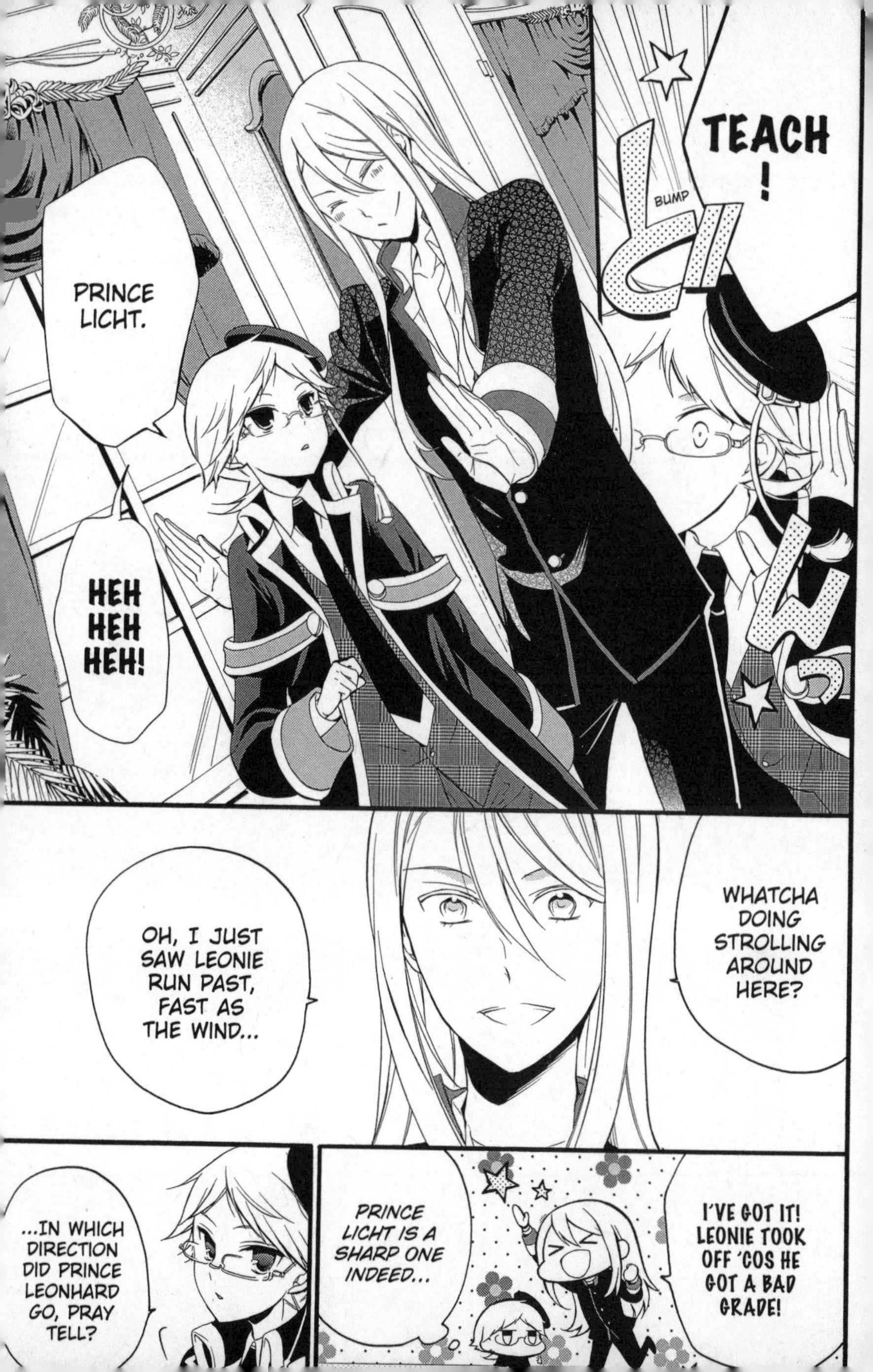
TEACH!
BUMP
PRINCE LICHT.
HEH HEH HEH!
WHATCHA DOING STROLLING AROUND HERE?
OH, I JUST SAW LEONIE RUN PAST, FAST AS THE WIND...
I'VE GOT IT! LEONIE TOOK OFF 'COS HE GOT A BAD GRADE!
PRINCE LICHT IS A SHARP ONE INDEED...
...IN WHICH DIRECTION DID PRINCE LEONHARD GO, PRAY TELL?

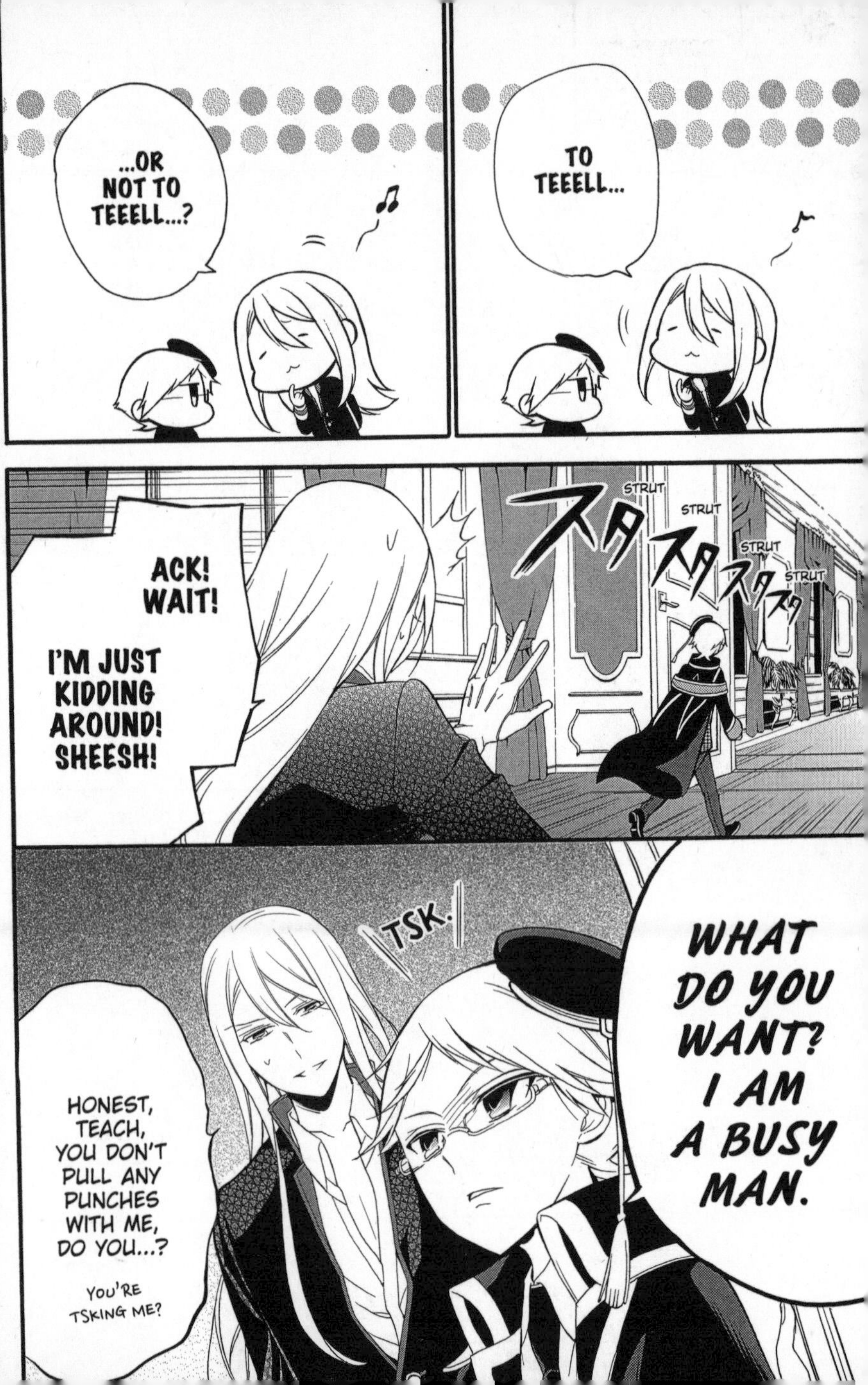
TO TEEELL...
...OR NOT TO TEEELL...?
スタスタスタスタ
STRUT STRUT STRUT STRUT
ACK! WAIT!
I'M JUST KIDDING AROUND! SHEESH!
WHAT DO YOU WANT? I AM A BUSY MAN.
TSK.
HONEST, TEACH, YOU DON'T PULL ANY PUNCHES WITH ME, DO YOU...?
YOU'RE TSKING ME?

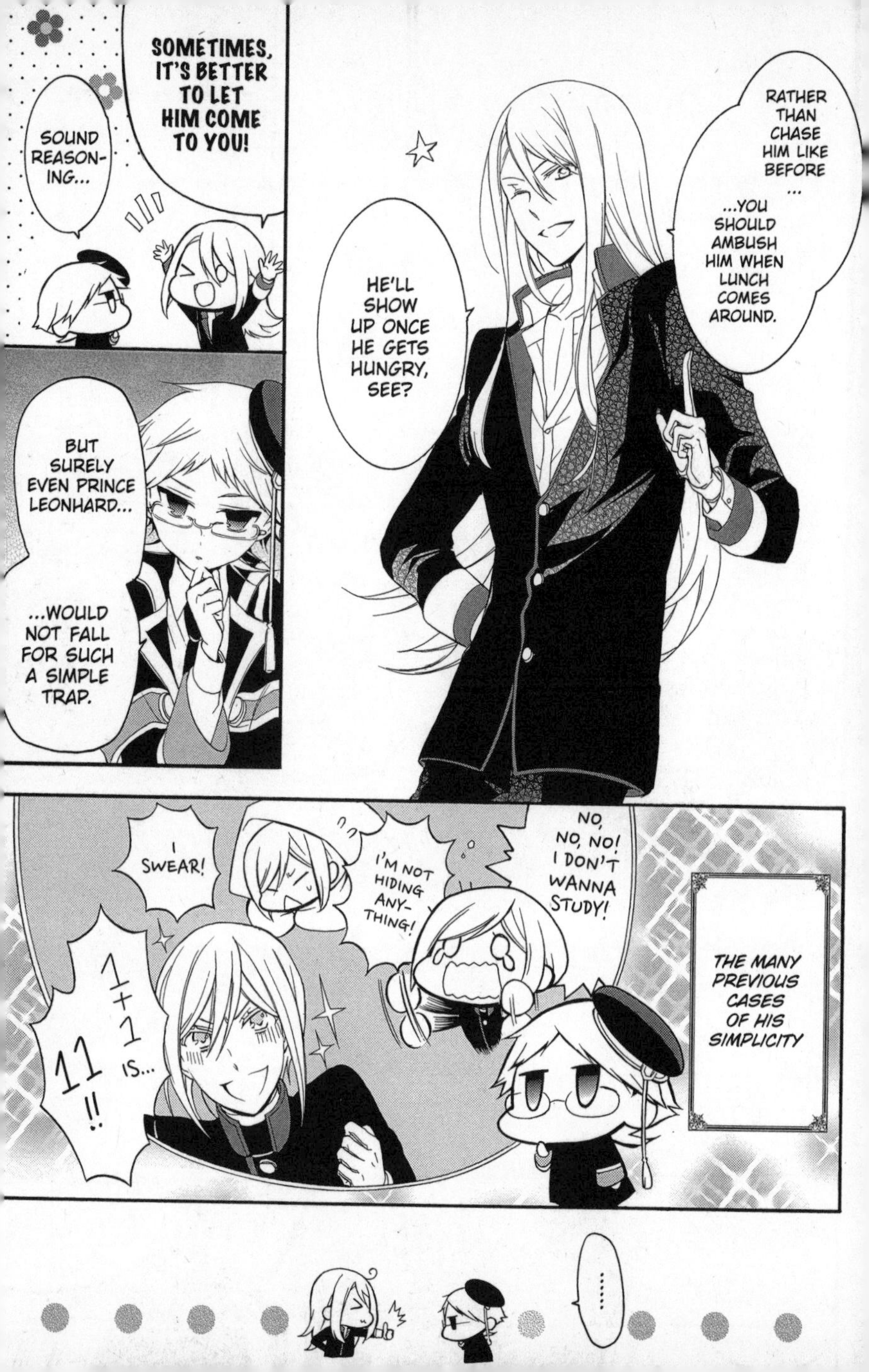
RATHER THAN CHASE HIM LIKE BEFORE ...
...YOU SHOULD AMBUSH HIM WHEN LUNCH COMES AROUND.
HE'LL SHOW UP ONCE HE GETS HUNGRY, SEE?
SOMETIMES, IT'S BETTER TO LET HIM COME TO YOU!
SOUND REASONING...
BUT SURELY EVEN PRINCE LEONHARD...
...WOULD NOT FALL FOR SUCH A SIMPLE TRAP.
THE MANY PREVIOUS CASES OF HIS SIMPLICITY
NO, NO, NO! I DON'T WANNA STUDY!
I'M NOT HIDING ANYTHING!
I SWEAR!
1+1 IS...
11!!
......

もぞっ
SNEAK

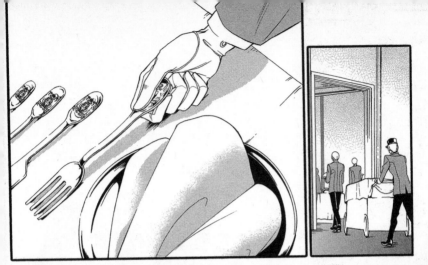

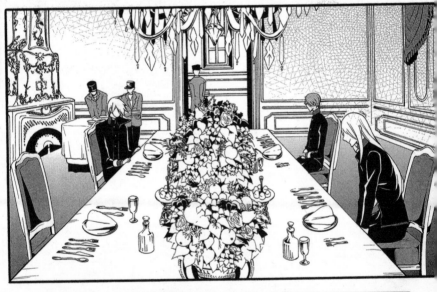

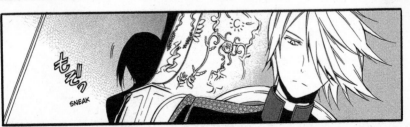

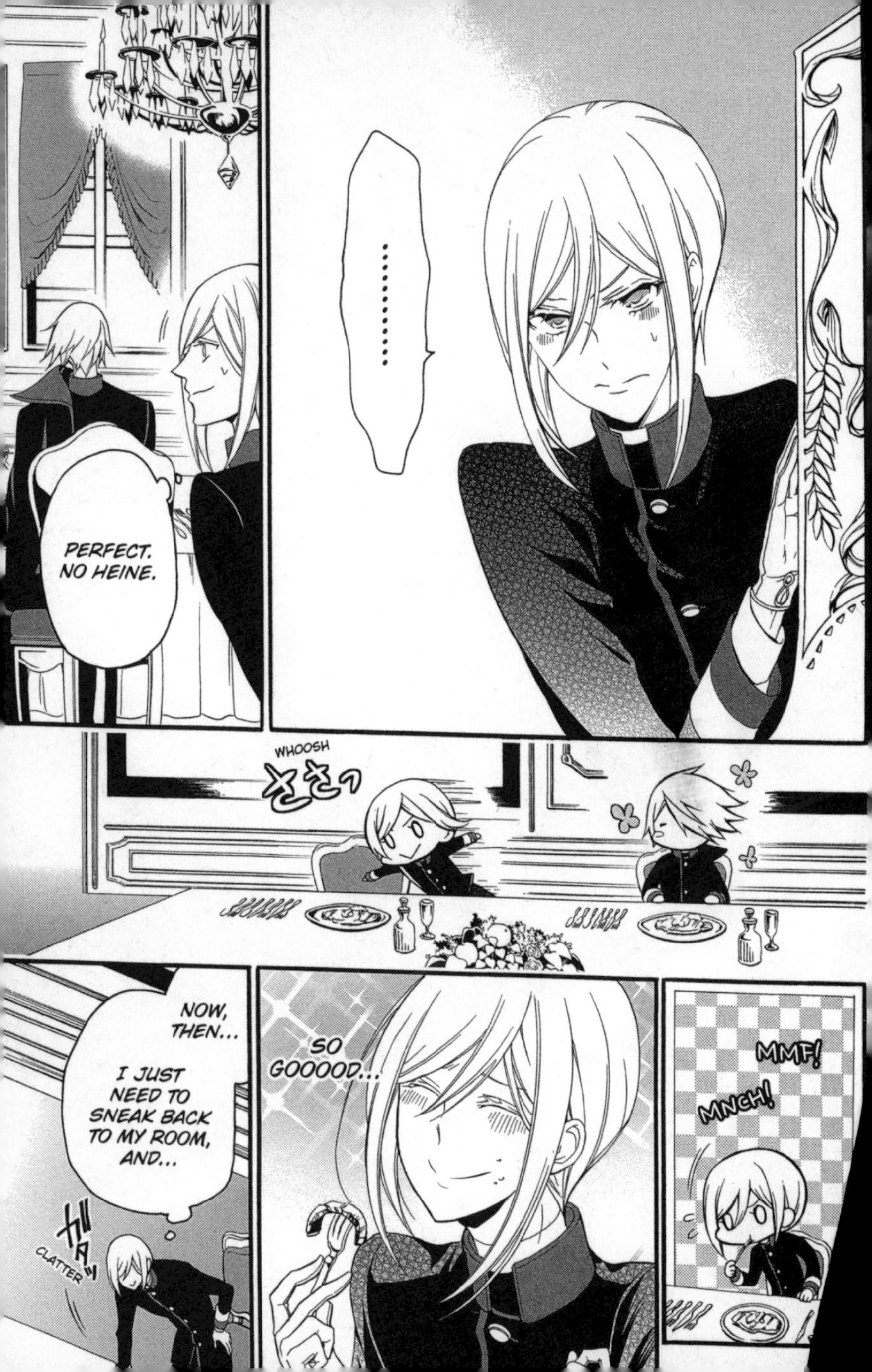
......
PERFECT. NO HEINE.
WHOOSH
MMF!
MNCH!
SO GOOOOD...
NOW, THEN...
I JUST NEED TO SNEAK BACK TO MY ROOM, AND...
CLATTER

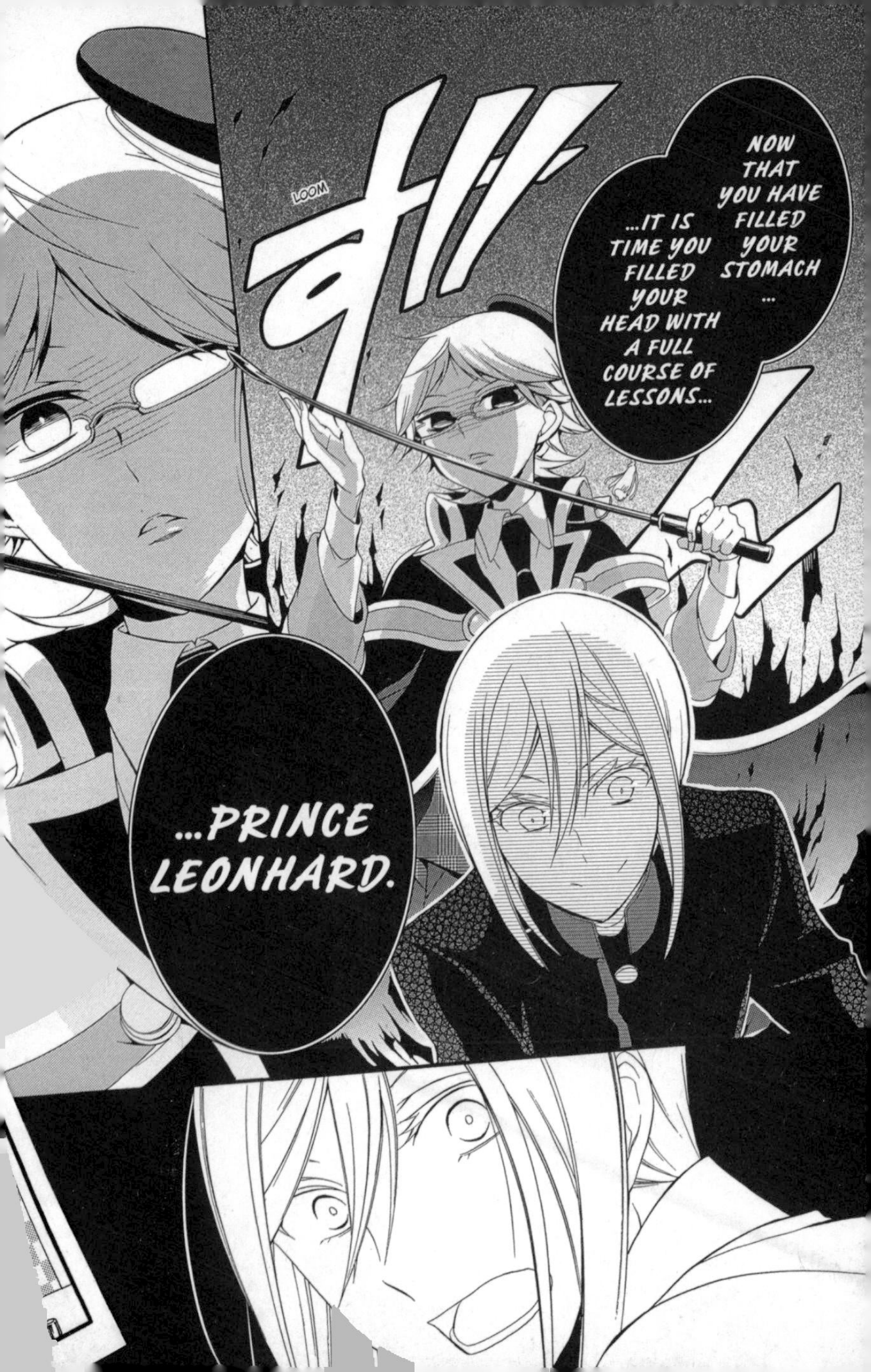
NOW THAT YOU HAVE FILLED YOUR STOMACH ...
...IT IS TIME YOU FILLED YOUR HEAD WITH A FULL COURSE OF LESSONS...
LOOM
...PRINCE LEONHARD.

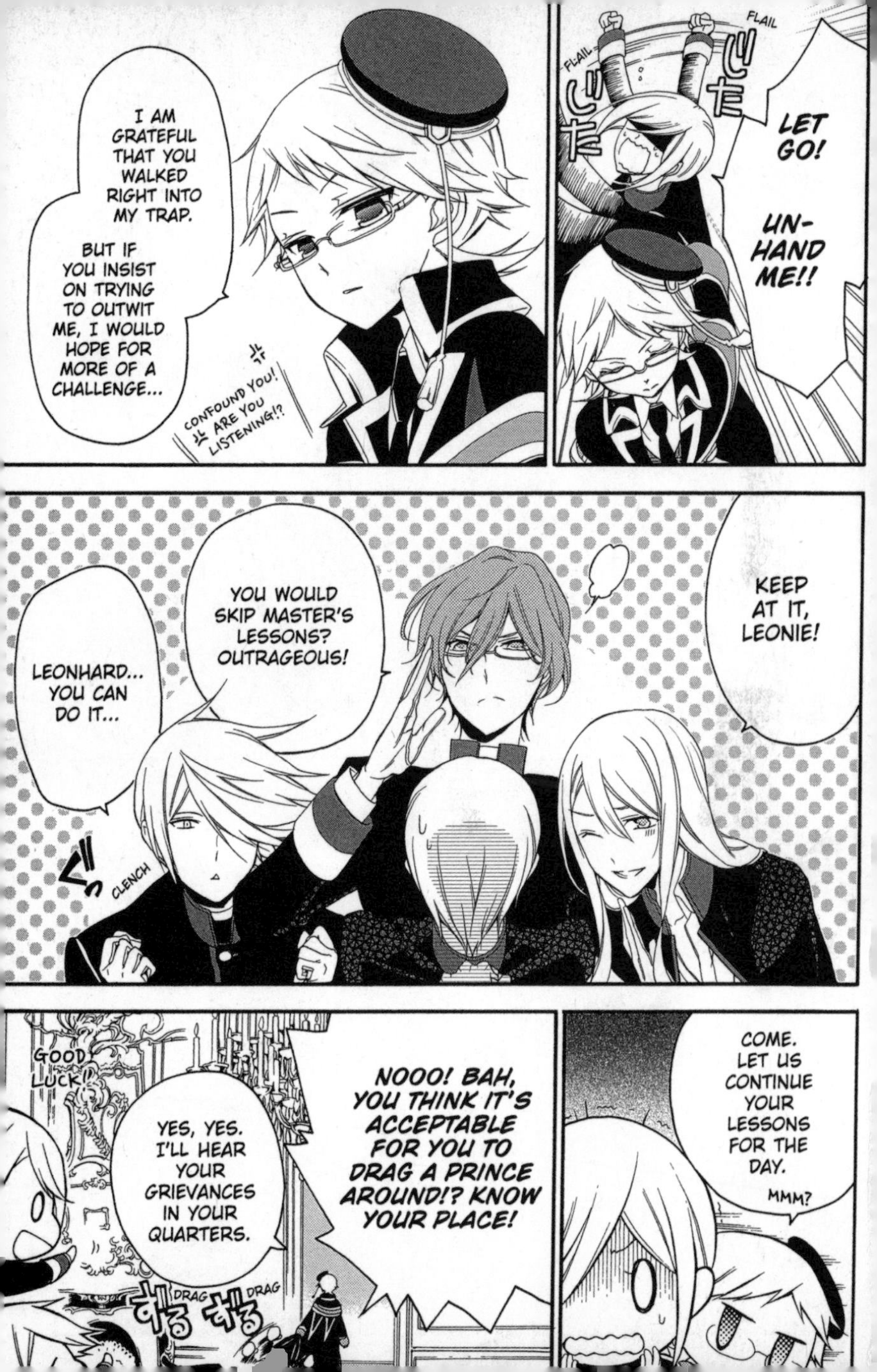
FLAIL FLAIL
LET GO!
UN-HAND ME!!
I AM GRATEFUL THAT YOU WALKED RIGHT INTO MY TRAP.
BUT IF YOU INSIST ON TRYING TO OUTWIT ME, I WOULD HOPE FOR MORE OF A CHALLENGE...
CONFOUND YOU! ARE YOU LISTENING!?
KEEP AT IT, LEONIE!
YOU WOULD SKIP MASTER'S LESSONS? OUTRAGEOUS!
LEONHARD... YOU CAN DO IT...
CLENCH
COME. LET US CONTINUE YOUR LESSONS FOR THE DAY.
MMM?
NOOO! BAH, YOU THINK IT'S ACCEPTABLE FOR YOU TO DRAG A PRINCE AROUND!? KNOW YOUR PLACE!
YES, YES. I'LL HEAR YOUR GRIEVANCES IN YOUR QUARTERS.
GOOD LUCK!
DRAG DRAG

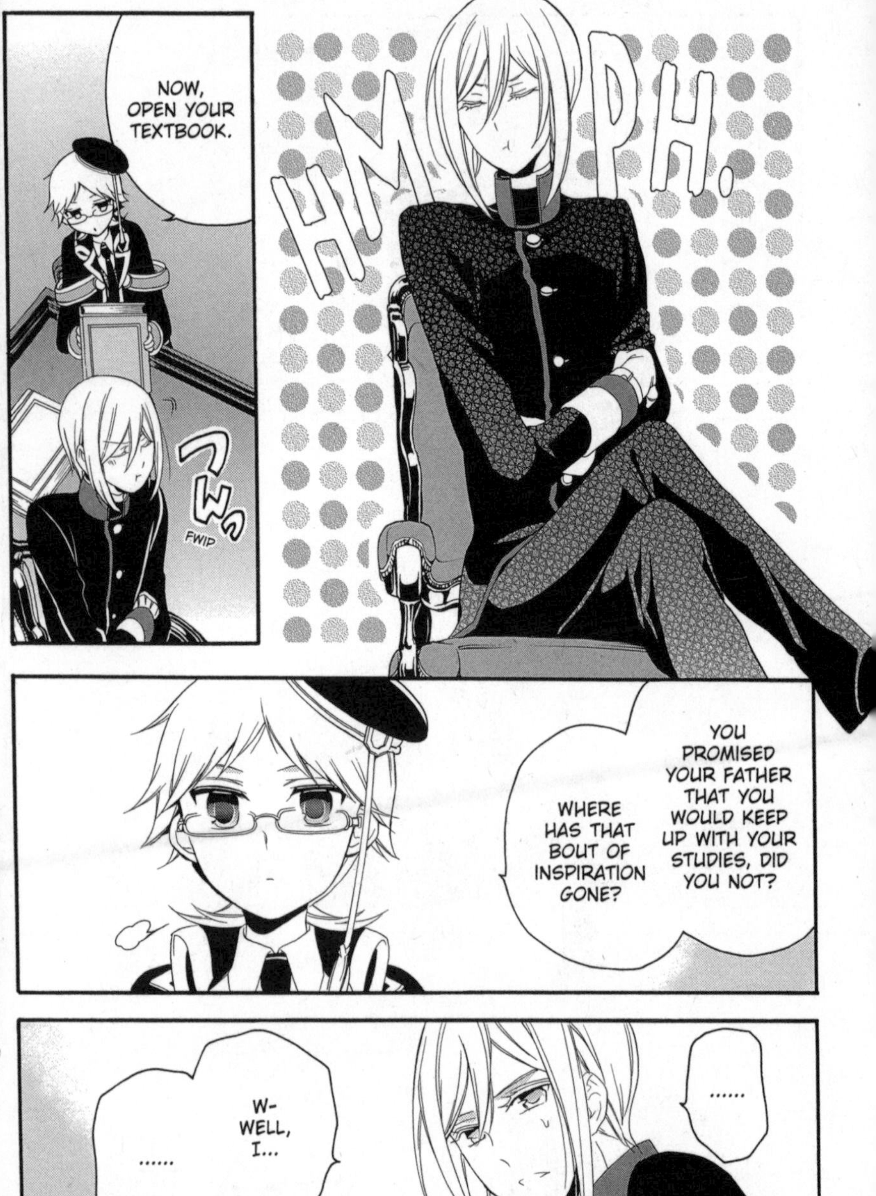
HMPH.
NOW, OPEN YOUR TEXTBOOK.
FWIP
YOU PROMISED YOUR FATHER THAT YOU WOULD KEEP UP WITH YOUR STUDIES, DID YOU NOT?
WHERE HAS THAT BOUT OF INSPIRATION GONE?
......
W-WELL, I...
......

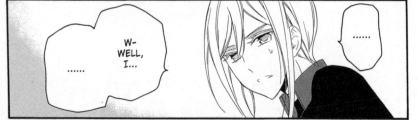

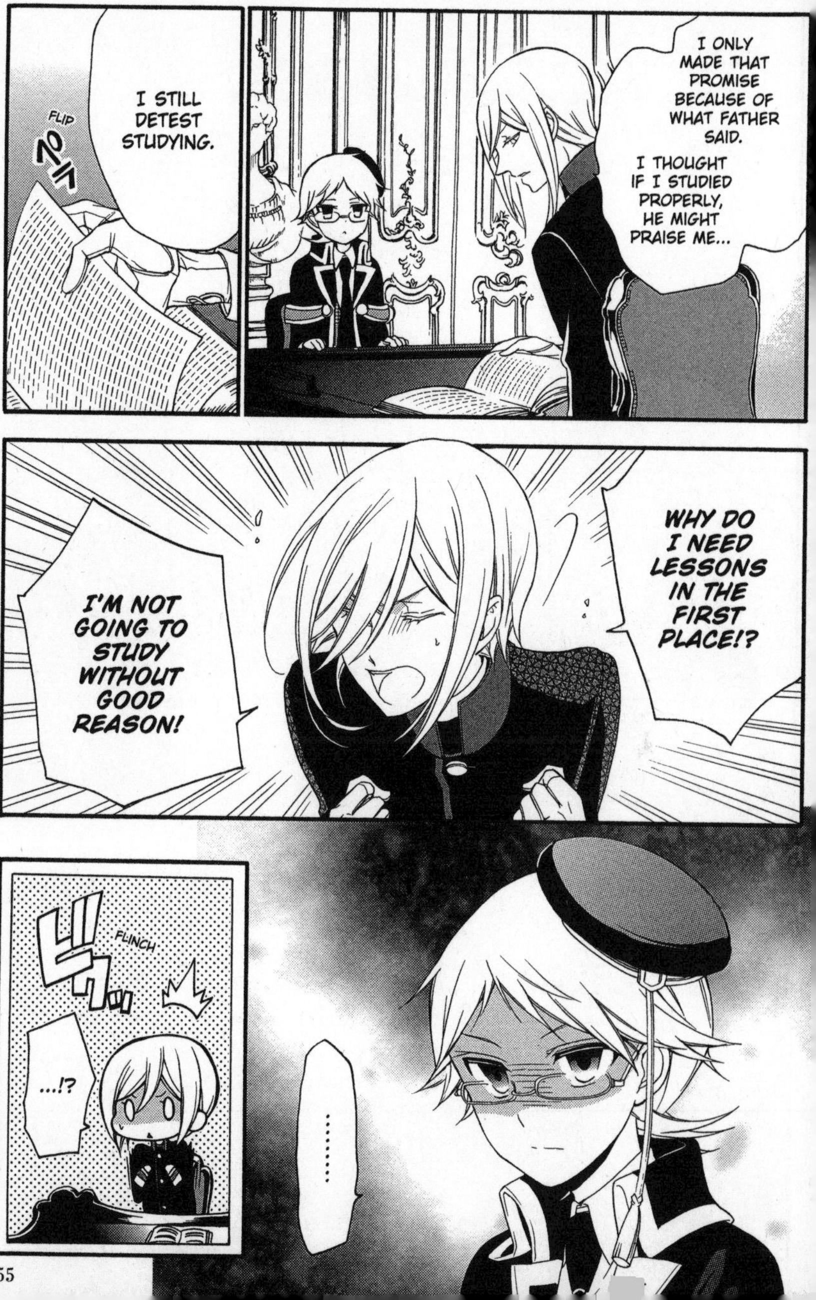
I ONLY MADE THAT PROMISE BECAUSE OF WHAT FATHER SAID.
I THOUGHT IF I STUDIED PROPERLY, HE MIGHT PRAISE ME...
FLIP
I STILL DETEST STUDYING.
WHY DO I NEED LESSONS IN THE FIRST PLACE!?
I'M NOT GOING TO STUDY WITHOUT GOOD REASON!
......
FLINCH
...!?

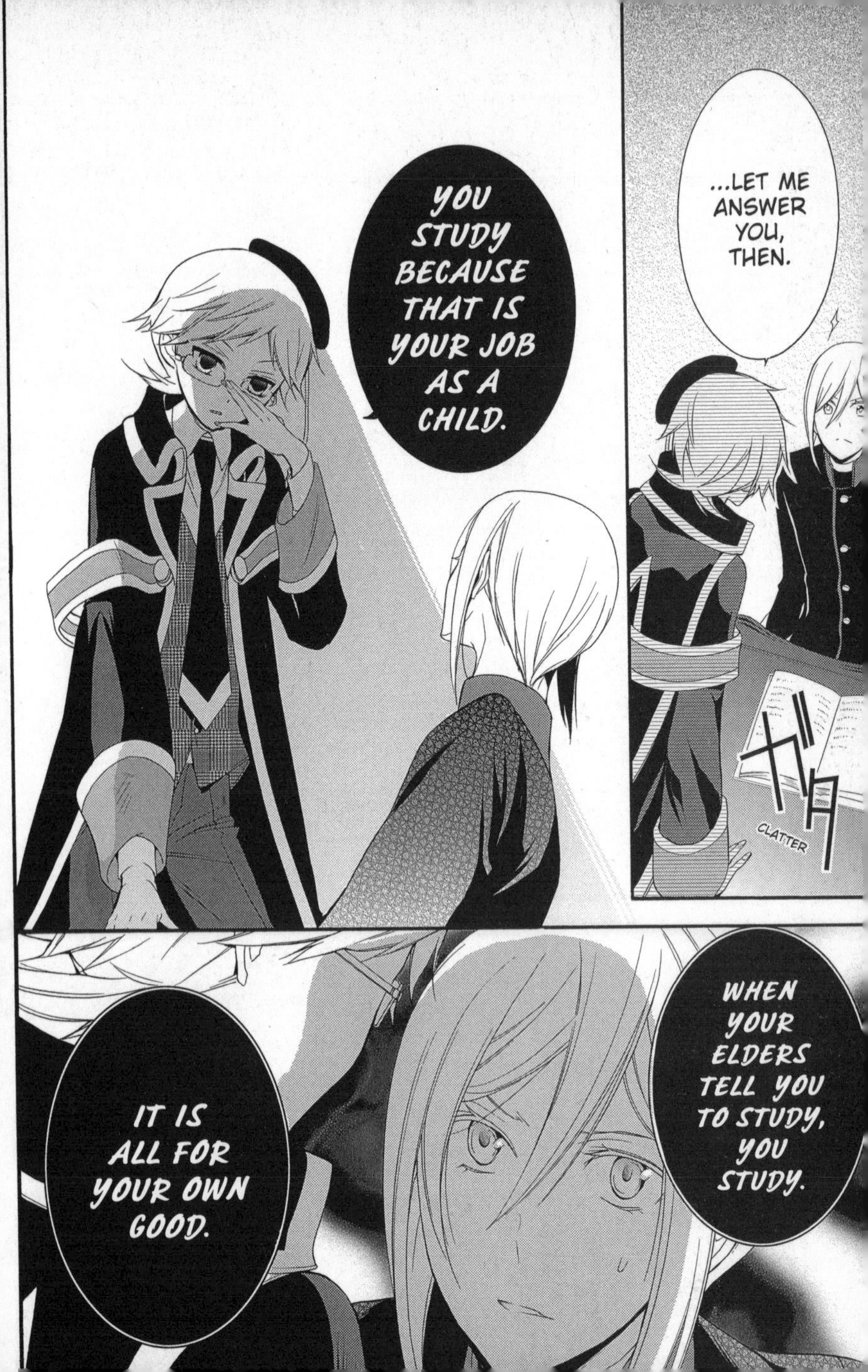
...LET ME ANSWER YOU, THEN.
CLATTER
YOU STUDY BECAUSE THAT IS YOUR JOB AS A CHILD.
WHEN YOUR ELDERS TELL YOU TO STUDY, YOU STUDY.
IT IS ALL FOR YOUR OWN GOOD.

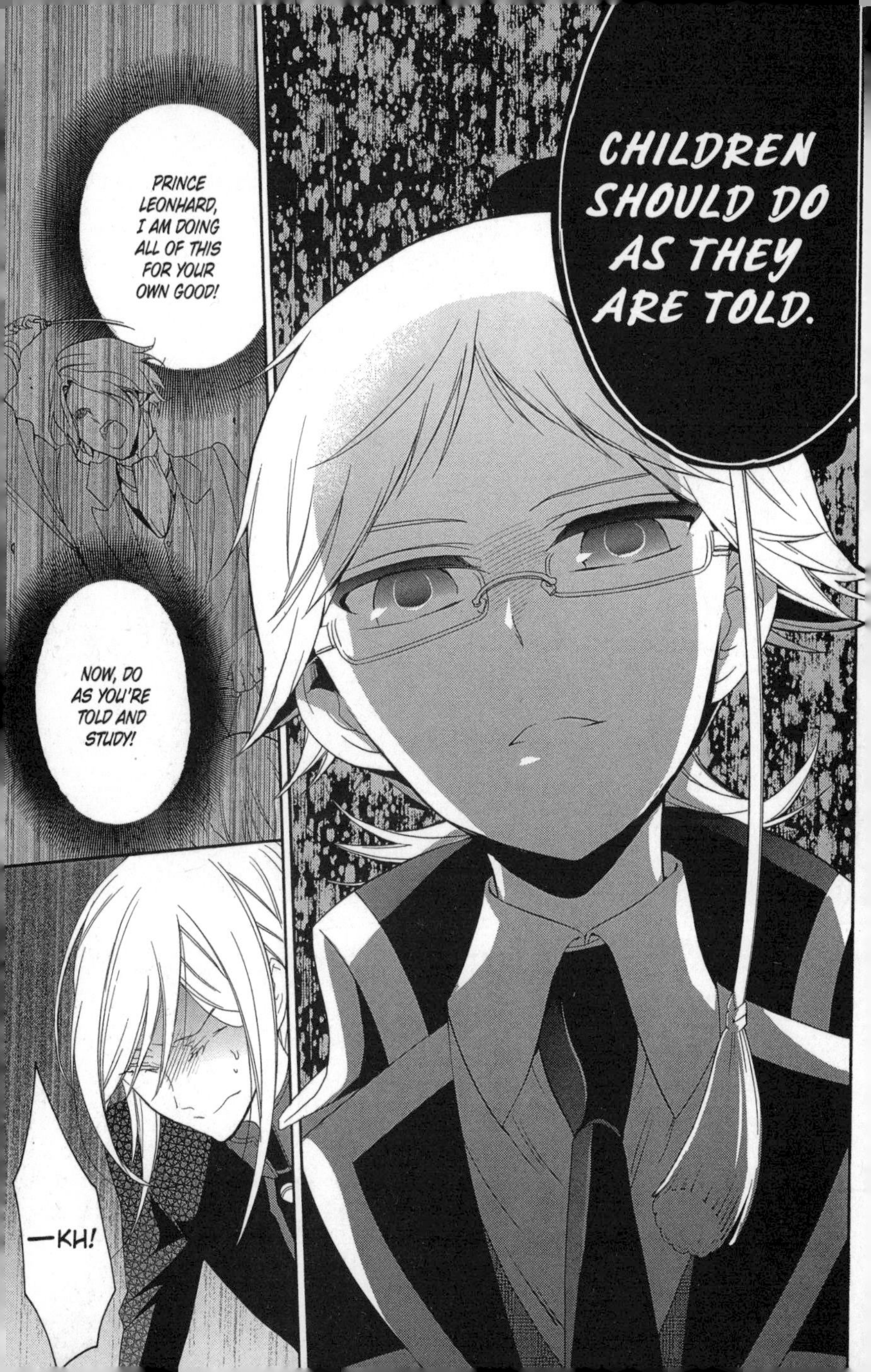
CHILDREN SHOULD DO AS THEY ARE TOLD.
PRINCE LEONHARD, I AM DOING ALL OF THIS FOR YOUR OWN GOOD!
NOW, DO AS YOU'RE TOLD AND STUDY!
—KH!

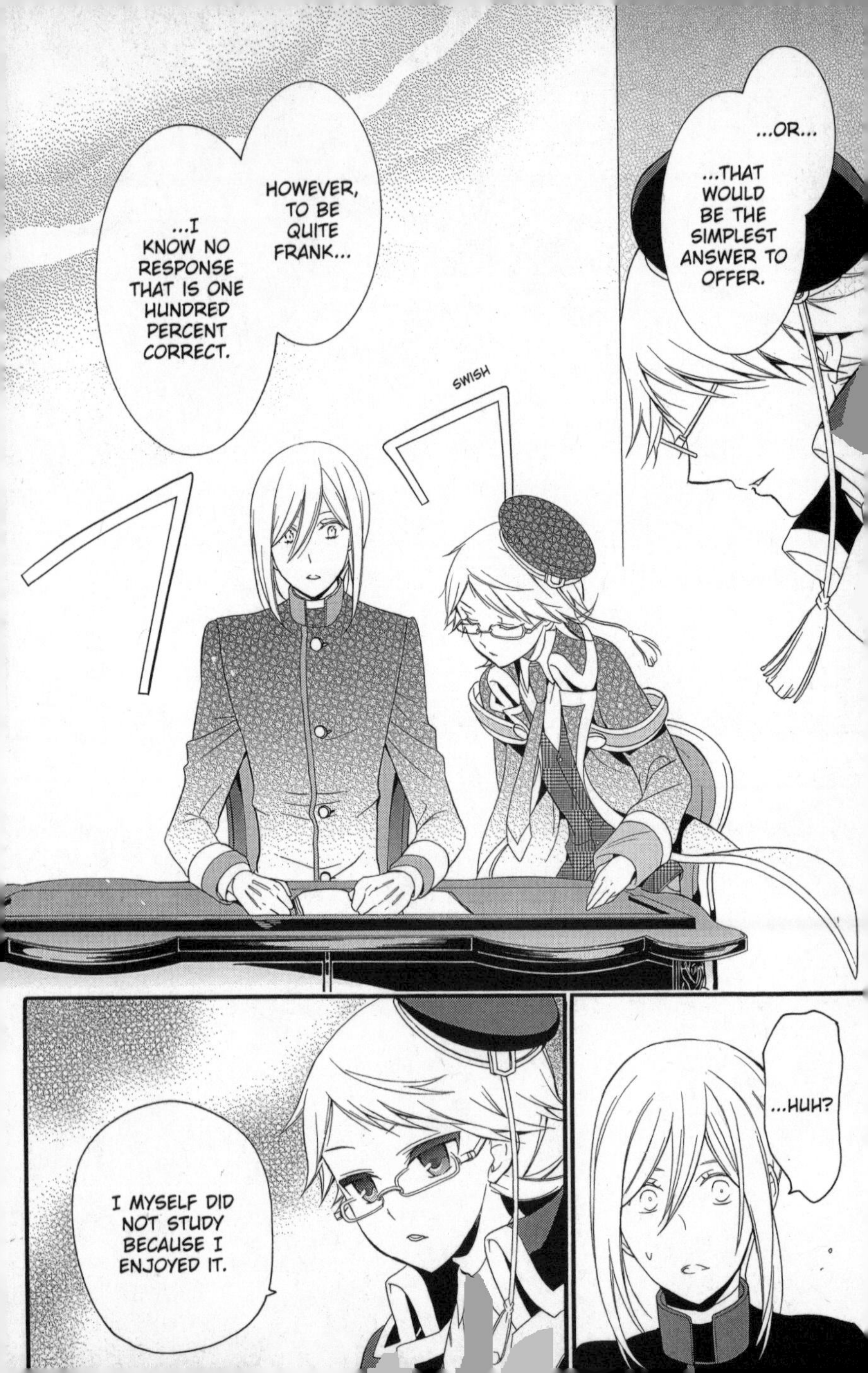
...OR...
...THAT WOULD BE THE SIMPLEST ANSWER TO OFFER.
HOWEVER, TO BE QUITE FRANK...
...I KNOW NO RESPONSE THAT IS ONE HUNDRED PERCENT CORRECT.
SWISH
...HUH?
I MYSELF DID NOT STUDY BECAUSE I ENJOYED IT.

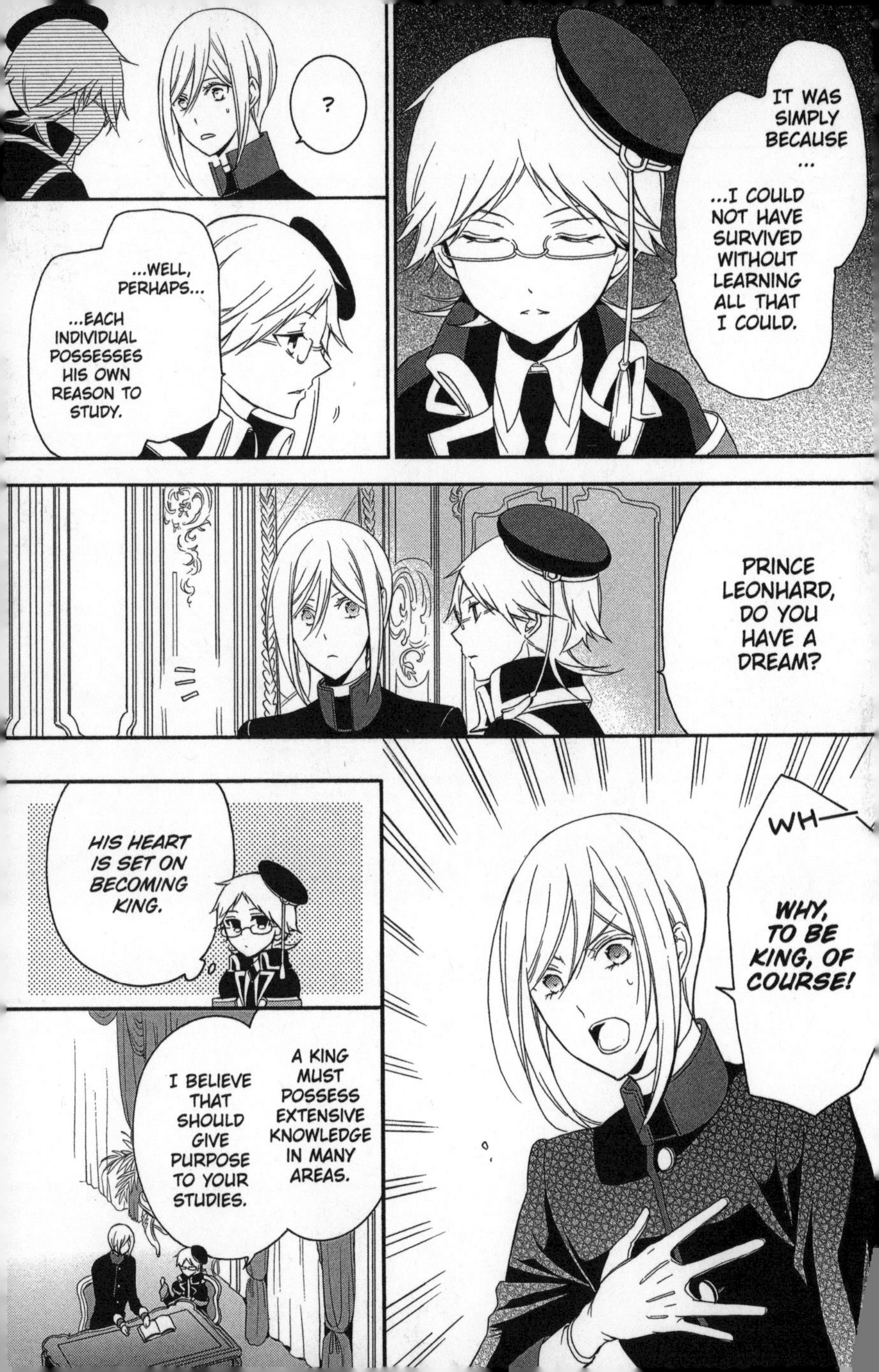
IT WAS SIMPLY BECAUSE ...
...I COULD NOT HAVE SURVIVED WITHOUT LEARNING ALL THAT I COULD.
?
...WELL, PERHAPS...
...EACH INDIVIDUAL POSSESSES HIS OWN REASON TO STUDY.
PRINCE LEONHARD, DO YOU HAVE A DREAM?
WH—
WHY, TO BE KING, OF COURSE!
HIS HEART IS SET ON BECOMING KING.
A KING MUST POSSESS EXTENSIVE KNOWLEDGE IN MANY AREAS.
I BELIEVE THAT SHOULD GIVE PURPOSE TO YOUR STUDIES.

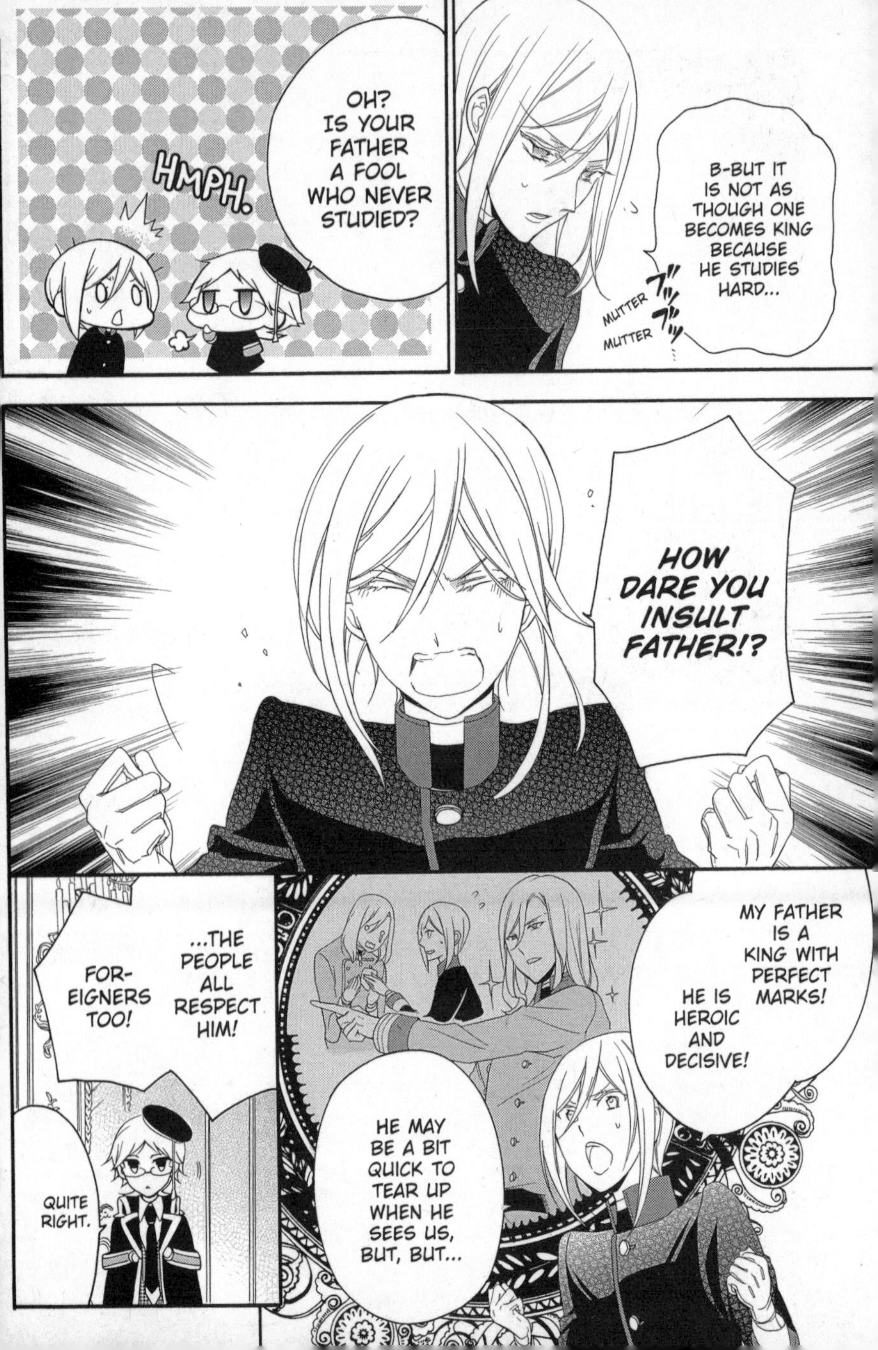
B-BUT IT IS NOT AS THOUGH ONE BECOMES KING BECAUSE HE STUDIES HARD...
MUTTER
MUTTER
OH? IS YOUR FATHER A FOOL WHO NEVER STUDIED?
HMPH.
HOW DARE YOU INSULT FATHER!?
MY FATHER IS A KING WITH PERFECT MARKS!
HE IS HEROIC AND DECISIVE!
HE MAY BE A BIT QUICK TO TEAR UP WHEN HE SEES US, BUT, BUT...
...THE PEOPLE ALL RESPECT HIM!
FOR-EIGNERS TOO!
QUITE RIGHT.

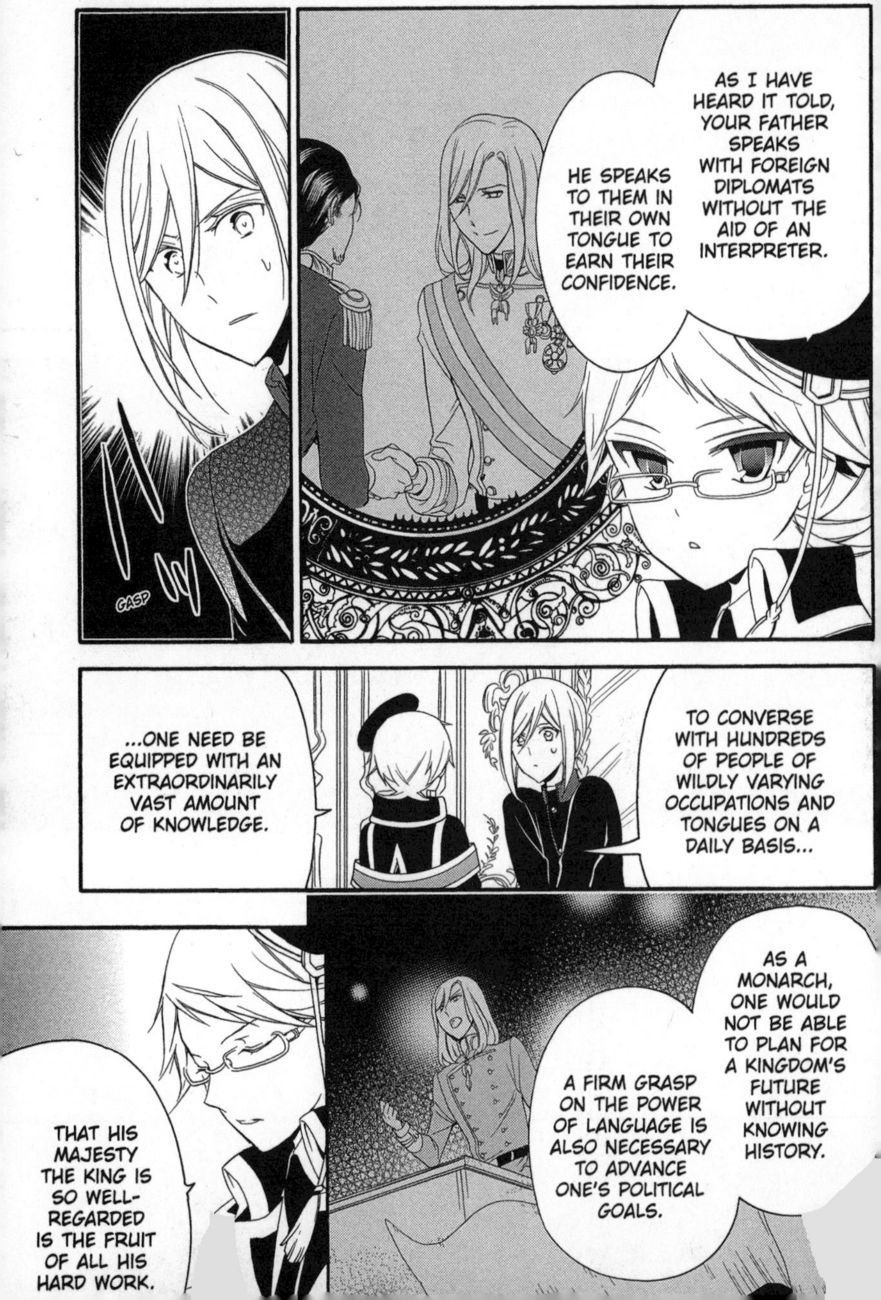
AS I HAVE HEARD IT TOLD, YOUR FATHER SPEAKS WITH FOREIGN DIPLOMATS WITHOUT THE AID OF AN INTERPRETER.
HE SPEAKS TO THEM IN THEIR OWN TONGUE TO EARN THEIR CONFIDENCE.
GASP
TO CONVERSE WITH HUNDREDS OF PEOPLE OF WILDLY VARYING OCCUPATIONS AND TONGUES ON A DAILY BASIS...
...ONE NEED BE EQUIPPED WITH AN EXTRAORDINARILY VAST AMOUNT OF KNOWLEDGE.
AS A MONARCH, ONE WOULD NOT BE ABLE TO PLAN FOR A KINGDOM'S FUTURE WITHOUT KNOWING HISTORY.
A FIRM GRASP ON THE POWER OF LANGUAGE IS ALSO NECESSARY TO ADVANCE ONE'S POLITICAL GOALS.
THAT HIS MAJESTY THE KING IS SO WELL-REGARDED IS THE FRUIT OF ALL HIS HARD WORK.

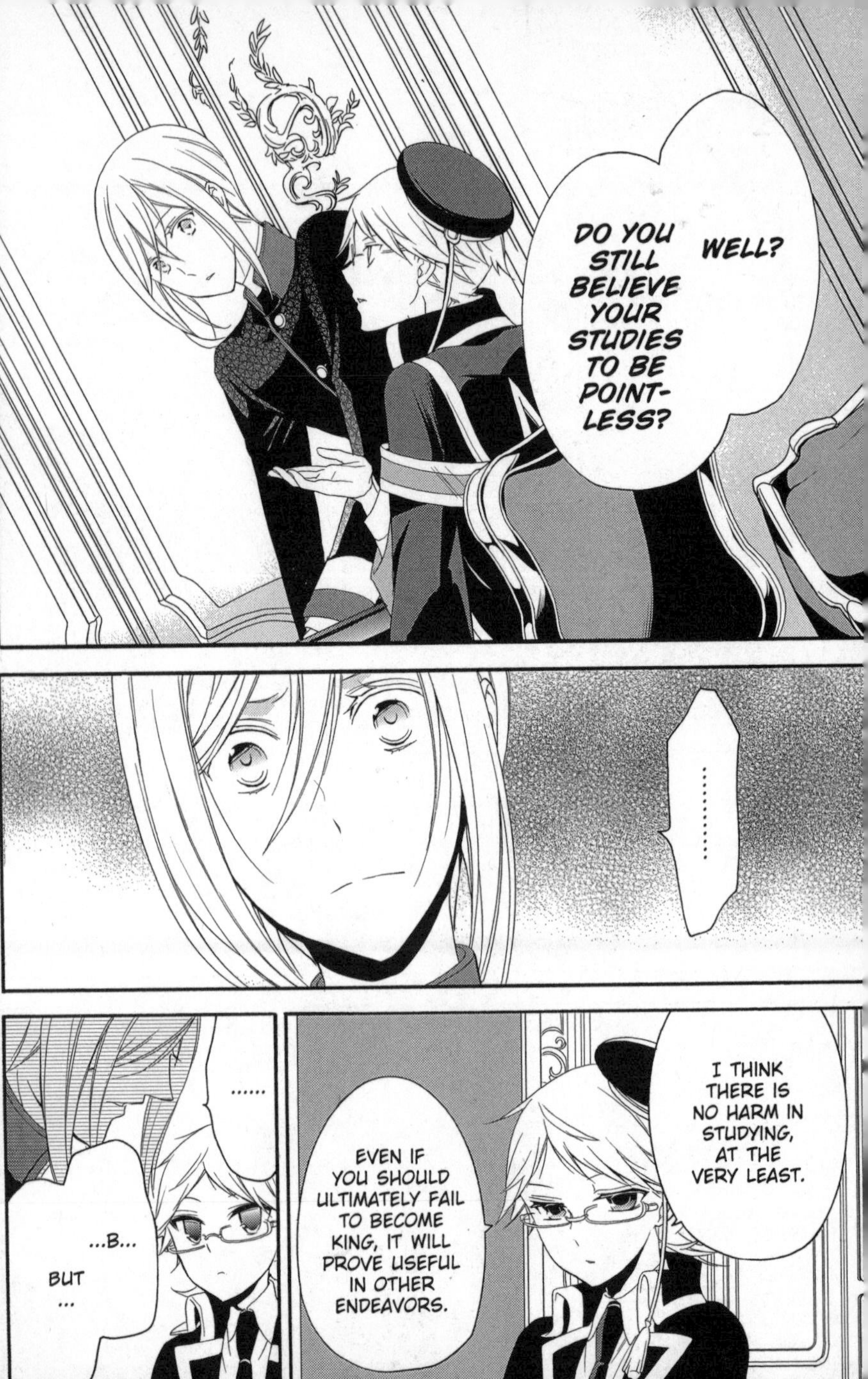
WELL?
DO YOU STILL BELIEVE YOUR STUDIES TO BE POINTLESS?
......
I THINK THERE IS NO HARM IN STUDYING, AT THE VERY LEAST.
EVEN IF YOU SHOULD ULTIMATELY FAIL TO BECOME KING, IT WILL PROVE USEFUL IN OTHER ENDEAVORS.
......
...B...
BUT ...

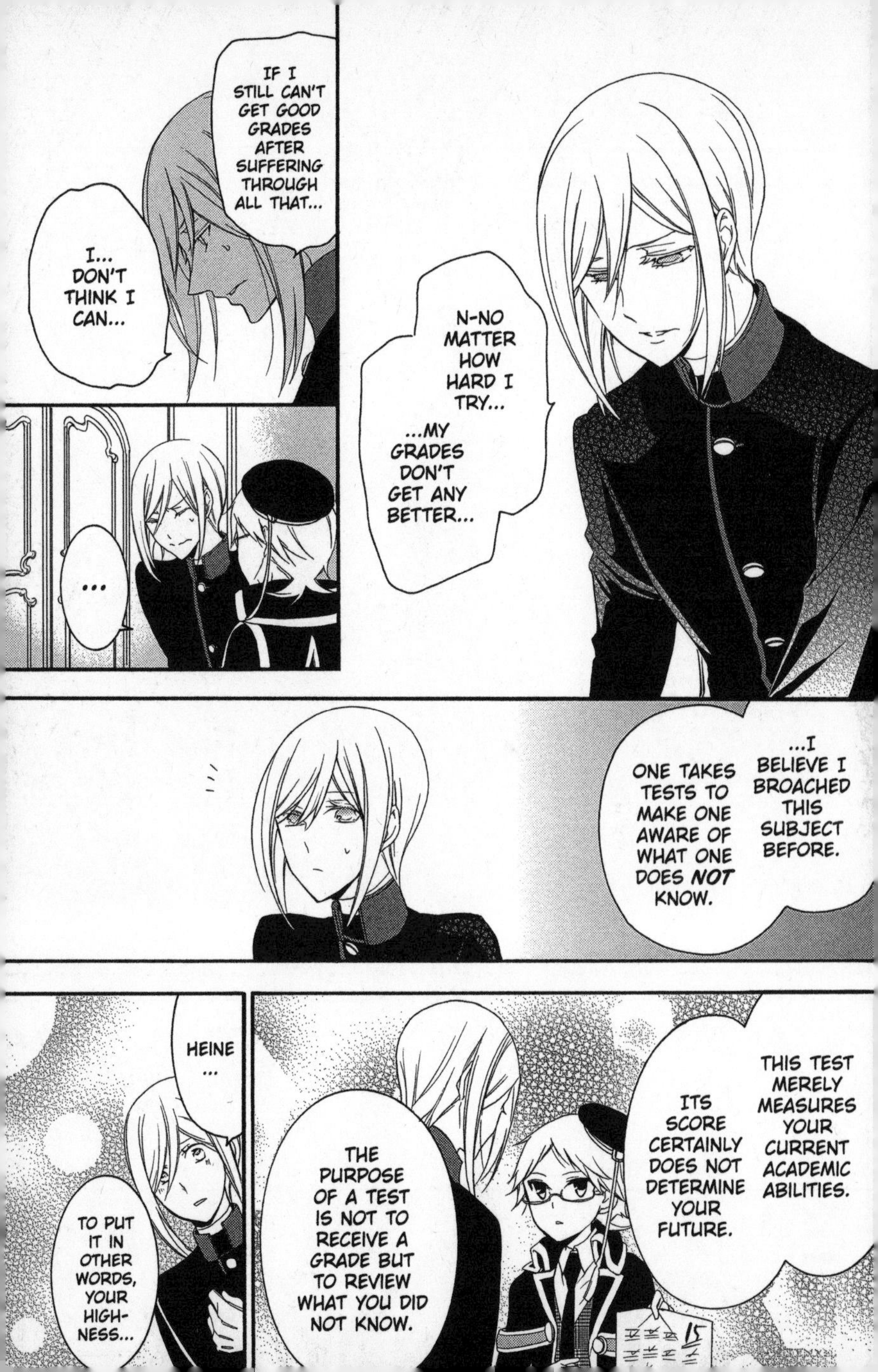
N-NO MATTER HOW HARD I TRY...
...MY GRADES DON'T GET ANY BETTER...
IF I STILL CAN'T GET GOOD GRADES AFTER SUFFERING THROUGH ALL THAT...
I... DON'T THINK I CAN...
...
...I BELIEVE I BROACHED THIS SUBJECT BEFORE.
ONE TAKES TESTS TO MAKE ONE AWARE OF WHAT ONE DOES *NOT* KNOW.
THIS TEST MERELY MEASURES YOUR CURRENT ACADEMIC ABILITIES.
ITS SCORE CERTAINLY DOES NOT DETERMINE YOUR FUTURE.
THE PURPOSE OF A TEST IS NOT TO RECEIVE A GRADE BUT TO REVIEW WHAT YOU DID NOT KNOW.
HEINE...
TO PUT IT IN OTHER WORDS, YOUR HIGHNESS...

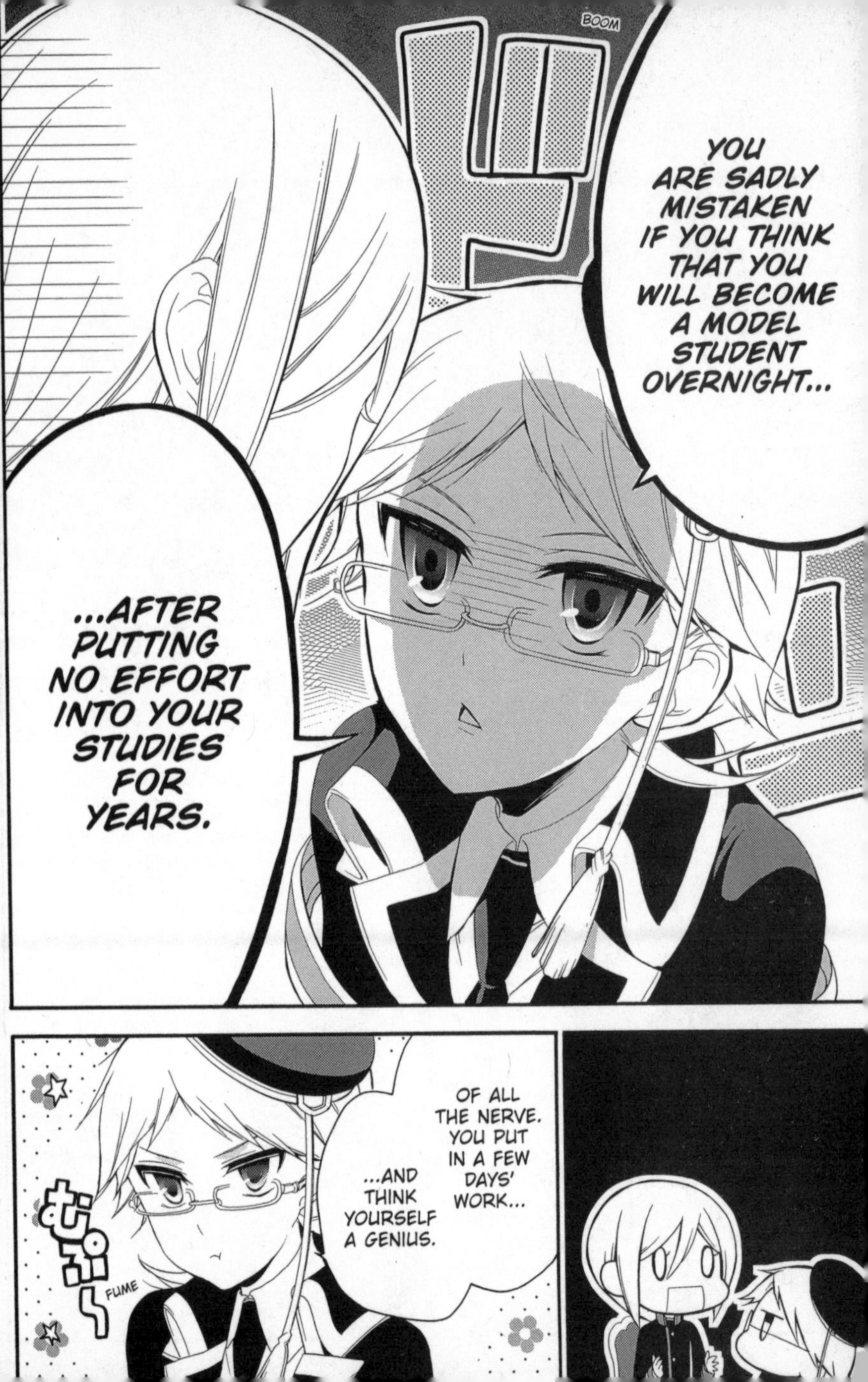
BOOM
YOU ARE SADLY MISTAKEN IF YOU THINK THAT YOU WILL BECOME A MODEL STUDENT OVERNIGHT...
...AFTER PUTTING NO EFFORT INTO YOUR STUDIES FOR YEARS.
OF ALL THE NERVE. YOU PUT IN A FEW DAYS' WORK...
...AND THINK YOURSELF A GENIUS.
むぷ～
FUME

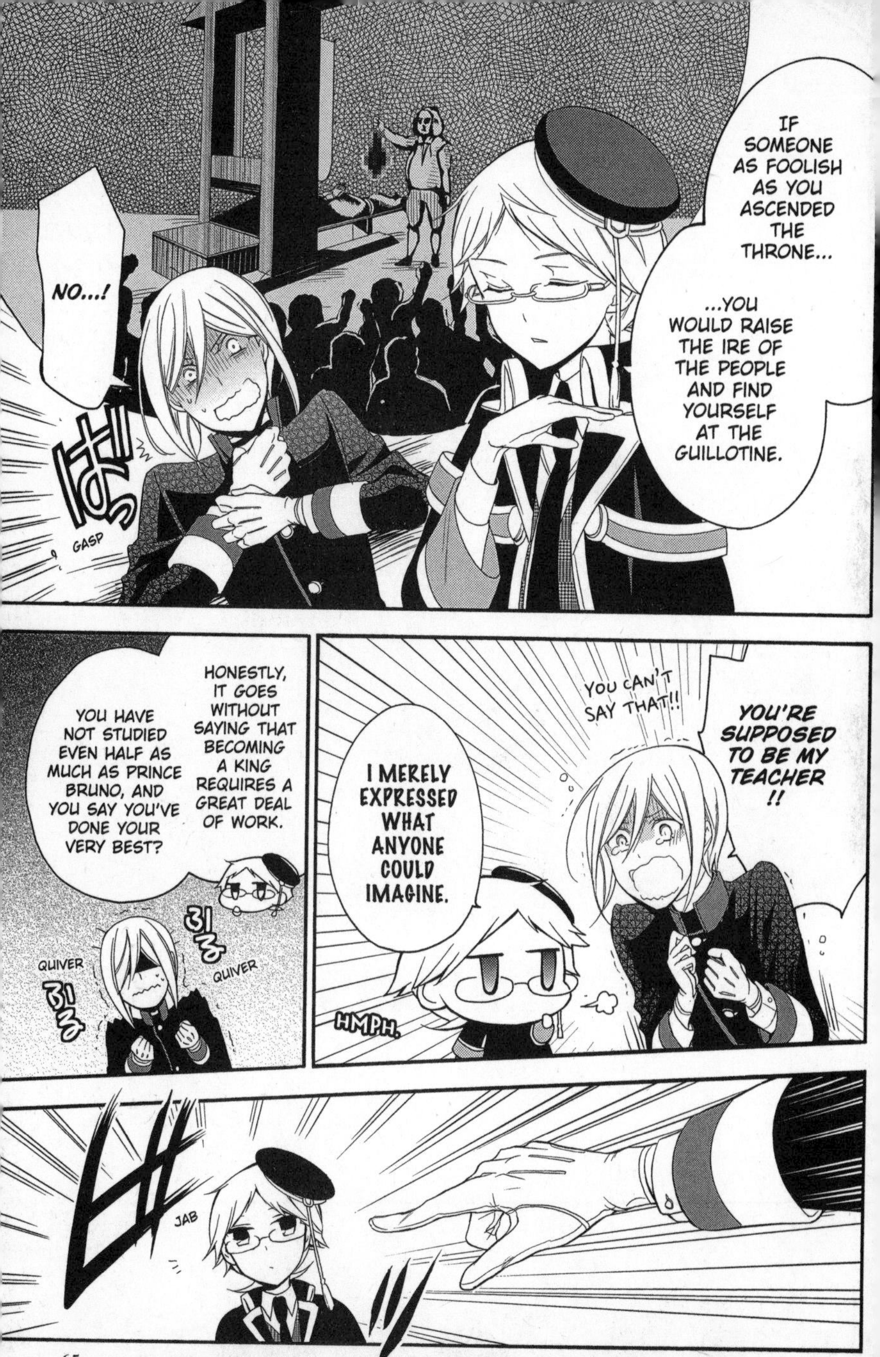
IF SOMEONE AS FOOLISH AS YOU ASCENDED THE THRONE...
...YOU WOULD RAISE THE IRE OF THE PEOPLE AND FIND YOURSELF AT THE GUILLOTINE.
NO...!
はっ
GASP
YOU'RE SUPPOSED TO BE MY TEACHER!!
YOU CAN'T SAY THAT!!
I MERELY EXPRESSED WHAT ANYONE COULD IMAGINE.
HMPH.
HONESTLY, IT GOES WITHOUT SAYING THAT BECOMING A KING REQUIRES A GREAT DEAL OF WORK.
YOU HAVE NOT STUDIED EVEN HALF AS MUCH AS PRINCE BRUNO, AND YOU SAY YOU'VE DONE YOUR VERY BEST?
ふる
QUIVER
ふる
QUIVER
JAB

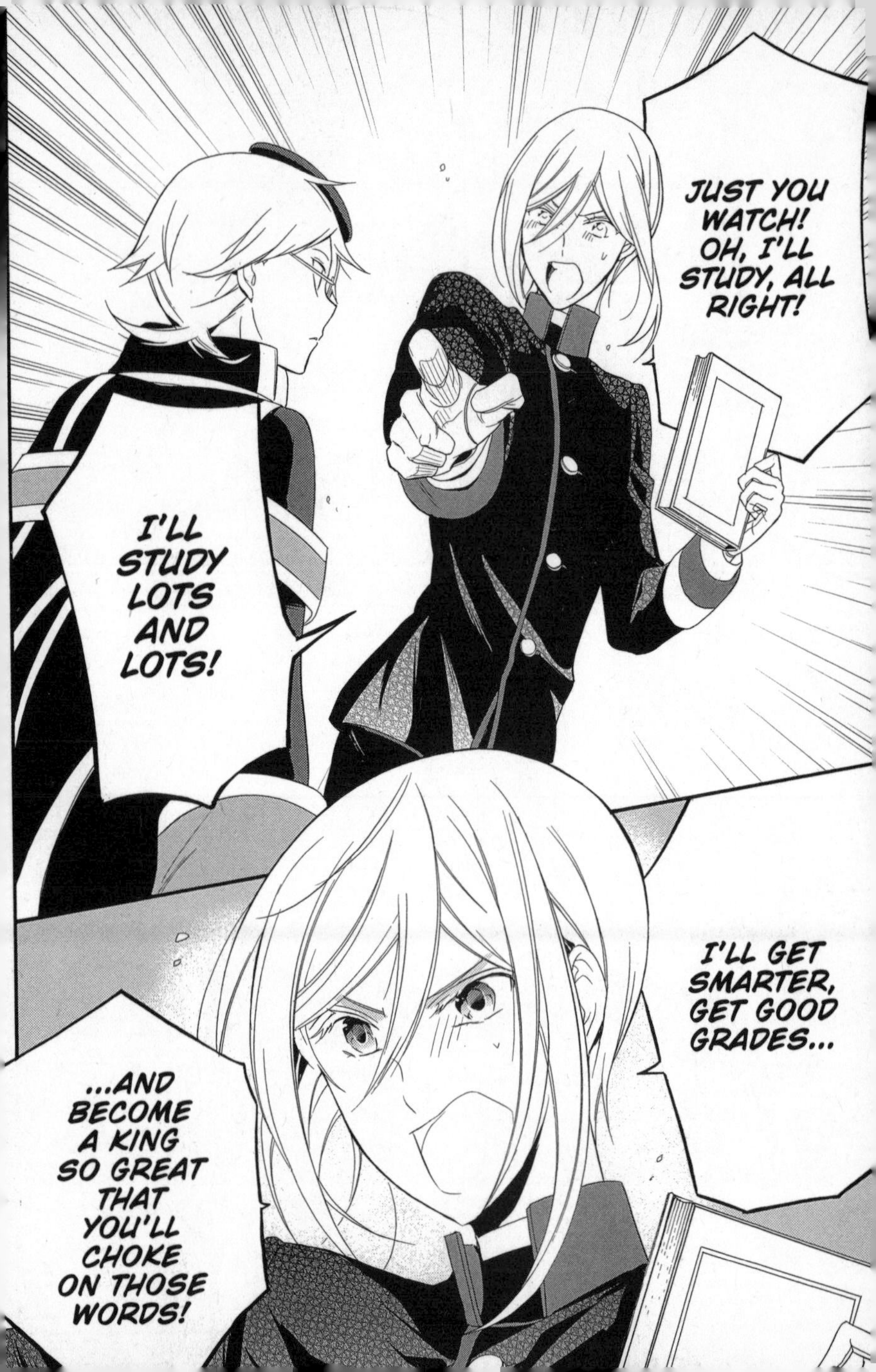
JUST YOU WATCH! OH, I'LL STUDY, ALL RIGHT!
I'LL STUDY LOTS AND LOTS!
I'LL GET SMARTER, GET GOOD GRADES...
...AND BECOME A KING SO GREAT THAT YOU'LL CHOKE ON THOSE WORDS!

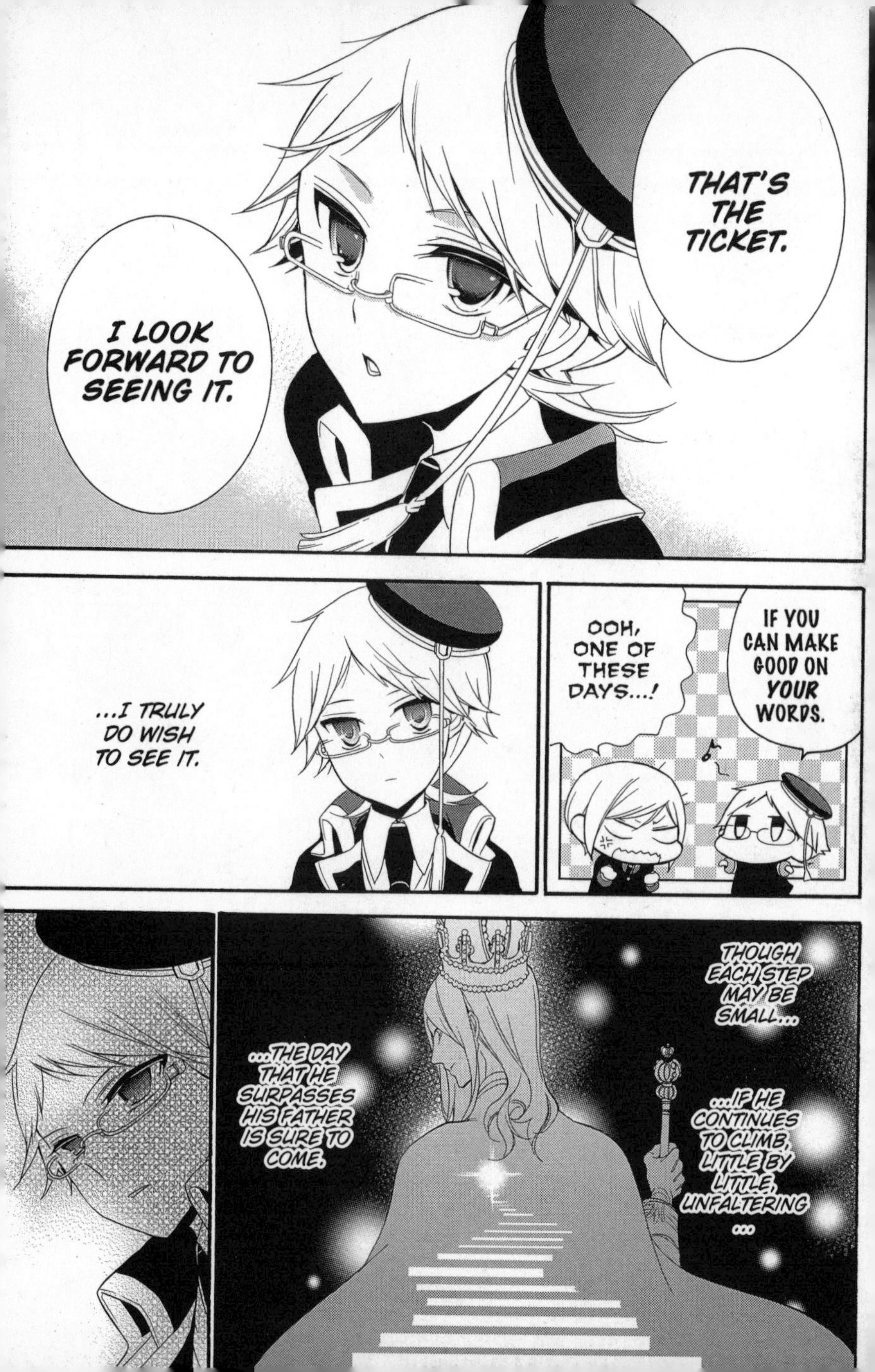
THAT'S THE TICKET.
I LOOK FORWARD TO SEEING IT.
IF YOU CAN MAKE GOOD ON YOUR WORDS.
OOH, ONE OF THESE DAYS...!
...I TRULY DO WISH TO SEE IT.
THOUGH EACH STEP MAY BE SMALL...
...IF HE CONTINUES TO CLIMB, LITTLE BY LITTLE, UNFALTERING...
...THE DAY THAT HE SURPASSES HIS FATHER IS SURE TO COME.

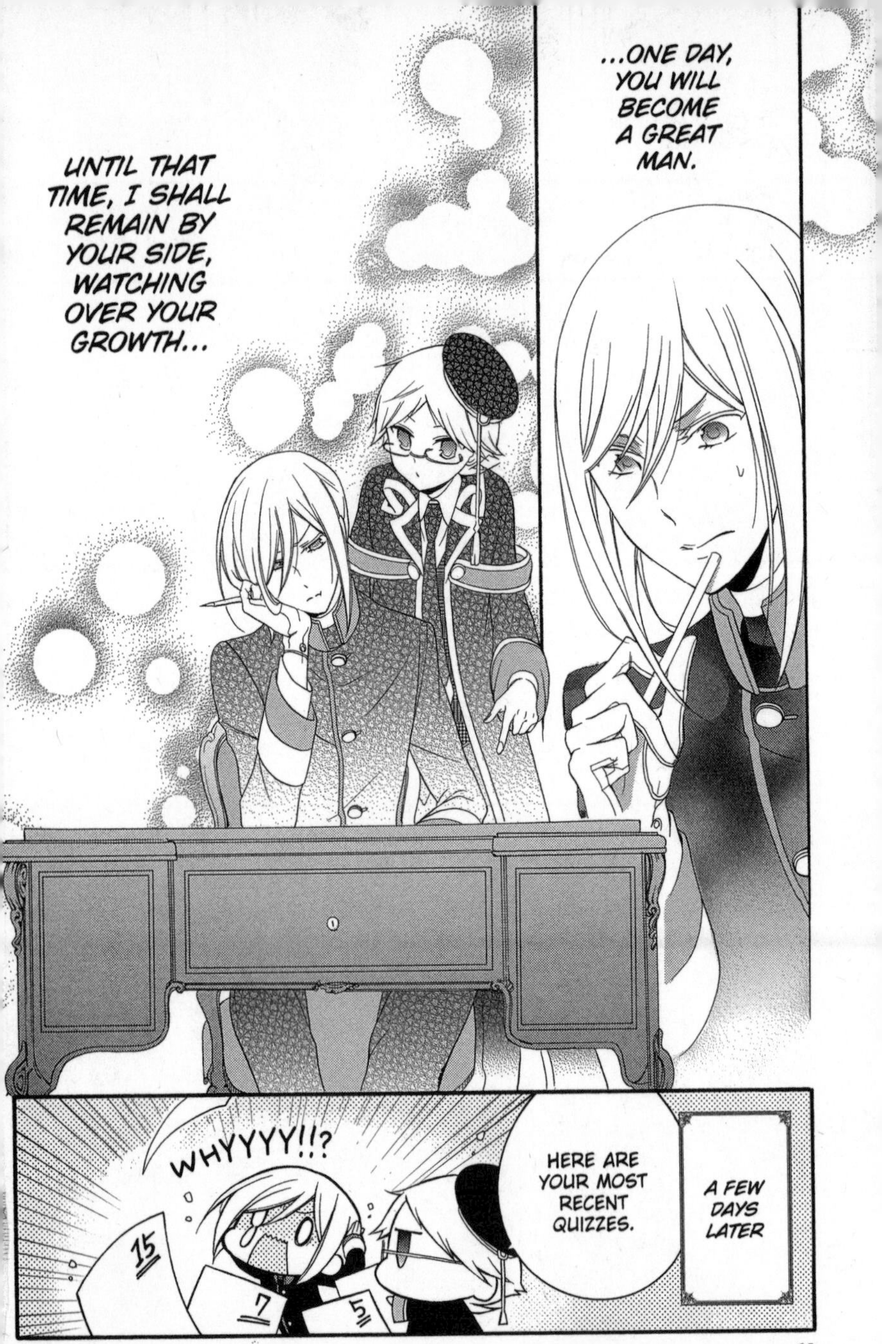
...ONE DAY, YOU WILL BECOME A GREAT MAN.
UNTIL THAT TIME, I SHALL REMAIN BY YOUR SIDE, WATCHING OVER YOUR GROWTH...
A FEW DAYS LATER
HERE ARE YOUR MOST RECENT QUIZZES.
WHYYYY!!?
15
7
5

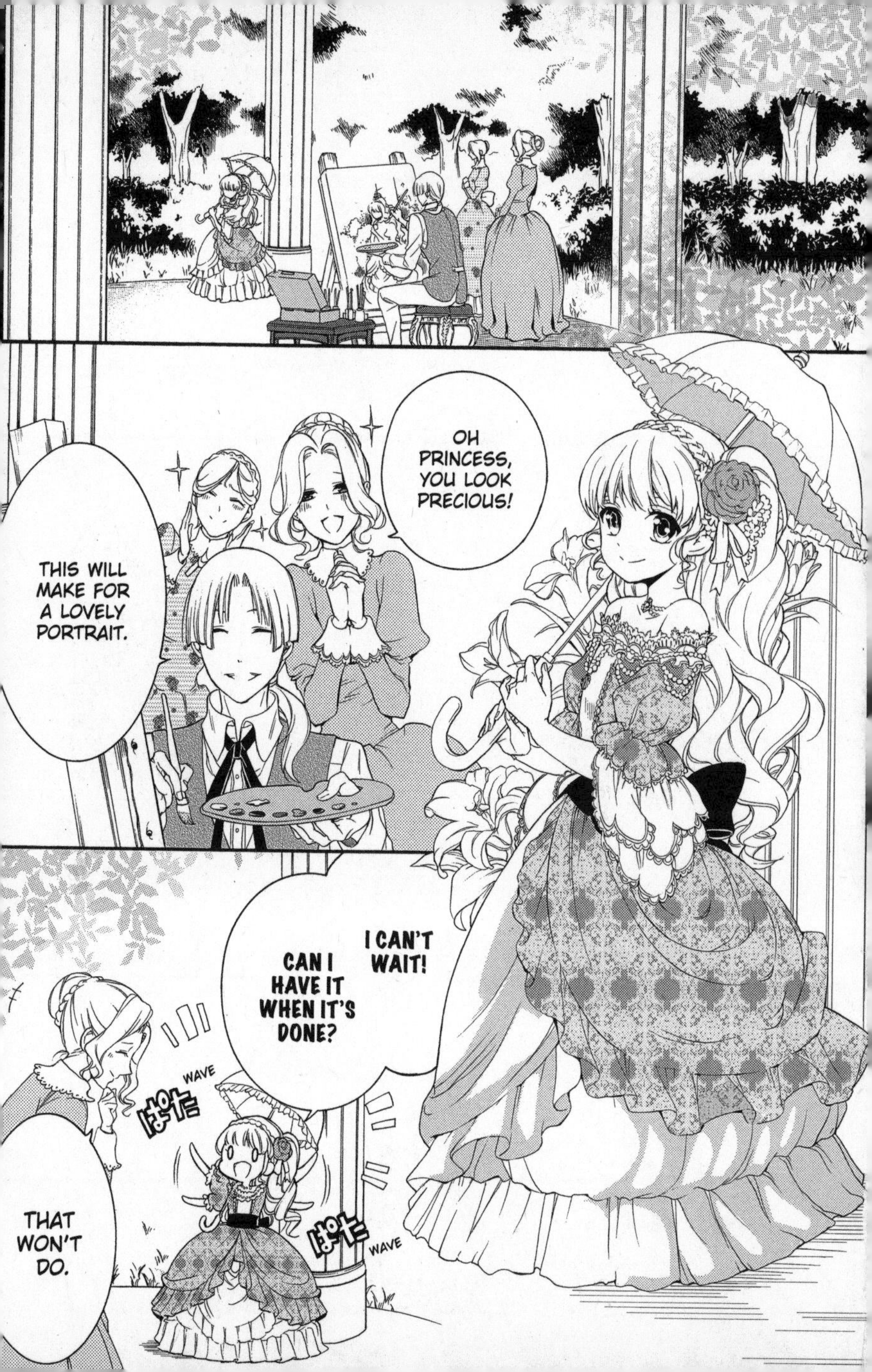
OH PRINCESS, YOU LOOK PRECIOUS!
THIS WILL MAKE FOR A LOVELY PORTRAIT.
I CAN'T WAIT!
CAN I HAVE IT WHEN IT'S DONE?
WAVE
WAVE
THAT WON'T DO.

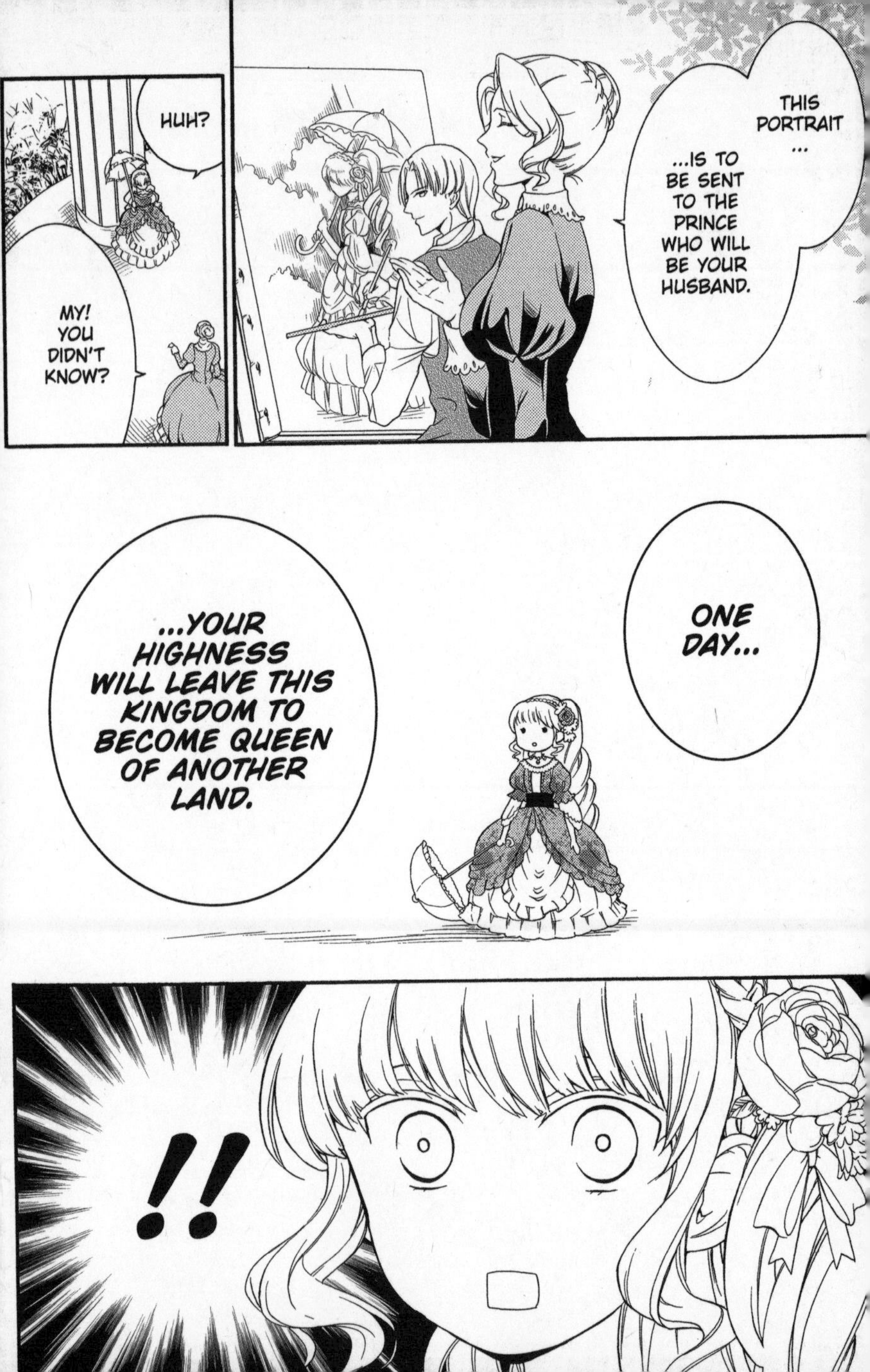
THIS PORTRAIT ...
...IS TO BE SENT TO THE PRINCE WHO WILL BE YOUR HUSBAND.
HUH?
MY! YOU DIDN'T KNOW?
ONE DAY...
...YOUR HIGHNESS WILL LEAVE THIS KINGDOM TO BECOME QUEEN OF ANOTHER LAND.
!!

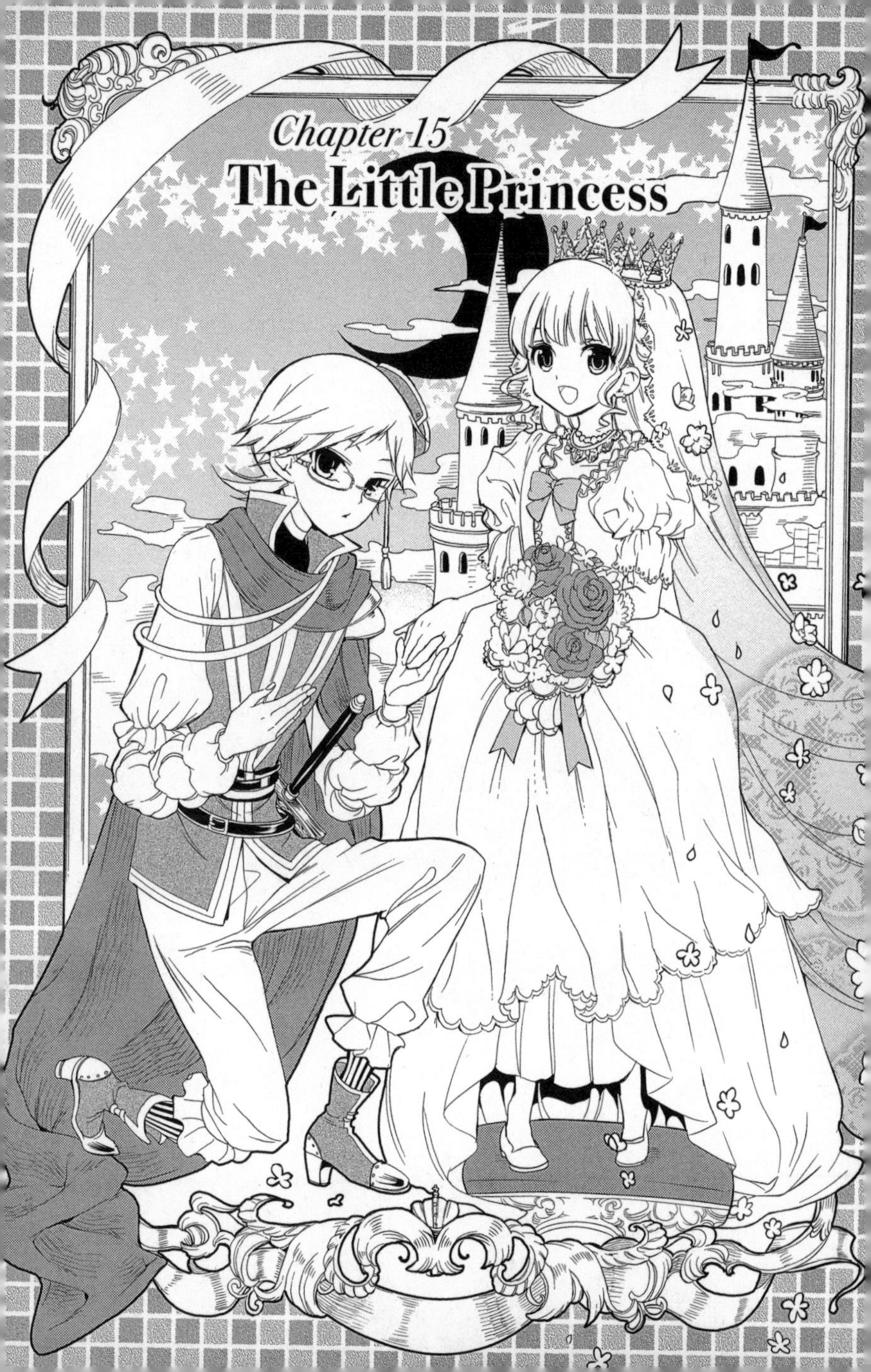
Chapter 15
The Little Princess

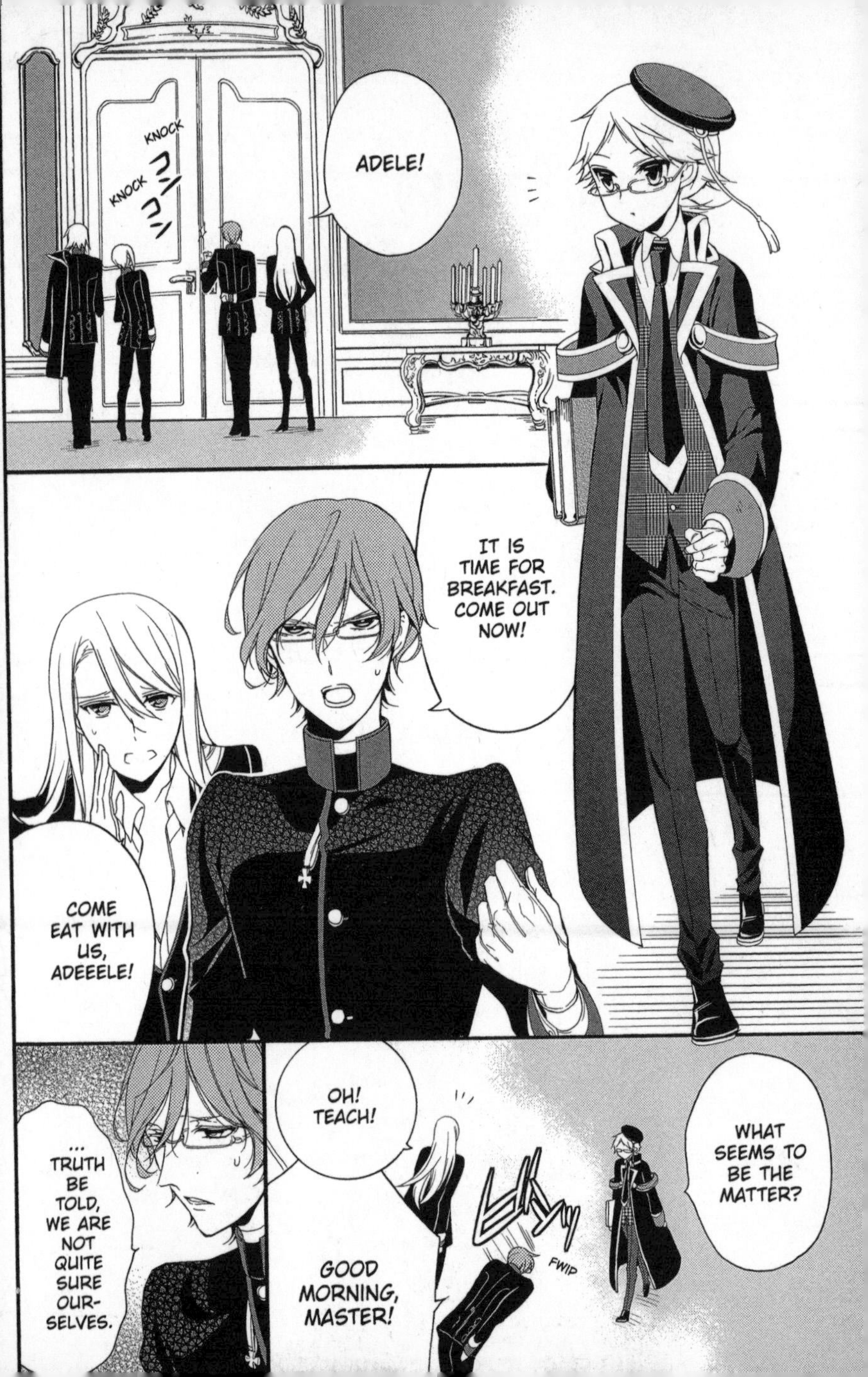
KNOCK
KNOCK
コンコン
ADELE!
IT IS TIME FOR BREAKFAST. COME OUT NOW!
COME EAT WITH US, ADEEELE!
WHAT SEEMS TO BE THE MATTER?
FWIP
OH! TEACH!
GOOD MORNING, MASTER!
... TRUTH BE TOLD, WE ARE NOT QUITE SURE OURSELVES.

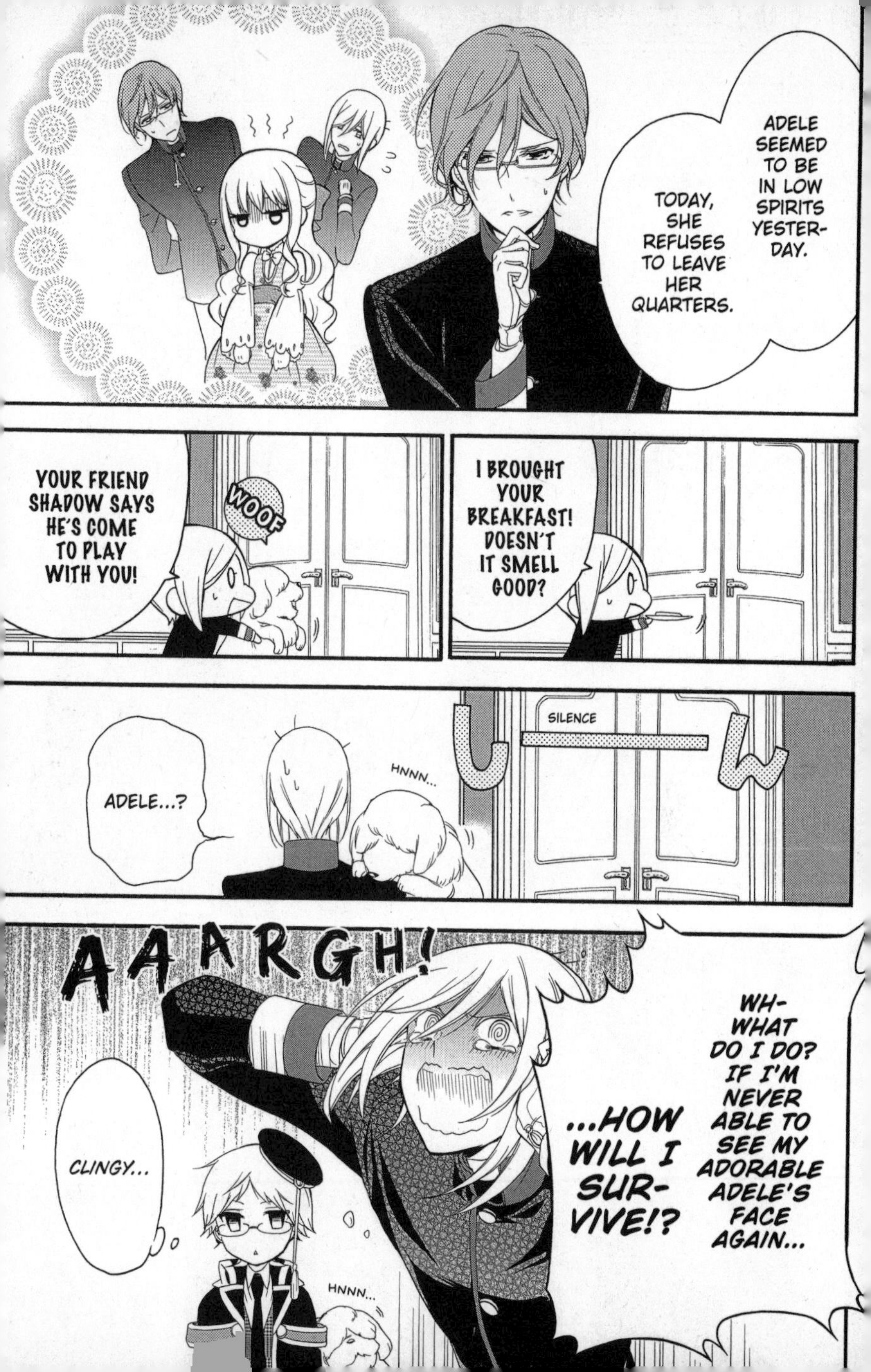
ADELE SEEMED TO BE IN LOW SPIRITS YESTERDAY.
TODAY, SHE REFUSES TO LEAVE HER QUARTERS.
I BROUGHT YOUR BREAKFAST! DOESN'T IT SMELL GOOD?
YOUR FRIEND SHADOW SAYS HE'S COME TO PLAY WITH YOU!
WOOF
SILENCE
U—W
HNNN...
ADELE...?
AAARGH!
WH-WHAT DO I DO? IF I'M NEVER ABLE TO SEE MY ADORABLE ADELE'S FACE AGAIN...
...HOW WILL I SUR-VIVE!?
CLINGY...
HNNN...

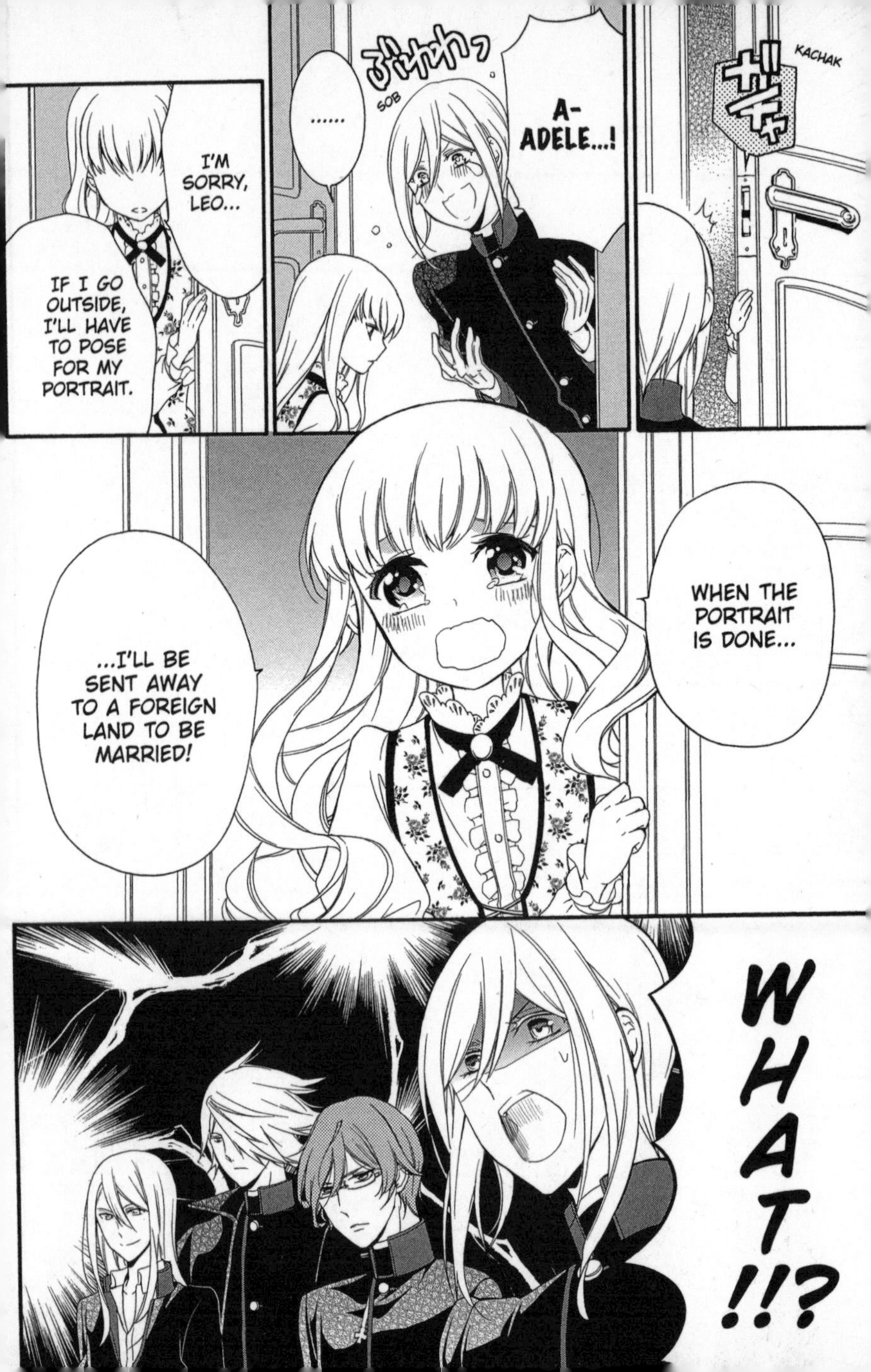

KACHAK
ガチャ
A-ADELE...!
SOB
......
I'M SORRY, LEO...
IF I GO OUTSIDE, I'LL HAVE TO POSE FOR MY PORTRAIT.
WHEN THE PORTRAIT IS DONE...
...I'LL BE SENT AWAY TO A FOREIGN LAND TO BE MARRIED!
WHAT!!?

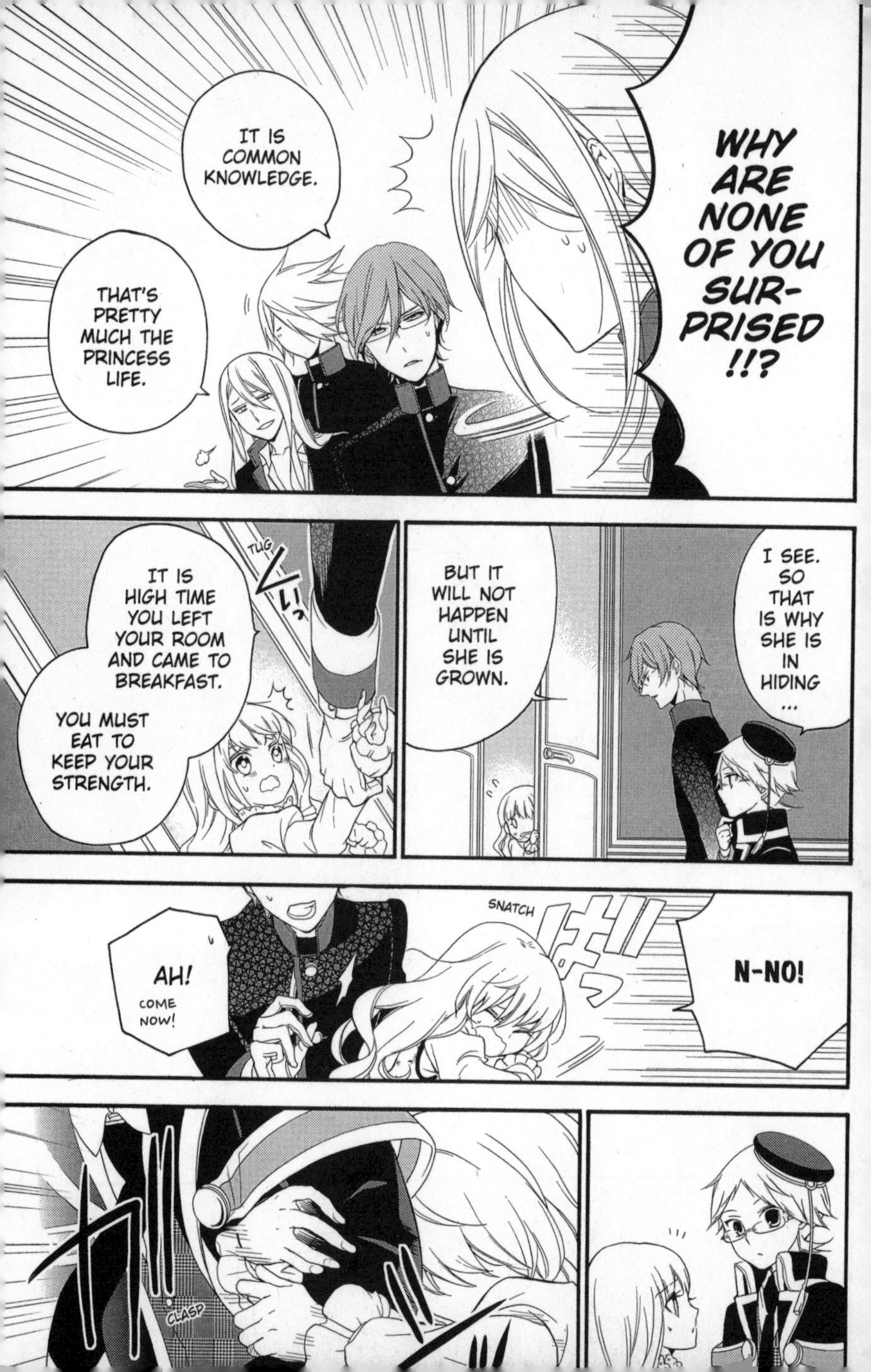
WHY ARE NONE OF YOU SURPRISED!!?
IT IS COMMON KNOWLEDGE.
THAT'S PRETTY MUCH THE PRINCESS LIFE.
I SEE. SO THAT IS WHY SHE IS IN HIDING...
BUT IT WILL NOT HAPPEN UNTIL SHE IS GROWN.
TUG
IT IS HIGH TIME YOU LEFT YOUR ROOM AND CAME TO BREAKFAST.
YOU MUST EAT TO KEEP YOUR STRENGTH.
N-NO!
SNATCH
AH!
COME NOW!
CLASP

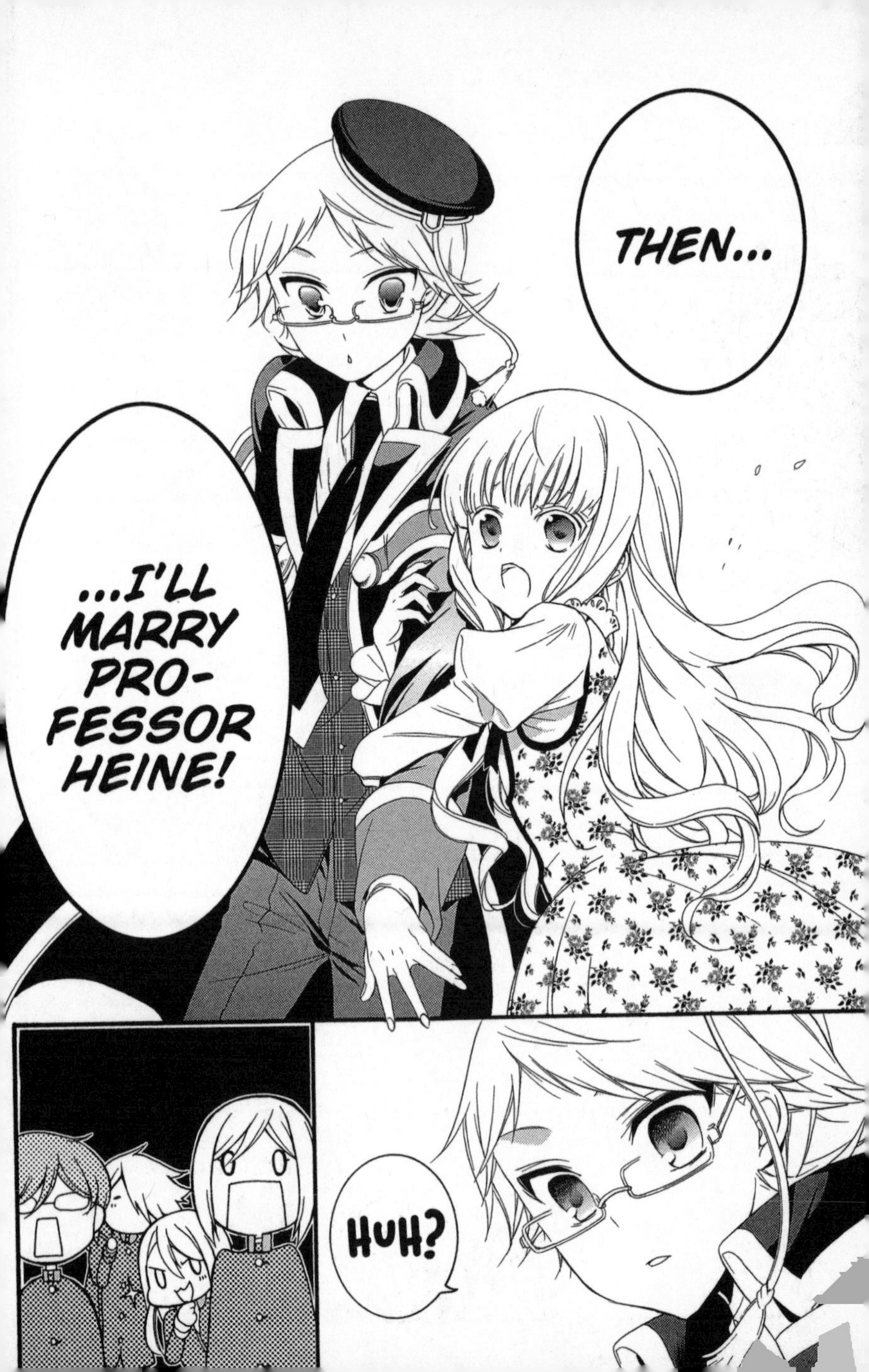
THEN...
...I'LL MARRY PRO-FESSOR HEINE!
HUH?

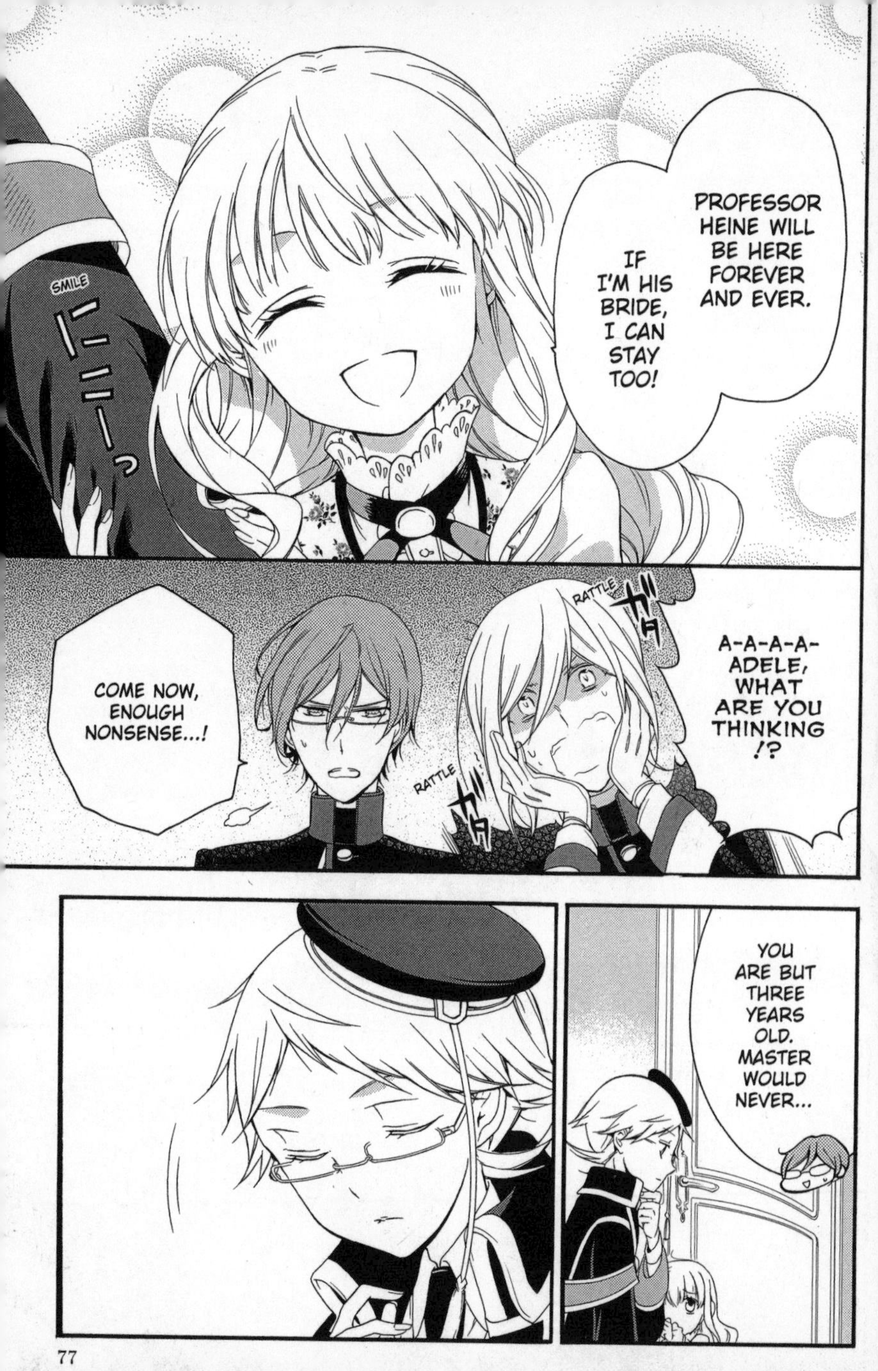
PROFESSOR HEINE WILL BE HERE FOREVER AND EVER.
IF I'M HIS BRIDE, I CAN STAY TOO!
SMILE
RATTLE
A-A-A-A-ADELE, WHAT ARE YOU THINKING!?
RATTLE
COME NOW, ENOUGH NONSENSE...!
YOU ARE BUT THREE YEARS OLD. MASTER WOULD NEVER...

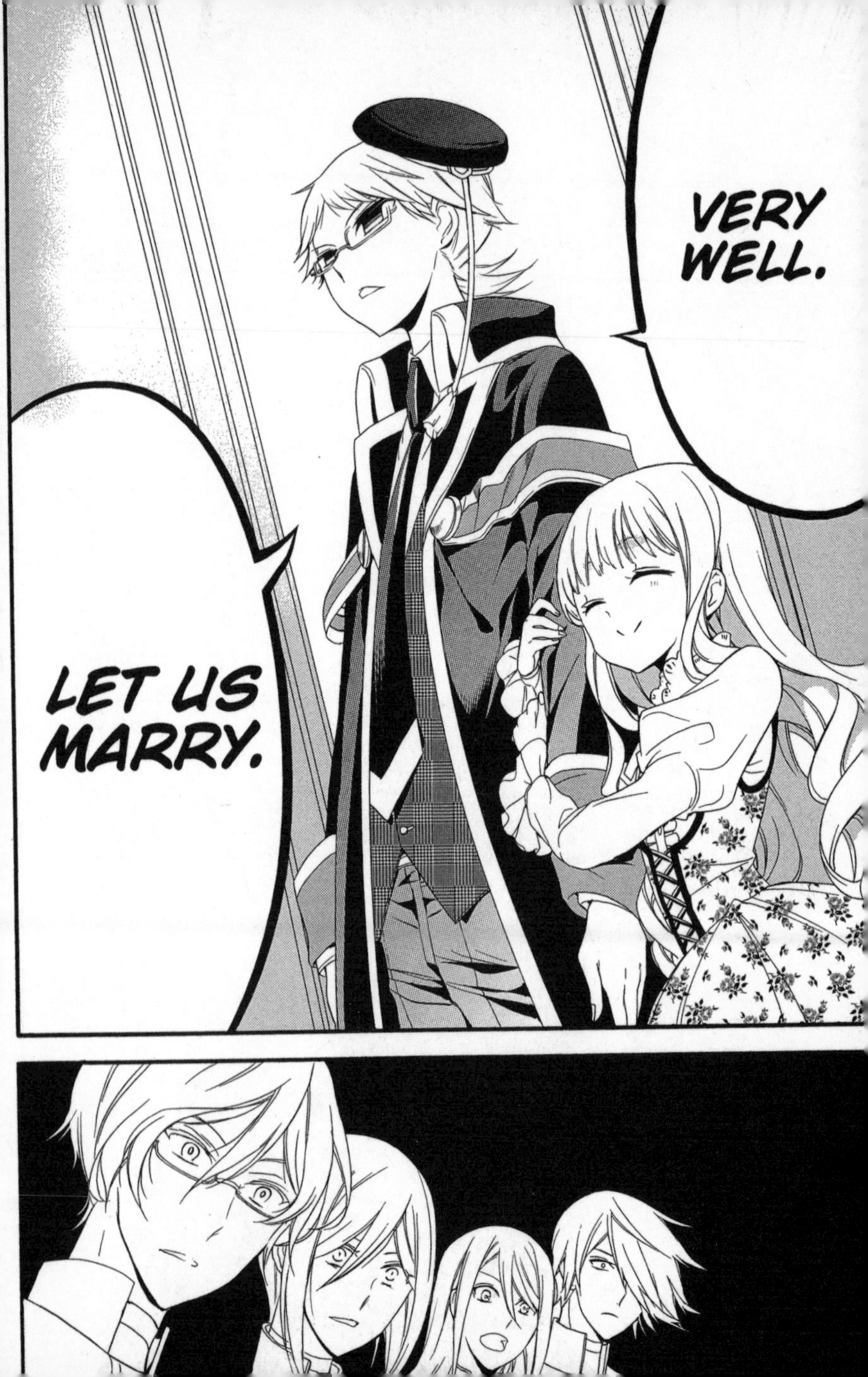
VERY WELL.
LET US MARRY.

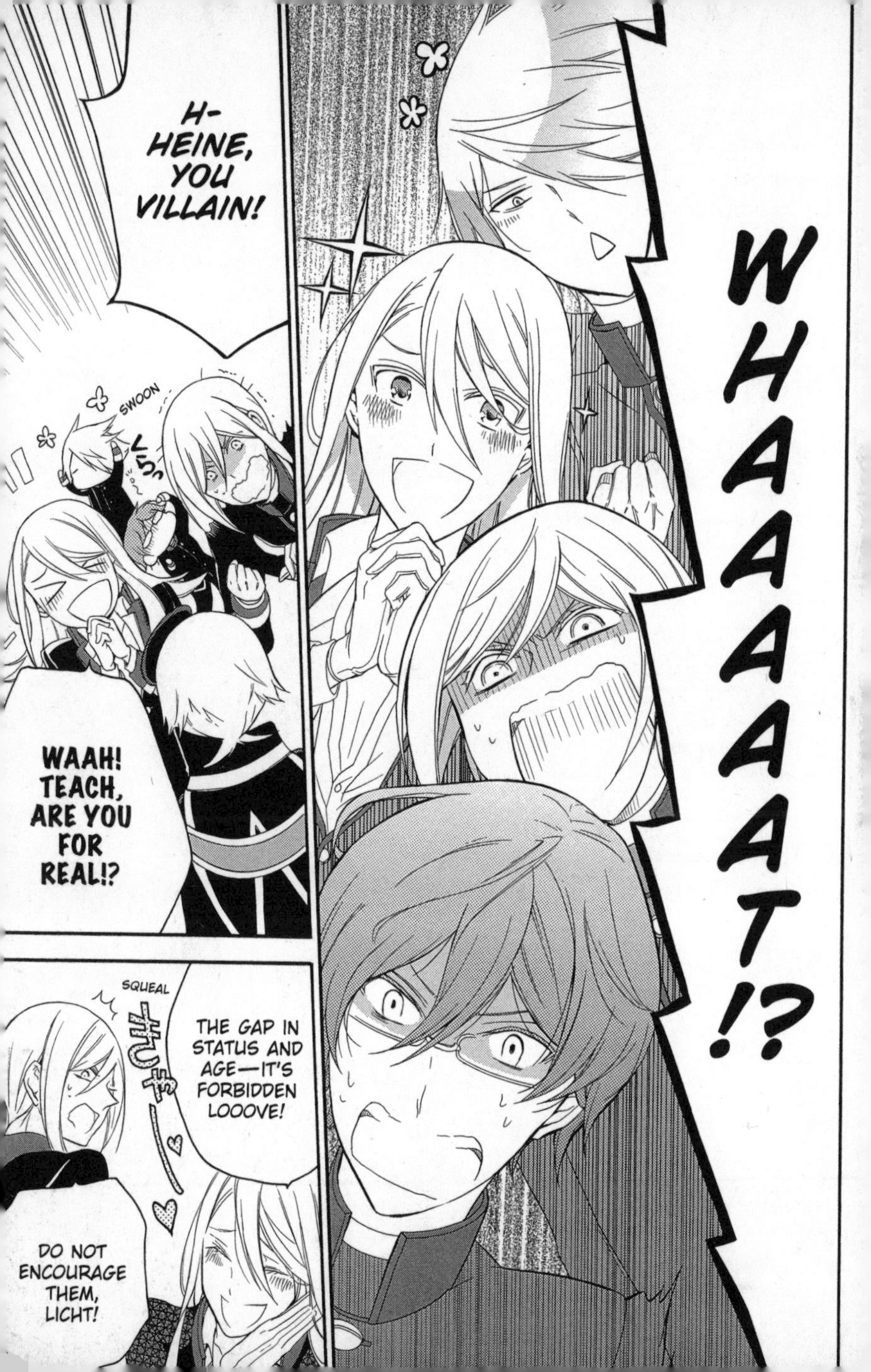
WHAAAAAT!?
H-HEINE, YOU VILLAIN!
SWOON
WAAH! TEACH, ARE YOU FOR REAL!?
SQUEAL
THE GAP IN STATUS AND AGE—IT'S FORBIDDEN LOOOVE!
DO NOT ENCOURAGE THEM, LICHT!

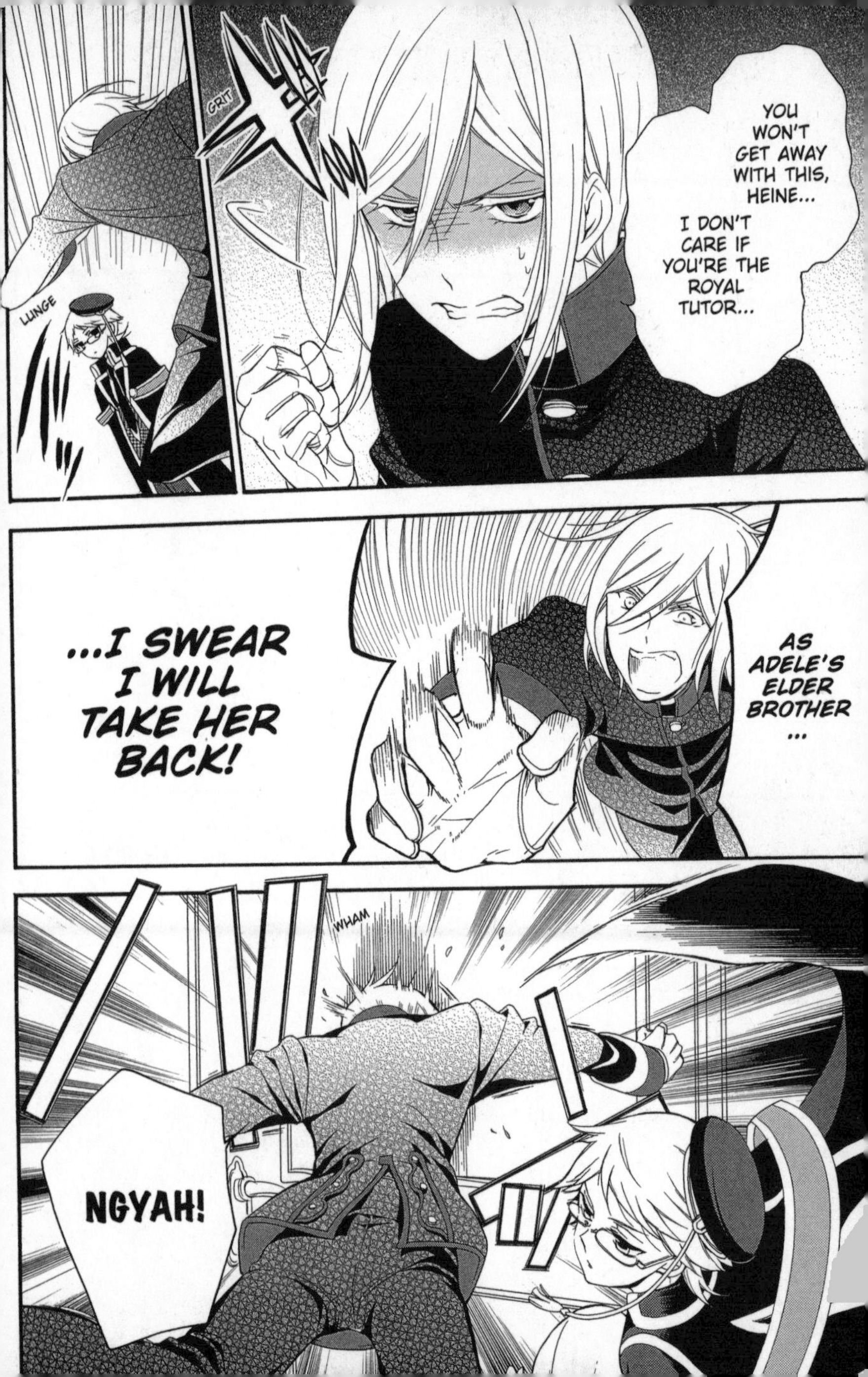
YOU WON'T GET AWAY WITH THIS, HEINE...
I DON'T CARE IF YOU'RE THE ROYAL TUTOR...
GRIT
LUNGE
AS ADELE'S ELDER BROTHER...
...I SWEAR I WILL TAKE HER BACK!
WHAM
NGYAH!

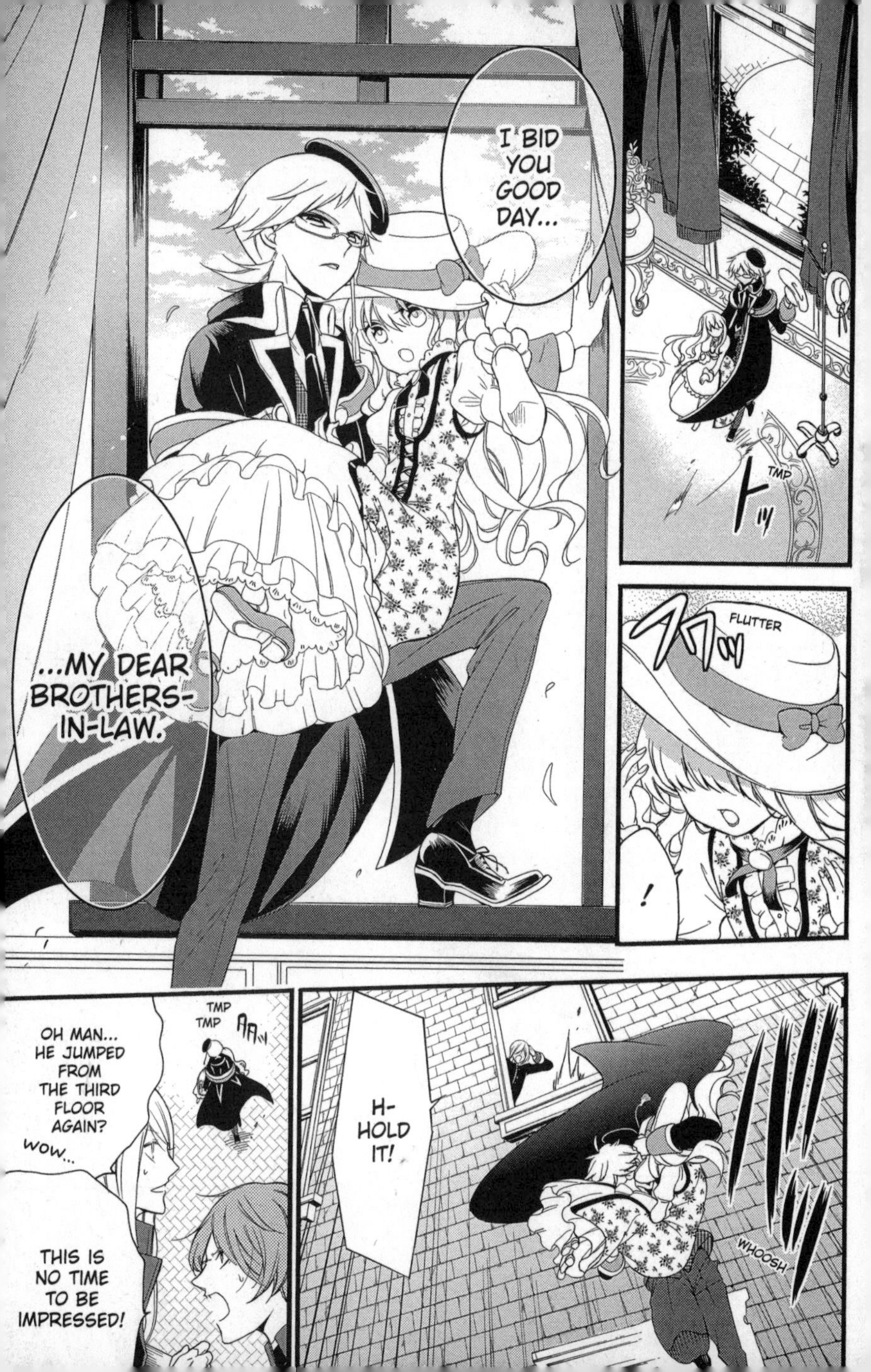
TMP
FLUTTER
I BID YOU GOOD DAY...
...MY DEAR BROTHERS-IN-LAW.
H-HOLD IT!
WHOOSH
TMP TMP
OH MAN... HE JUMPED FROM THE THIRD FLOOR AGAIN?
WOW...
THIS IS NO TIME TO BE IMPRESSED!

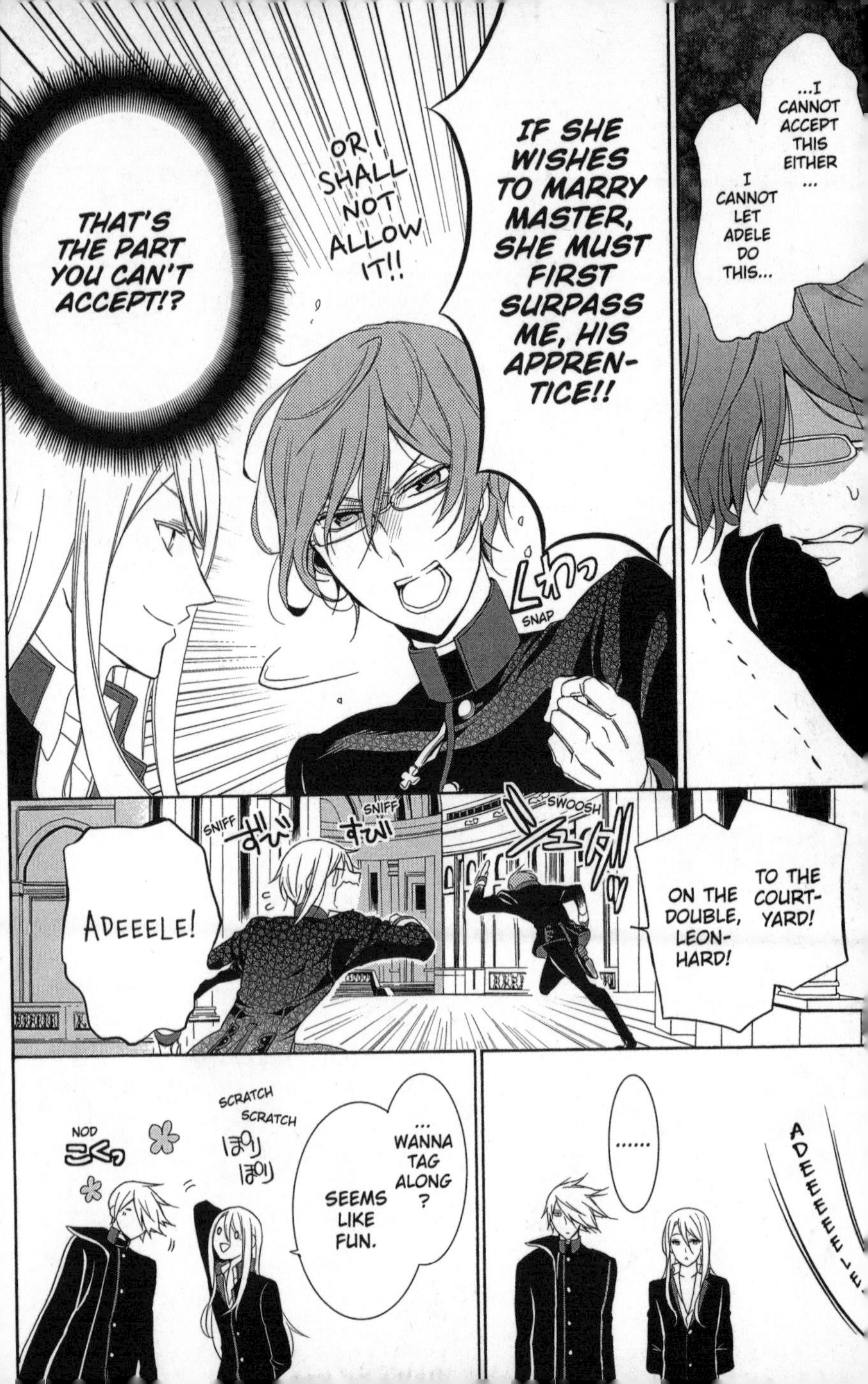
...I CANNOT ACCEPT THIS EITHER...
I CANNOT LET ADELE DO THIS...
IF SHE WISHES TO MARRY MASTER, SHE MUST FIRST SURPASS ME, HIS APPRENTICE!!
OR I SHALL NOT ALLOW IT!!
SNAP
THAT'S THE PART YOU CAN'T ACCEPT!?
TO THE COURTYARD!
ON THE DOUBLE, LEONHARD!
SWOOSH
SNIFF
SNIFF
ADEEEELE!
ADEEEEEE
......
...WANNA TAG ALONG?
SEEMS LIKE FUN.
SCRATCH SCRATCH
NOD

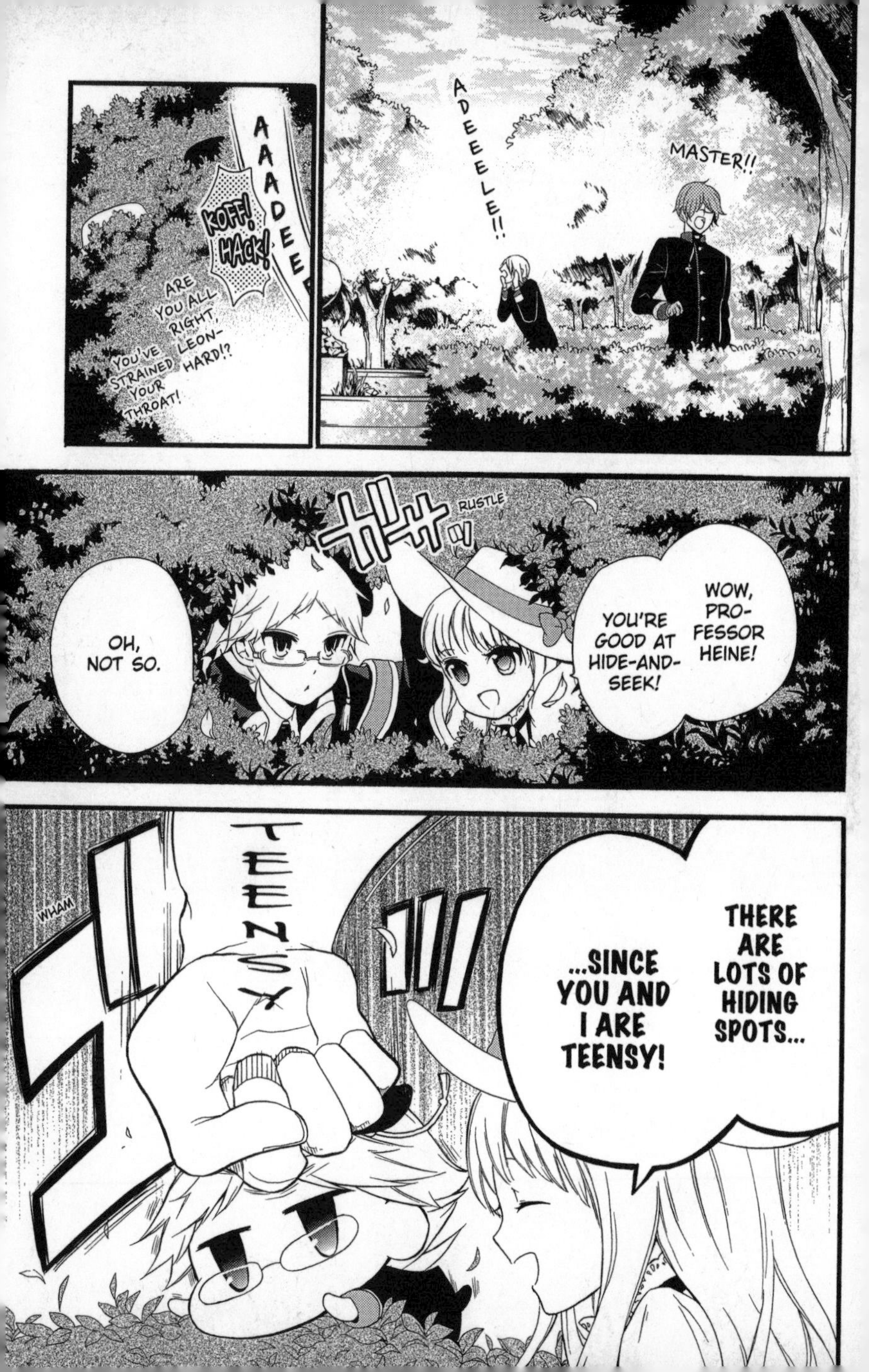
MASTER!!
ADEEEELE!!
AAAADEEE
KOFF! HACK!
ARE YOU ALL RIGHT, LEON-HARD!?
YOU'VE STRAINED YOUR THROAT!
RUSTLE
WOW, PRO-FESSOR HEINE!
YOU'RE GOOD AT HIDE-AND-SEEK!
OH, NOT SO.
THERE ARE LOTS OF HIDING SPOTS...
...SINCE YOU AND I ARE TEENSY!
TEENSY
WHAM

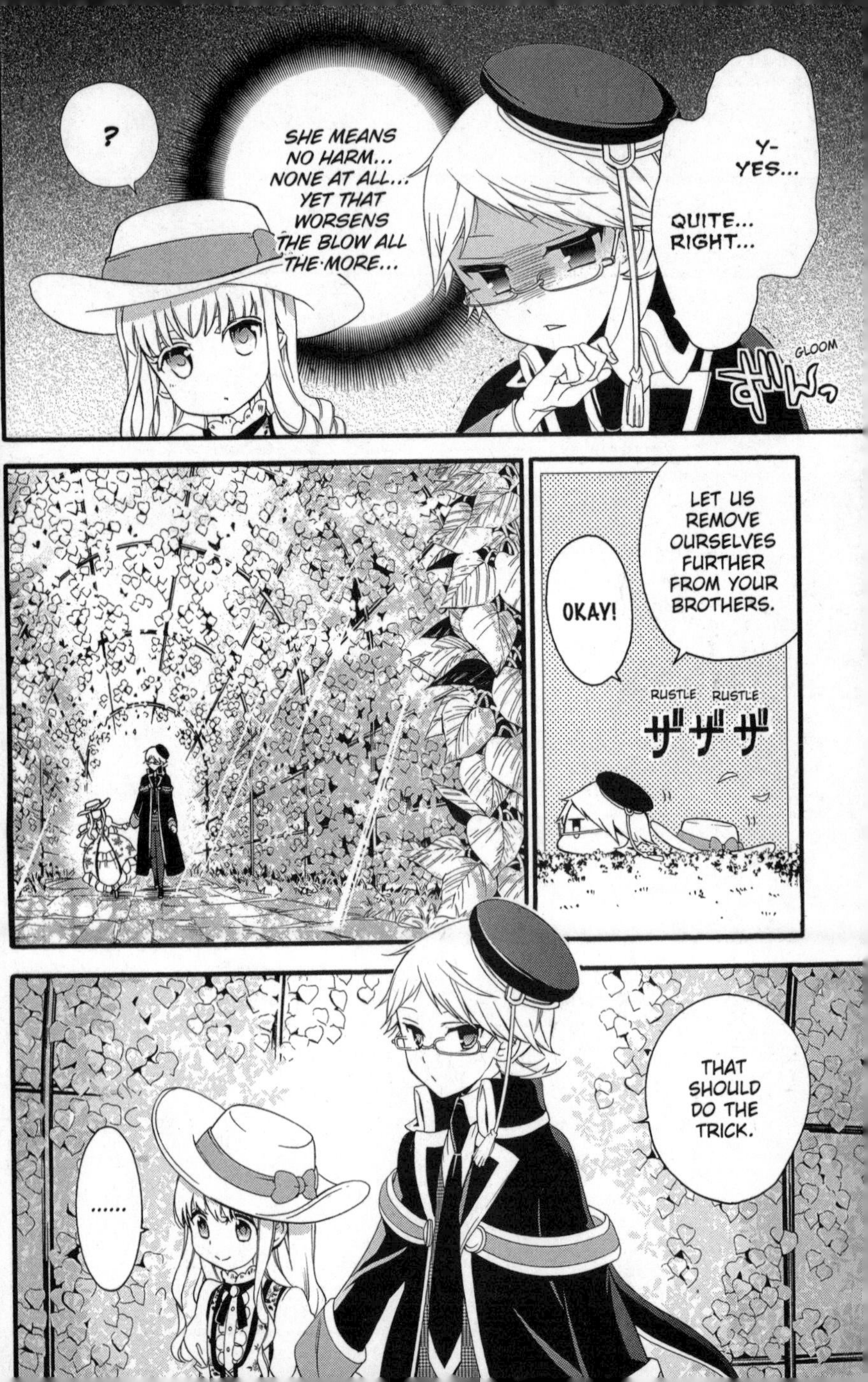
Y- YES...
QUITE... RIGHT...
SHE MEANS NO HARM... NONE AT ALL... YET THAT WORSENS THE BLOW ALL THE MORE...
?
GLOOM
LET US REMOVE OURSELVES FURTHER FROM YOUR BROTHERS.
OKAY!
RUSTLE RUSTLE
ザザザ
THAT SHOULD DO THE TRICK.
......

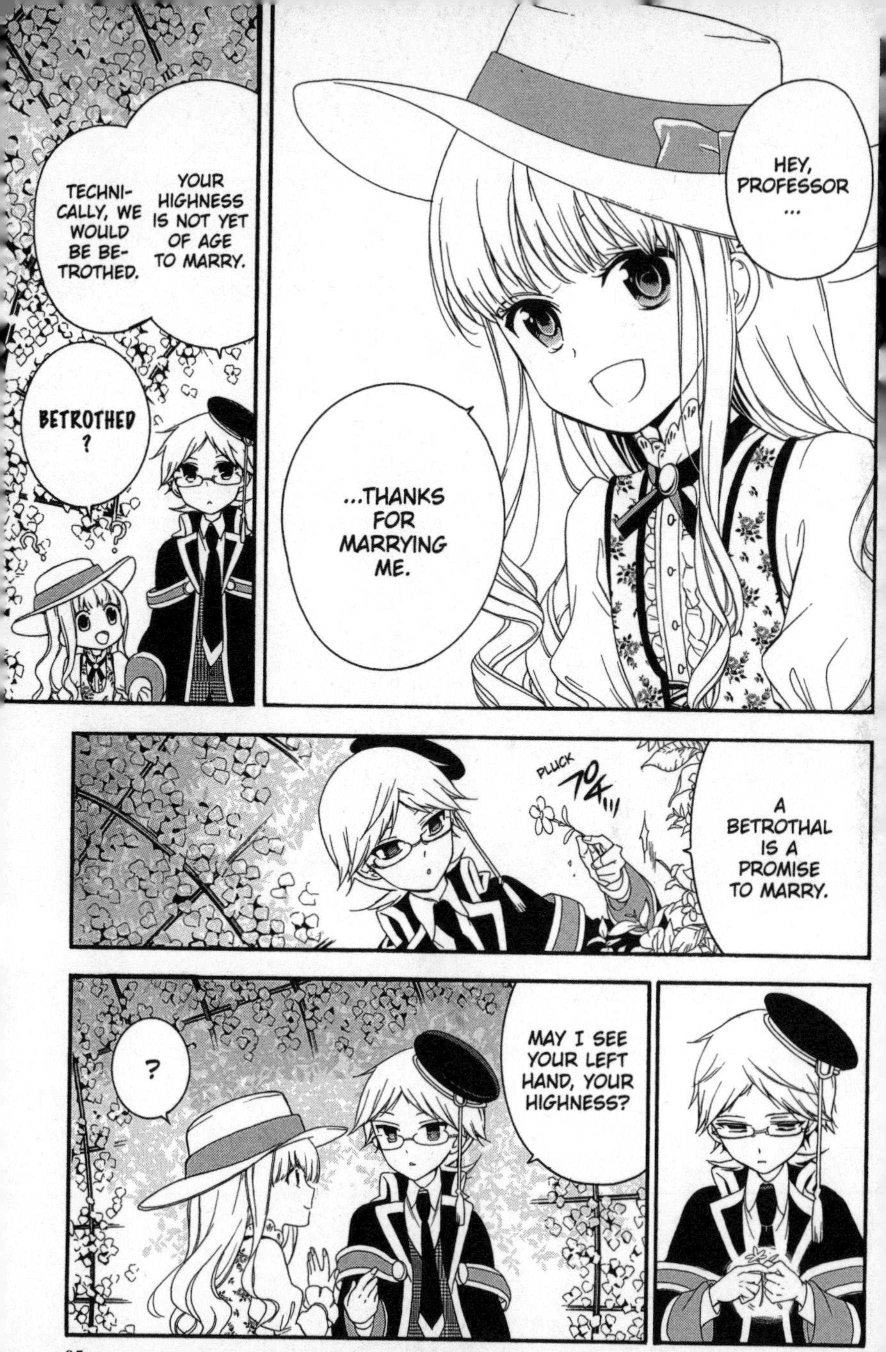
HEY, PROFESSOR ...
...THANKS FOR MARRYING ME.
YOUR HIGHNESS IS NOT YET OF AGE TO MARRY.
TECHNI-CALLY, WE WOULD BE BE-TROTHED.
BETROTHED ?
A BETROTHAL IS A PROMISE TO MARRY.
PLUCK
MAY I SEE YOUR LEFT HAND, YOUR HIGHNESS?
?

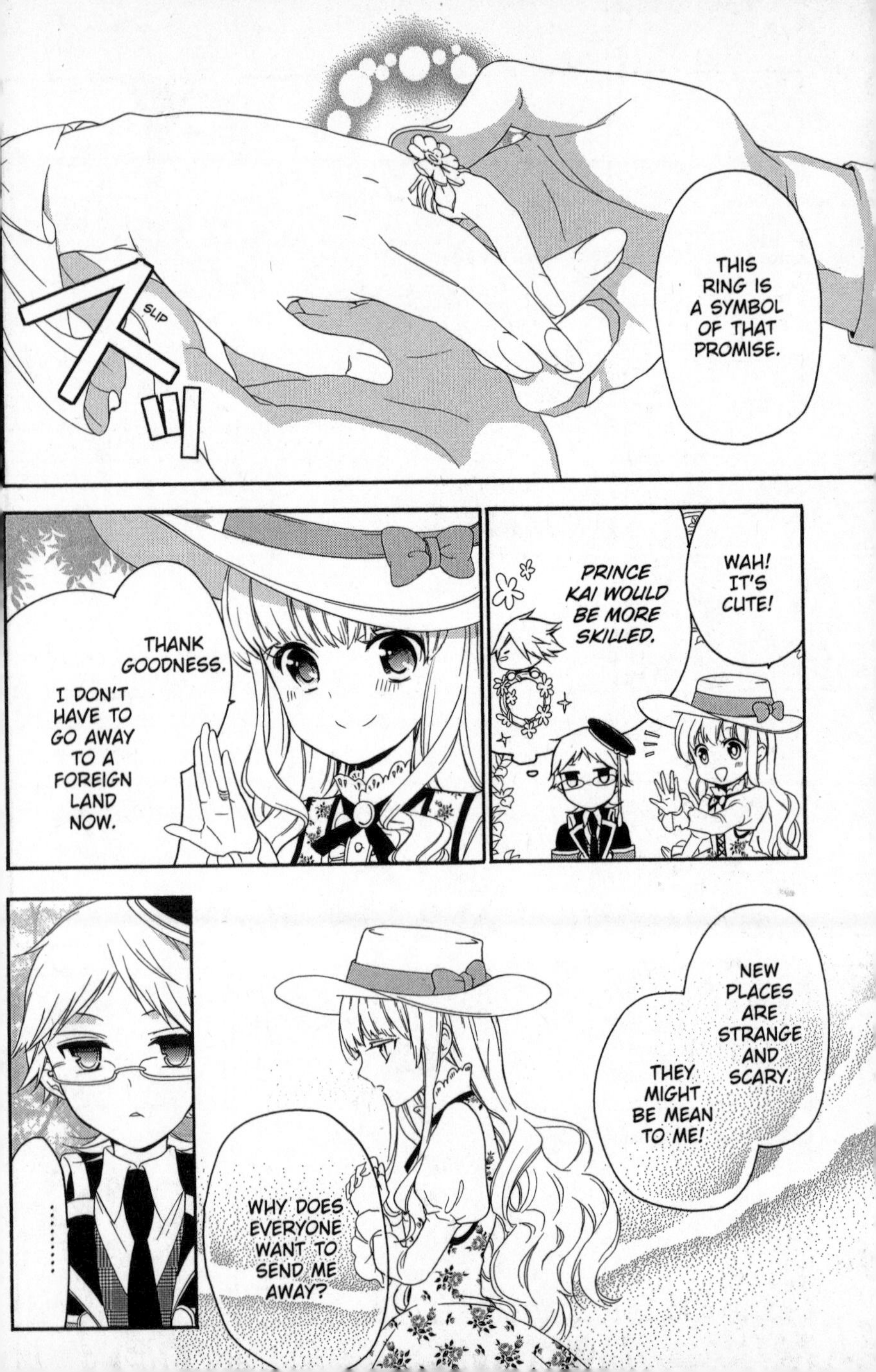
THIS RING IS A SYMBOL OF THAT PROMISE.
SLIP
WAH! IT'S CUTE!
PRINCE KAI WOULD BE MORE SKILLED.
THANK GOODNESS.
I DON'T HAVE TO GO AWAY TO A FOREIGN LAND NOW.
NEW PLACES ARE STRANGE AND SCARY.
THEY MIGHT BE MEAN TO ME!
WHY DOES EVERYONE WANT TO SEND ME AWAY?
......

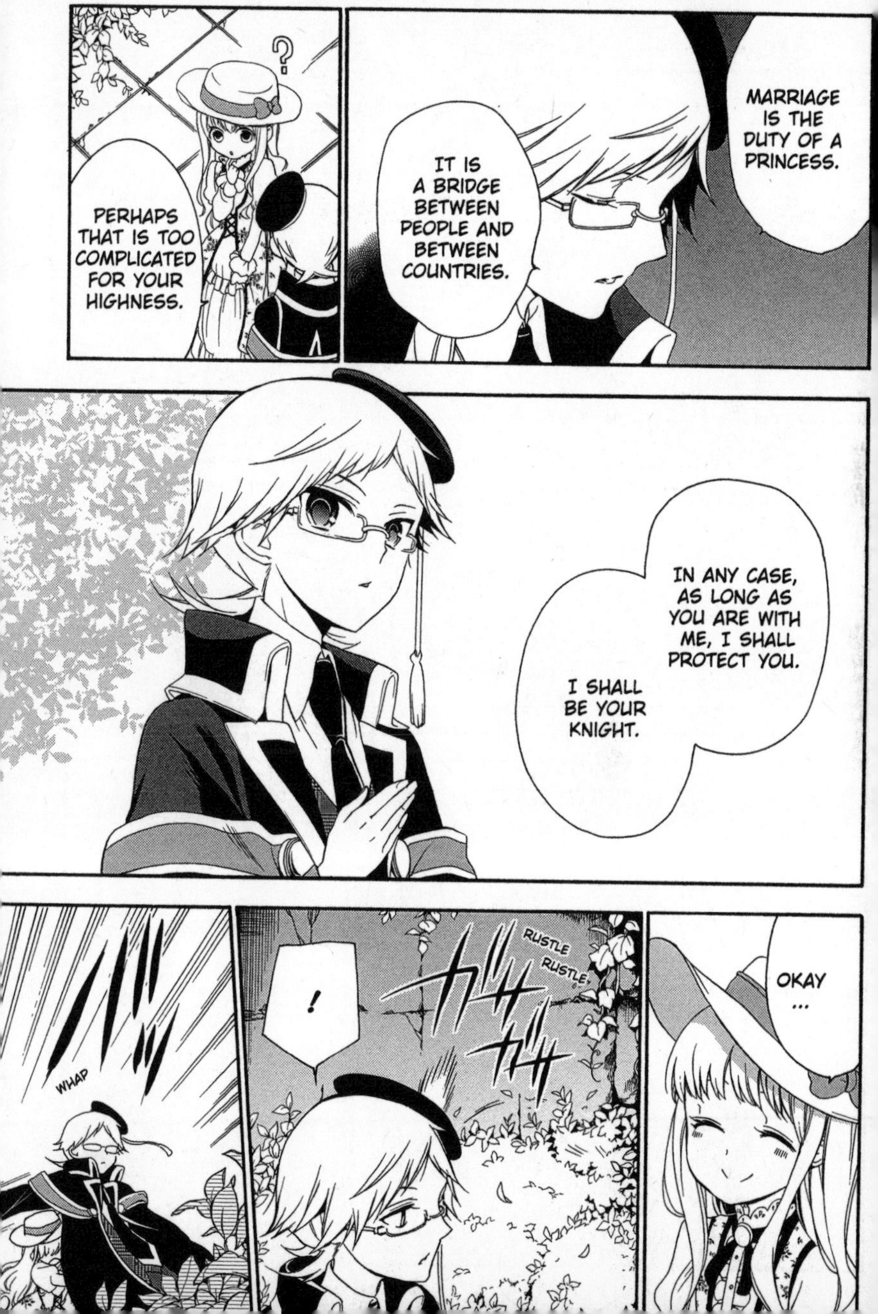
MARRIAGE IS THE DUTY OF A PRINCESS.
IT IS A BRIDGE BETWEEN PEOPLE AND BETWEEN COUNTRIES.
?
PERHAPS THAT IS TOO COMPLICATED FOR YOUR HIGHNESS.
IN ANY CASE, AS LONG AS YOU ARE WITH ME, I SHALL PROTECT YOU.
I SHALL BE YOUR KNIGHT.
OKAY ...
!
RUSTLE
RUSTLE
WHAP

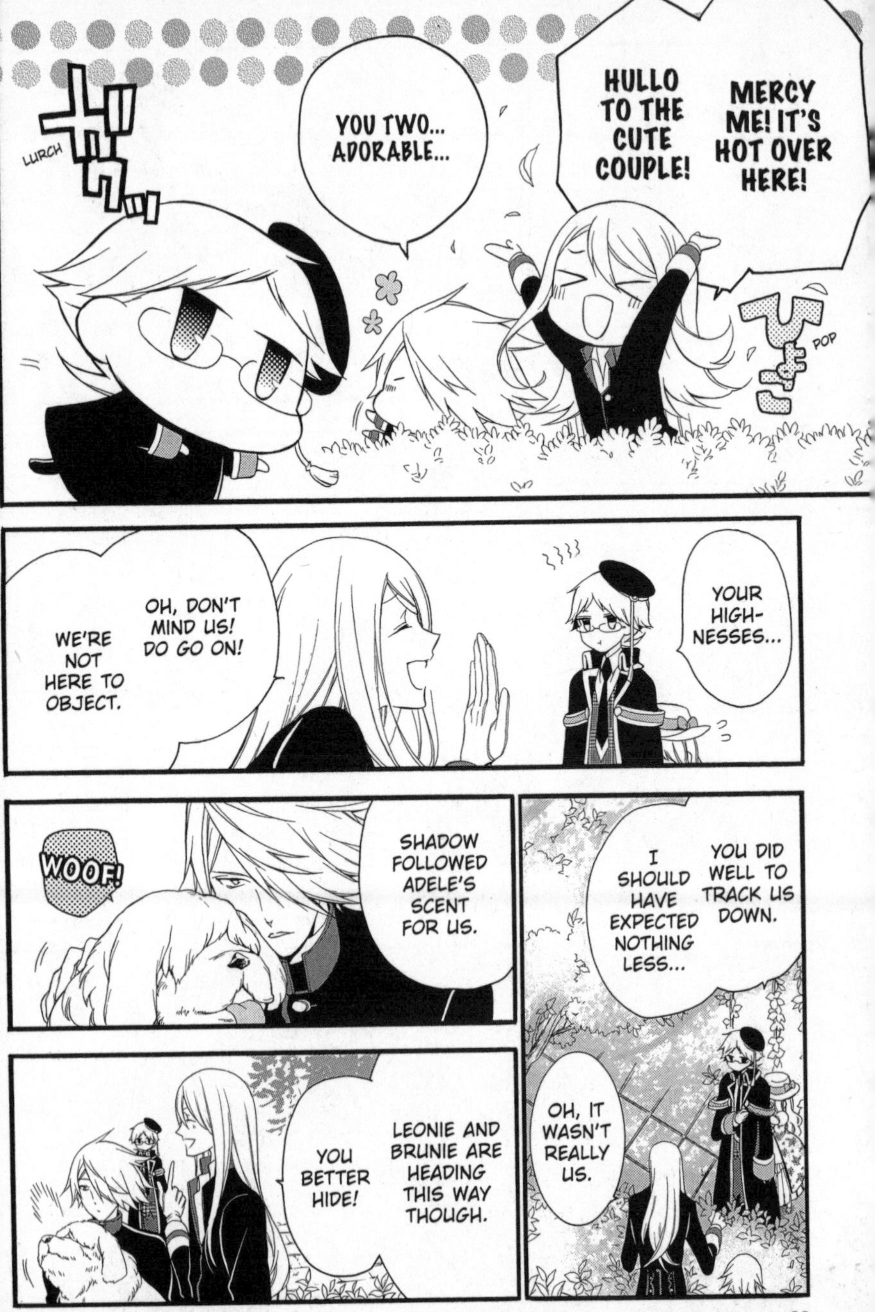

MERCY ME! IT'S HOT OVER HERE!
HULLO TO THE CUTE COUPLE!
POP
YOU TWO... ADORABLE...
LURCH
YOUR HIGH-NESSES...
OH, DON'T MIND US! DO GO ON!
WE'RE NOT HERE TO OBJECT.
YOU DID WELL TO TRACK US DOWN.
I SHOULD HAVE EXPECTED NOTHING LESS...
OH, IT WASN'T REALLY US.
SHADOW FOLLOWED ADELE'S SCENT FOR US.
WOOF!
LEONIE AND BRUNIE ARE HEADING THIS WAY THOUGH.
YOU BETTER HIDE!

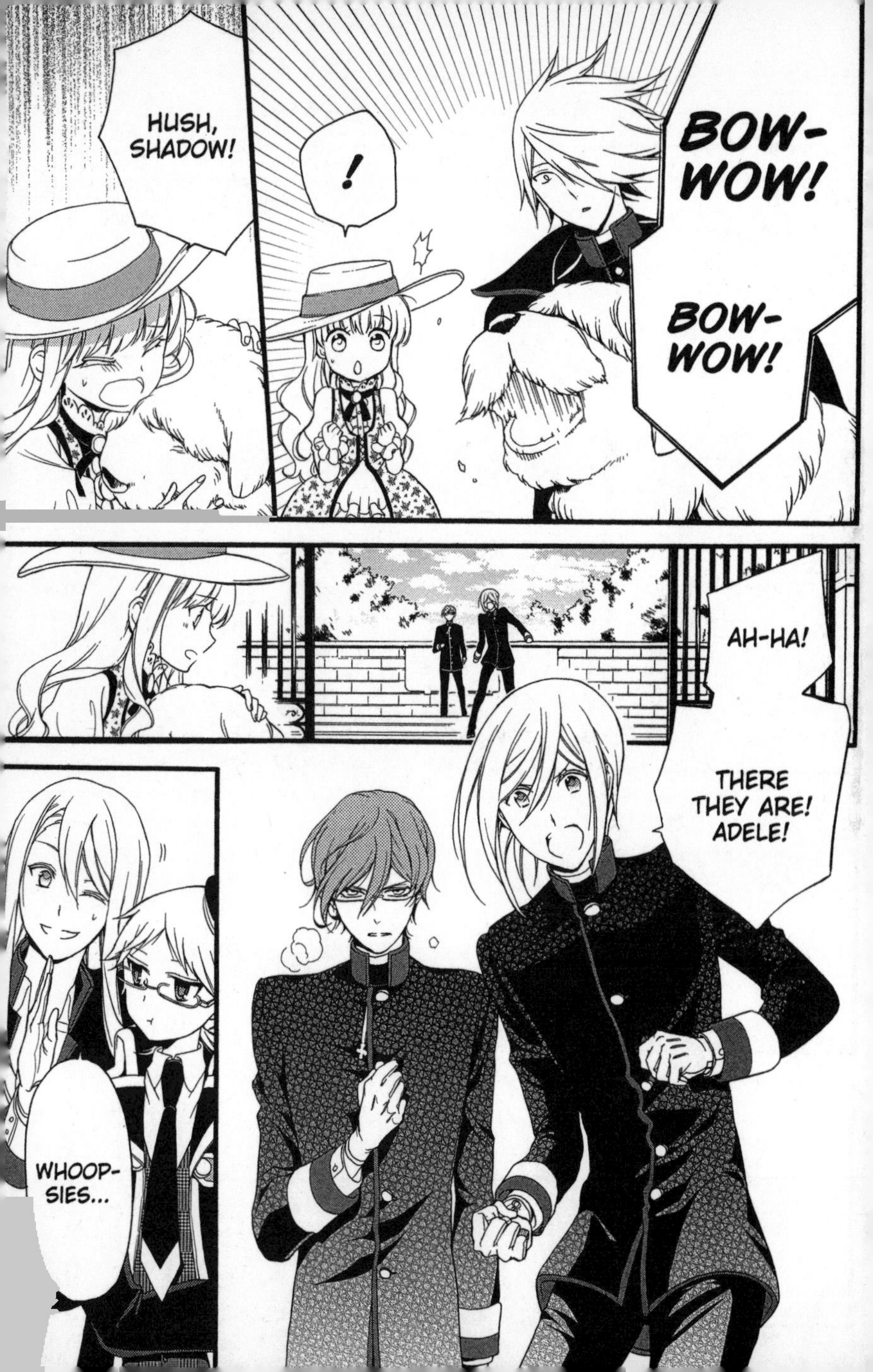
BOW-WOW!
!
BOW-WOW!
HUSH, SHADOW!
AH-HA!
THERE THEY ARE! ADELE!
WHOOP-SIES...

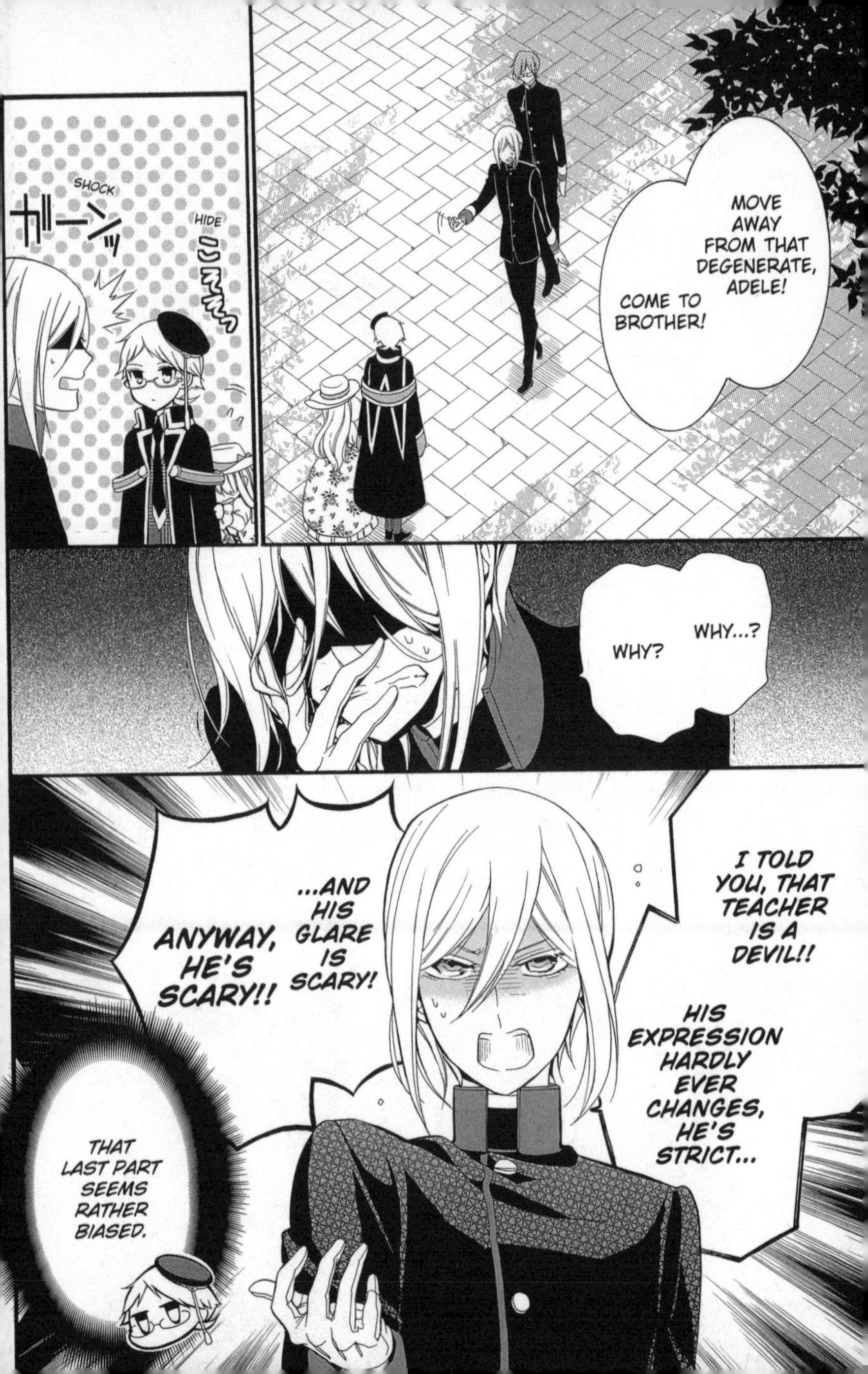
MOVE AWAY FROM THAT DEGENERATE, ADELE!
COME TO BROTHER!
SHOCK
ガーンッ
HIDE
WHY...?
WHY?
I TOLD YOU, THAT TEACHER IS A DEVIL!!
HIS EXPRESSION HARDLY EVER CHANGES, HE'S STRICT...
...AND HIS GLARE IS SCARY!
ANYWAY, HE'S SCARY!!
THAT LAST PART SEEMS RATHER BIASED.

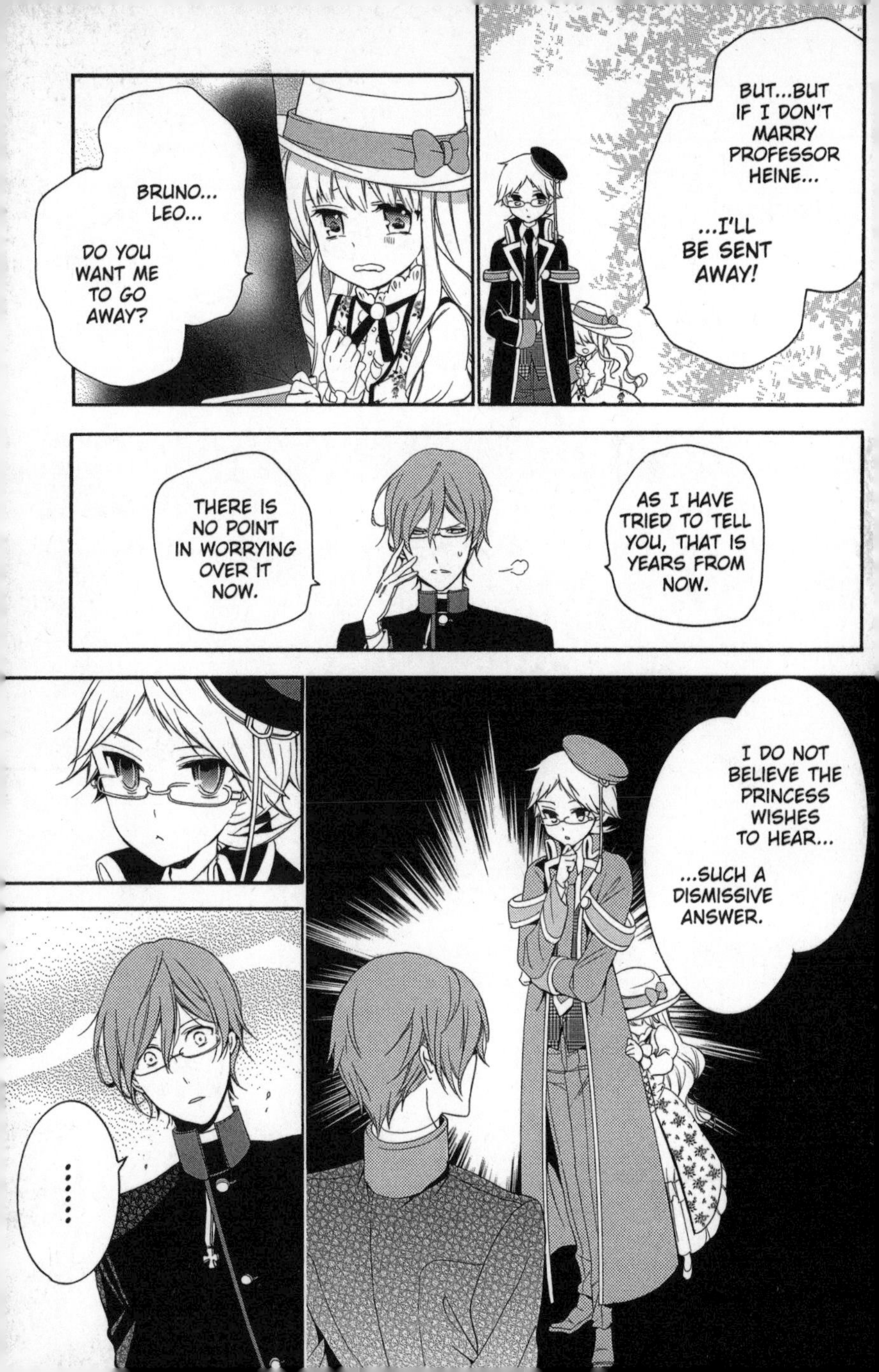
BUT...BUT IF I DON'T MARRY PROFESSOR HEINE...
...I'LL BE SENT AWAY!
BRUNO... LEO...
DO YOU WANT ME TO GO AWAY?
AS I HAVE TRIED TO TELL YOU, THAT IS YEARS FROM NOW.
THERE IS NO POINT IN WORRYING OVER IT NOW.
I DO NOT BELIEVE THE PRINCESS WISHES TO HEAR...
...SUCH A DISMISSIVE ANSWER.
......

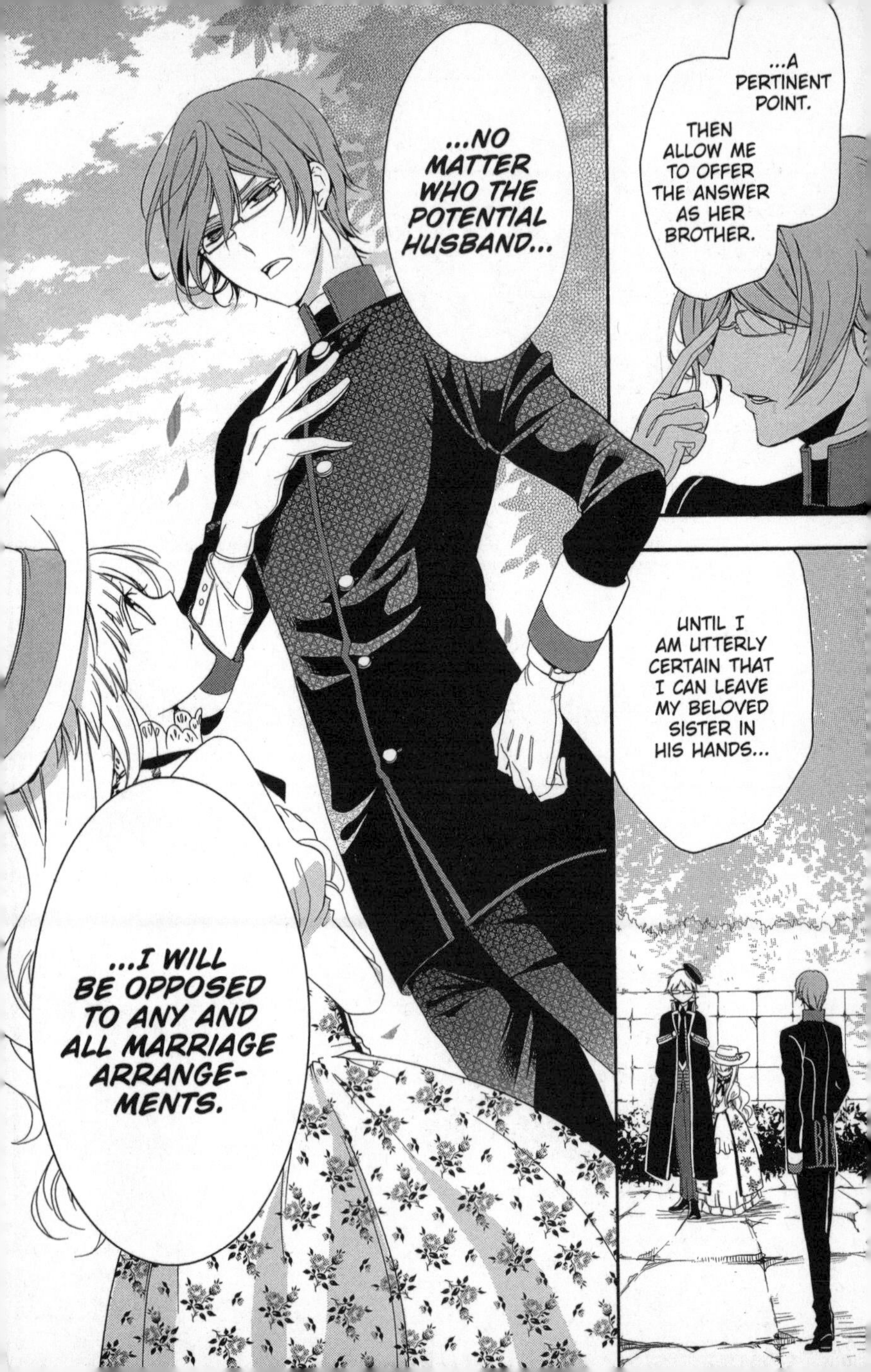
...A PERTINENT POINT.
THEN ALLOW ME TO OFFER THE ANSWER AS HER BROTHER.
UNTIL I AM UTTERLY CERTAIN THAT I CAN LEAVE MY BELOVED SISTER IN HIS HANDS...
...NO MATTER WHO THE POTENTIAL HUSBAND...
...I WILL BE OPPOSED TO ANY AND ALL MARRIAGE ARRANGE-MENTS.

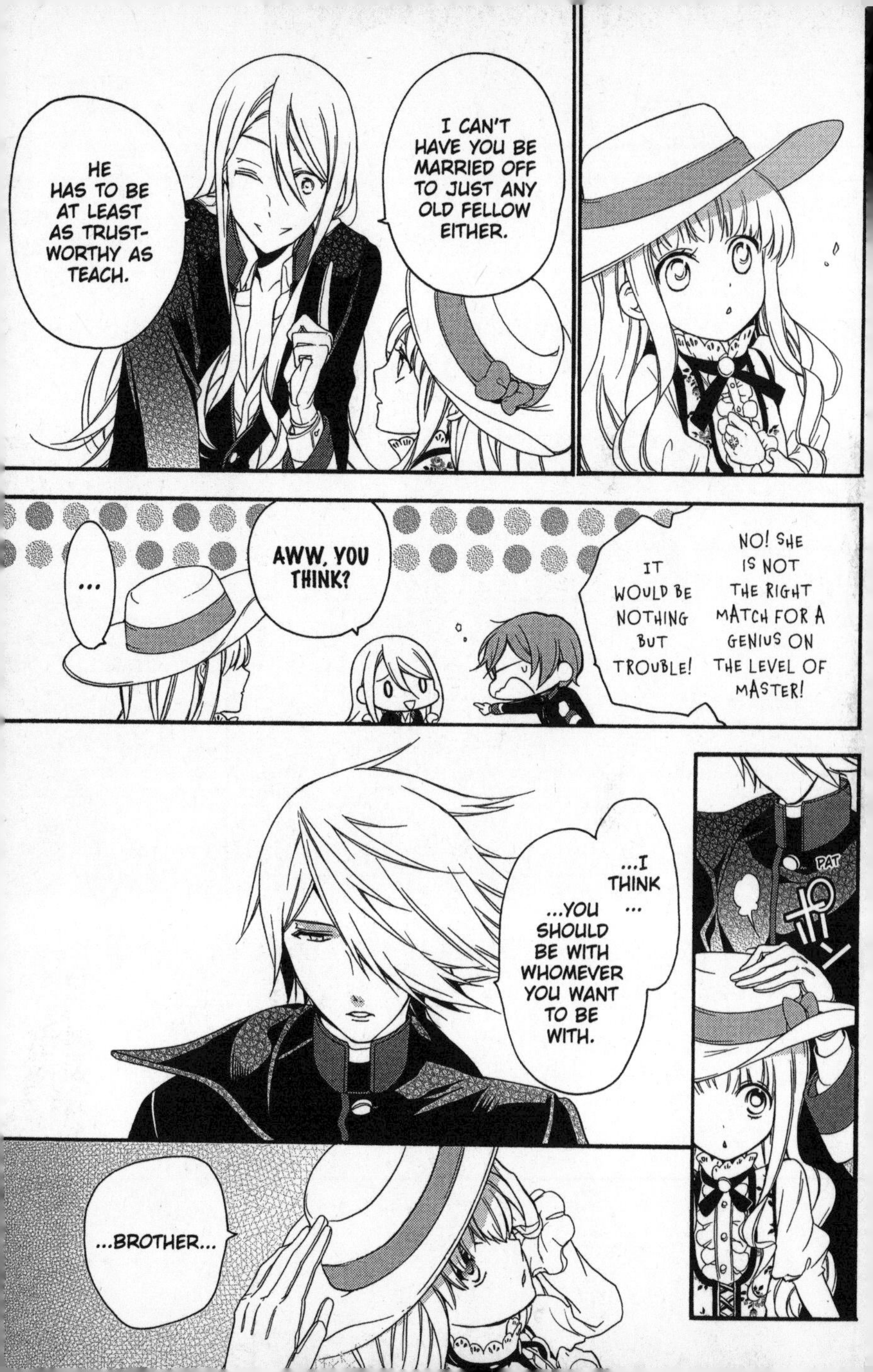
I CAN'T HAVE YOU BE MARRIED OFF TO JUST ANY OLD FELLOW EITHER.
HE HAS TO BE AT LEAST AS TRUST-WORTHY AS TEACH.
NO! SHE IS NOT THE RIGHT MATCH FOR A GENIUS ON THE LEVEL OF MASTER!
IT WOULD BE NOTHING BUT TROUBLE!
AWW, YOU THINK?
...
PAT
...I THINK ...
...YOU SHOULD BE WITH WHOMEVER YOU WANT TO BE WITH.
...BROTHER...

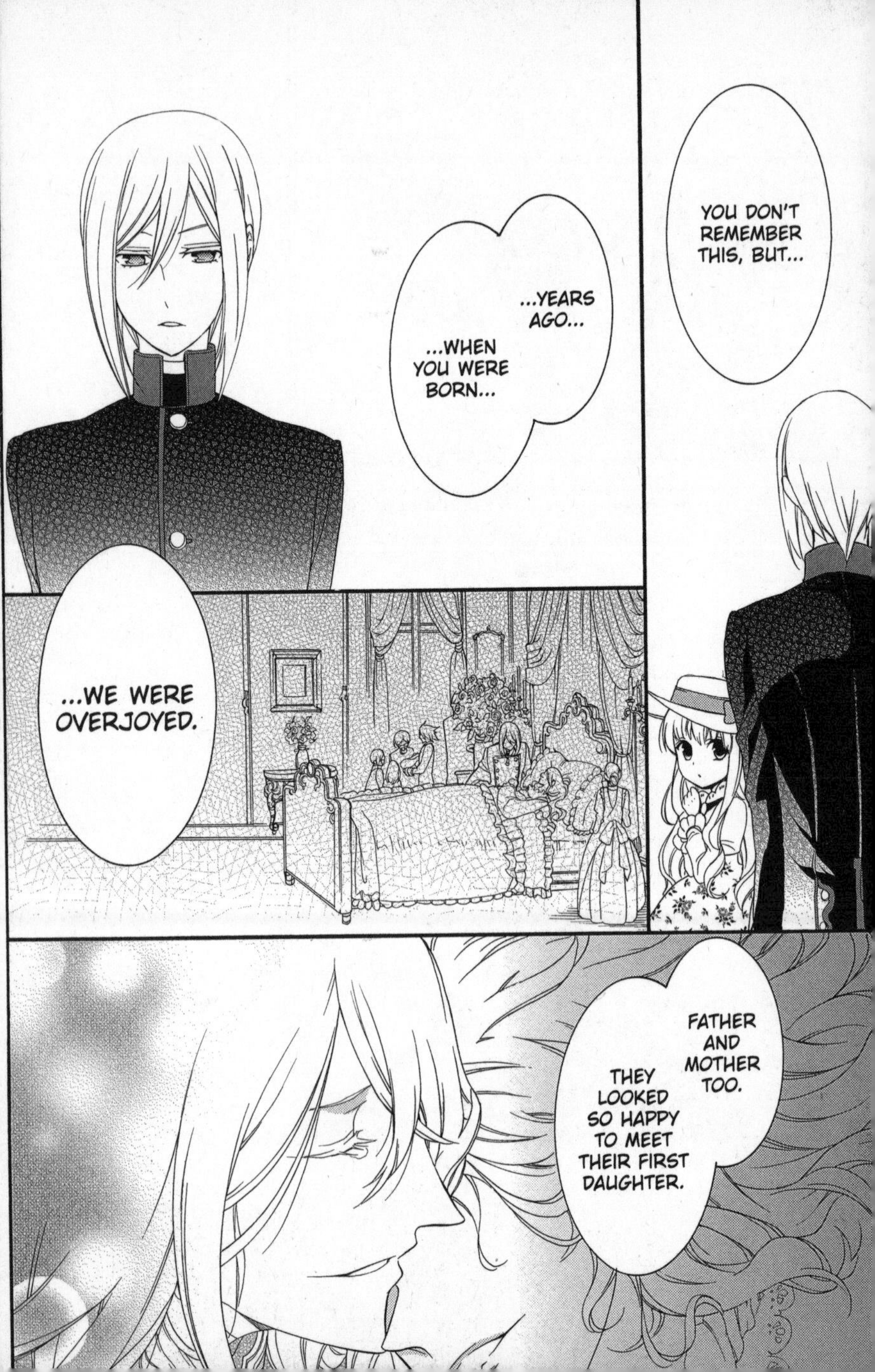
YOU DON'T REMEMBER THIS, BUT...
...YEARS AGO...
...WHEN YOU WERE BORN...
...WE WERE OVERJOYED.
FATHER AND MOTHER TOO.
THEY LOOKED SO HAPPY TO MEET THEIR FIRST DAUGHTER.

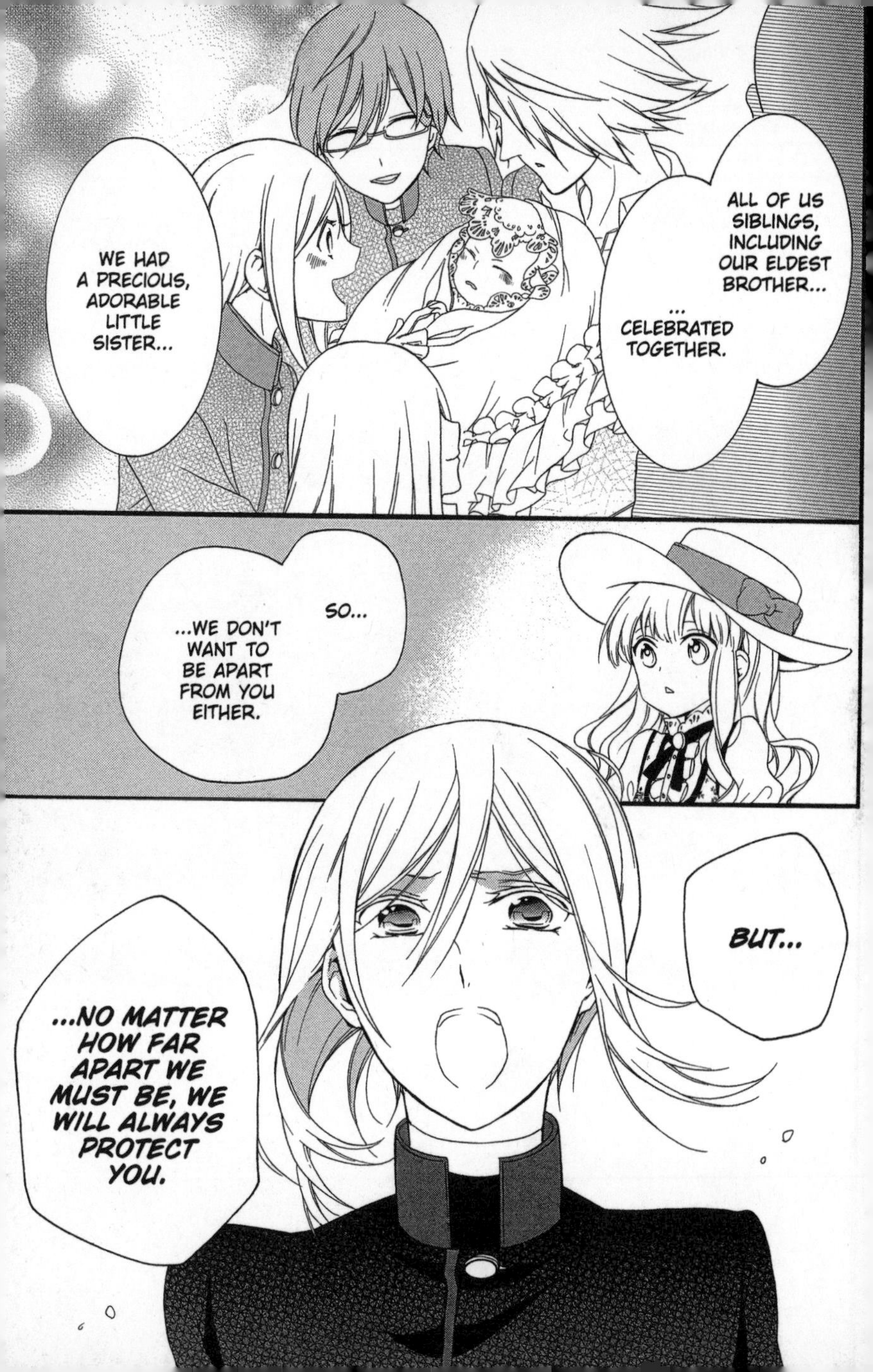
ALL OF US SIBLINGS, INCLUDING OUR ELDEST BROTHER...
... CELEBRATED TOGETHER.
WE HAD A PRECIOUS, ADORABLE LITTLE SISTER...
SO...
...WE DON'T WANT TO BE APART FROM YOU EITHER.
BUT...
...NO MATTER HOW FAR APART WE MUST BE, WE WILL ALWAYS PROTECT YOU.

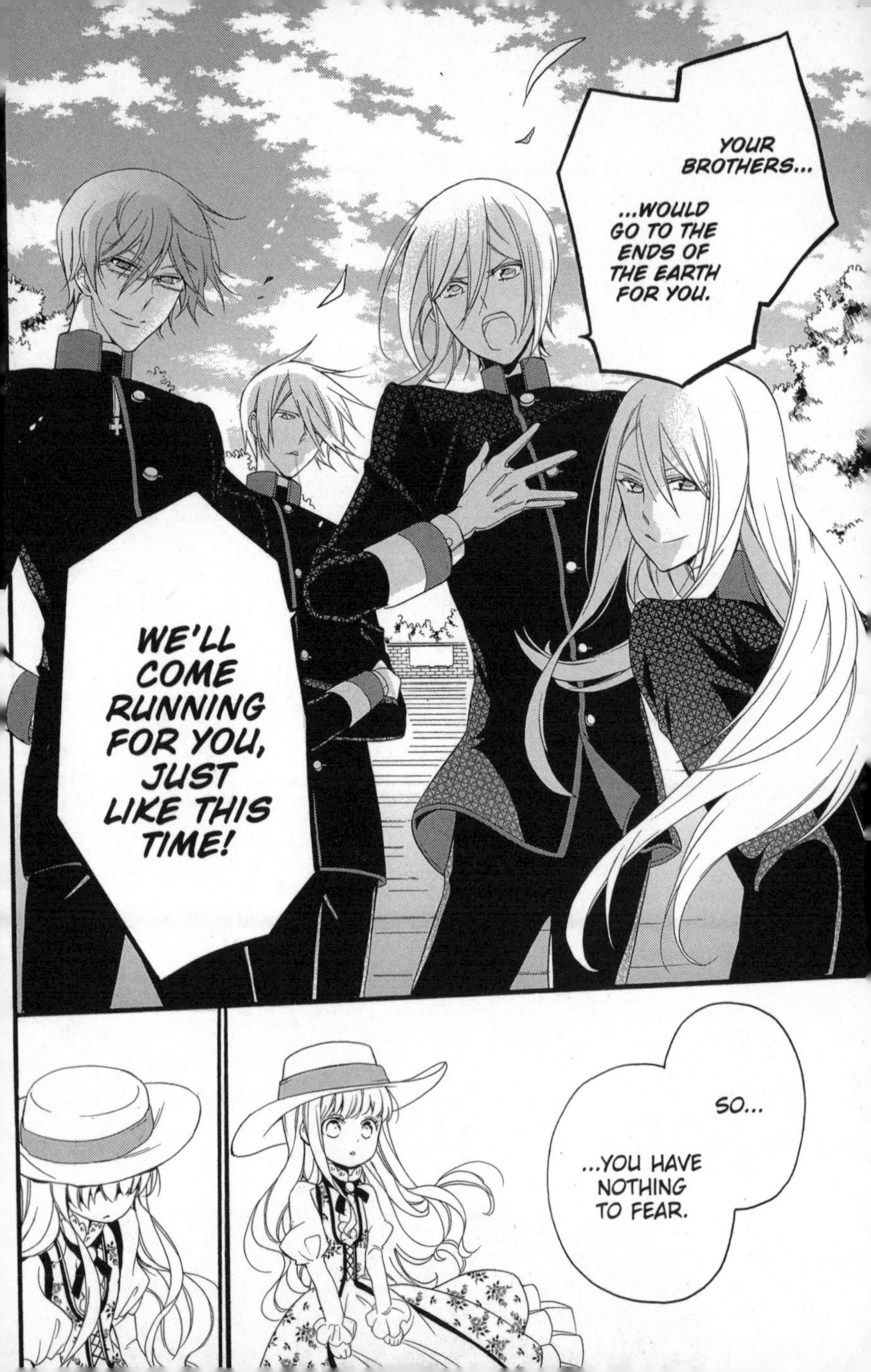
YOUR BROTHERS...
...WOULD GO TO THE ENDS OF THE EARTH FOR YOU.
WE'LL COME RUNNING FOR YOU, JUST LIKE THIS TIME!
SO...
...YOU HAVE NOTHING TO FEAR.

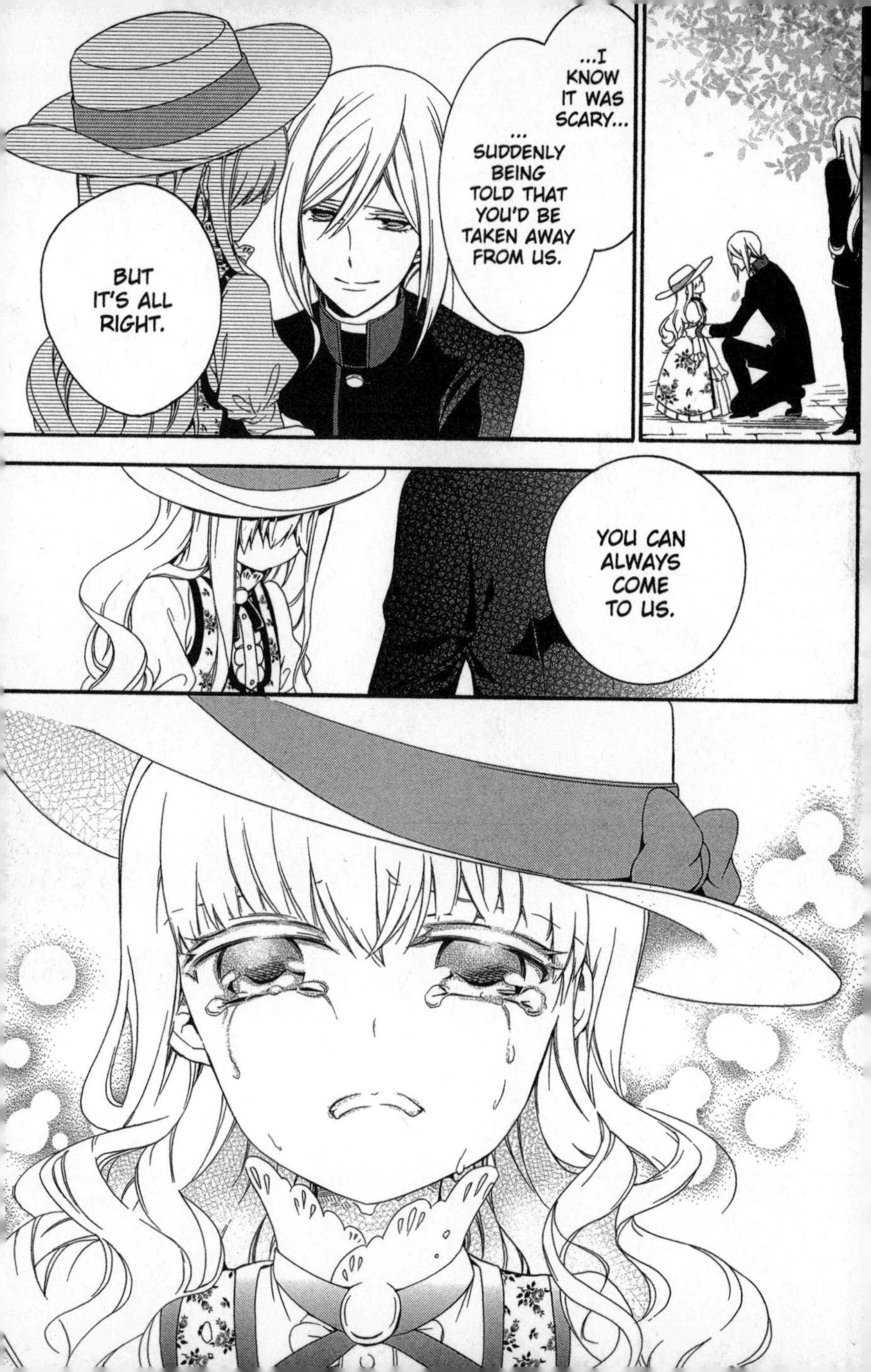
...I KNOW IT WAS SCARY...
...SUDDENLY BEING TOLD THAT YOU'D BE TAKEN AWAY FROM US.
BUT IT'S ALL RIGHT.
YOU CAN ALWAYS COME TO US.

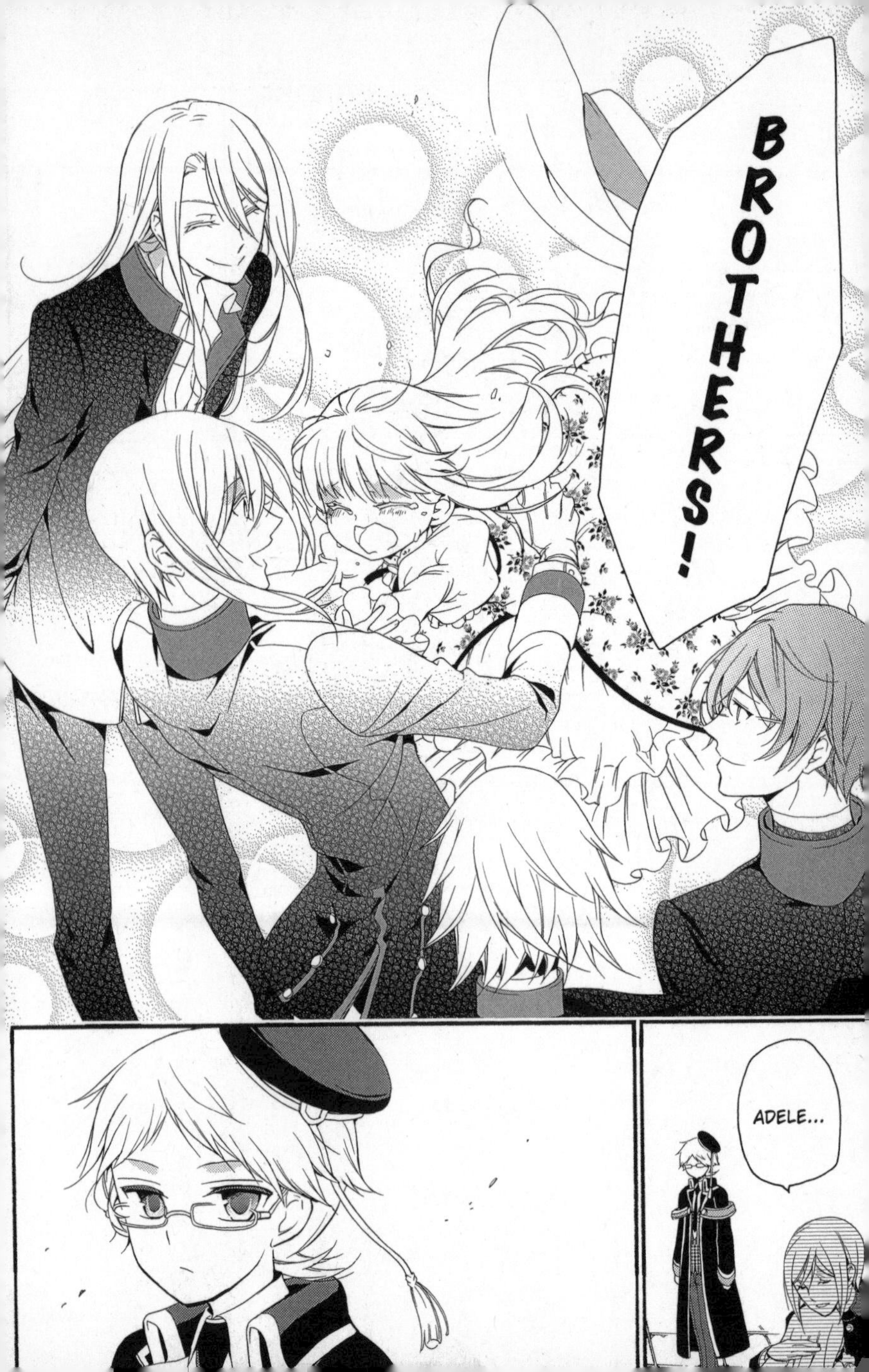
BROTHERS!
ADELE...

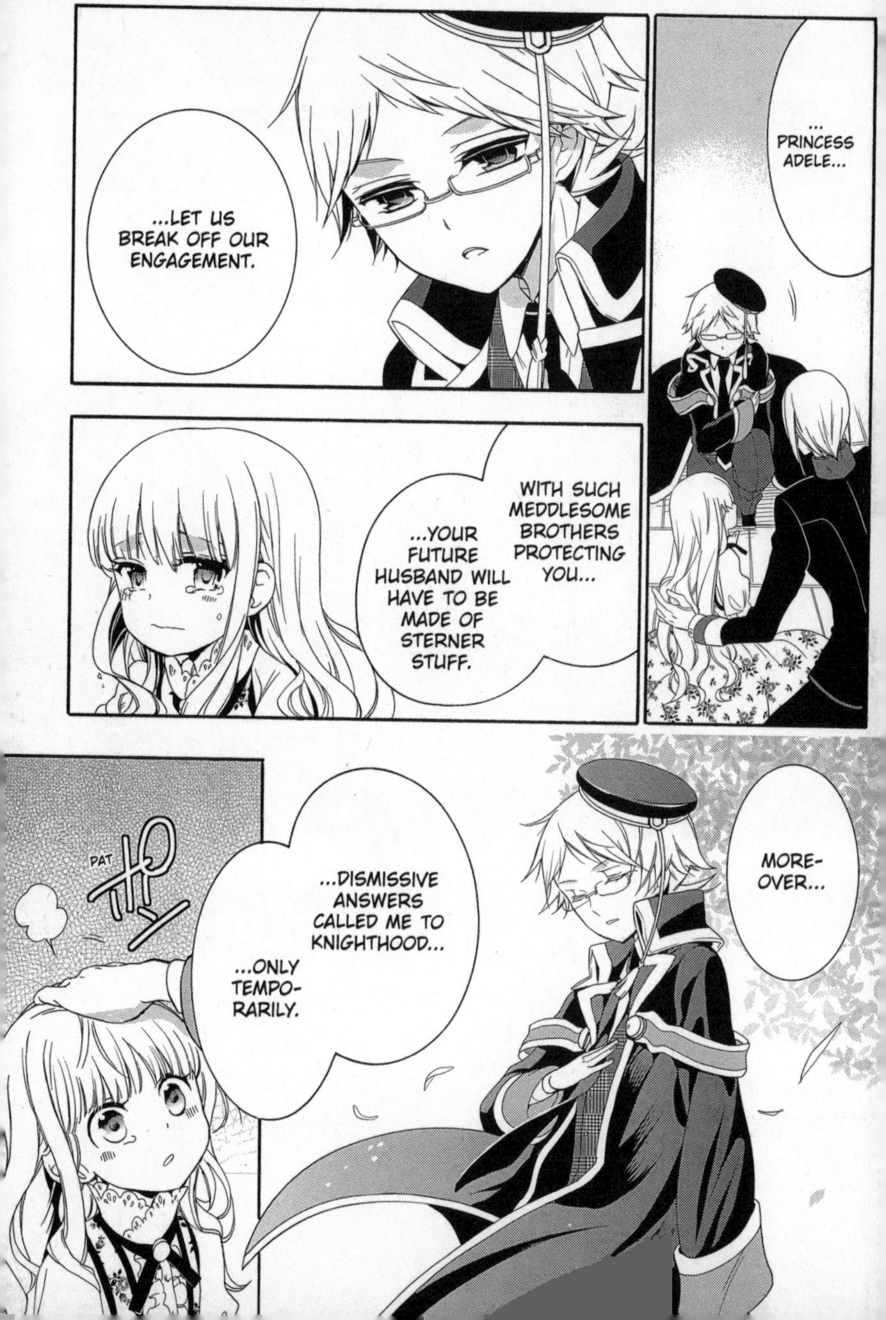
...PRINCESS ADELE...
...LET US BREAK OFF OUR ENGAGEMENT.
WITH SUCH MEDDLESOME BROTHERS PROTECTING YOU...
...YOUR FUTURE HUSBAND WILL HAVE TO BE MADE OF STERNER STUFF.
MORE-OVER...
...DISMISSIVE ANSWERS CALLED ME TO KNIGHTHOOD...
...ONLY TEMPO-RARILY.
PAT

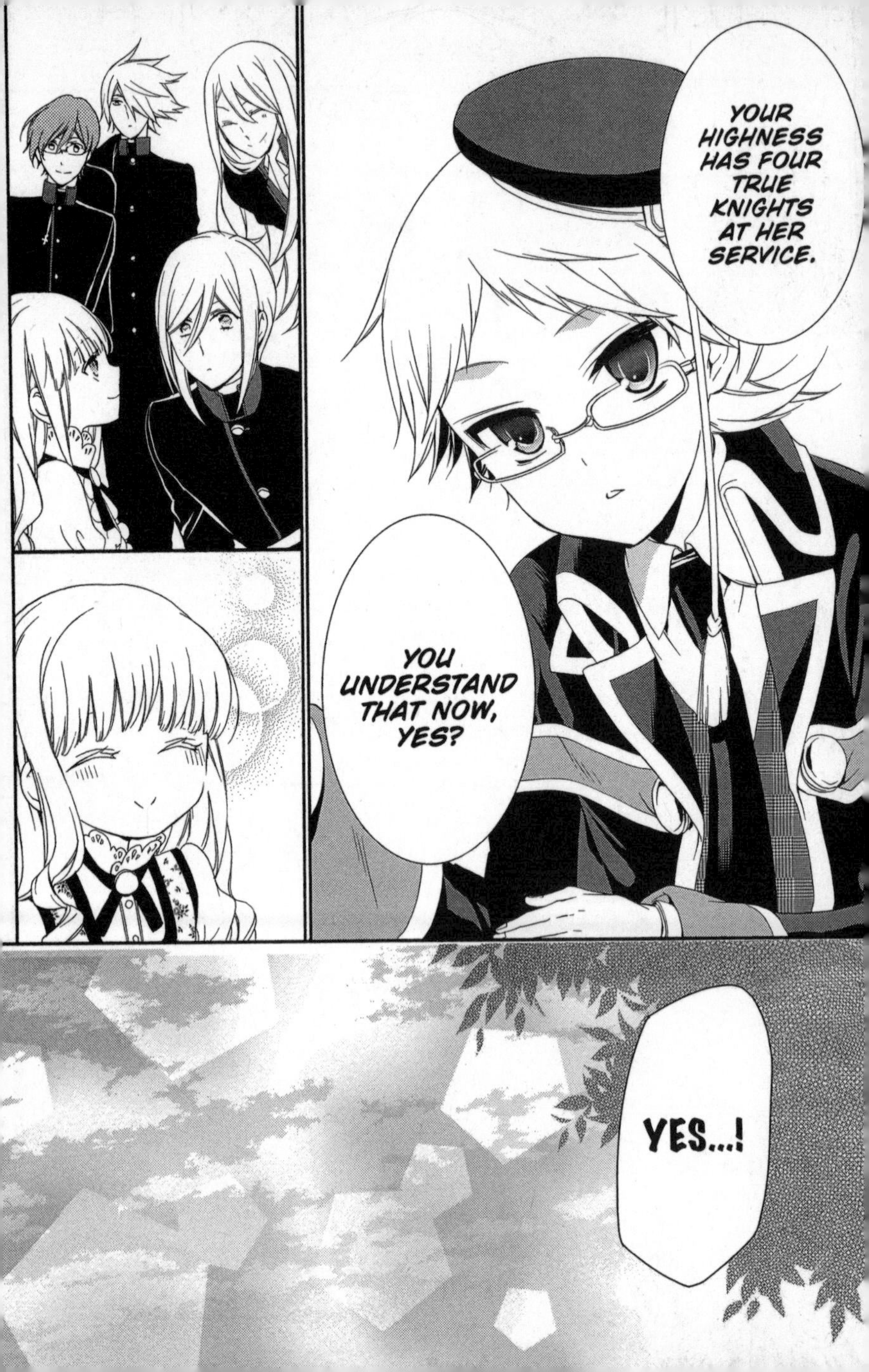
YOUR HIGHNESS HAS FOUR TRUE KNIGHTS AT HER SERVICE.
YOU UNDERSTAND THAT NOW, YES?
YES...!

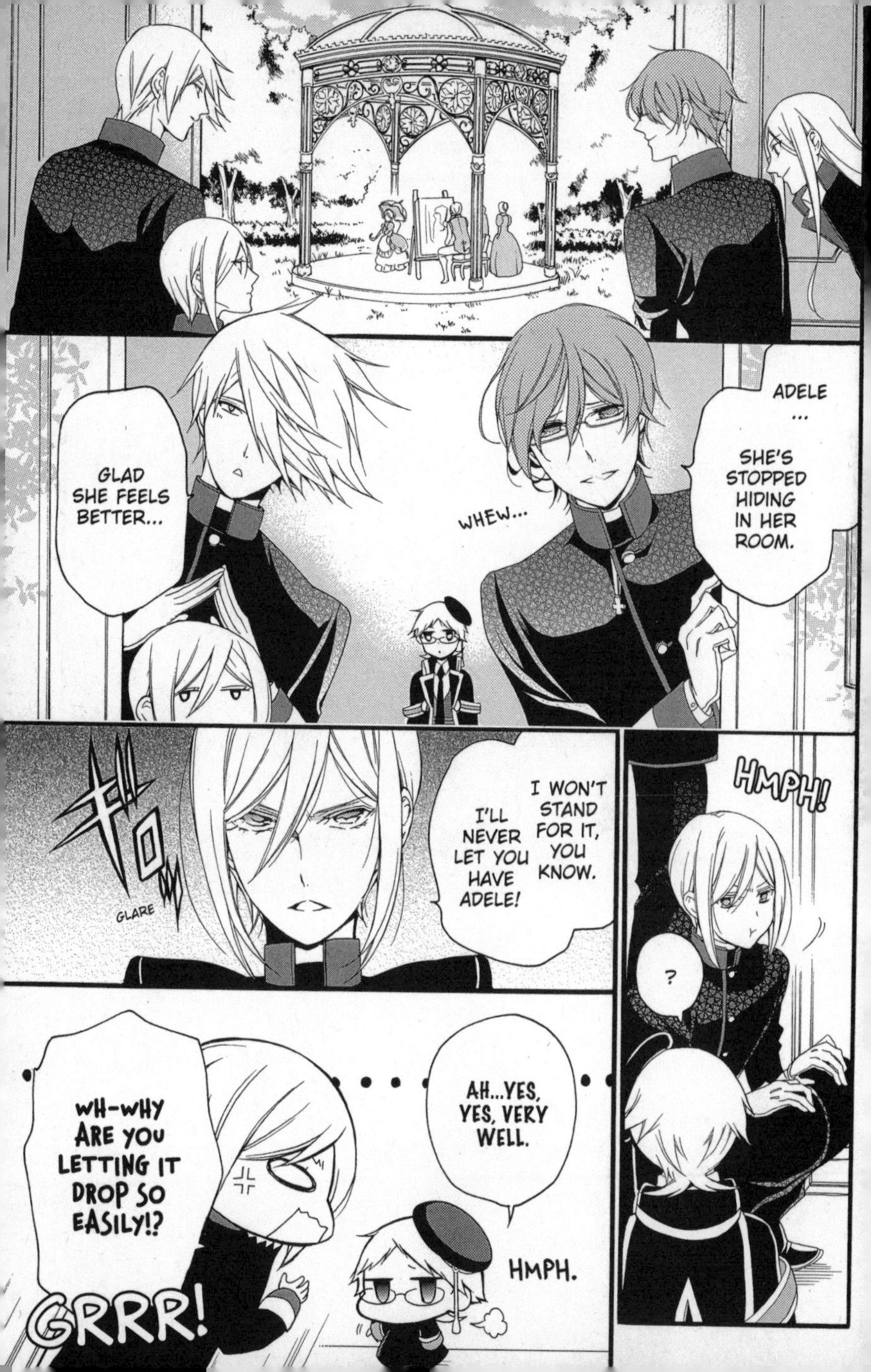
ADELE ...
SHE'S STOPPED HIDING IN HER ROOM.
WHEW...
GLAD SHE FEELS BETTER...
HMPH!
?
I WON'T STAND FOR IT, YOU KNOW.
I'LL NEVER LET YOU HAVE ADELE!
GLARE
AH...YES, YES, VERY WELL.
HMPH.
WH-WHY ARE YOU LETTING IT DROP SO EASILY!?
GRRR!

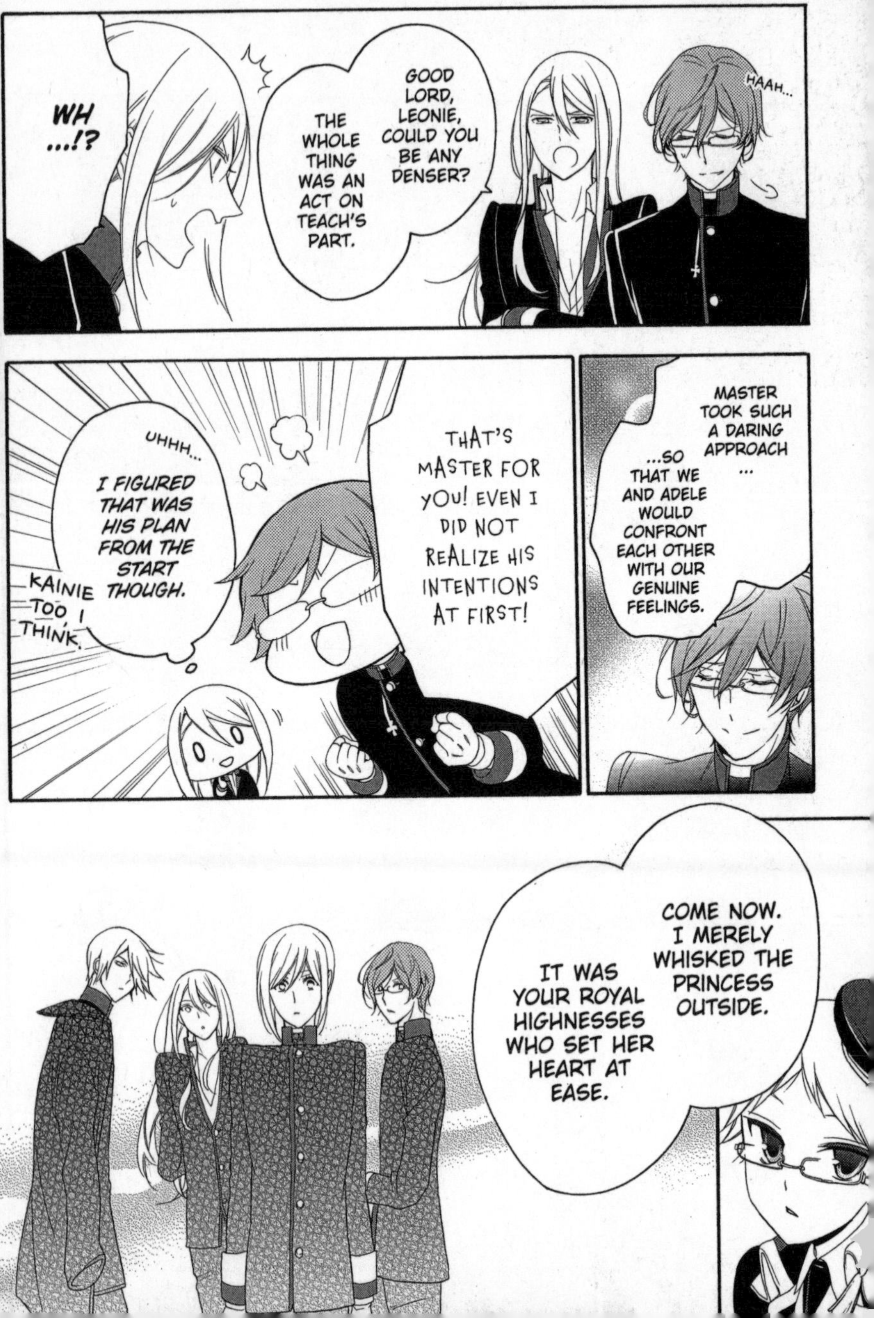
HAAH...
GOOD LORD, LEONIE, COULD YOU BE ANY DENSER?
THE WHOLE THING WAS AN ACT ON TEACH'S PART.
WH...!?
MASTER TOOK SUCH A DARING APPROACH...
...SO THAT WE AND ADELE WOULD CONFRONT EACH OTHER WITH OUR GENUINE FEELINGS.
THAT'S MASTER FOR YOU! EVEN I DID NOT REALIZE HIS INTENTIONS AT FIRST!
UHHH...
I FIGURED THAT WAS HIS PLAN FROM THE START THOUGH.
KAINIE TOO, I THINK.
COME NOW. I MERELY WHISKED THE PRINCESS OUTSIDE.
IT WAS YOUR ROYAL HIGHNESSES WHO SET HER HEART AT EASE.

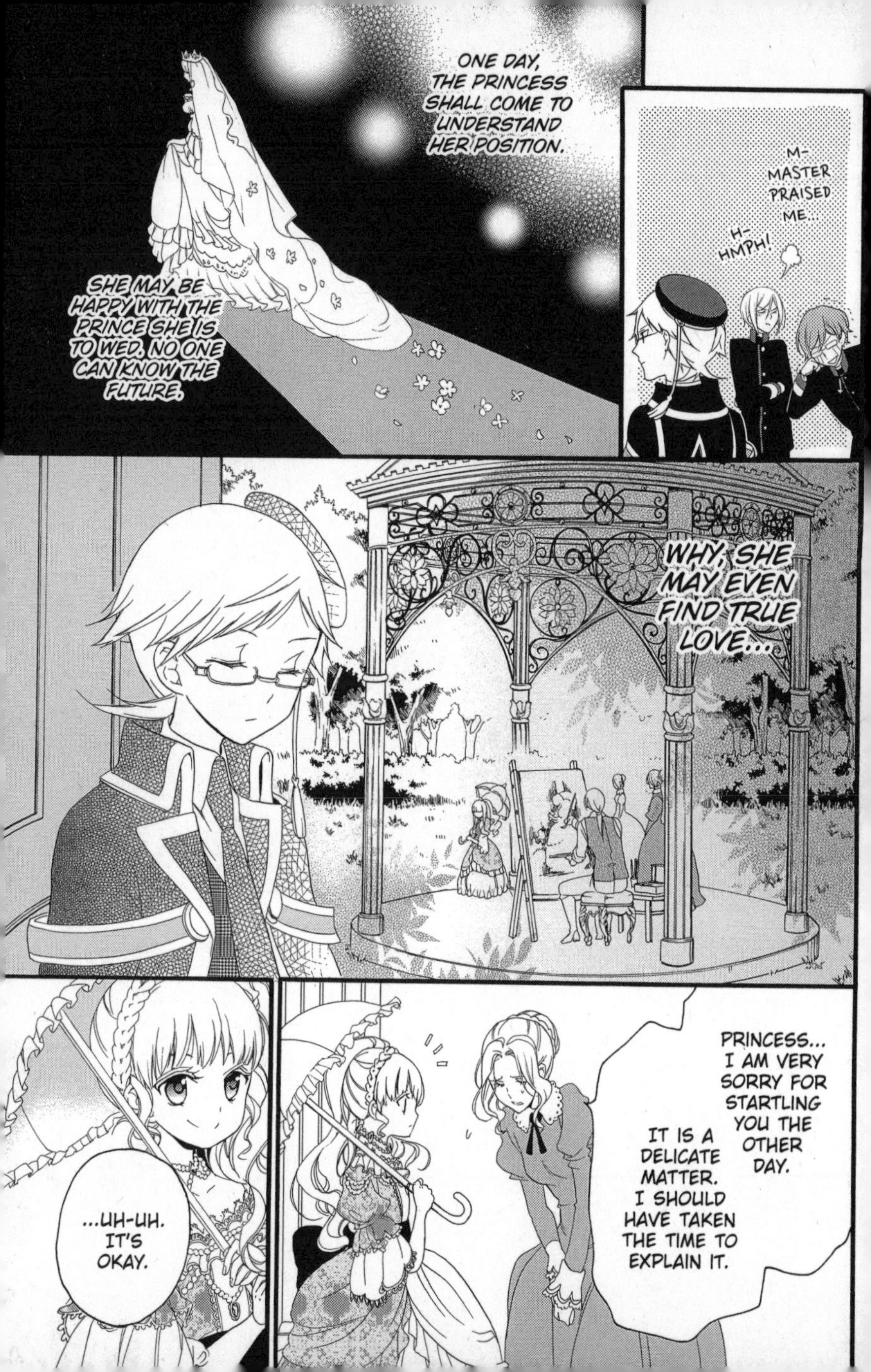
M-MASTER PRAISED ME...
H-HMPH!
ONE DAY, THE PRINCESS SHALL COME TO UNDERSTAND HER POSITION.
SHE MAY BE HAPPY WITH THE PRINCE SHE IS TO WED. NO ONE CAN KNOW THE FUTURE.
WHY, SHE MAY EVEN FIND TRUE LOVE...
PRINCESS... I AM VERY SORRY FOR STARTLING YOU THE OTHER DAY.
IT IS A DELICATE MATTER. I SHOULD HAVE TAKEN THE TIME TO EXPLAIN IT.
...UH-UH. IT'S OKAY.

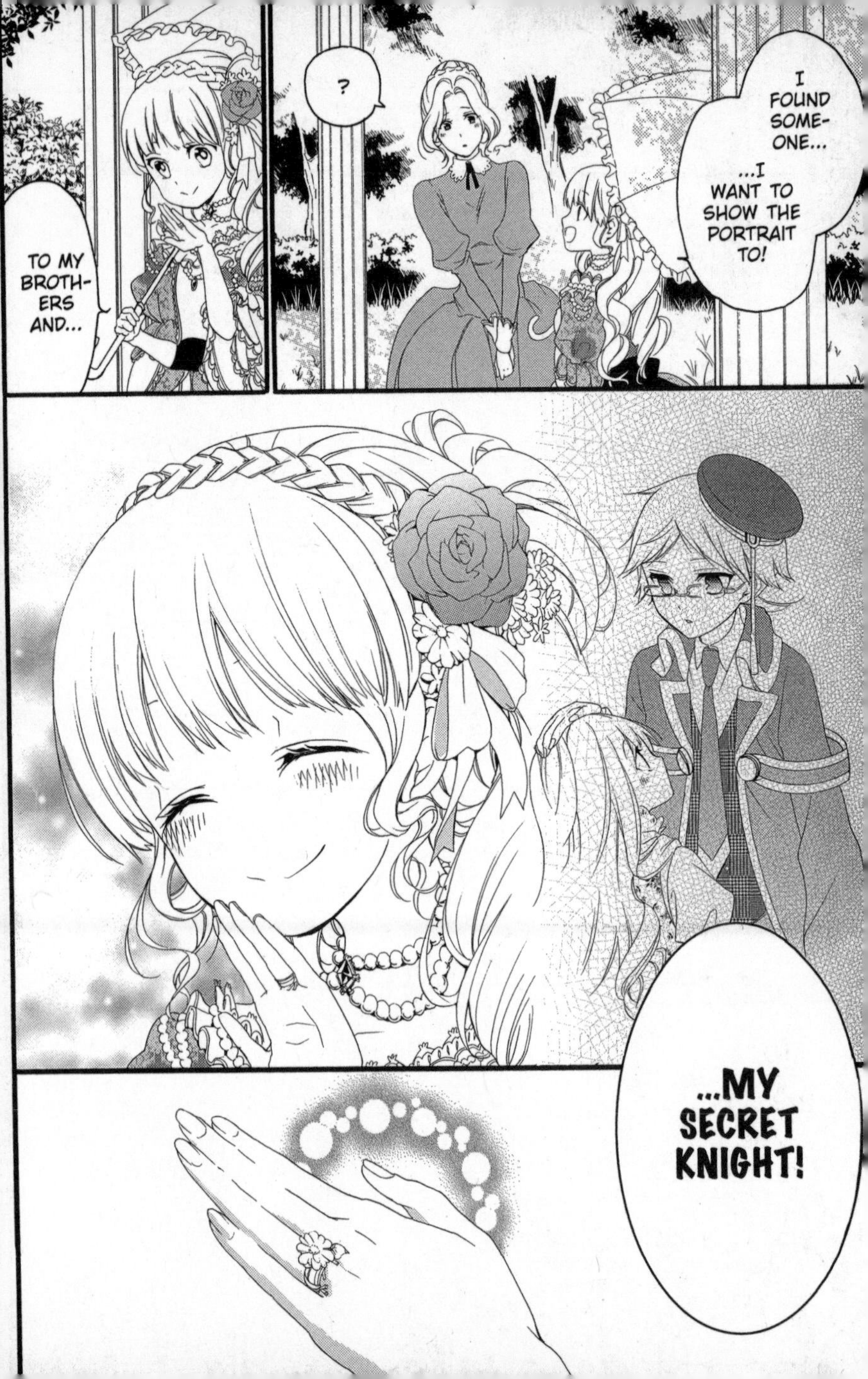
I FOUND SOME-ONE... ...I WANT TO SHOW THE PORTRAIT TO!
?
TO MY BROTH-ERS AND...
...MY SECRET KNIGHT!

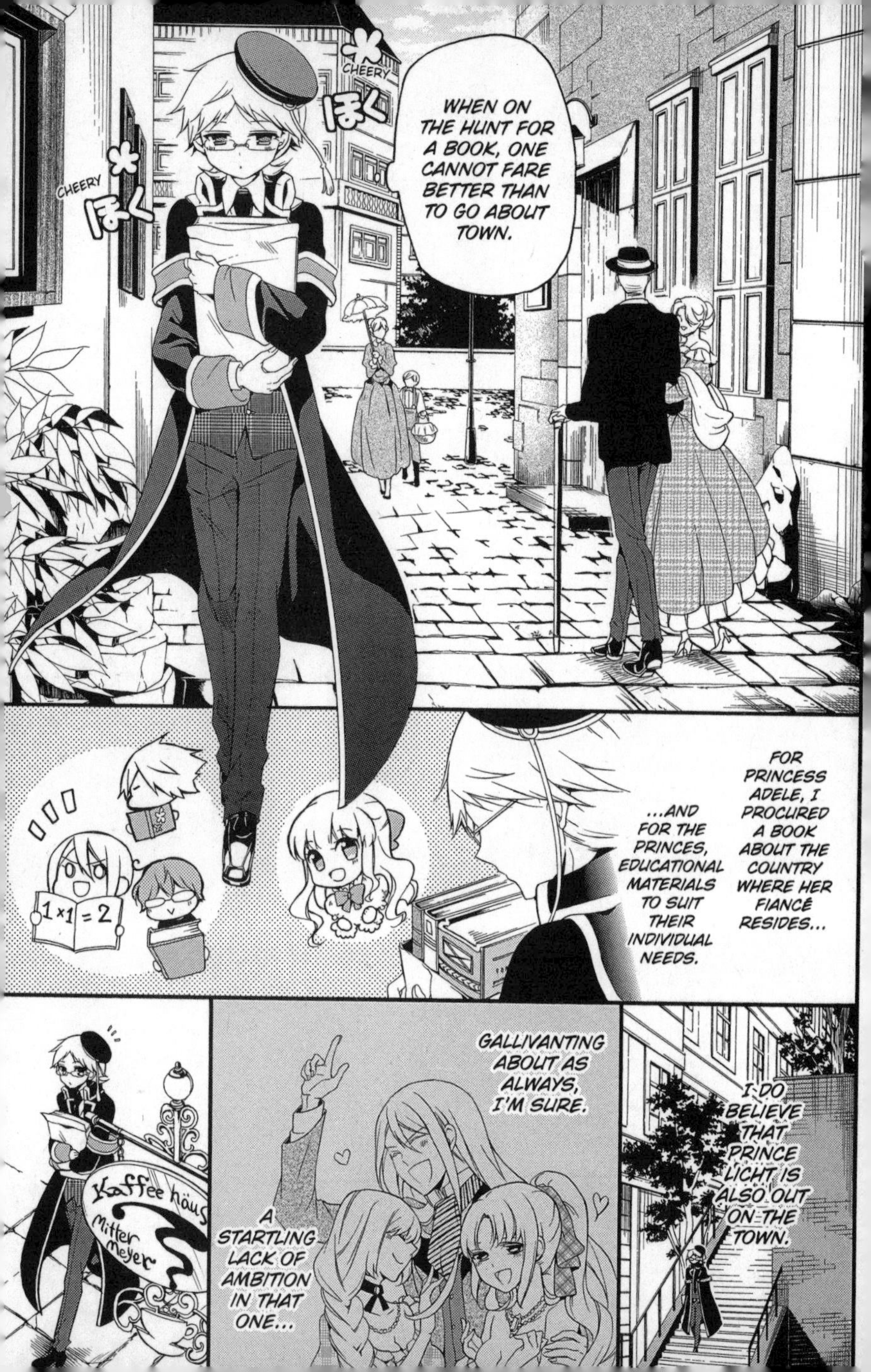
WHEN ON THE HUNT FOR A BOOK, ONE CANNOT FARE BETTER THAN TO GO ABOUT TOWN.
CHEERY ほく
CHEERY ほく
FOR PRINCESS ADELE, I PROCURED A BOOK ABOUT THE COUNTRY WHERE HER FIANCÉ RESIDES...
...AND FOR THE PRINCES, EDUCATIONAL MATERIALS TO SUIT THEIR INDIVIDUAL NEEDS.
1×1 = 2
I DO BELIEVE THAT PRINCE LICHT IS ALSO OUT ON THE TOWN.
GALLIVANTING ABOUT AS ALWAYS, I'M SURE.
A STARTLING LACK OF AMBITION IN THAT ONE...
Kaffee häus
Mitter meyer

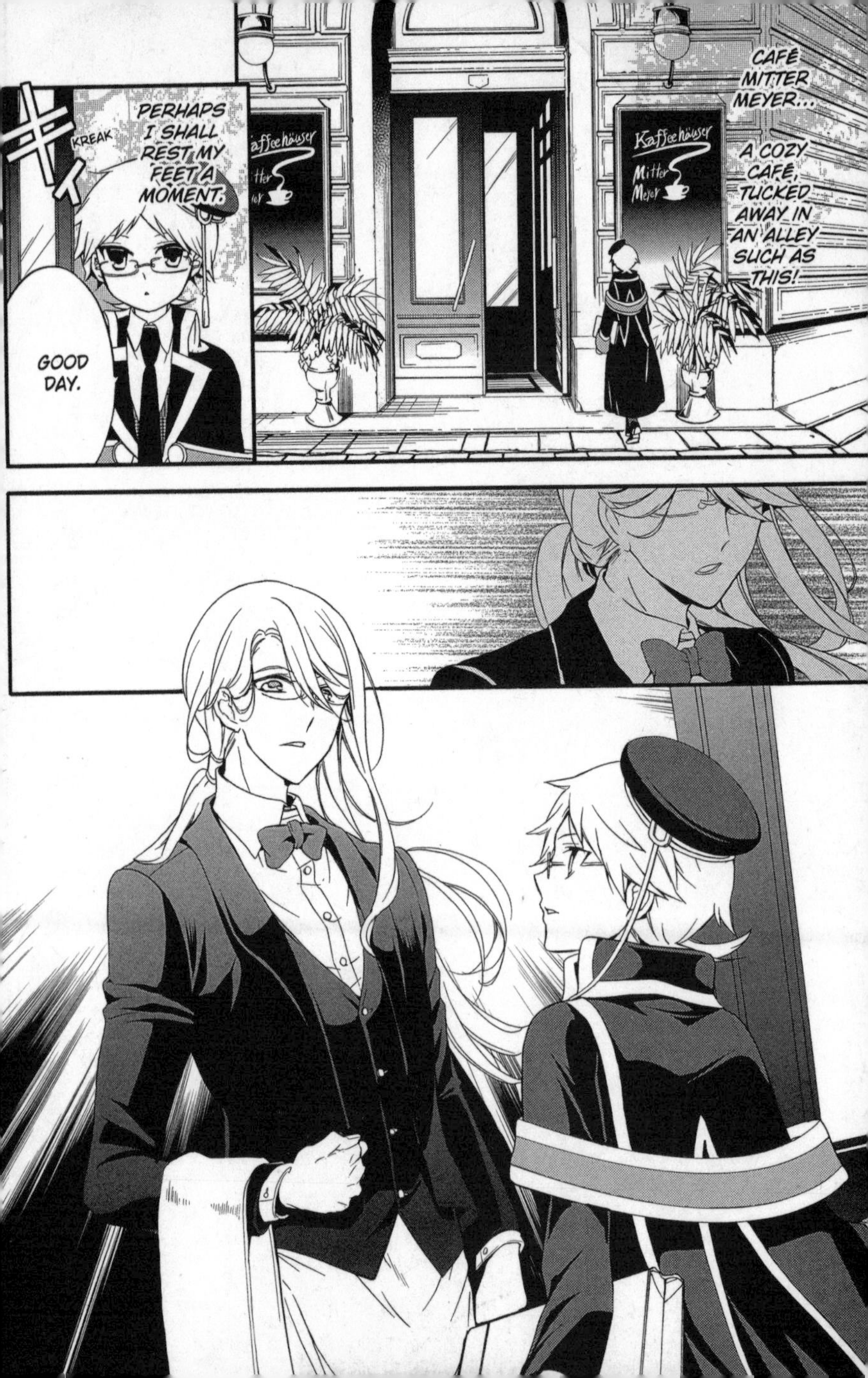
CAFÉ MITTER MEYER...
A COZY CAFÉ, TUCKED AWAY IN AN ALLEY SUCH AS THIS!
Kaffeehäuser Mitter Meyer
ギィ
KREAK
PERHAPS I SHALL REST MY FEET A MOMENT.
GOOD DAY.

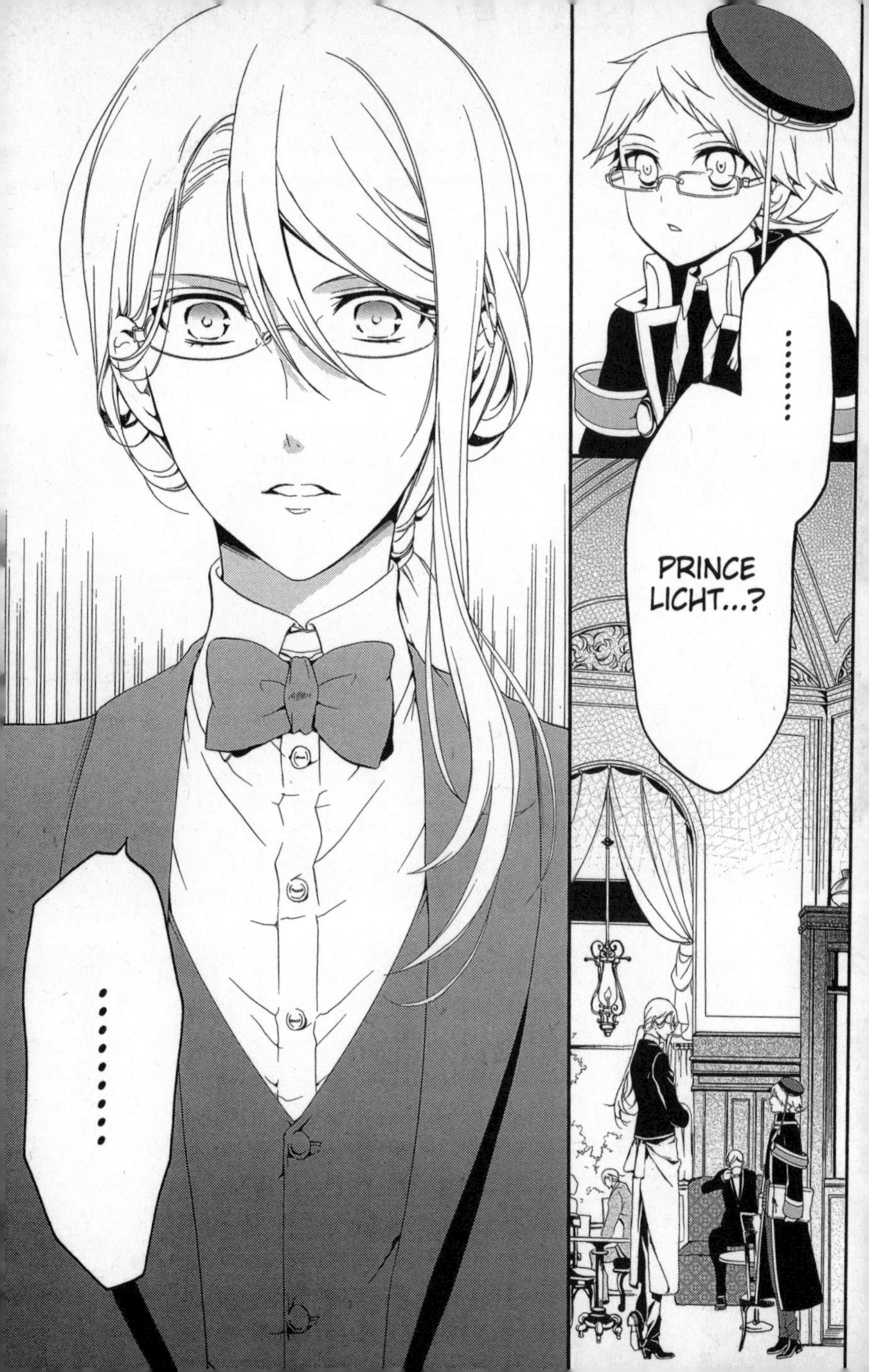
......
PRINCE LICHT...?
......

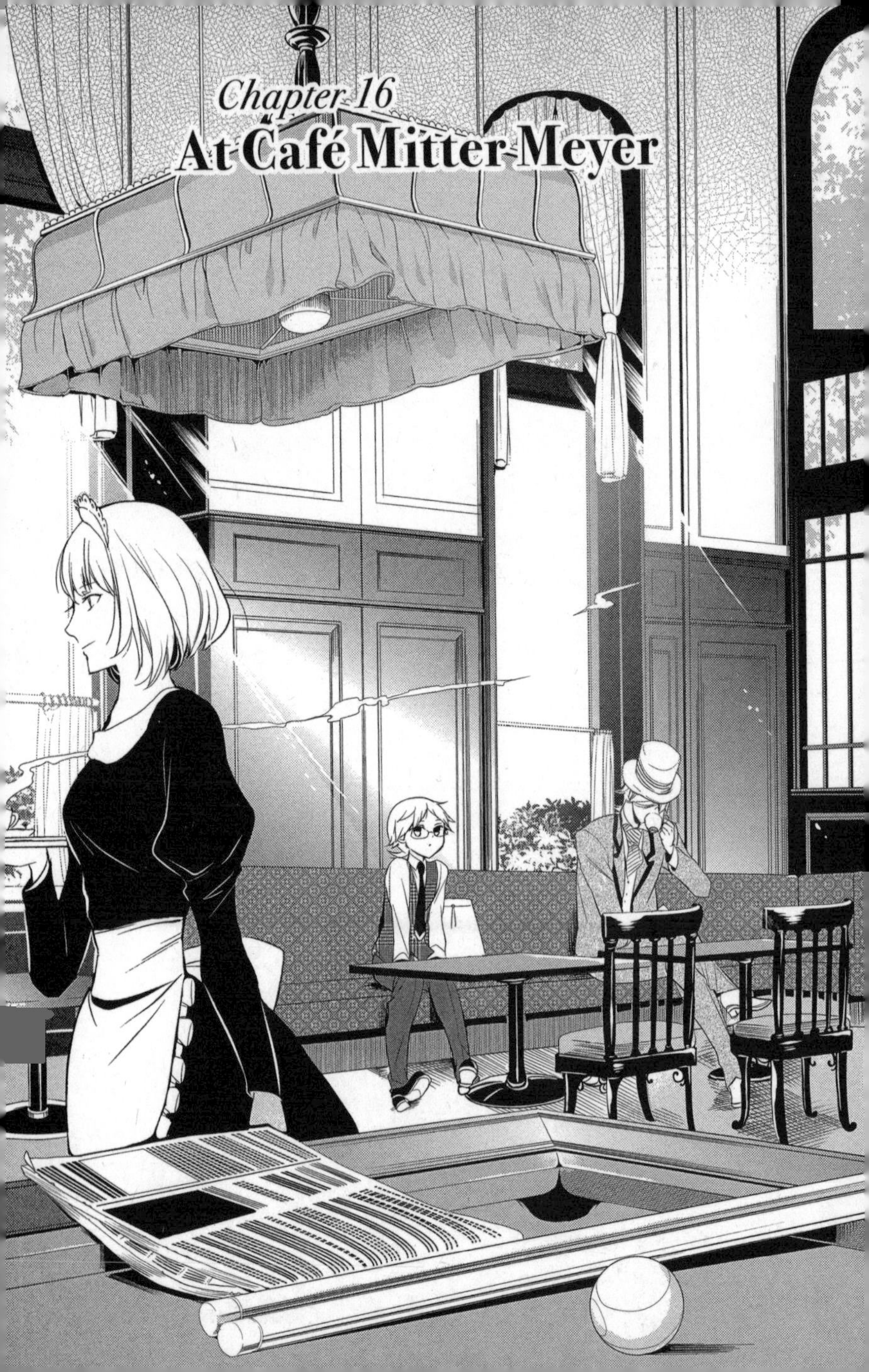
Chapter 16
At Café Mitter Meyer

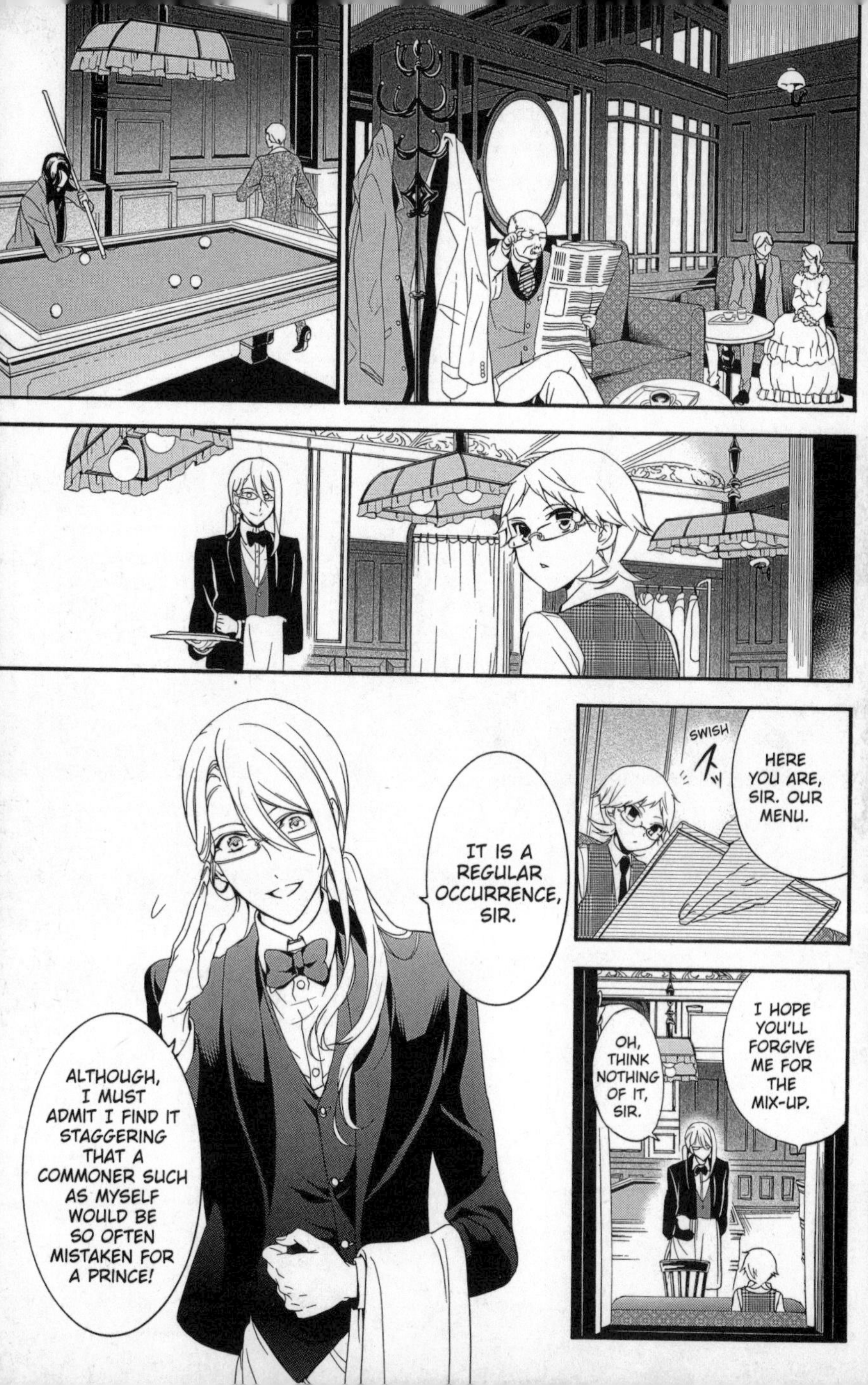
SWISH
HERE YOU ARE, SIR. OUR MENU.
I HOPE YOU'LL FORGIVE ME FOR THE MIX-UP.
OH, THINK NOTHING OF IT, SIR.
IT IS A REGULAR OCCURRENCE, SIR.
ALTHOUGH, I MUST ADMIT I FIND IT STAGGERING THAT A COMMONER SUCH AS MYSELF WOULD BE SO OFTEN MISTAKEN FOR A PRINCE!

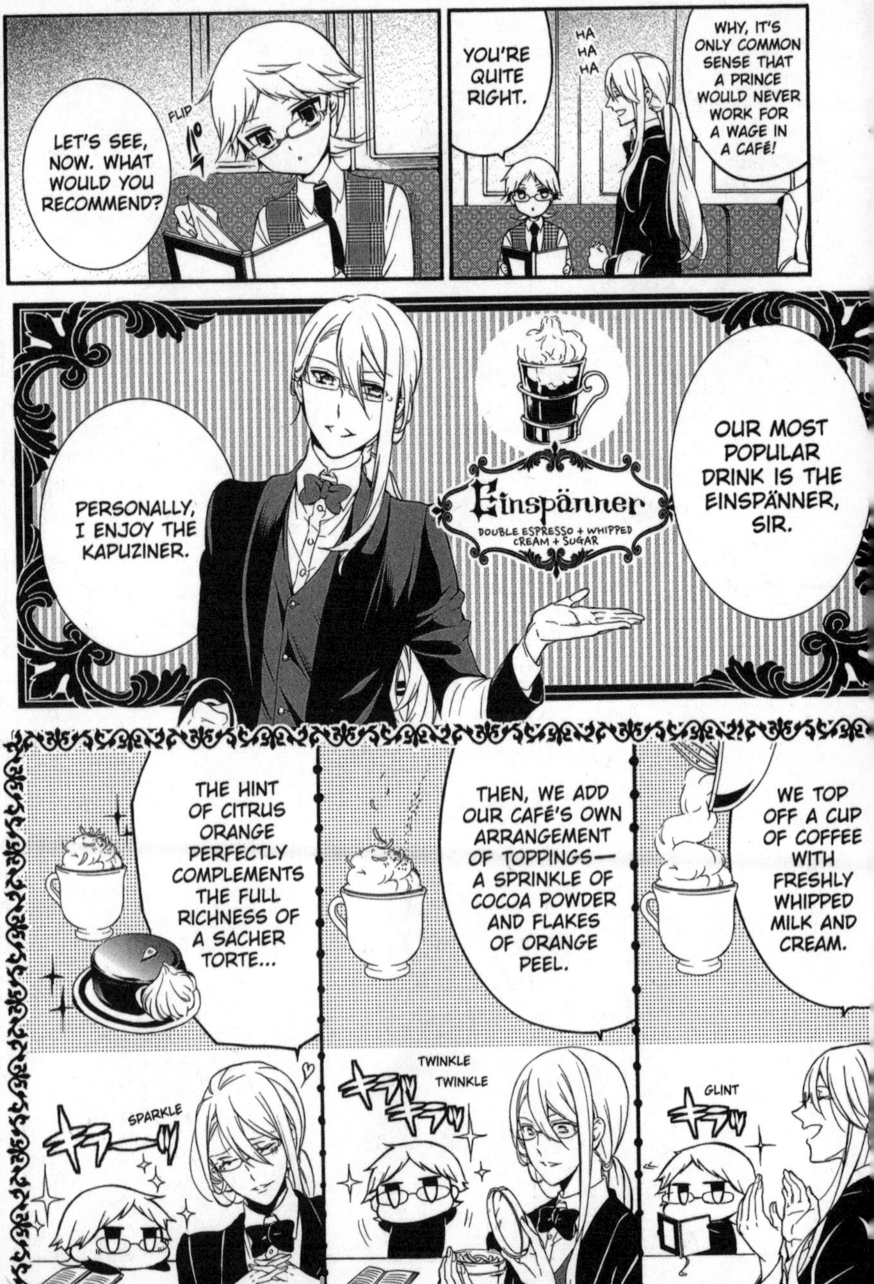
WHY, IT'S ONLY COMMON SENSE THAT A PRINCE WOULD NEVER WORK FOR A WAGE IN A CAFÉ!
HA HA HA
YOU'RE QUITE RIGHT.
FLIP
LET'S SEE, NOW. WHAT WOULD YOU RECOMMEND?
OUR MOST POPULAR DRINK IS THE EINSPÄNNER, SIR.
Einspänner
DOUBLE ESPRESSO + WHIPPED CREAM + SUGAR
PERSONALLY, I ENJOY THE KAPUZINER.
WE TOP OFF A CUP OF COFFEE WITH FRESHLY WHIPPED MILK AND CREAM.
GLINT
THEN, WE ADD OUR CAFÉ'S OWN ARRANGEMENT OF TOPPINGS—A SPRINKLE OF COCOA POWDER AND FLAKES OF ORANGE PEEL.
TWINKLE
TWINKLE
THE HINT OF CITRUS ORANGE PERFECTLY COMPLEMENTS THE FULL RICHNESS OF A SACHER TORTE...
SPARKLE

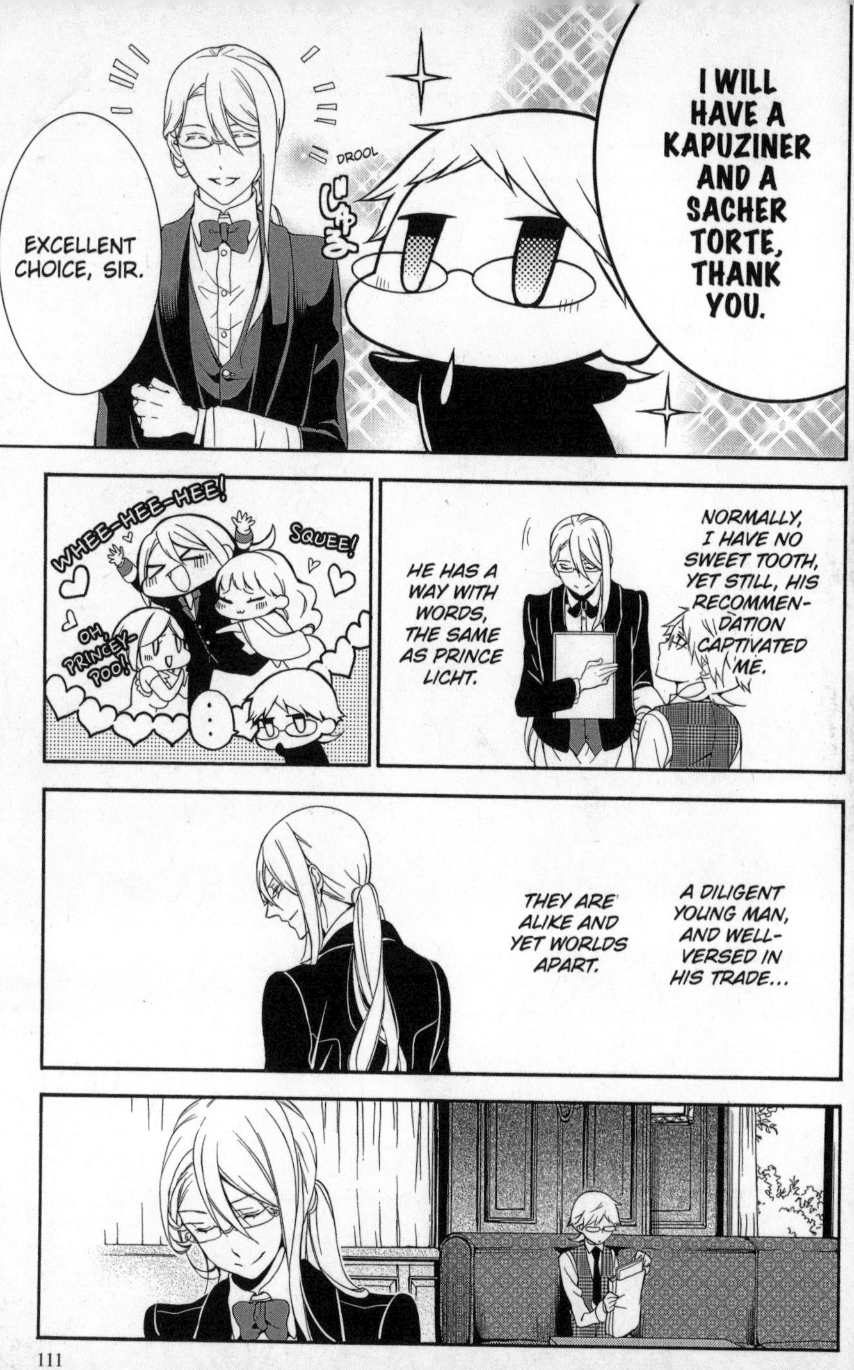
I WILL HAVE A KAPUZINER AND A SACHER TORTE, THANK YOU.
DROOL
じゅる
EXCELLENT CHOICE, SIR.
NORMALLY, I HAVE NO SWEET TOOTH, YET STILL, HIS RECOMMENDATION CAPTIVATED ME.
HE HAS A WAY WITH WORDS, THE SAME AS PRINCE LICHT.
SQUEE!
WHEE-HEE-HEE!
OH, PRINCEY-POO!
...
A DILIGENT YOUNG MAN, AND WELL-VERSED IN HIS TRADE...
THEY ARE ALIKE AND YET WORLDS APART.

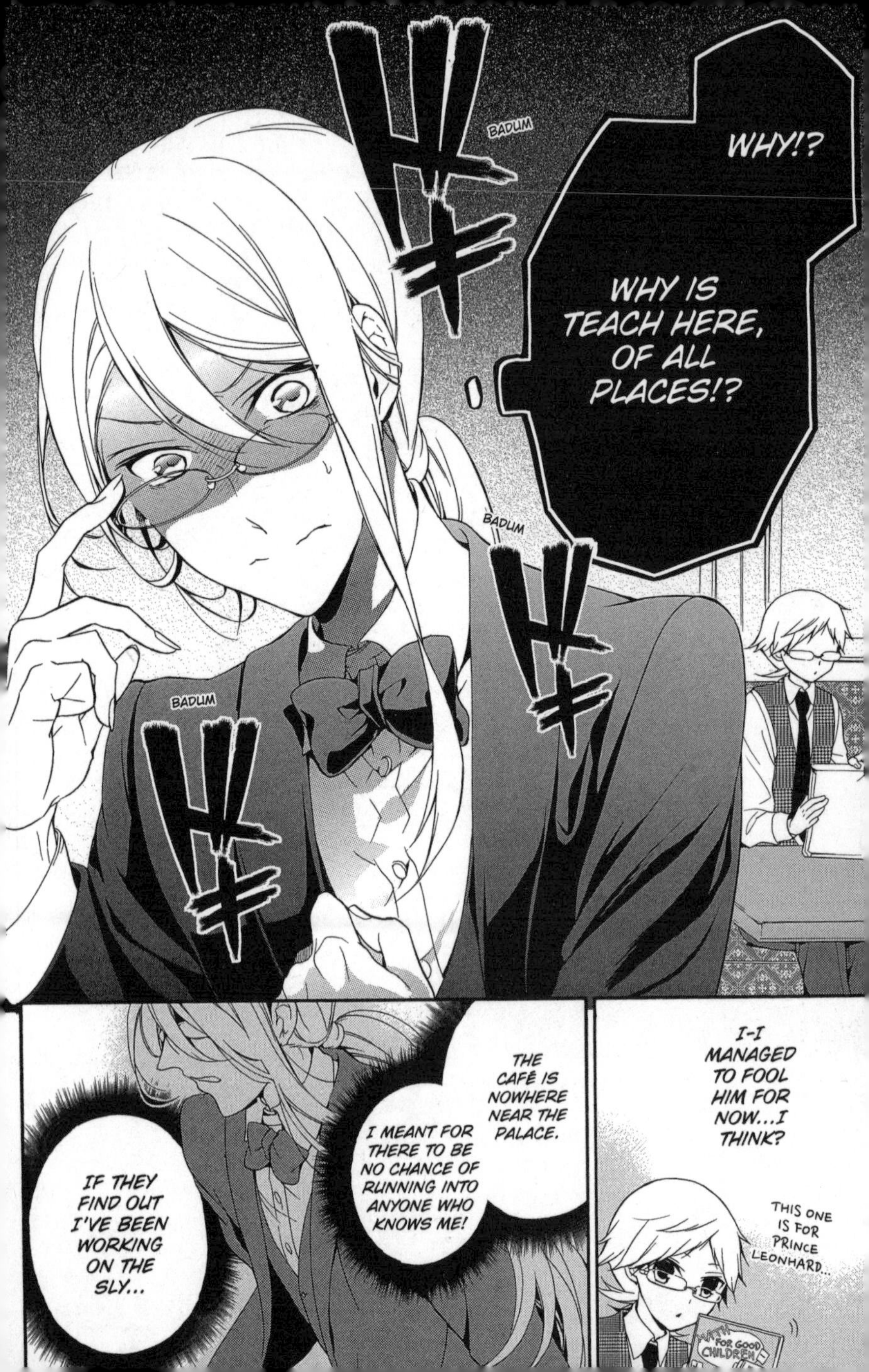
WHY!?
WHY IS TEACH HERE, OF ALL PLACES!?
BADUM
BADUM
BADUM
I-I MANAGED TO FOOL HIM FOR NOW...I THINK?
THIS ONE IS FOR PRINCE LEONHARD...
FOR GOOD CHILDREN
THE CAFÉ IS NOWHERE NEAR THE PALACE.
I MEANT FOR THERE TO BE NO CHANCE OF RUNNING INTO ANYONE WHO KNOWS ME!
IF THEY FIND OUT I'VE BEEN WORKING ON THE SLY...

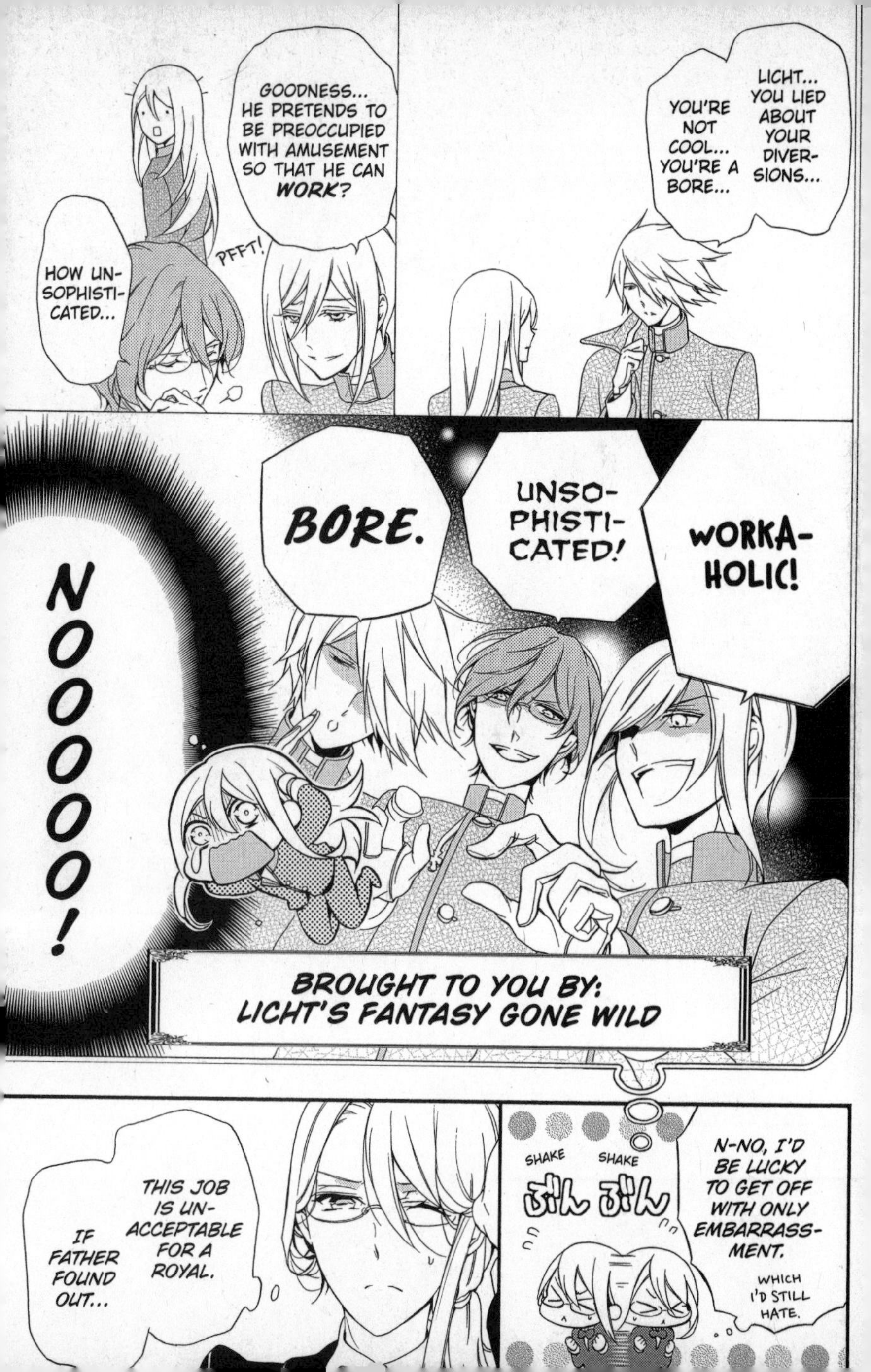
LICHT... YOU LIED ABOUT YOUR DIVERSIONS...
YOU'RE NOT COOL... YOU'RE A BORE...
GOODNESS... HE PRETENDS TO BE PREOCCUPIED WITH AMUSEMENT SO THAT HE CAN WORK?
PFFT!
HOW UN-SOPHISTICATED...
WORKA-HOLIC!
UNSO-PHISTI-CATED!
BORE.
NOOOOOO!
BROUGHT TO YOU BY: LICHT'S FANTASY GONE WILD
SHAKE SHAKE
ぶん ぶん
N-NO, I'D BE LUCKY TO GET OFF WITH ONLY EMBARRASS-MENT.
WHICH I'D STILL HATE.
THIS JOB IS UN-ACCEPTABLE FOR A ROYAL.
IF FATHER FOUND OUT...

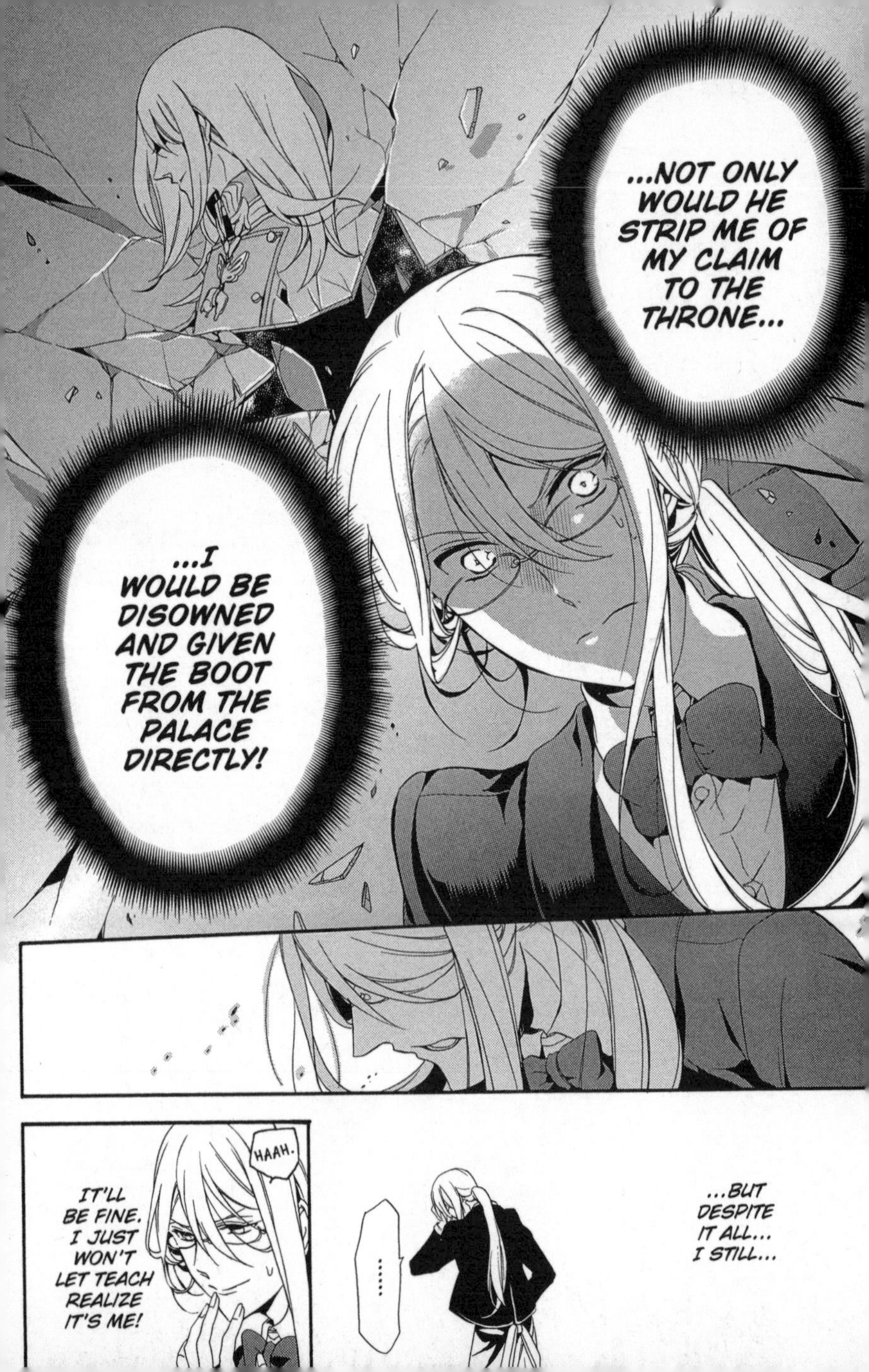
...NOT ONLY WOULD HE STRIP ME OF MY CLAIM TO THE THRONE...
...I WOULD BE DISOWNED AND GIVEN THE BOOT FROM THE PALACE DIRECTLY!
...BUT DESPITE IT ALL... I STILL...
......
HAAH.
IT'LL BE FINE. I JUST WON'T LET TEACH REALIZE IT'S ME!

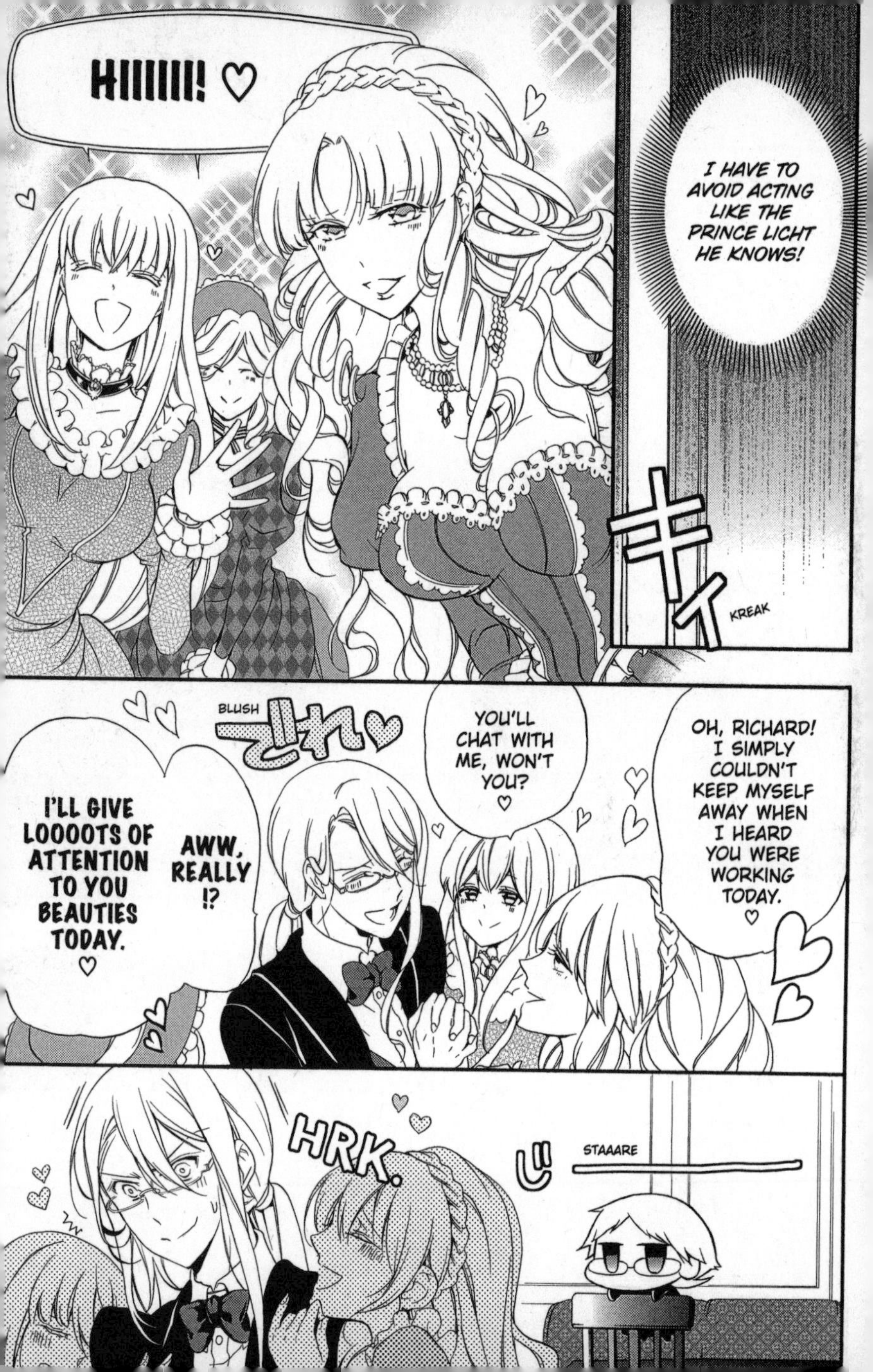
I HAVE TO AVOID ACTING LIKE THE PRINCE LICHT HE KNOWS!
キィ
KREAK
HIIIIII! ♡
OH, RICHARD! I SIMPLY COULDN'T KEEP MYSELF AWAY WHEN I HEARD YOU WERE WORKING TODAY. ♡
YOU'LL CHAT WITH ME, WON'T YOU? ♡
BLUSH
でれ
AWW, REALLY!?
I'LL GIVE LOOOOTS OF ATTENTION TO YOU BEAUTIES TODAY. ♡
STAAARE
じ
HRK.

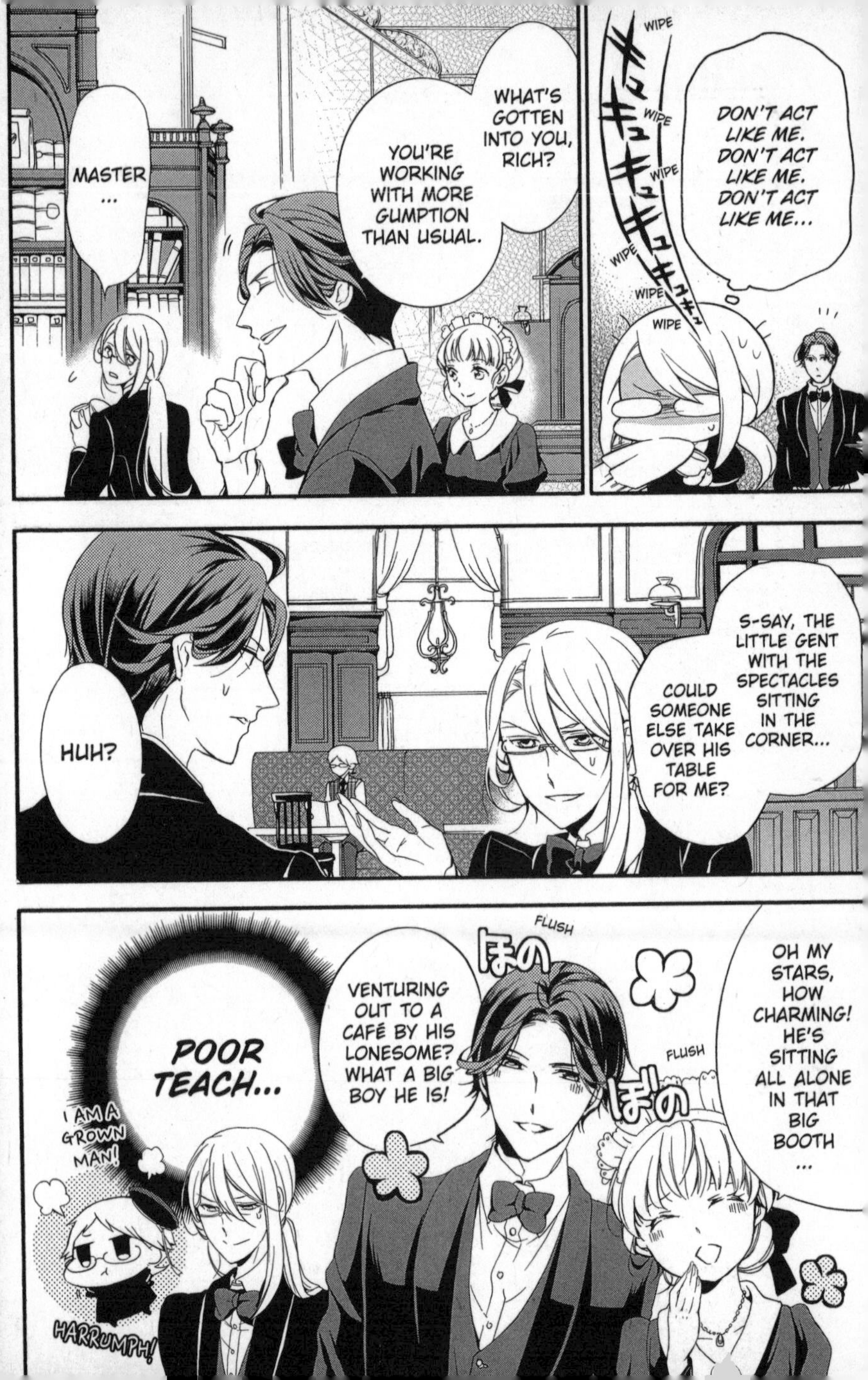
WIPE
WIPE
WIPE
WIPE
WIPE
WIPE
DON'T ACT LIKE ME. DON'T ACT LIKE ME. DON'T ACT LIKE ME...
WHAT'S GOTTEN INTO YOU, RICH?
YOU'RE WORKING WITH MORE GUMPTION THAN USUAL.
MASTER...
S-SAY, THE LITTLE GENT WITH THE SPECTACLES SITTING IN THE CORNER...
COULD SOMEONE ELSE TAKE OVER HIS TABLE FOR ME?
HUH?
OH MY STARS, HOW CHARMING! HE'S SITTING ALL ALONE IN THAT BIG BOOTH...
FLUSH
ぽの
FLUSH
ほの
VENTURING OUT TO A CAFÉ BY HIS LONESOME? WHAT A BIG BOY HE IS!
POOR TEACH...
I AM A GROWN MAN!
HARRUMPH!

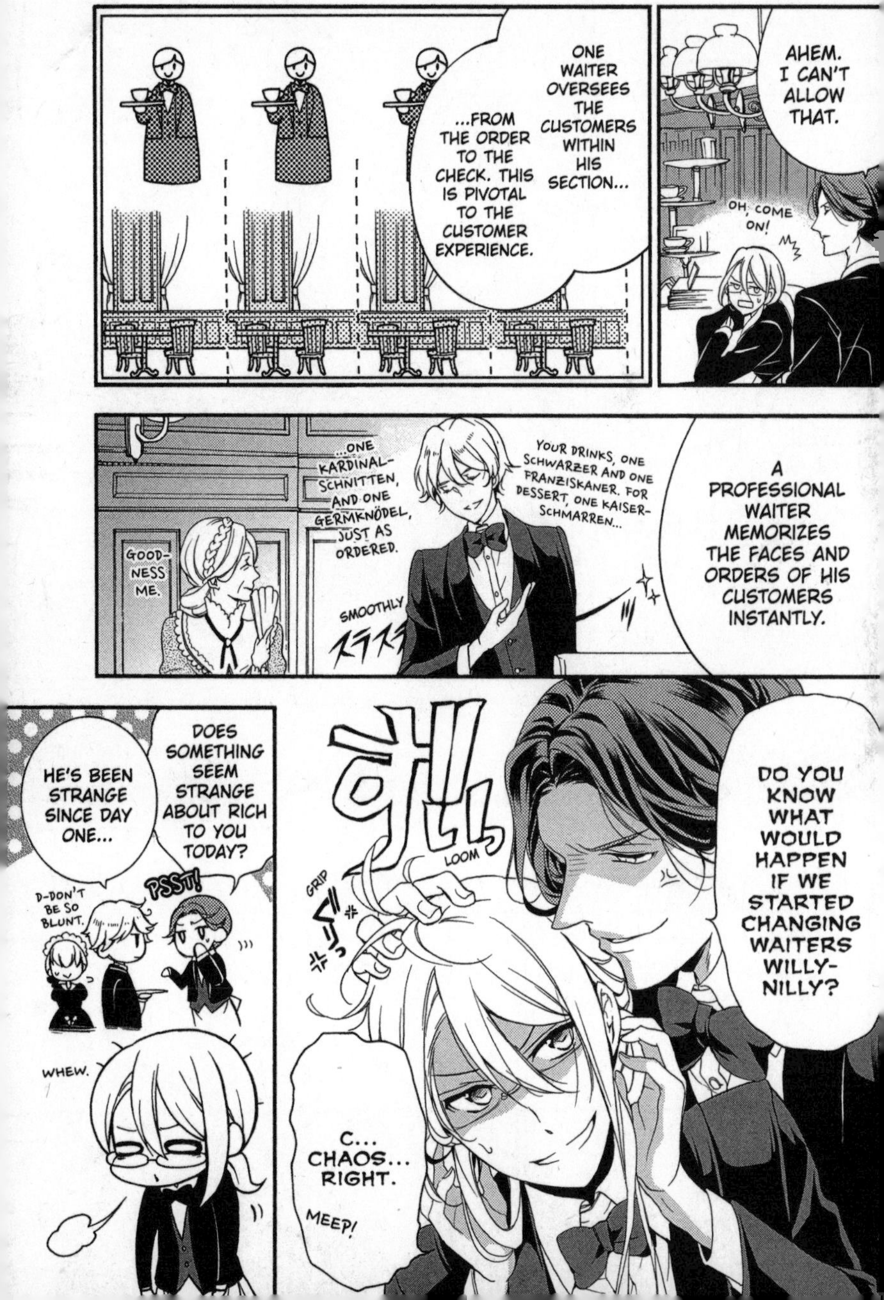
AHEM. I CAN'T ALLOW THAT.
OH, COME ON!
ONE WAITER OVERSEES THE CUSTOMERS WITHIN HIS SECTION...
...FROM THE ORDER TO THE CHECK. THIS IS PIVOTAL TO THE CUSTOMER EXPERIENCE.
A PROFESSIONAL WAITER MEMORIZES THE FACES AND ORDERS OF HIS CUSTOMERS INSTANTLY.
YOUR DRINKS, ONE SCHWARZER AND ONE FRANZISKANER. FOR DESSERT, ONE KAISER-SCHMARREN...
...ONE KARDINAL-SCHNITTEN, AND ONE GERMKNÖDEL, JUST AS ORDERED.
GOOD-NESS ME.
SMOOTHLY
LOOM
DO YOU KNOW WHAT WOULD HAPPEN IF WE STARTED CHANGING WAITERS WILLY-NILLY?
GRIP
C... CHAOS... RIGHT.
MEEP!
DOES SOMETHING SEEM STRANGE ABOUT RICH TO YOU TODAY?
HE'S BEEN STRANGE SINCE DAY ONE...
PSSST!
D-DON'T BE SO BLUNT.
WHEW.

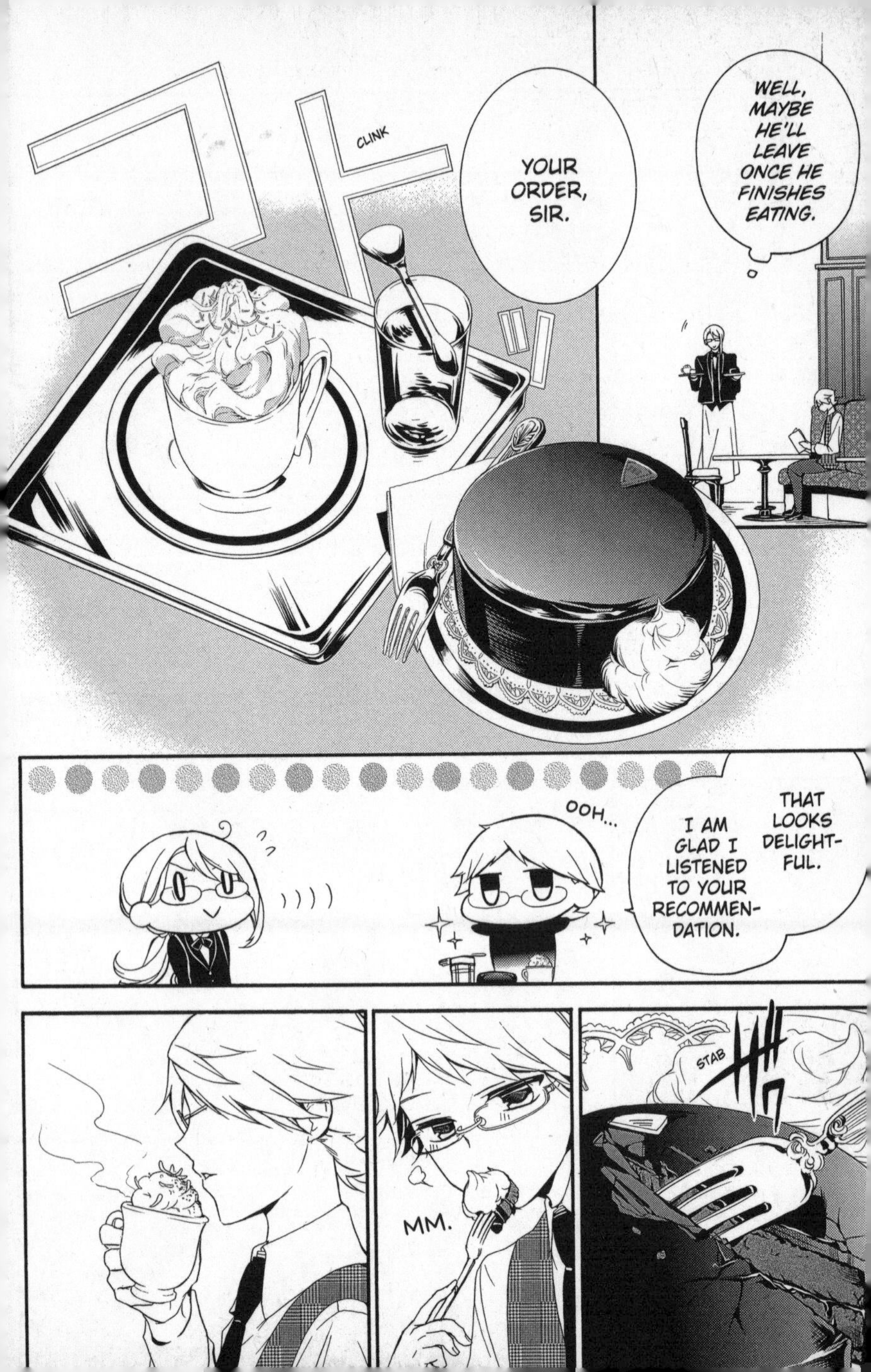
WELL, MAYBE HE'LL LEAVE ONCE HE FINISHES EATING.
CLINK
YOUR ORDER, SIR.
THAT LOOKS DELIGHTFUL.
I AM GLAD I LISTENED TO YOUR RECOMMENDATION.
OOH...
STAB
MM.

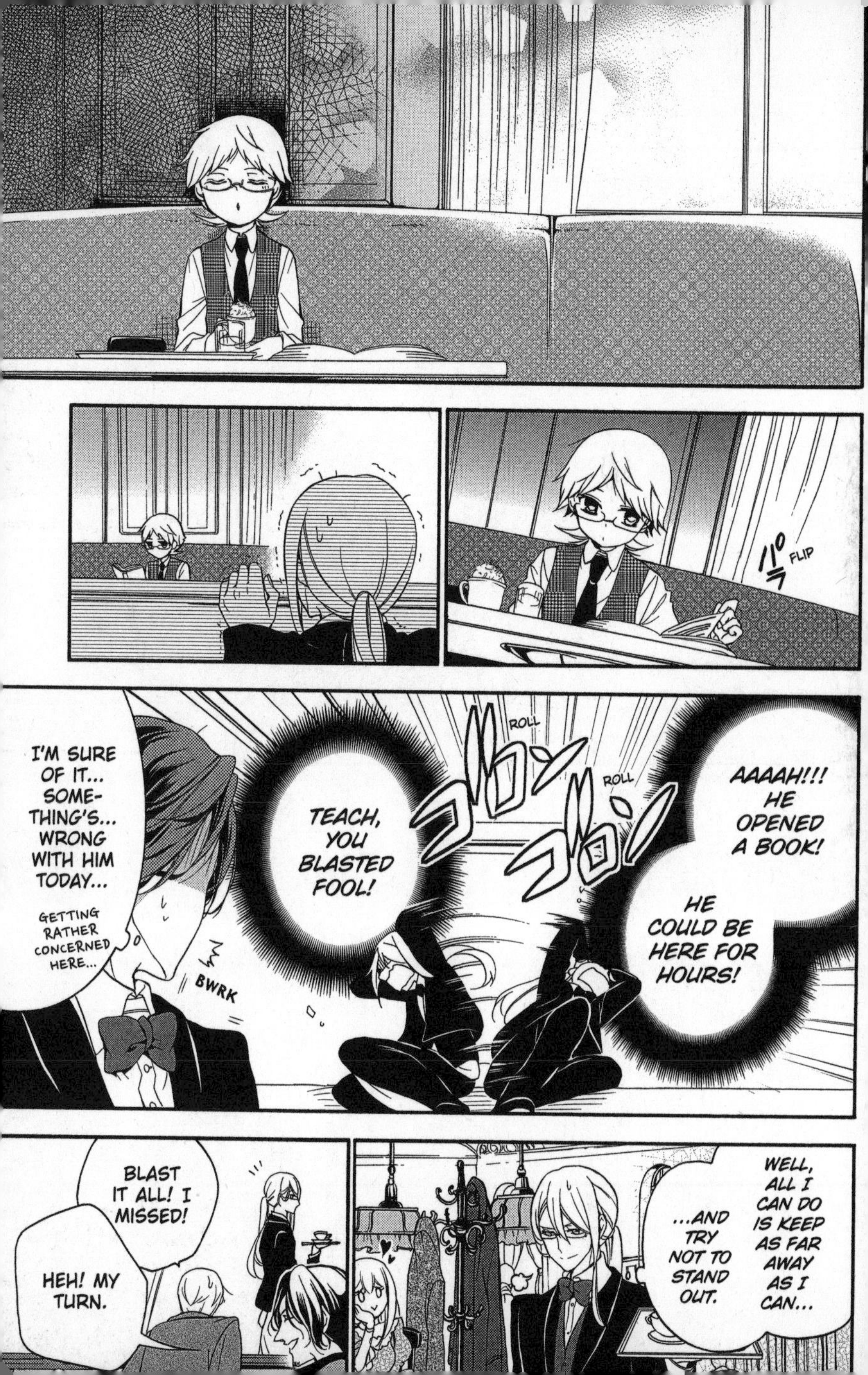
FLIP
AAAAH!!! HE OPENED A BOOK!
HE COULD BE HERE FOR HOURS!
ROLL
ROLL
TEACH, YOU BLASTED FOOL!
BWRK
I'M SURE OF IT... SOME-THING'S... WRONG WITH HIM TODAY...
GETTING RATHER CONCERNED HERE...
WELL, ALL I CAN DO IS KEEP AS FAR AWAY AS I CAN...
...AND TRY NOT TO STAND OUT.
BLAST IT ALL! I MISSED!
HEH! MY TURN.

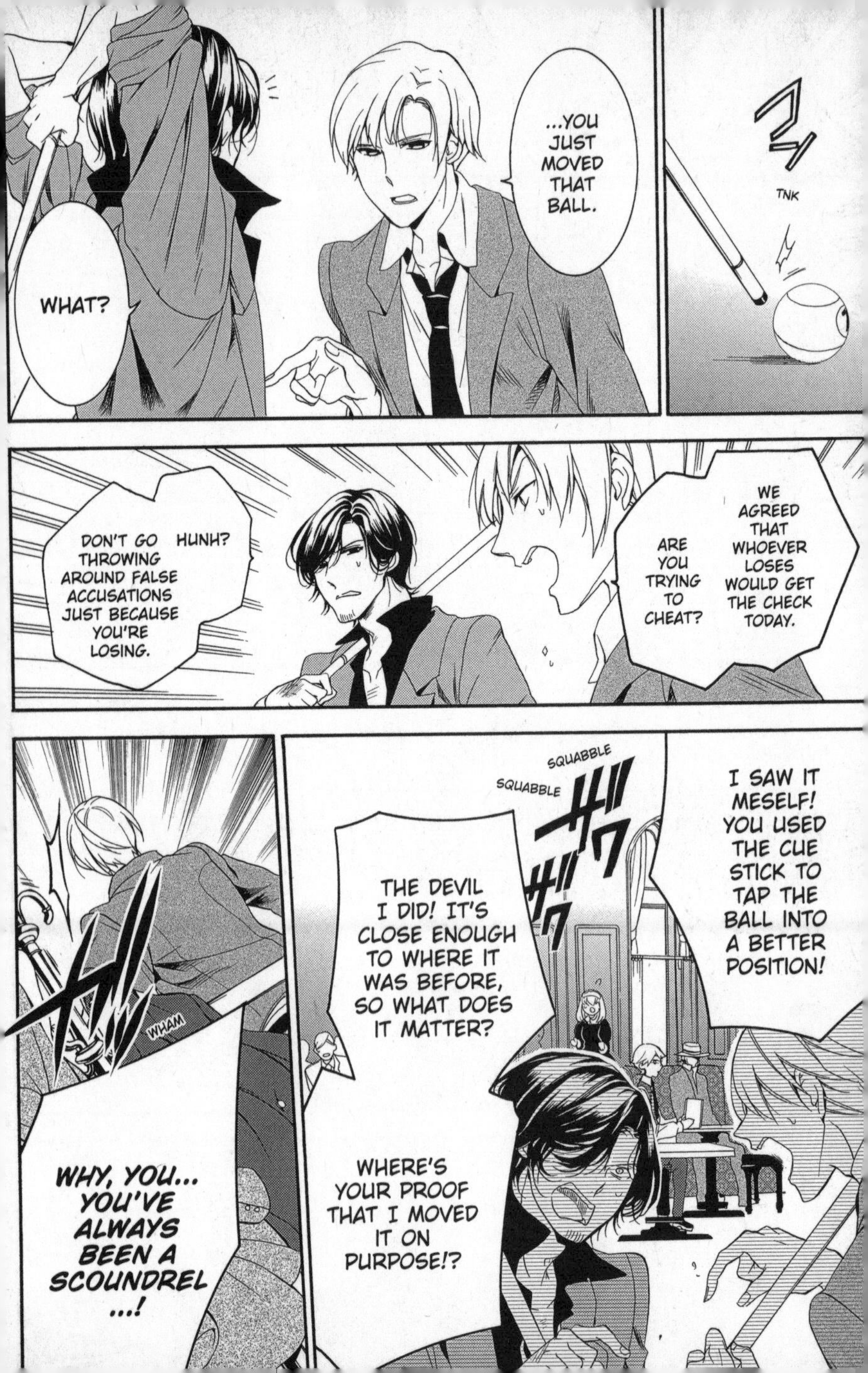
TNK
...YOU JUST MOVED THAT BALL.
WHAT?
WE AGREED THAT WHOEVER LOSES WOULD GET THE CHECK TODAY.
ARE YOU TRYING TO CHEAT?
HUNH?
DON'T GO THROWING AROUND FALSE ACCUSATIONS JUST BECAUSE YOU'RE LOSING.
SQUABBLE
SQUABBLE
I SAW IT MESELF! YOU USED THE CUE STICK TO TAP THE BALL INTO A BETTER POSITION!
THE DEVIL I DID! IT'S CLOSE ENOUGH TO WHERE IT WAS BEFORE, SO WHAT DOES IT MATTER?
WHERE'S YOUR PROOF THAT I MOVED IT ON PURPOSE!?
WHAM
WHY, YOU... YOU'VE ALWAYS BEEN A SCOUNDREL ...!

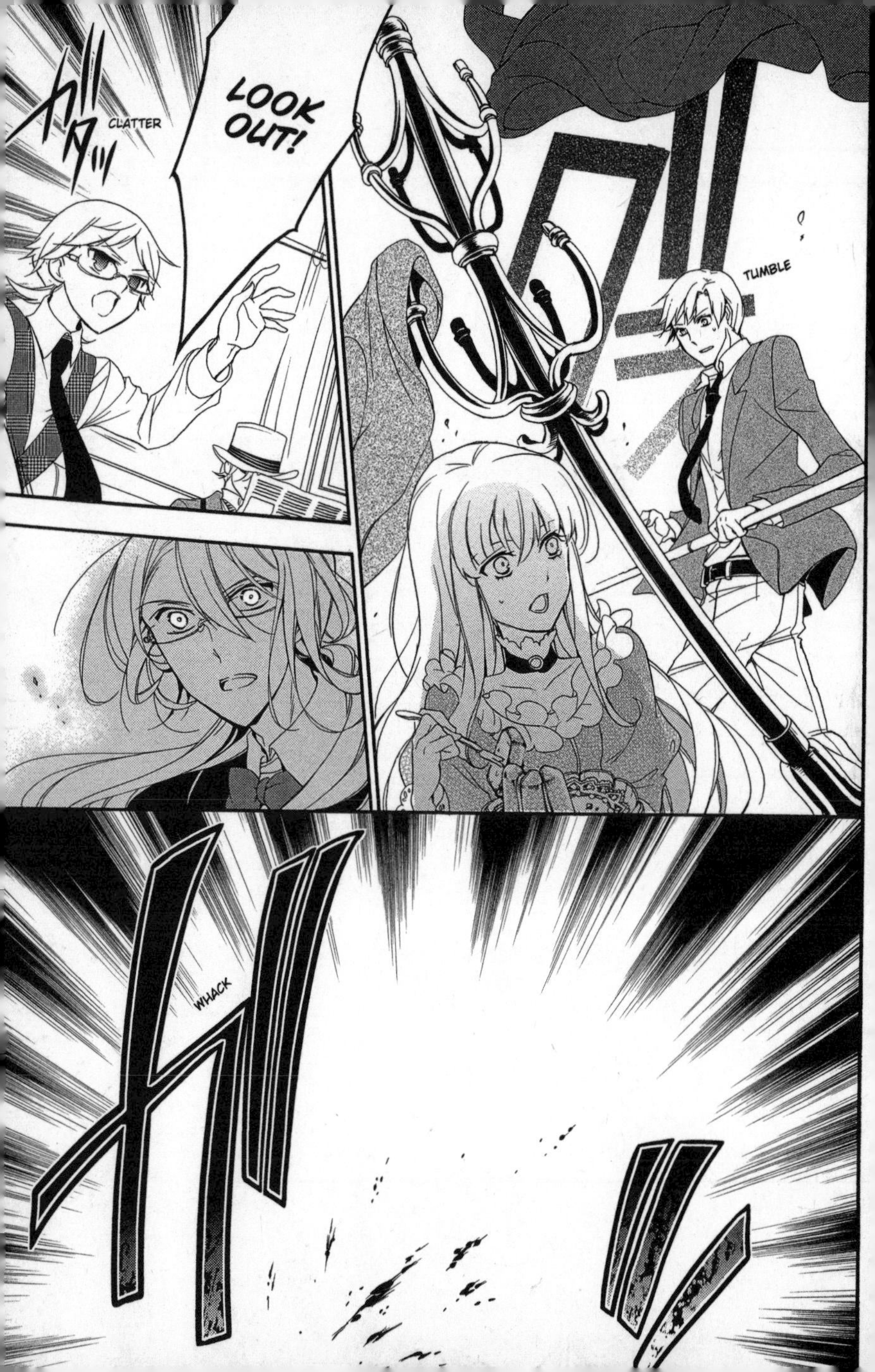
TUMBLE
LOOK OUT!
CLATTER
WHACK

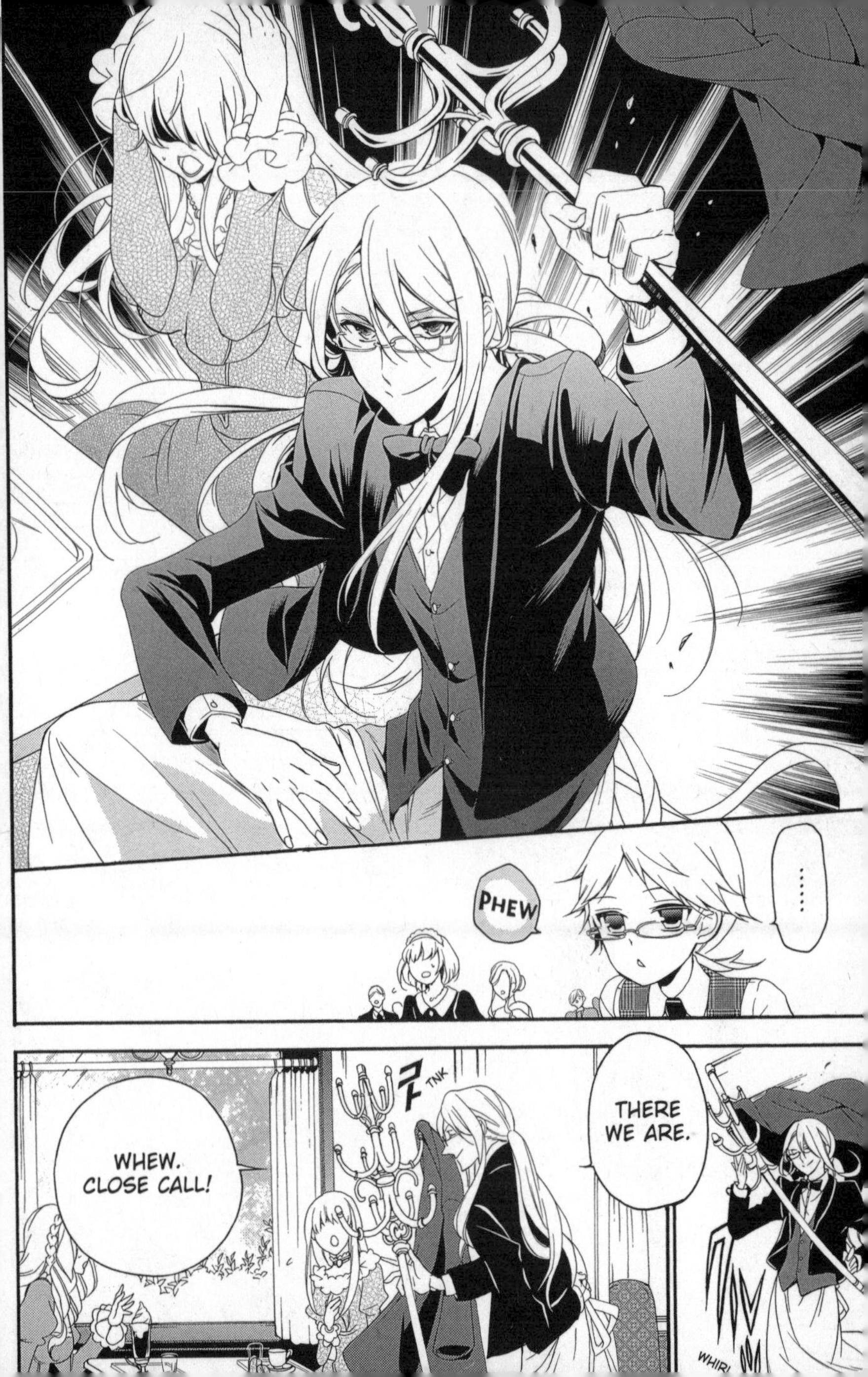
......
PHEW
WHIR!
THERE WE ARE.
TNK
WHEW. CLOSE CALL!

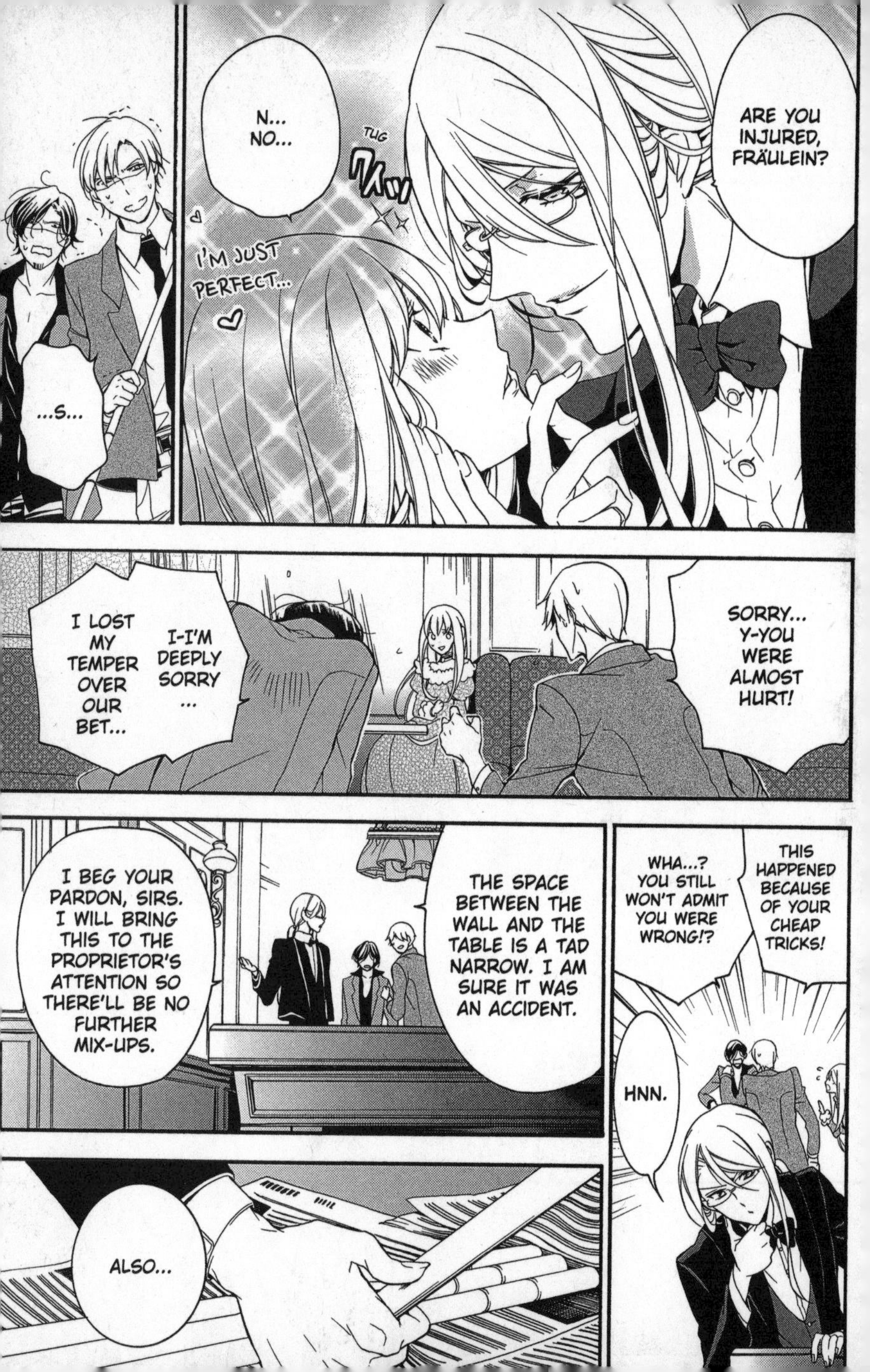
ARE YOU INJURED, FRÄULEIN?
N... NO...
TUG
クイッ
I'M JUST PERFECT...
...S...
SORRY... Y-YOU WERE ALMOST HURT!
I-I'M DEEPLY SORRY ...
I LOST MY TEMPER OVER OUR BET...
THIS HAPPENED BECAUSE OF YOUR CHEAP TRICKS!
WHA...? YOU STILL WON'T ADMIT YOU WERE WRONG!?
HNN.
THE SPACE BETWEEN THE WALL AND THE TABLE IS A TAD NARROW. I AM SURE IT WAS AN ACCIDENT.
I BEG YOUR PARDON, SIRS. I WILL BRING THIS TO THE PROPRIETOR'S ATTENTION SO THERE'LL BE NO FURTHER MIX-UPS.
ALSO...

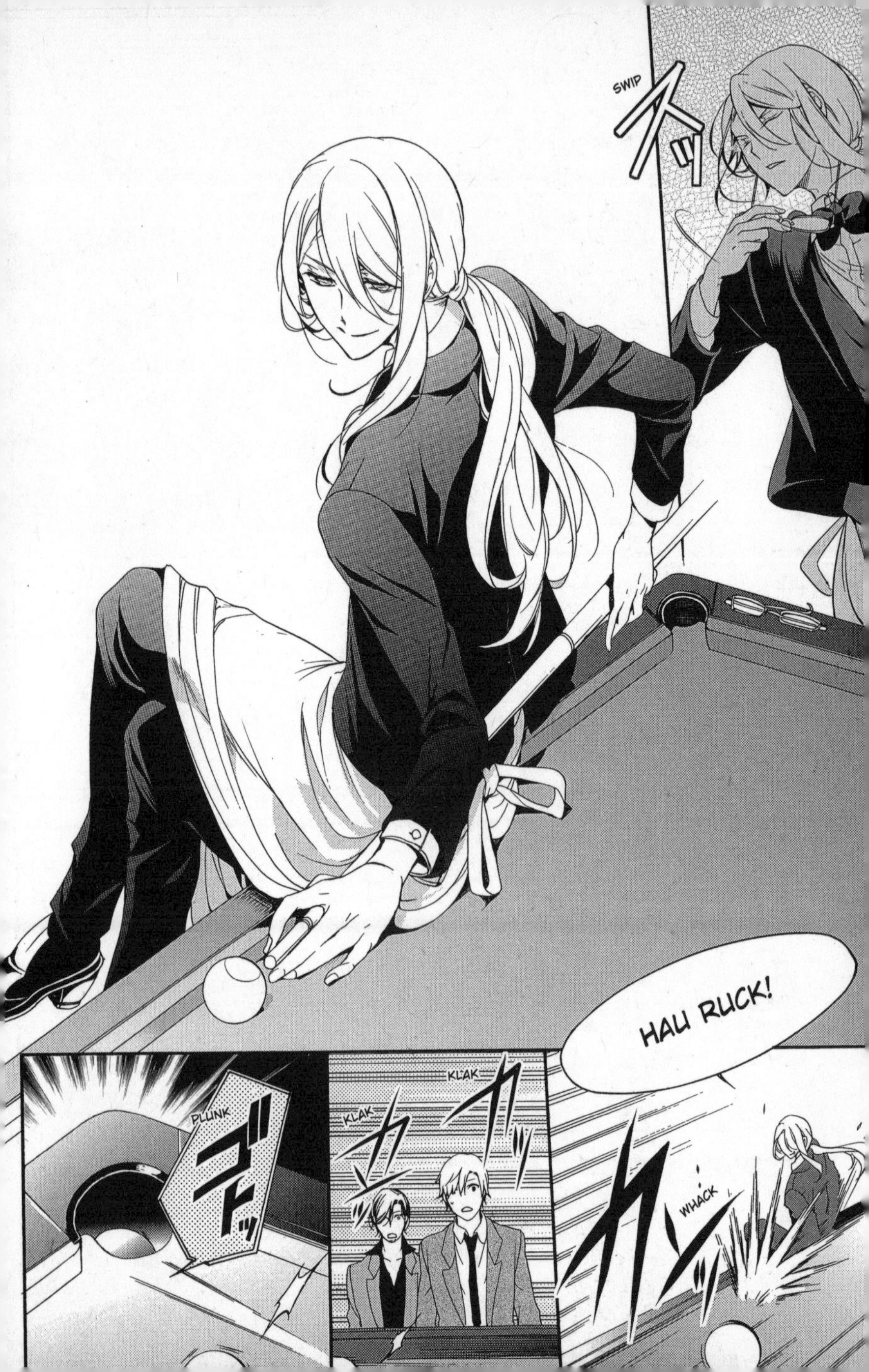
SWIP
HAU RUCK!
WHACK
KLAK
KLAK
PLUNK

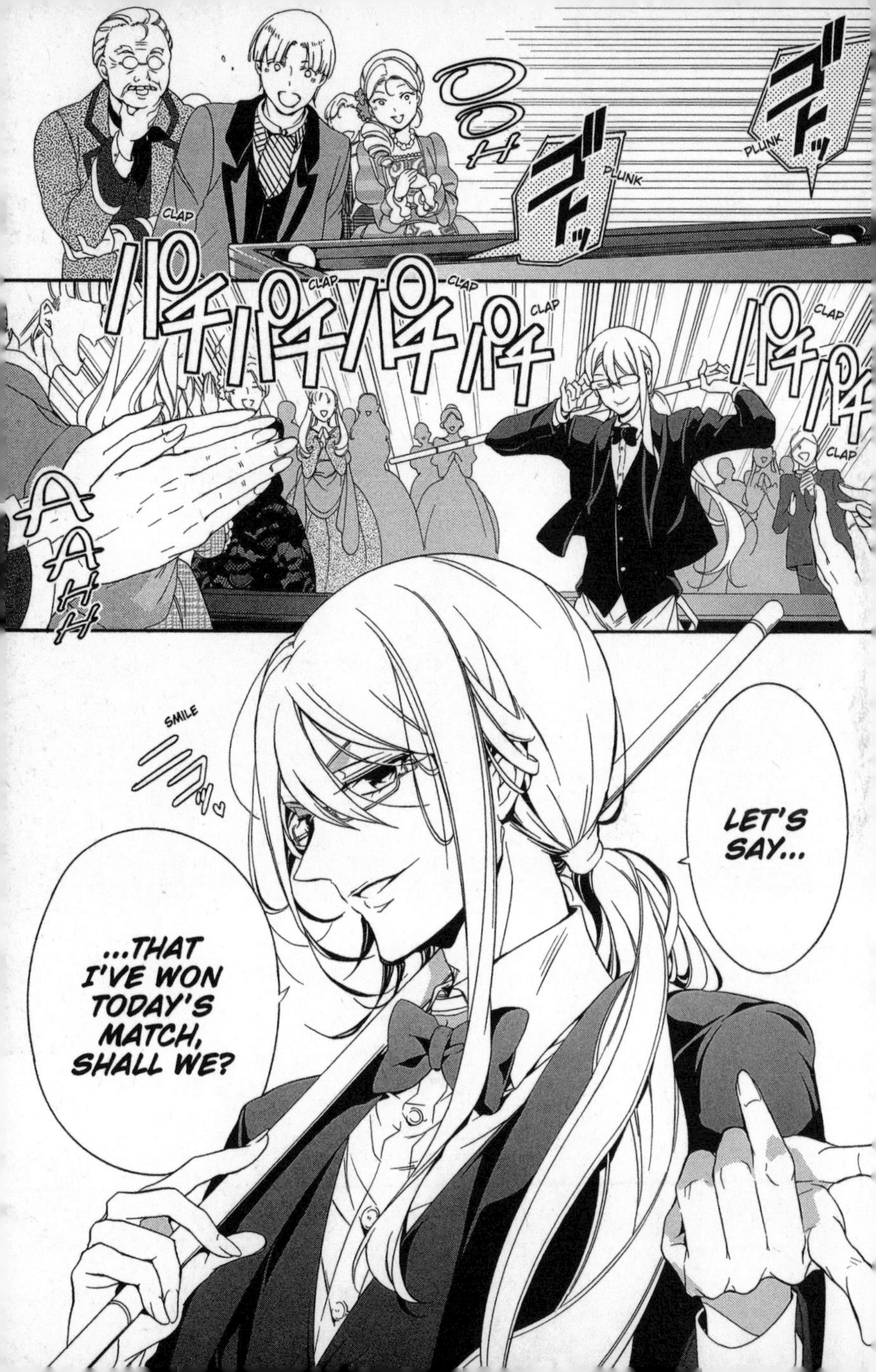
PLUNK
PLUNK
OOH
CLAP
CLAP
CLAP
CLAP
CLAP
CLAP
CLAP
AAHH
LET'S SAY...
SMILE
...THAT I'VE WON TODAY'S MATCH, SHALL WE?

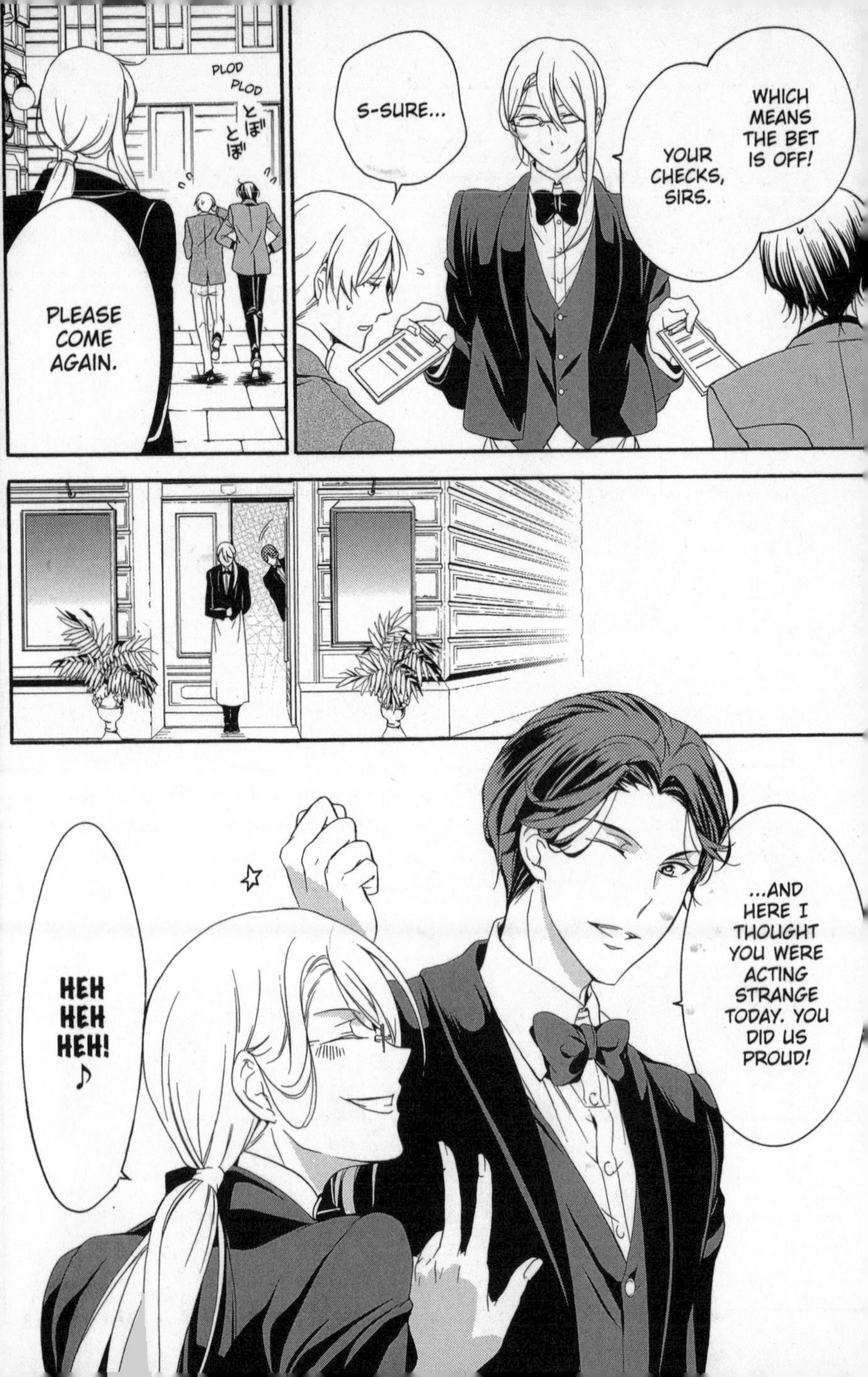
WHICH MEANS THE BET IS OFF!
YOUR CHECKS, SIRS.
S-SURE...
PLOD PLOD
とぼとぼ
PLEASE COME AGAIN.
...AND HERE I THOUGHT YOU WERE ACTING STRANGE TODAY. YOU DID US PROUD!
HEH HEH HEH! ♪

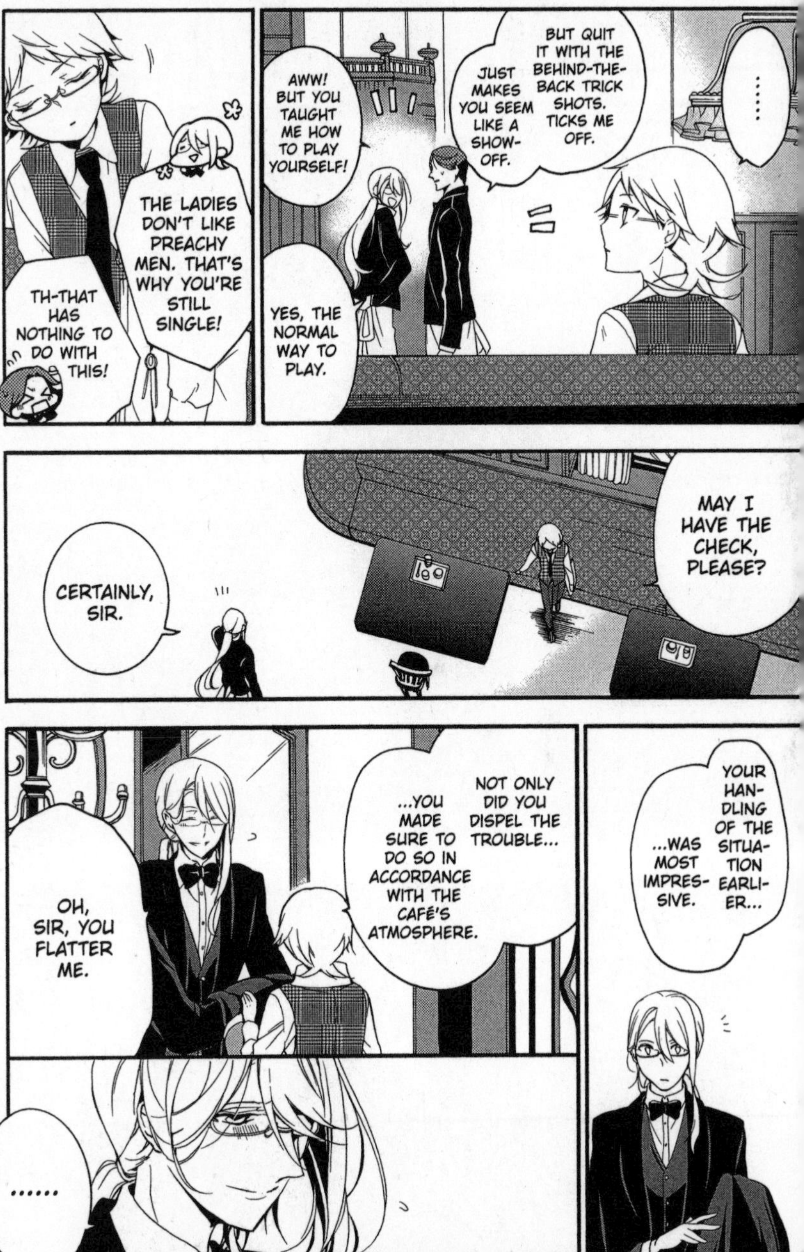
......
BUT QUIT IT WITH THE BEHIND-THE-BACK TRICK SHOTS. TICKS ME OFF.
JUST MAKES YOU SEEM LIKE A SHOW-OFF.
AWW! BUT YOU TAUGHT ME HOW TO PLAY YOURSELF!
YES, THE NORMAL WAY TO PLAY.
THE LADIES DON'T LIKE PREACHY MEN. THAT'S WHY YOU'RE STILL SINGLE!
TH-THAT HAS NOTHING TO DO WITH THIS!
MAY I HAVE THE CHECK, PLEASE?
CERTAINLY, SIR.
YOUR HANDLING OF THE SITUATION EARLIER...
...WAS MOST IMPRESSIVE.
NOT ONLY DID YOU DISPEL THE TROUBLE...
...YOU MADE SURE TO DO SO IN ACCORDANCE WITH THE CAFÉ'S ATMOSPHERE.
OH, SIR, YOU FLATTER ME.
......

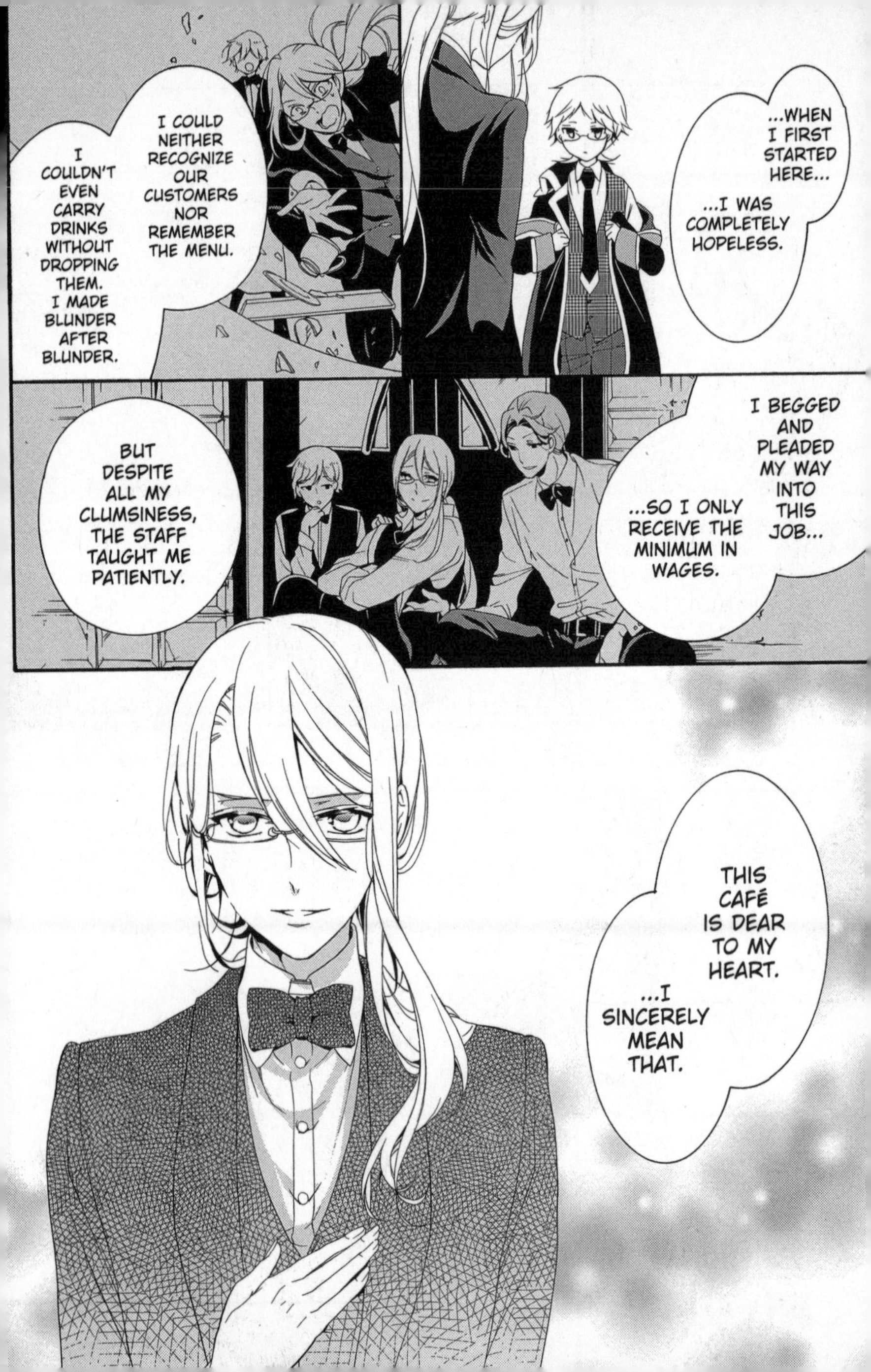
...WHEN I FIRST STARTED HERE...
...I WAS COMPLETELY HOPELESS.
I COULD NEITHER RECOGNIZE OUR CUSTOMERS NOR REMEMBER THE MENU.
I COULDN'T EVEN CARRY DRINKS WITHOUT DROPPING THEM. I MADE BLUNDER AFTER BLUNDER.
I BEGGED AND PLEADED MY WAY INTO THIS JOB...
...SO I ONLY RECEIVE THE MINIMUM IN WAGES.
BUT DESPITE ALL MY CLUMSINESS, THE STAFF TAUGHT ME PATIENTLY.
THIS CAFÉ IS DEAR TO MY HEART.
...I SINCERELY MEAN THAT.

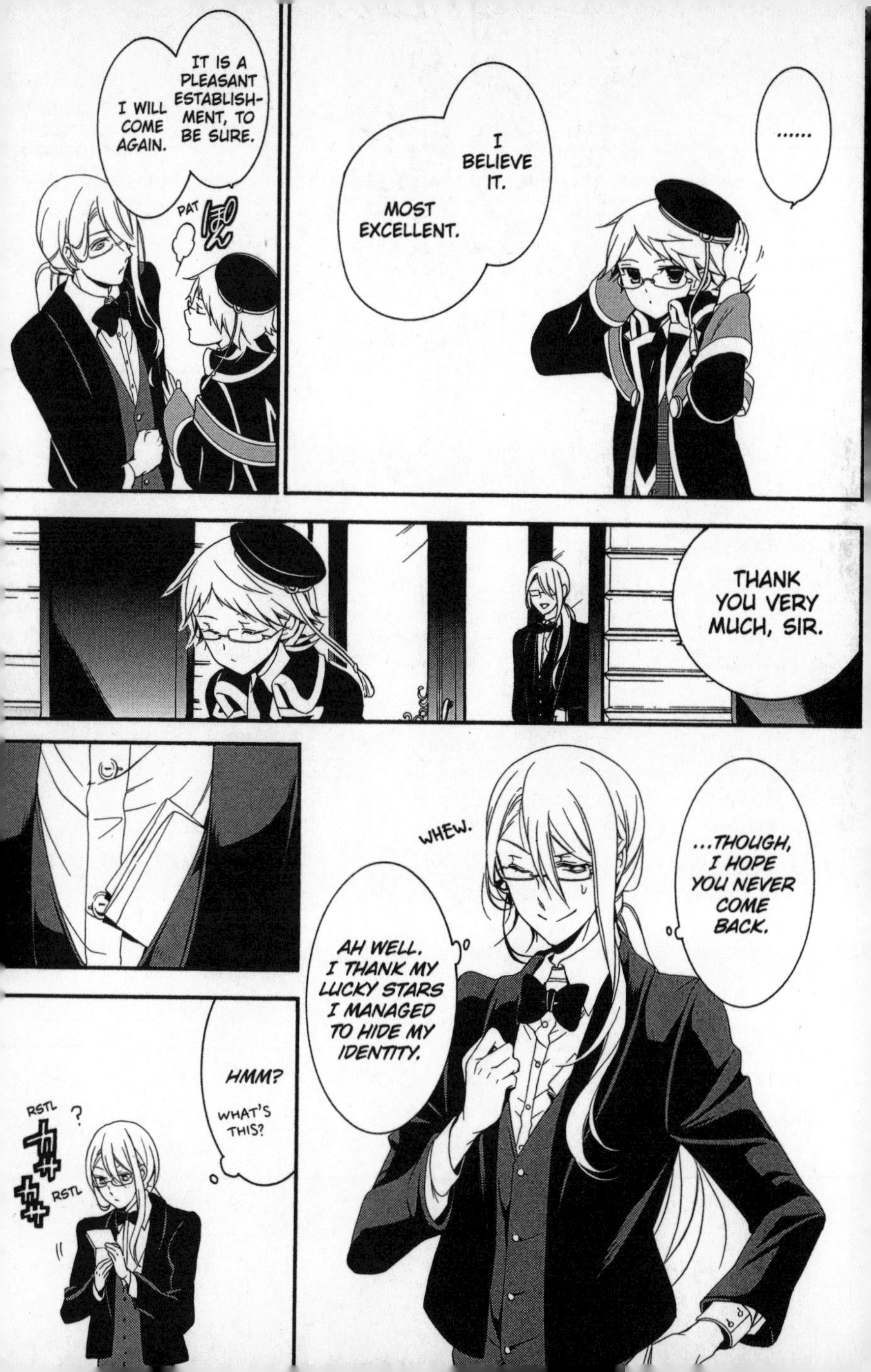
......
I BELIEVE IT.
MOST EXCELLENT.
IT IS A PLEASANT ESTABLISHMENT, TO BE SURE.
I WILL COME AGAIN.
PAT
THANK YOU VERY MUCH, SIR.
...THOUGH, I HOPE YOU NEVER COME BACK.
WHEW.
AH WELL. I THANK MY LUCKY STARS I MANAGED TO HIDE MY IDENTITY.
HMM?
WHAT'S THIS?
RSTL
RSTL

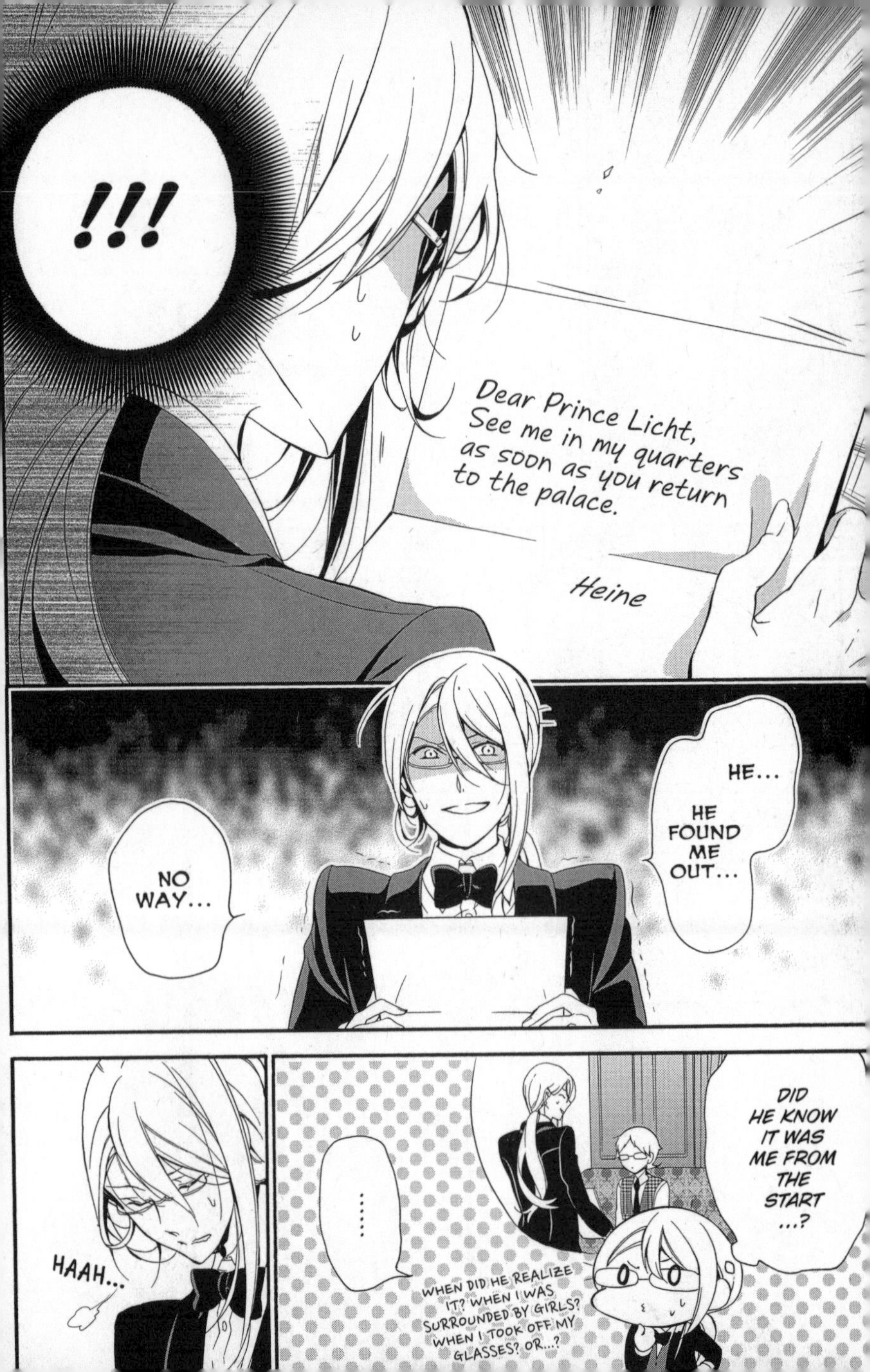
Dear Prince Licht,
See me in my quarters as soon as you return to the palace.
Heine
!!!
HE...
HE FOUND ME OUT...
NO WAY...
DID HE KNOW IT WAS ME FROM THE START...?
......
WHEN DID HE REALIZE IT? WHEN I WAS SURROUNDED BY GIRLS? WHEN I TOOK OFF MY GLASSES? OR...?
HAAH...

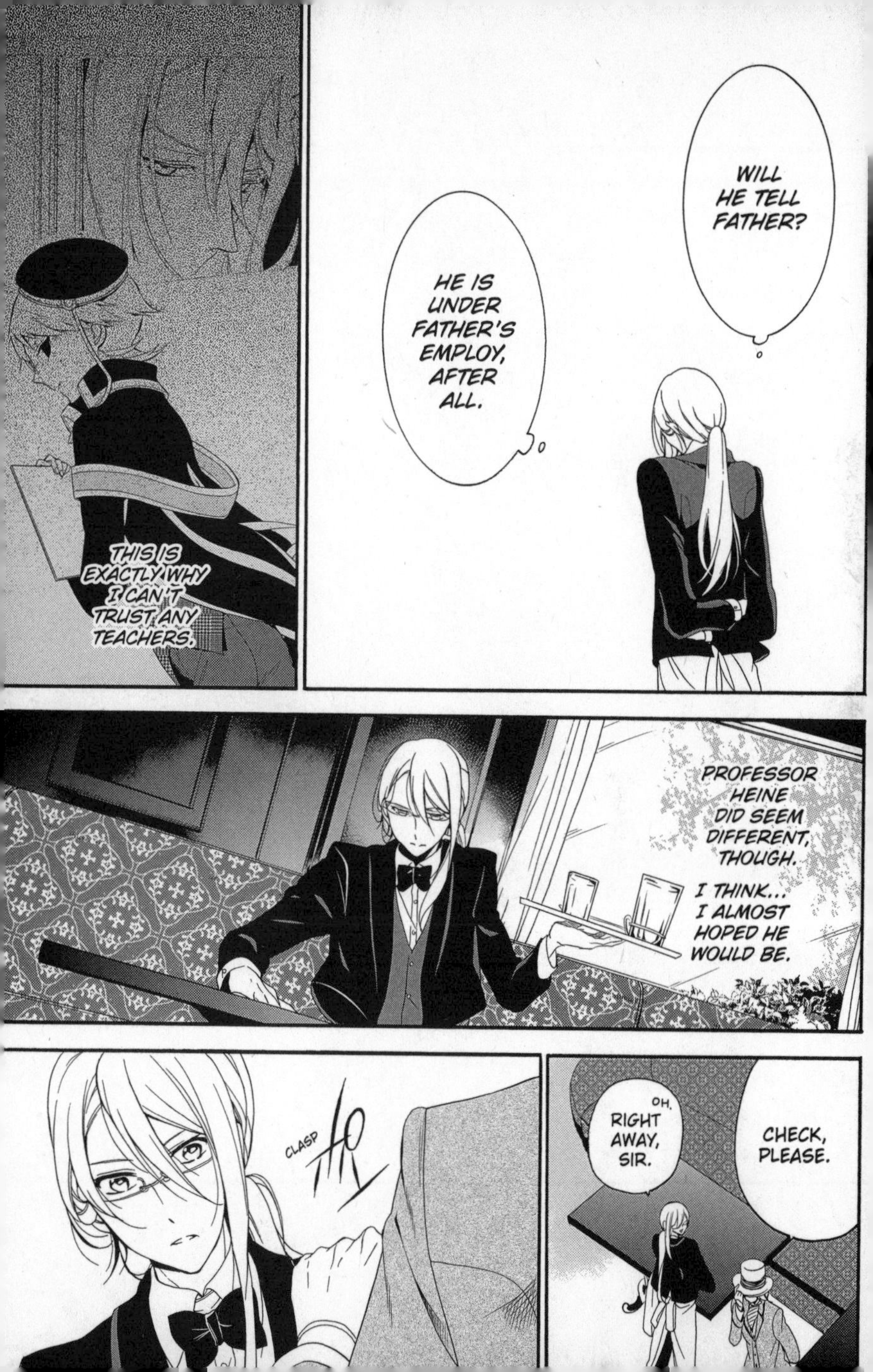
WILL HE TELL FATHER?
HE IS UNDER FATHER'S EMPLOY, AFTER ALL.
THIS IS EXACTLY WHY I CAN'T TRUST ANY TEACHERS.
PROFESSOR HEINE DID SEEM DIFFERENT, THOUGH.
I THINK... I ALMOST HOPED HE WOULD BE.
CHECK, PLEASE.
OH, RIGHT AWAY, SIR.
CLASP

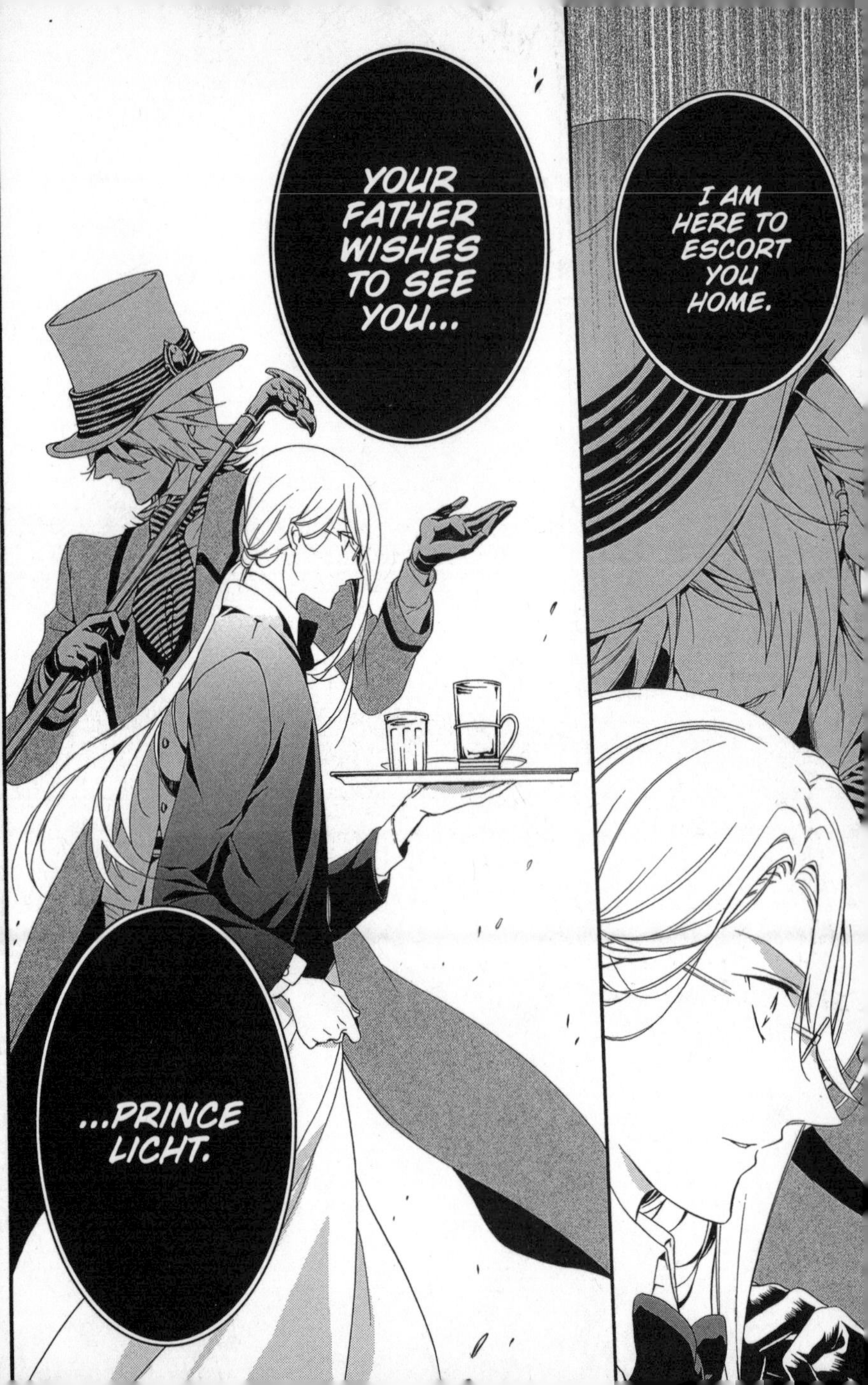
I AM HERE TO ESCORT YOU HOME.
YOUR FATHER WISHES TO SEE YOU...
...PRINCE LICHT.

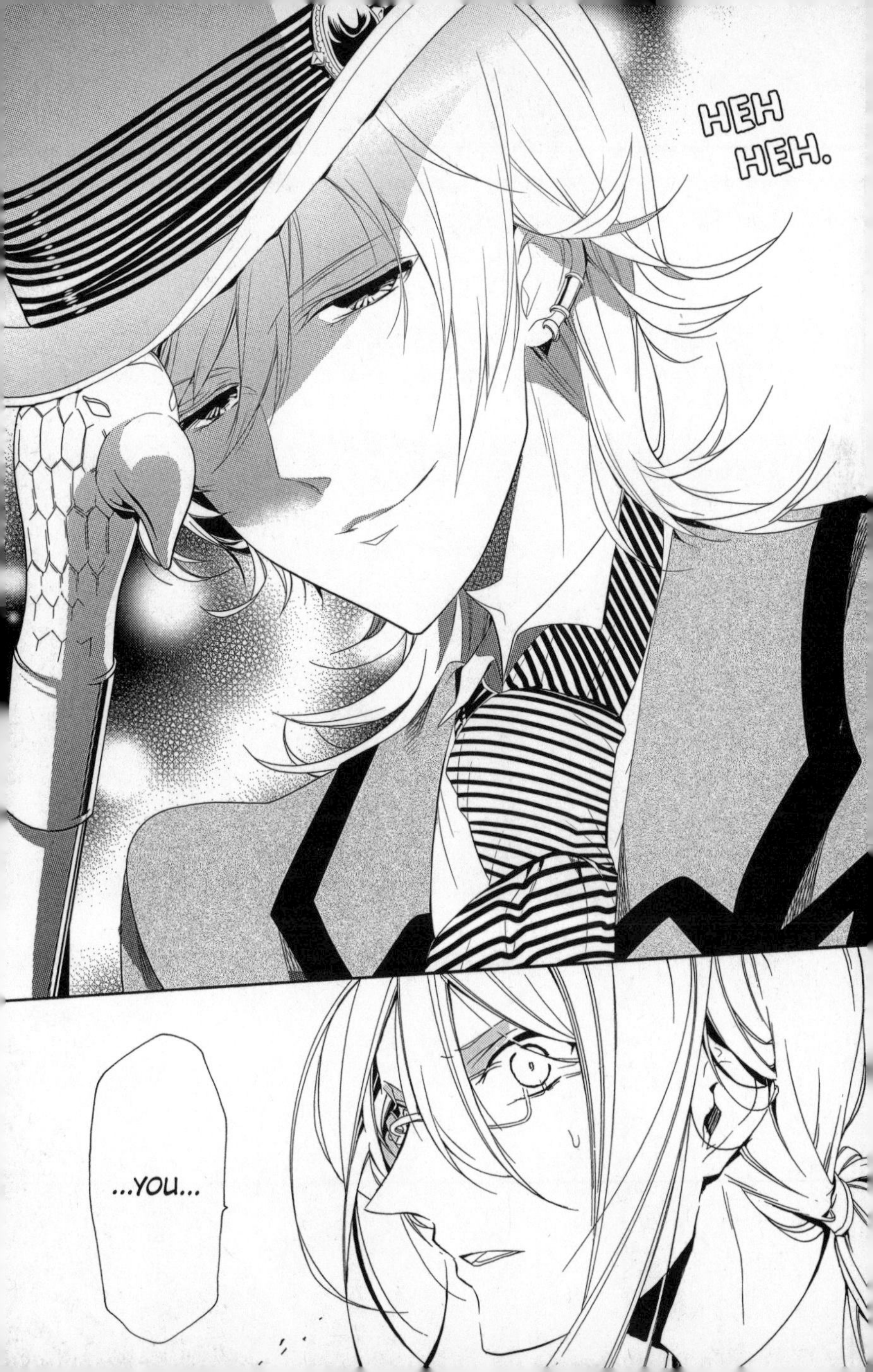
HEH HEH.
...YOU...

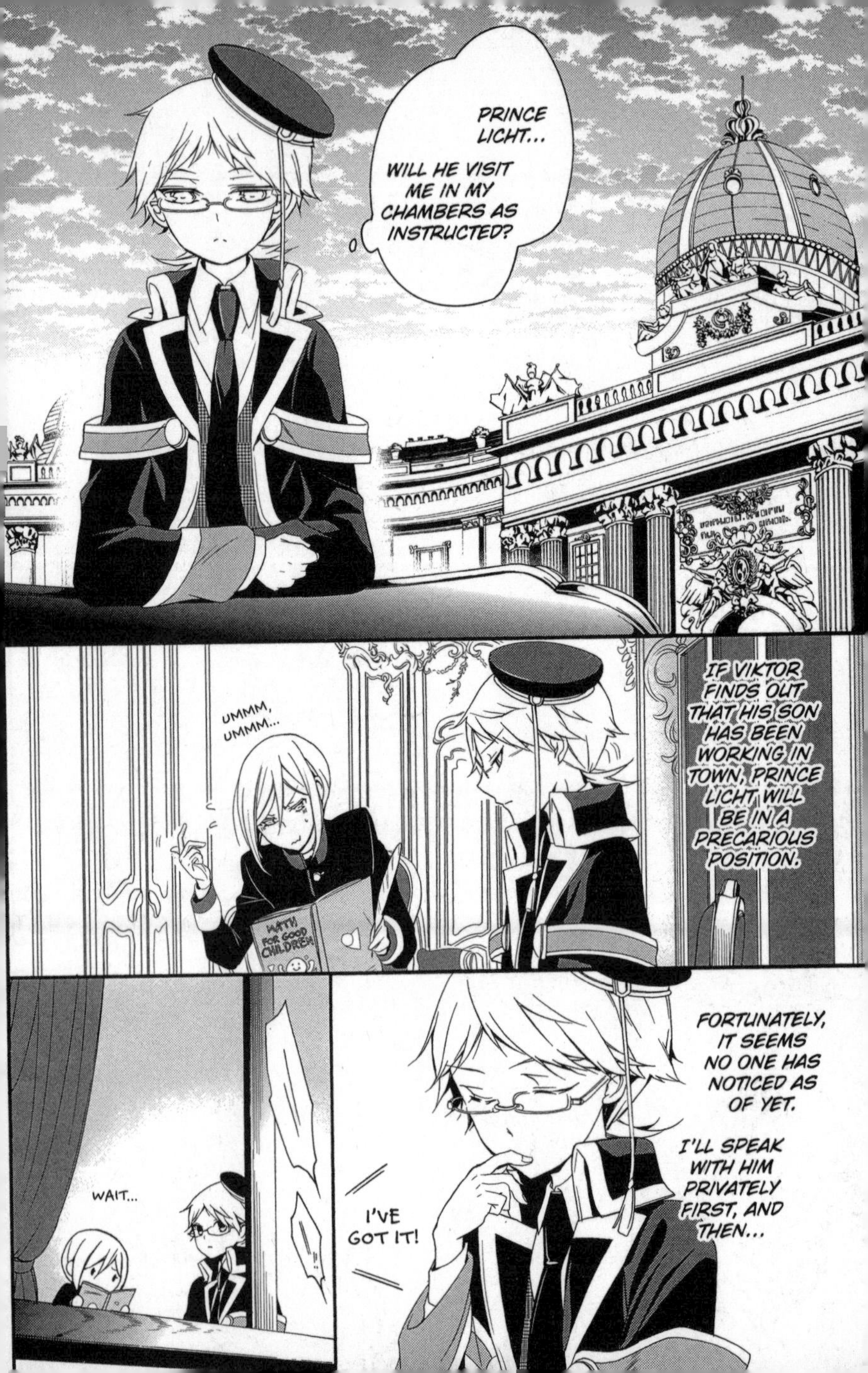
PRINCE LICHT...
WILL HE VISIT ME IN MY CHAMBERS AS INSTRUCTED?
IF VIKTOR FINDS OUT THAT HIS SON HAS BEEN WORKING IN TOWN, PRINCE LICHT WILL BE IN A PRECARIOUS POSITION.
UMMM, UMMM...
MATH FOR GOOD CHILDREN
FORTUNATELY, IT SEEMS NO ONE HAS NOTICED AS OF YET.
I'LL SPEAK WITH HIM PRIVATELY FIRST, AND THEN...
I'VE GOT IT!
WAIT...

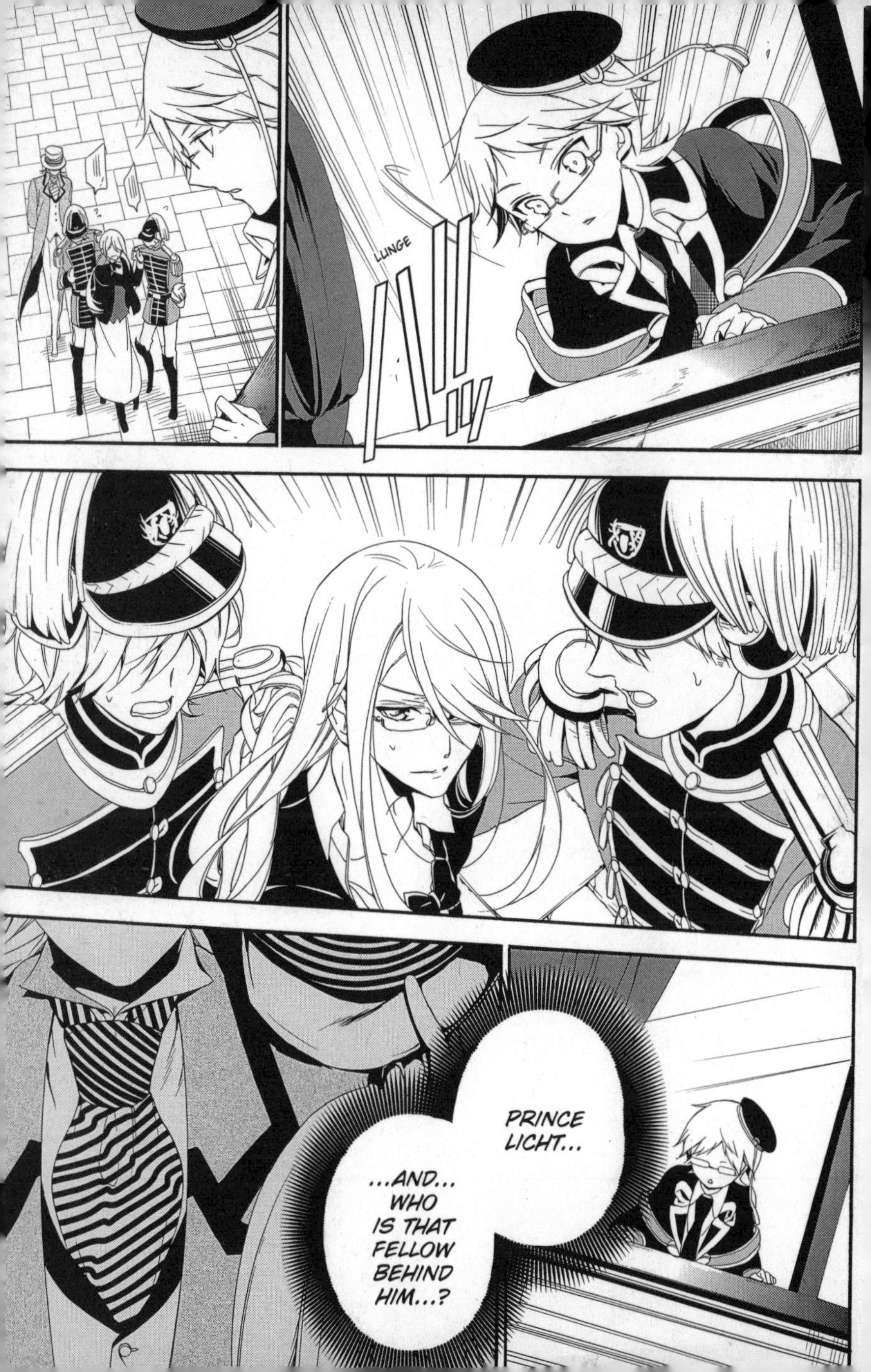
LUNGE
PRINCE LICHT...
...AND... WHO IS THAT FELLOW BEHIND HIM...?

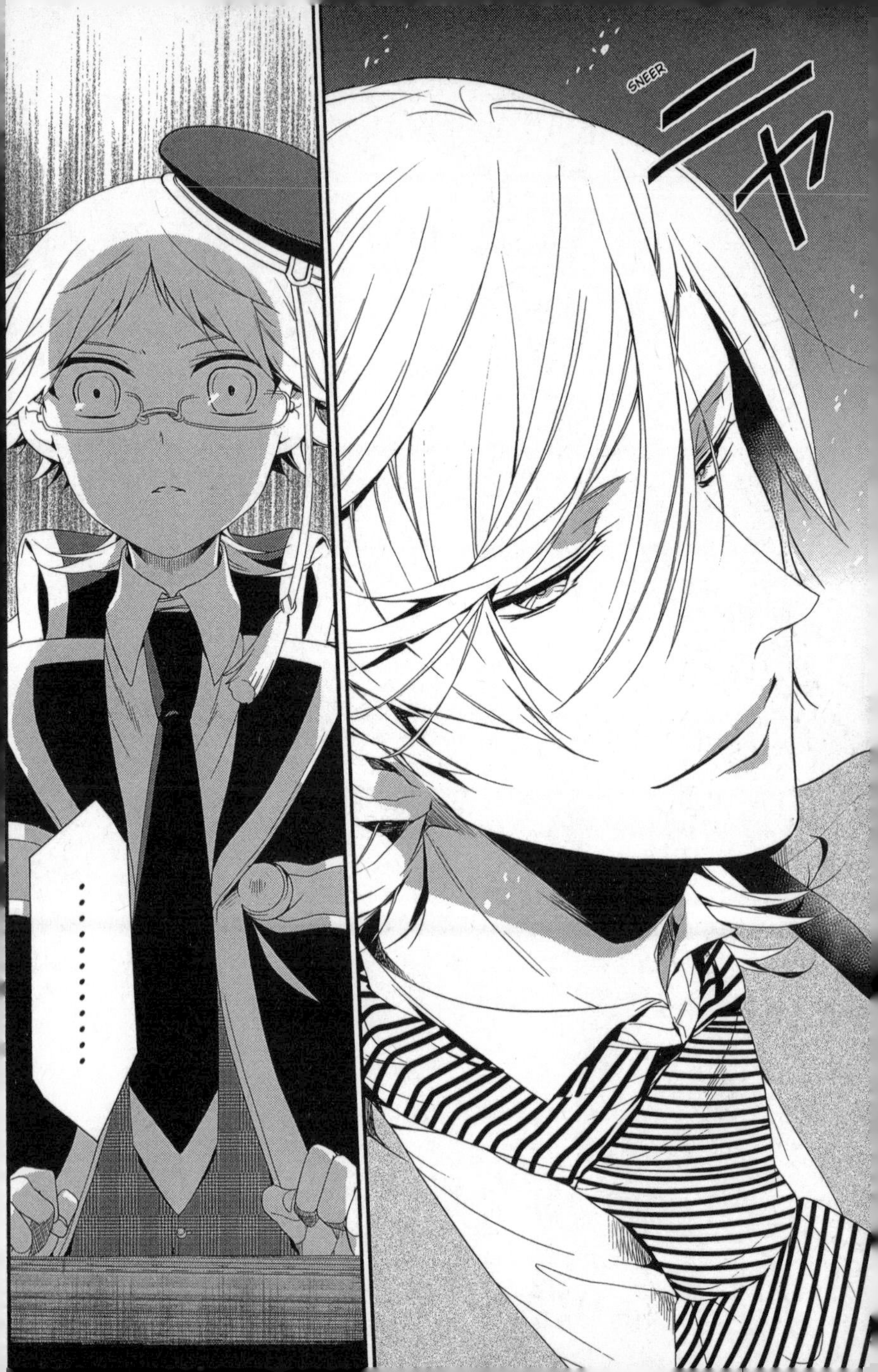
SNEER
ニヤ
……………

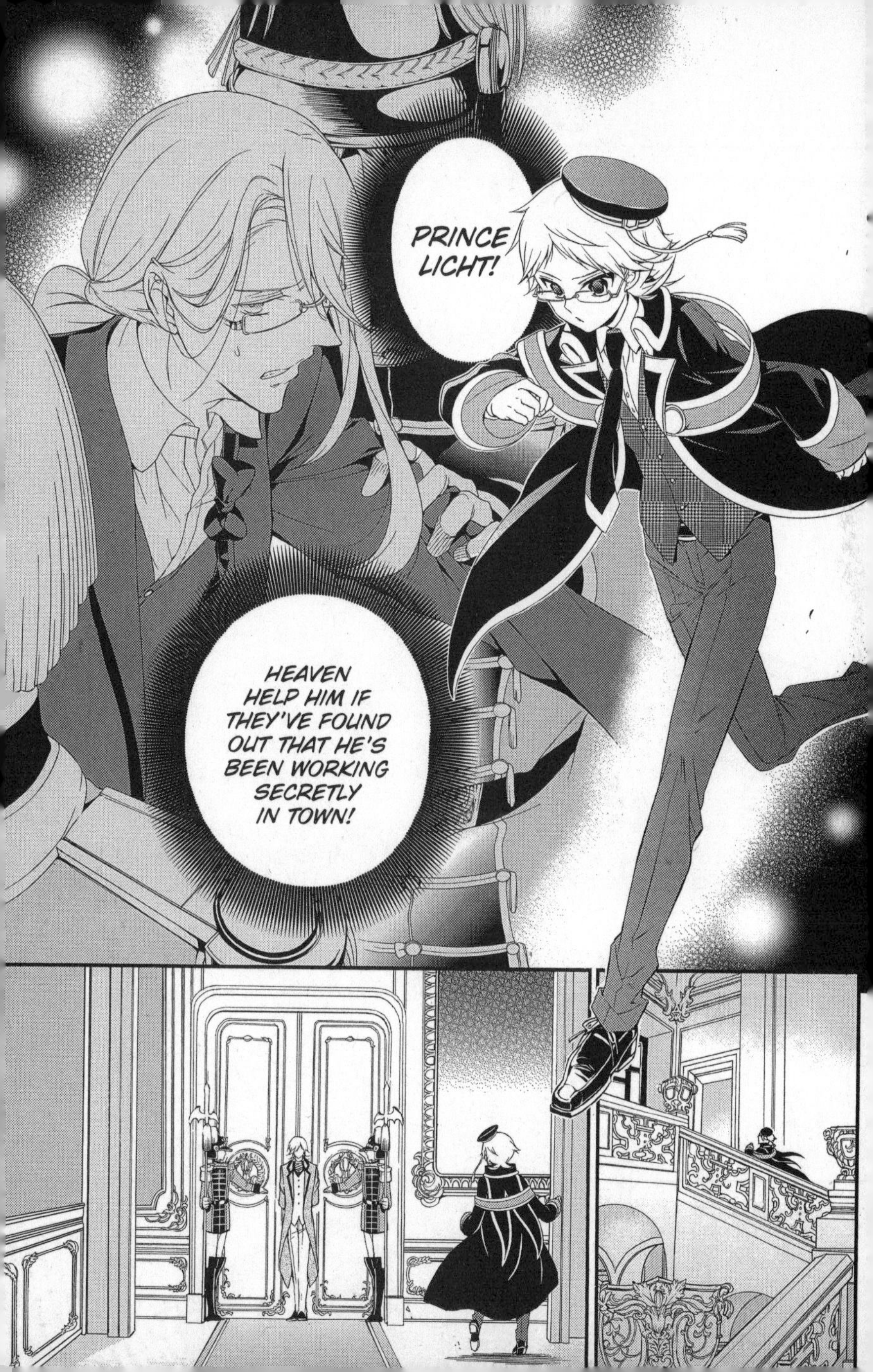
PRINCE LICHT!
HEAVEN HELP HIM IF THEY'VE FOUND OUT THAT HE'S BEEN WORKING SECRETLY IN TOWN!

Chapter 17
You Don't Understand

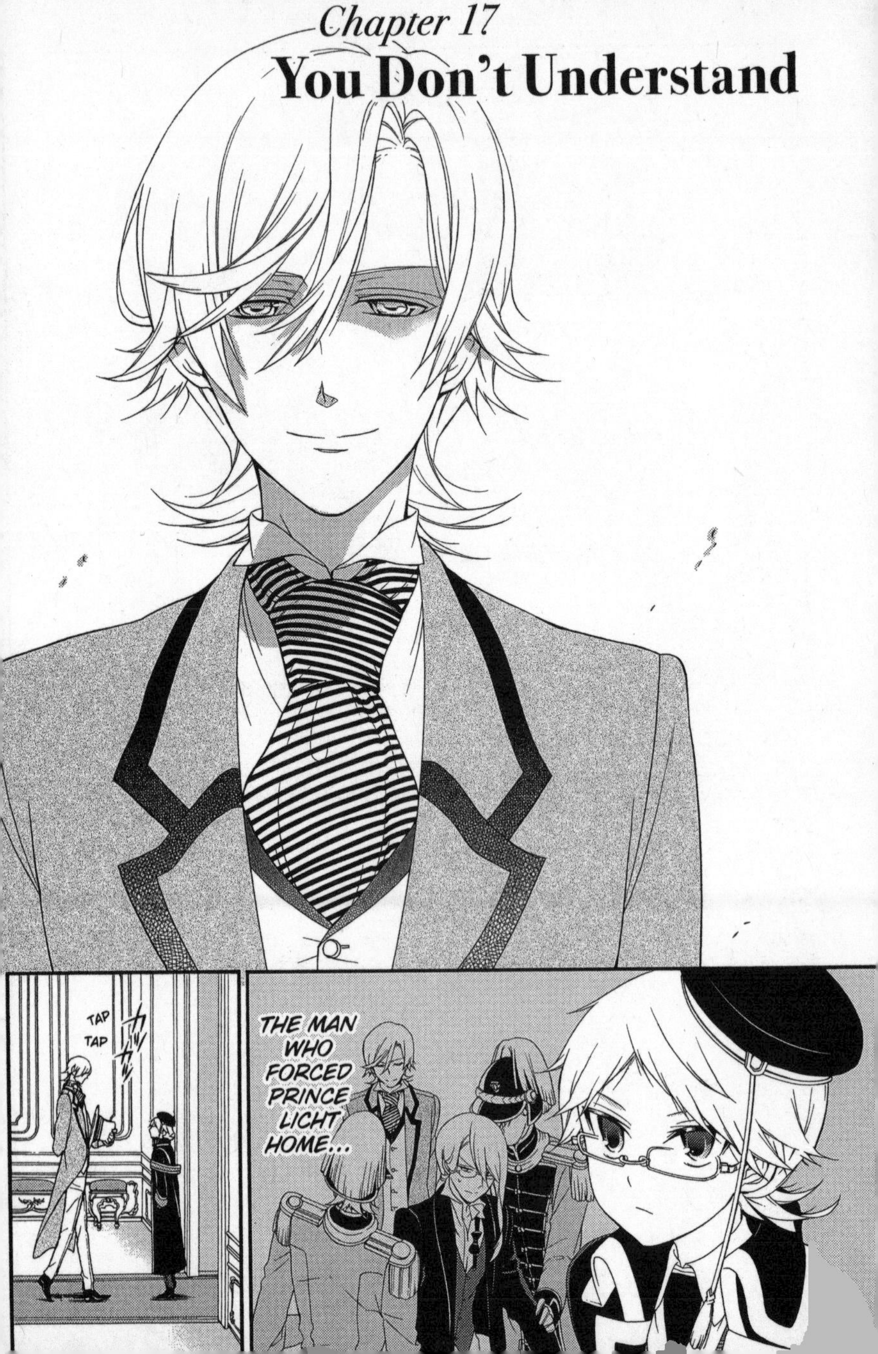
THE MAN WHO FORCED PRINCE LICHT HOME...
TAP TAP

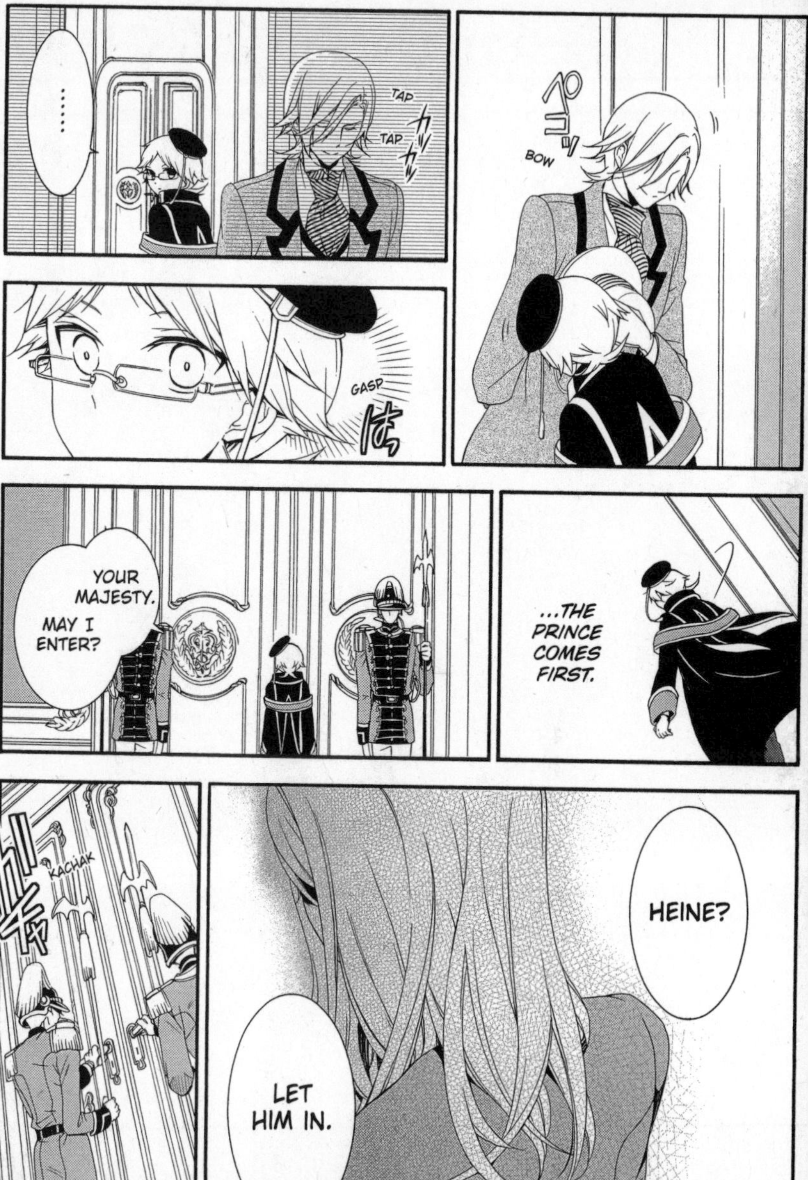
ペコッ
BOW
......
TAP TAP
カツカツ
GASP
はっ
...THE PRINCE COMES FIRST.
YOUR MAJESTY. MAY I ENTER?
HEINE?
LET HIM IN.
ガチャ
KACHAK

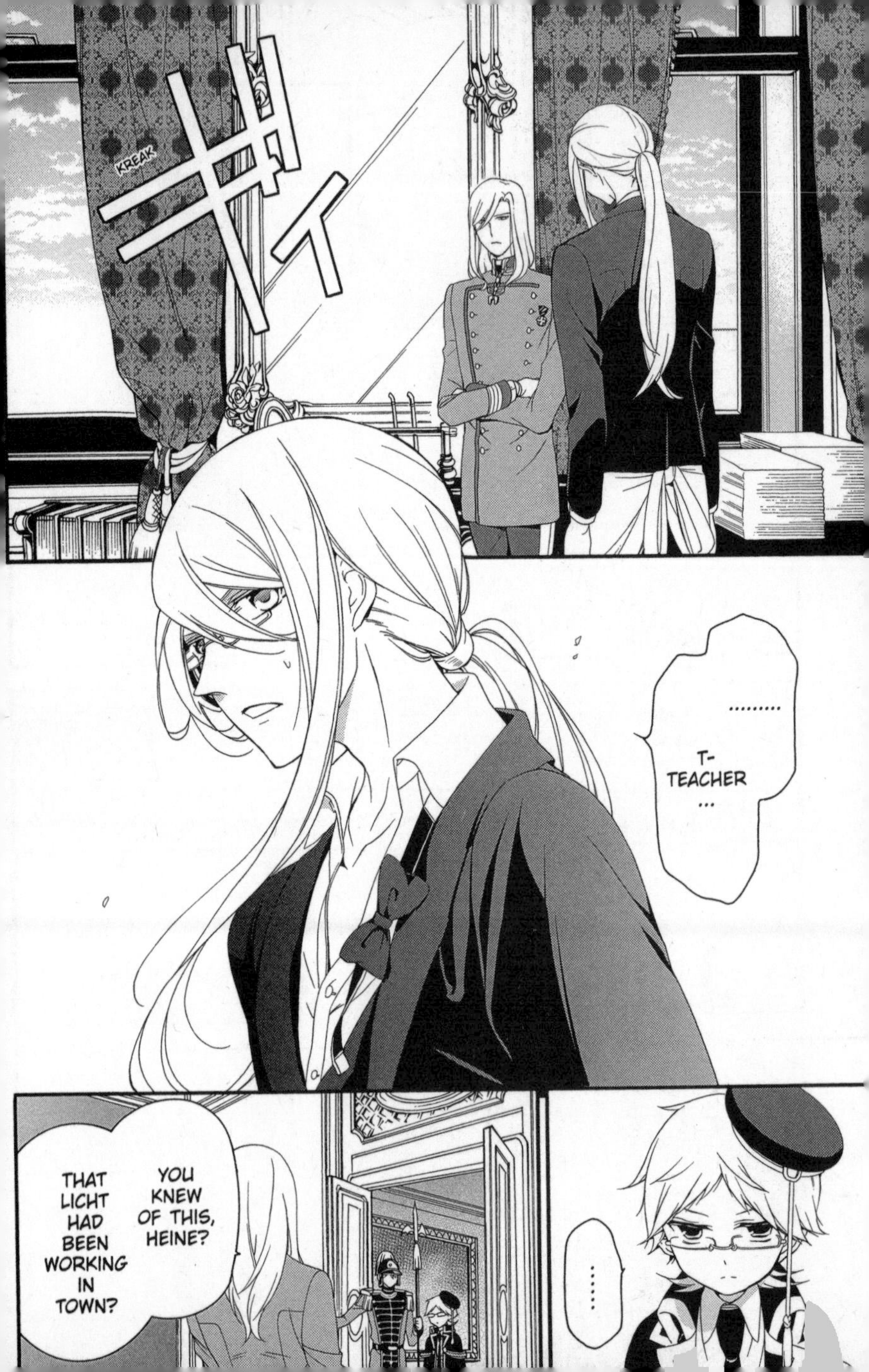
KREAK
....
T-TEACHER...
......
YOU KNEW OF THIS, HEINE?
THAT LICHT HAD BEEN WORKING IN TOWN?

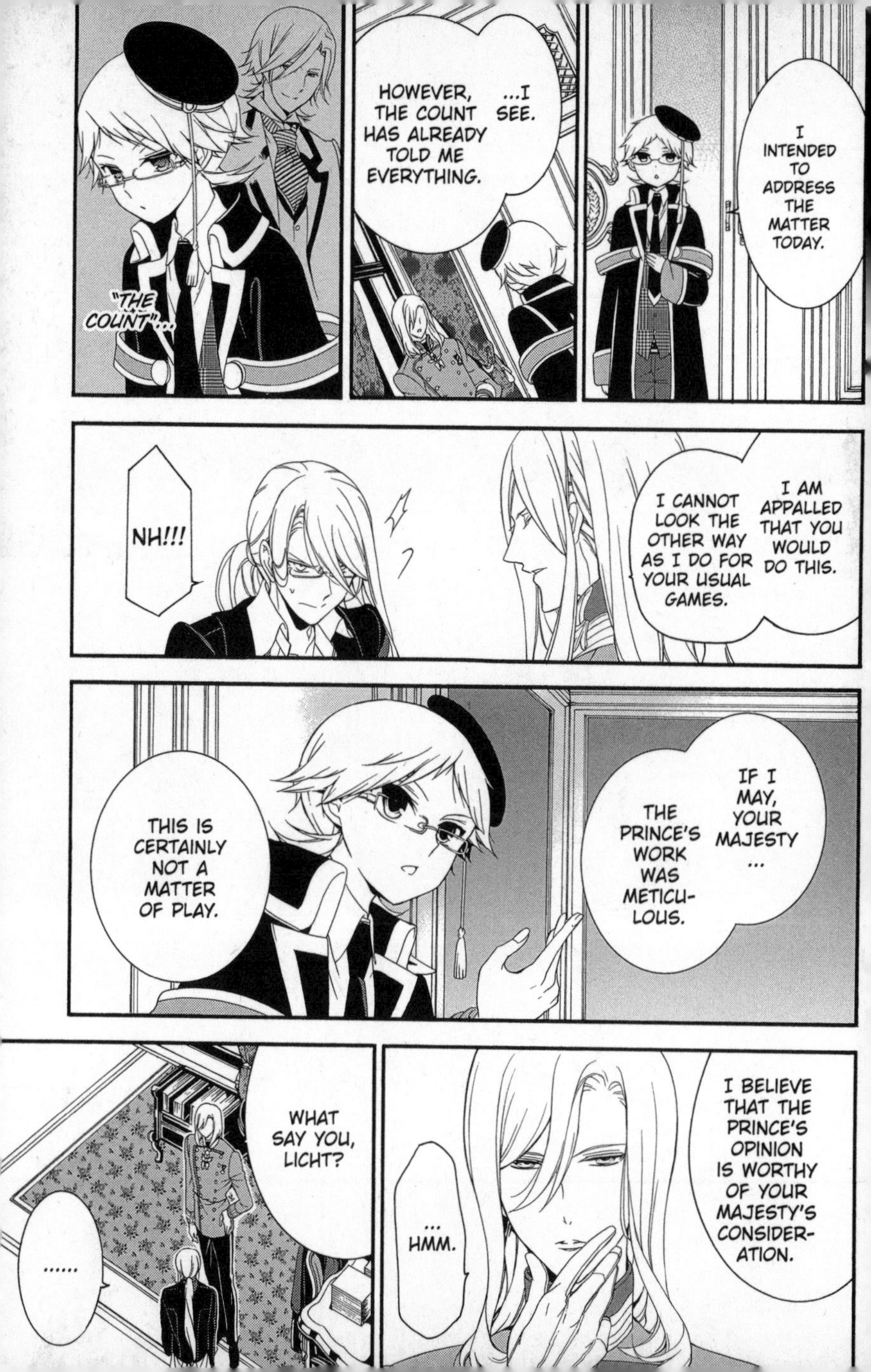
I INTENDED TO ADDRESS THE MATTER TODAY.
...I SEE.
HOWEVER, THE COUNT HAS ALREADY TOLD ME EVERYTHING.
"THE COUNT"...
I AM APPALLED THAT YOU WOULD DO THIS.
I CANNOT LOOK THE OTHER WAY AS I DO FOR YOUR USUAL GAMES.
NH!!!
IF I MAY, YOUR MAJESTY...
THE PRINCE'S WORK WAS METICU-LOUS.
THIS IS CERTAINLY NOT A MATTER OF PLAY.
I BELIEVE THAT THE PRINCE'S OPINION IS WORTHY OF YOUR MAJESTY'S CONSIDER-ATION.
...HMM.
WHAT SAY YOU, LICHT?
......

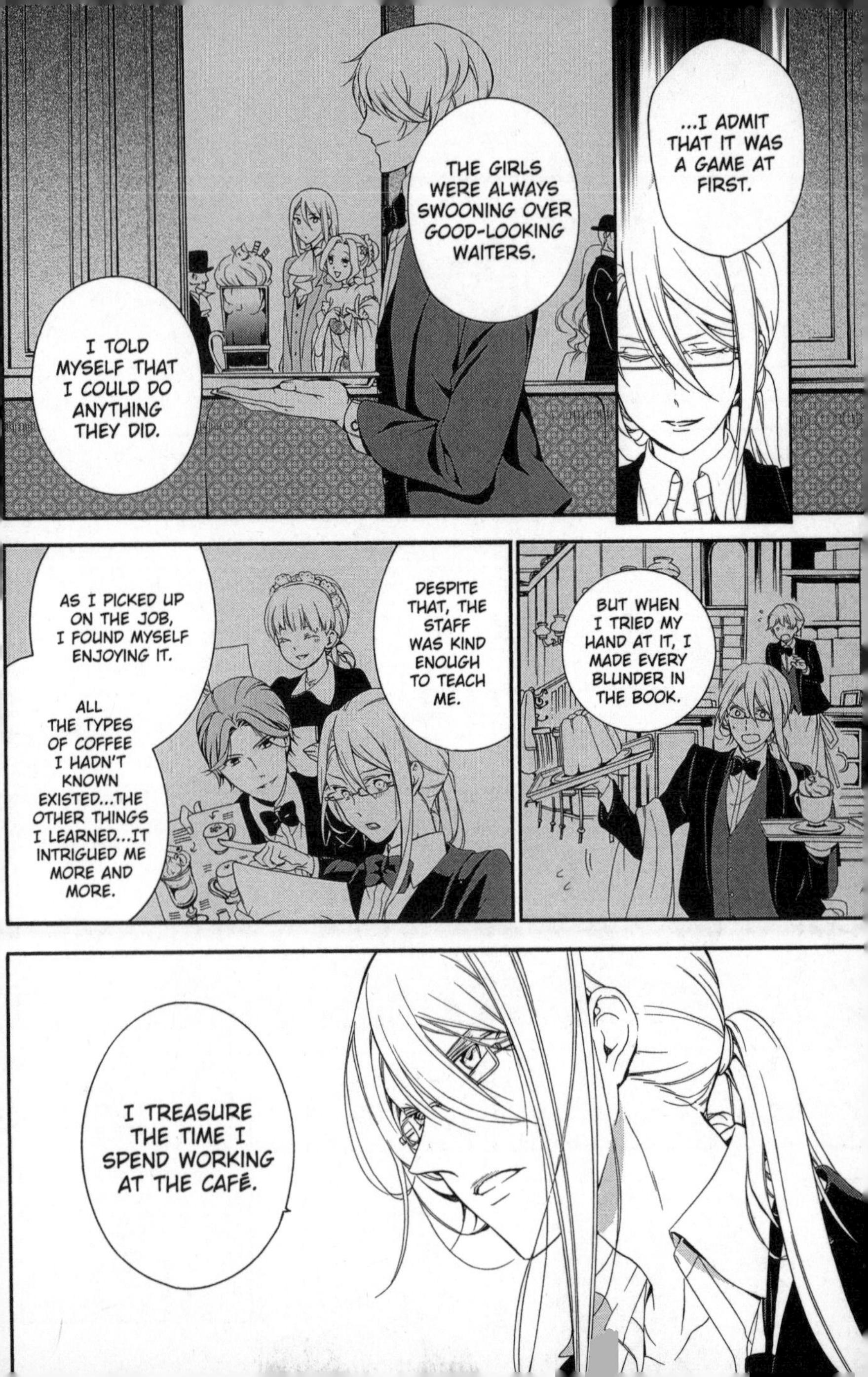
...I ADMIT THAT IT WAS A GAME AT FIRST.
THE GIRLS WERE ALWAYS SWOONING OVER GOOD-LOOKING WAITERS.
I TOLD MYSELF THAT I COULD DO ANYTHING THEY DID.
BUT WHEN I TRIED MY HAND AT IT, I MADE EVERY BLUNDER IN THE BOOK.
DESPITE THAT, THE STAFF WAS KIND ENOUGH TO TEACH ME.
AS I PICKED UP ON THE JOB, I FOUND MYSELF ENJOYING IT.
ALL THE TYPES OF COFFEE I HADN'T KNOWN EXISTED...THE OTHER THINGS I LEARNED...IT INTRIGUED ME MORE AND MORE.
I TREASURE THE TIME I SPEND WORKING AT THE CAFÉ.

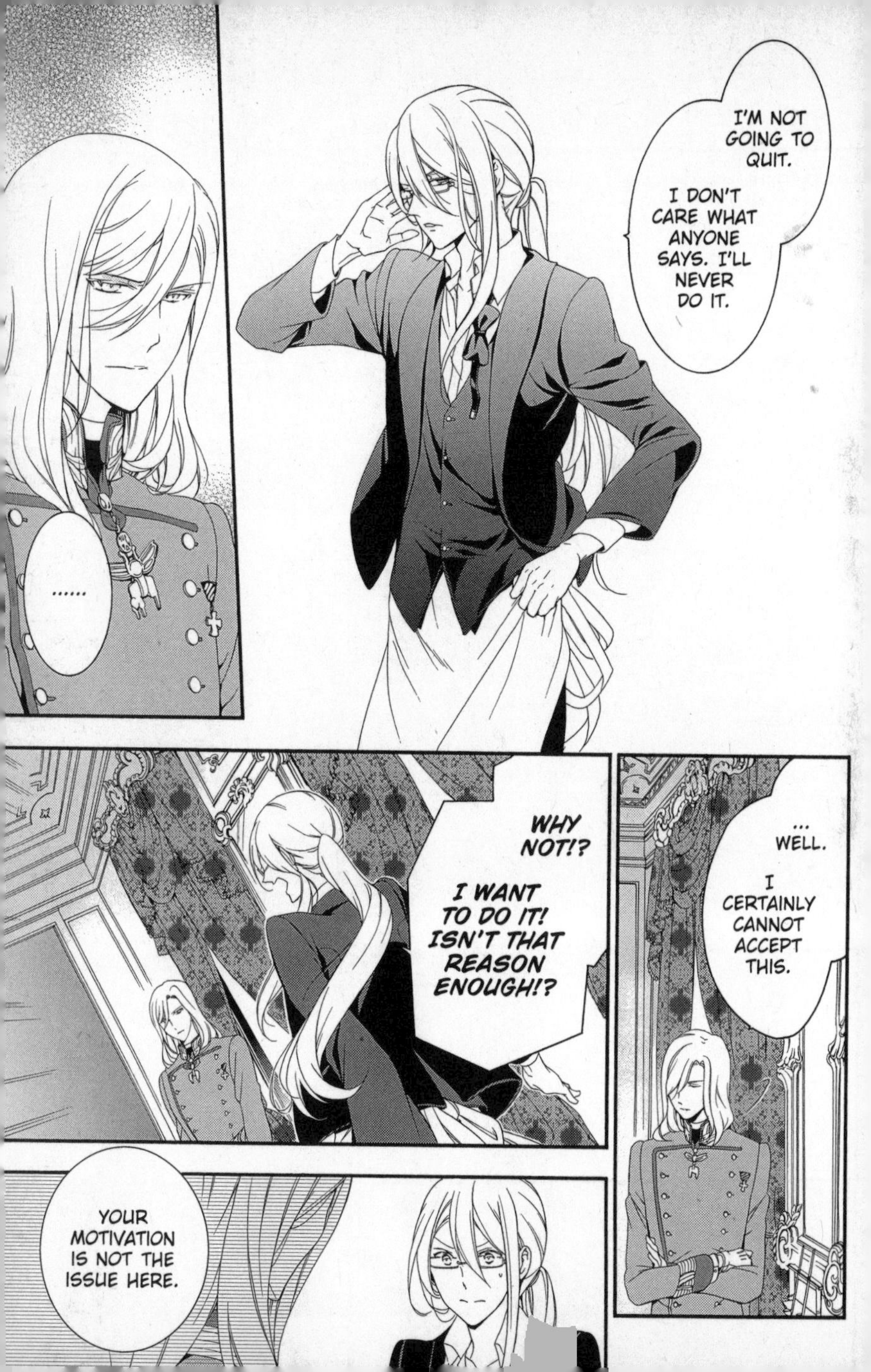
I'M NOT GOING TO QUIT.
I DON'T CARE WHAT ANYONE SAYS. I'LL NEVER DO IT.
......
... WELL.
I CERTAINLY CANNOT ACCEPT THIS.
WHY NOT!?
I WANT TO DO IT! ISN'T THAT REASON ENOUGH!?
YOUR MOTIVATION IS NOT THE ISSUE HERE.

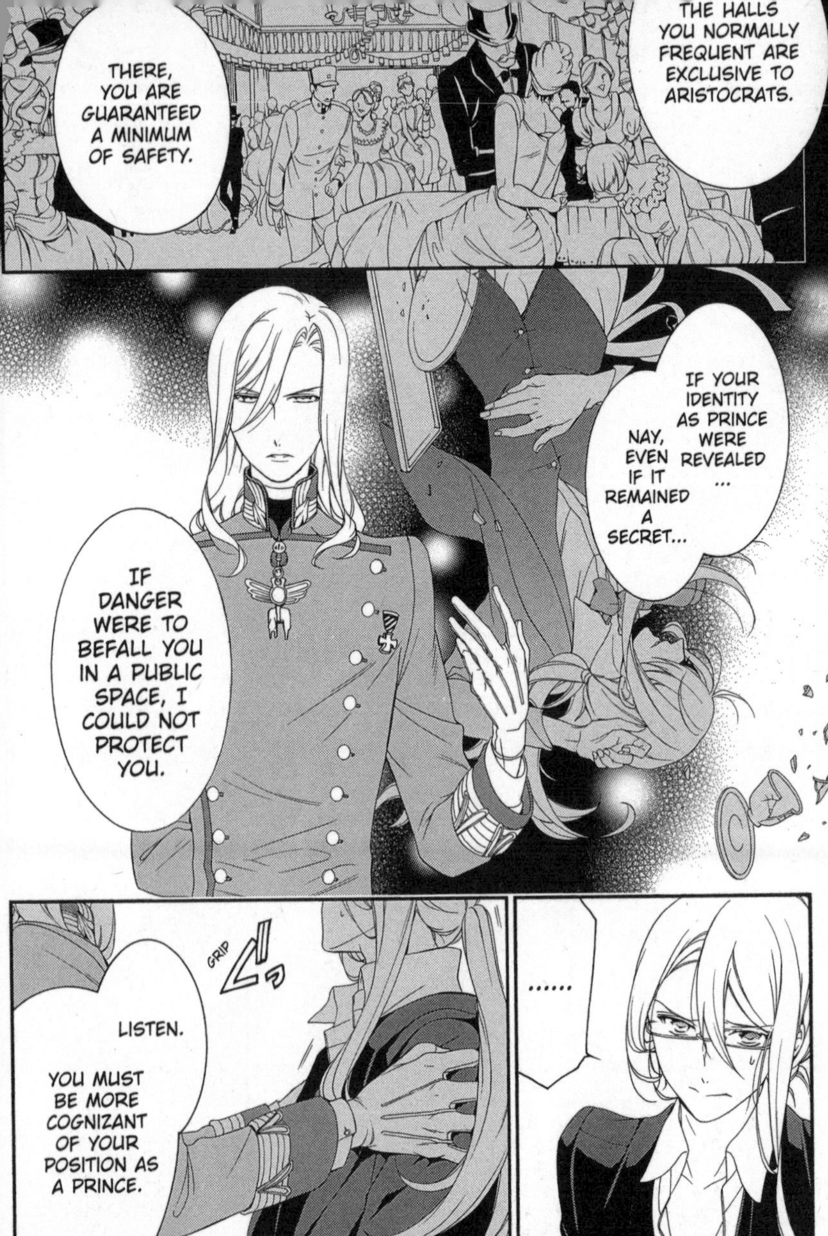
THE HALLS YOU NORMALLY FREQUENT ARE EXCLUSIVE TO ARISTOCRATS.
THERE, YOU ARE GUARANTEED A MINIMUM OF SAFETY.
IF YOUR IDENTITY AS PRINCE WERE REVEALED ...
NAY, EVEN IF IT REMAINED A SECRET...
IF DANGER WERE TO BEFALL YOU IN A PUBLIC SPACE, I COULD NOT PROTECT YOU.
......
GRIP
LISTEN.
YOU MUST BE MORE COGNIZANT OF YOUR POSITION AS A PRINCE.

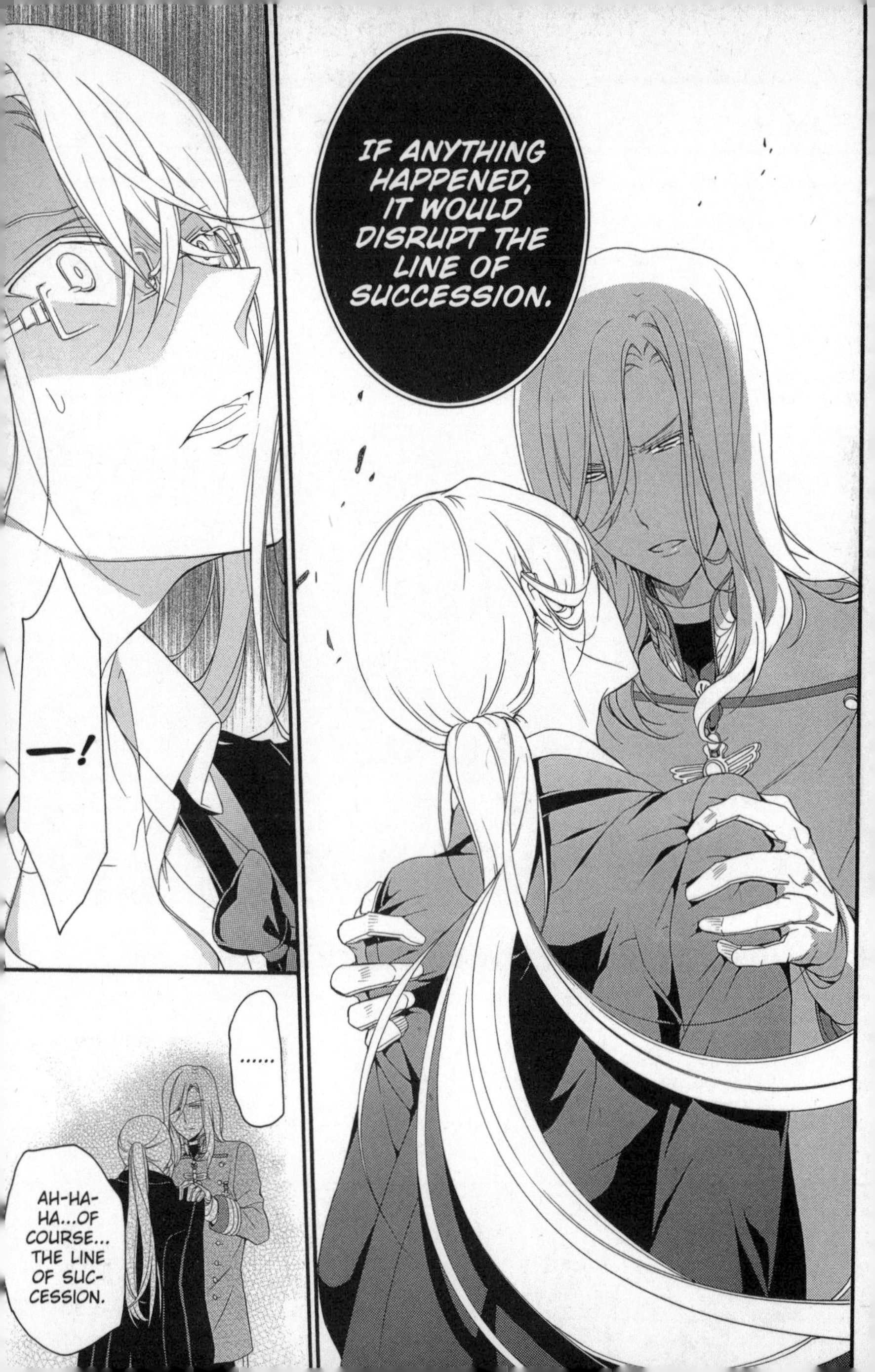
IF ANYTHING HAPPENED, IT WOULD DISRUPT THE LINE OF SUCCESSION.
—!
......
AH-HA-HA...OF COURSE... THE LINE OF SUCCESSION.

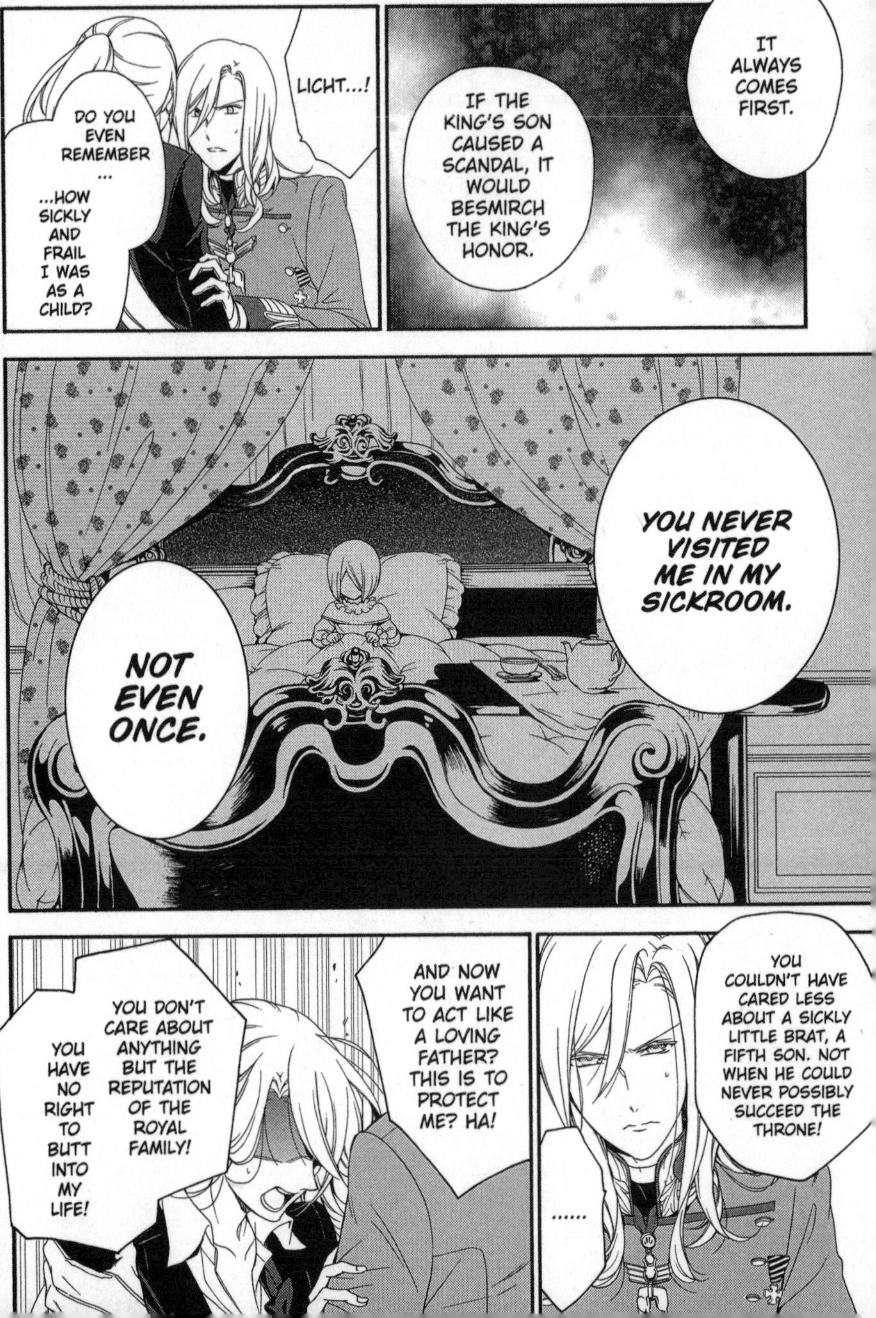
IT ALWAYS COMES FIRST.
IF THE KING'S SON CAUSED A SCANDAL, IT WOULD BESMIRCH THE KING'S HONOR.
LICHT...!
DO YOU EVEN REMEMBER ...
...HOW SICKLY AND FRAIL I WAS AS A CHILD?
YOU NEVER VISITED ME IN MY SICKROOM.
NOT EVEN ONCE.
YOU COULDN'T HAVE CARED LESS ABOUT A SICKLY LITTLE BRAT, A FIFTH SON. NOT WHEN HE COULD NEVER POSSIBLY SUCCEED THE THRONE!
......
AND NOW YOU WANT TO ACT LIKE A LOVING FATHER? THIS IS TO PROTECT ME? HA!
YOU DON'T CARE ABOUT ANYTHING BUT THE REPUTATION OF THE ROYAL FAMILY!
YOU HAVE NO RIGHT TO BUTT INTO MY LIFE!

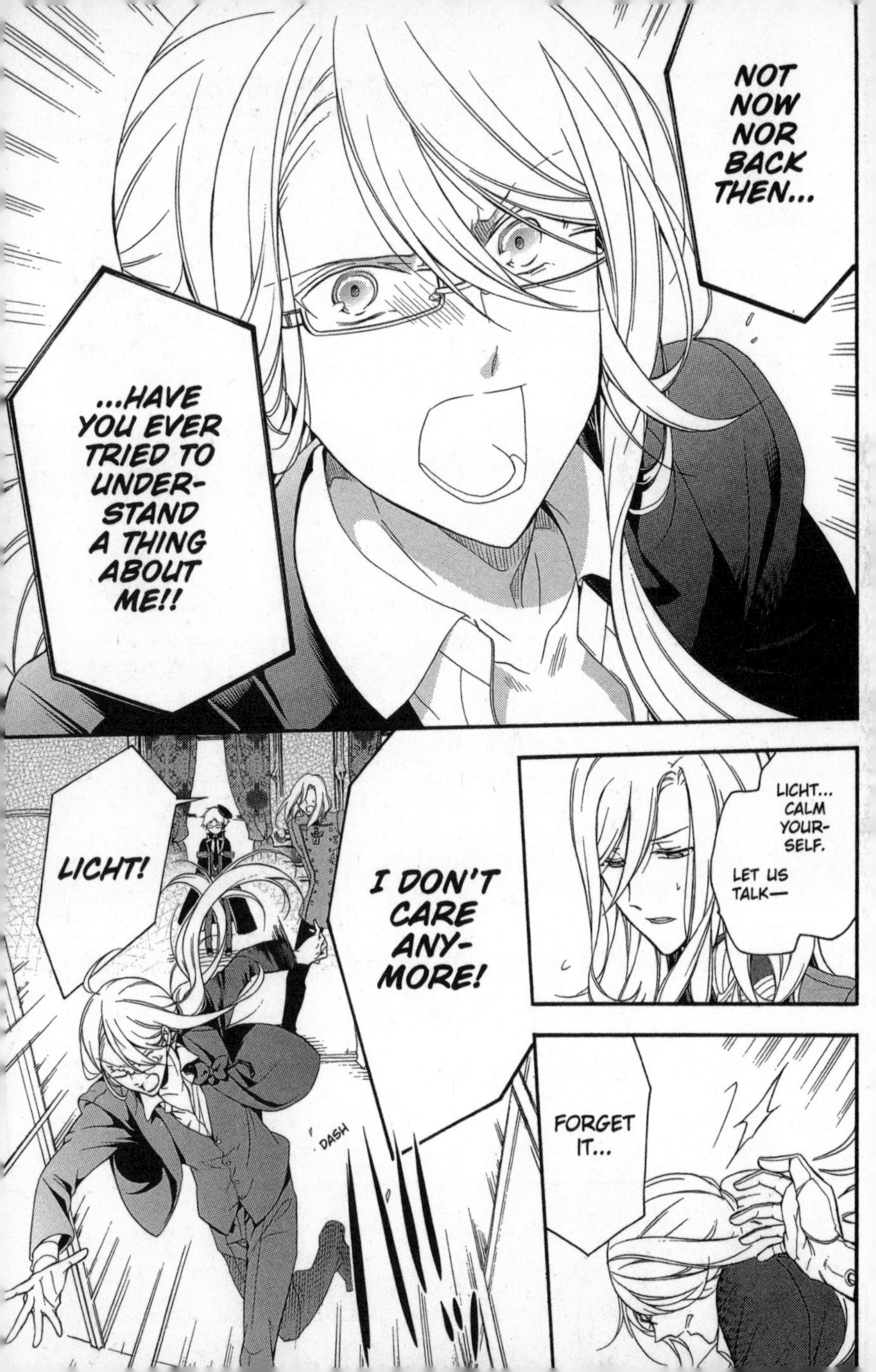
NOT NOW NOR BACK THEN...
...HAVE YOU EVER TRIED TO UNDER-STAND A THING ABOUT ME!!
LICHT... CALM YOUR-SELF.
LET US TALK—
FORGET IT...
I DON'T CARE ANY-MORE!
LICHT!
DASH

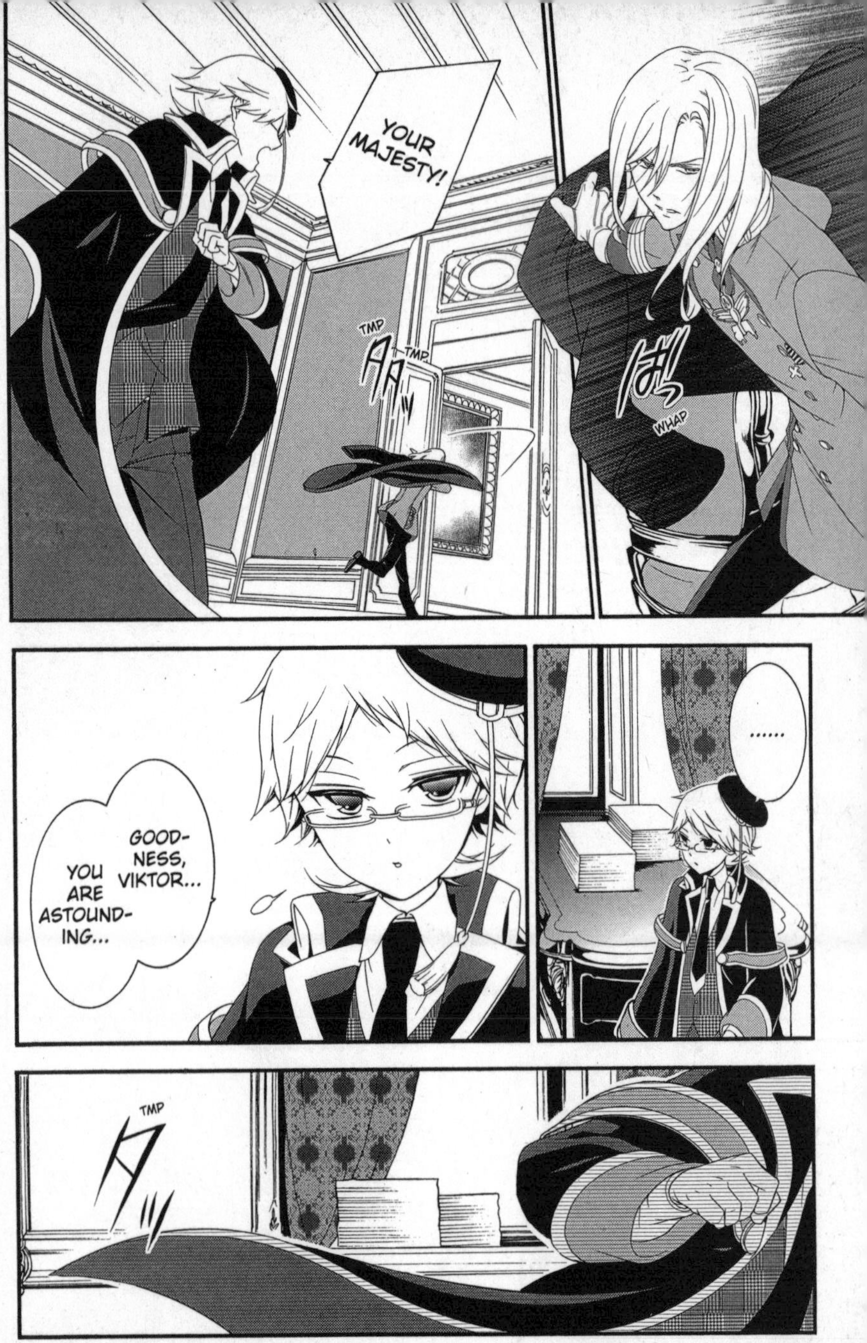
WHAP
YOUR MAJESTY!
TMP
TMP
......
GOODNESS, VIKTOR...
YOU ARE ASTOUNDING...
TMP

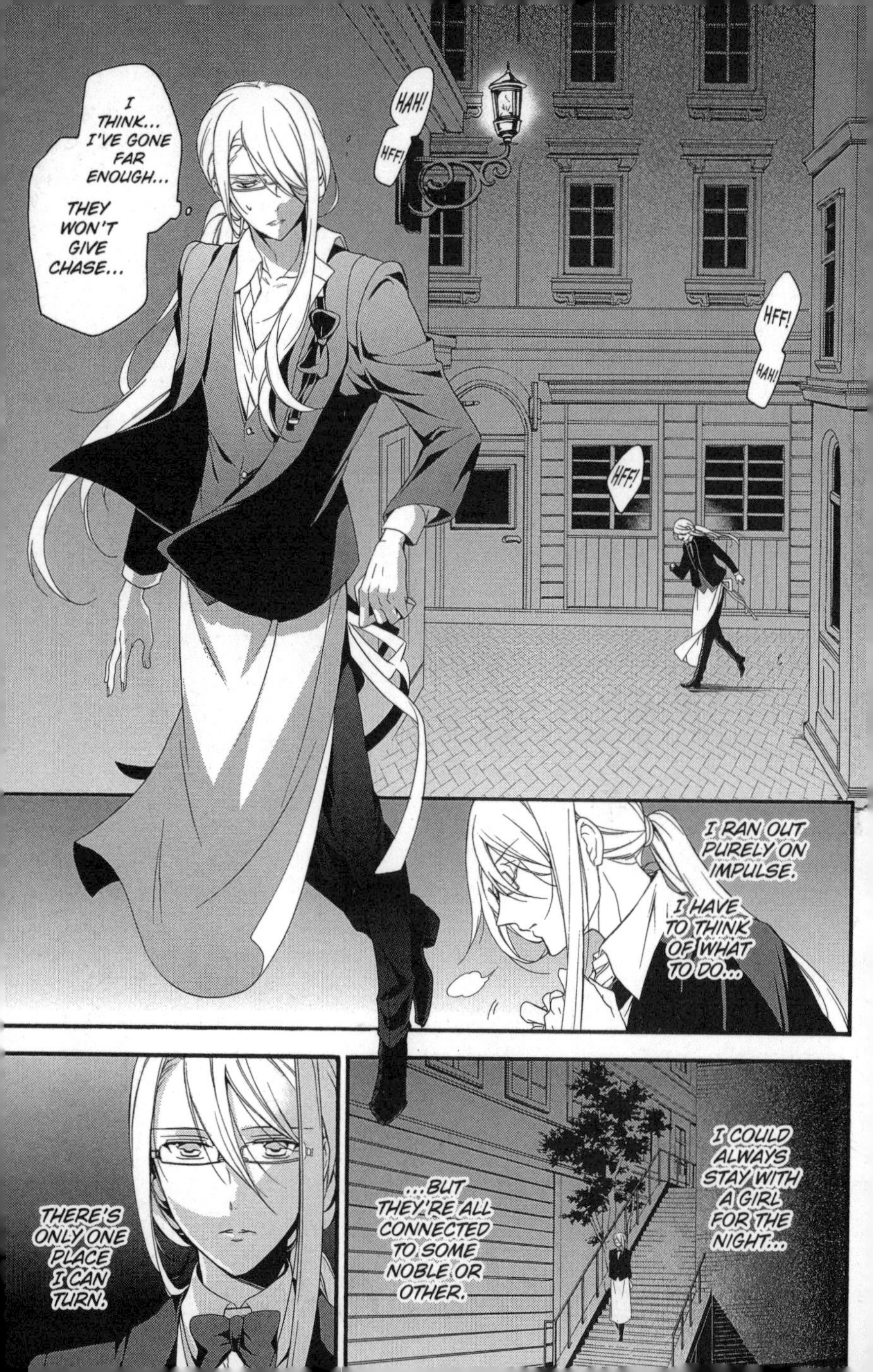
HAH!
HFF!
I THINK... I'VE GONE FAR ENOUGH...
THEY WON'T GIVE CHASE...
HFF!
HAH!
HFF!
I RAN OUT PURELY ON IMPULSE.
I HAVE TO THINK OF WHAT TO DO...
I COULD ALWAYS STAY WITH A GIRL FOR THE NIGHT...
...BUT THEY'RE ALL CONNECTED TO SOME NOBLE OR OTHER.
THERE'S ONLY ONE PLACE I CAN TURN.

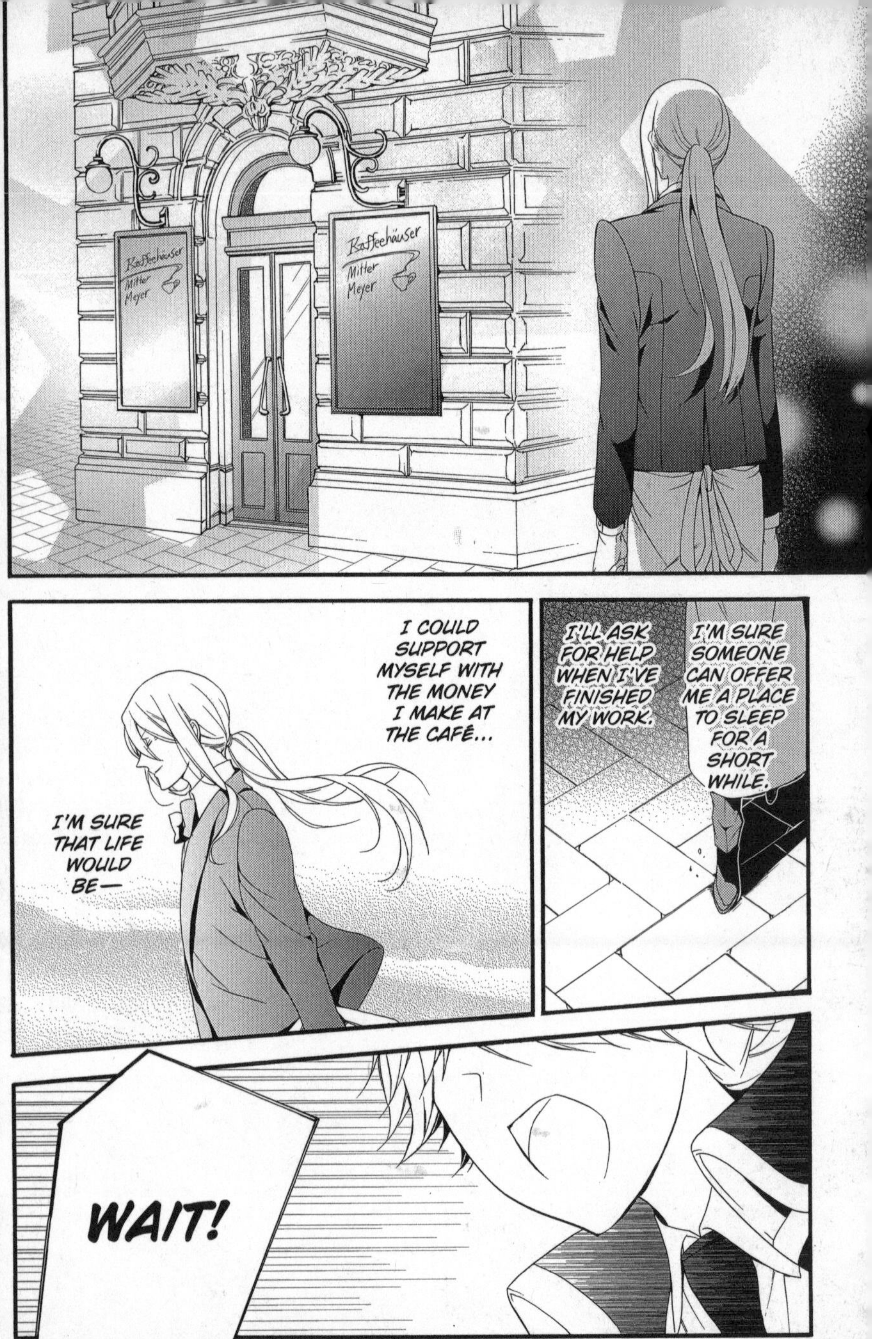
Kaffeehäuser Mitter Meyer
Kaffeehäuser Mitter Meyer
I'M SURE SOMEONE CAN OFFER ME A PLACE TO SLEEP FOR A SHORT WHILE.
I'LL ASK FOR HELP WHEN I'VE FINISHED MY WORK.
I COULD SUPPORT MYSELF WITH THE MONEY I MAKE AT THE CAFÉ...
I'M SURE THAT LIFE WOULD BE—
WAIT!

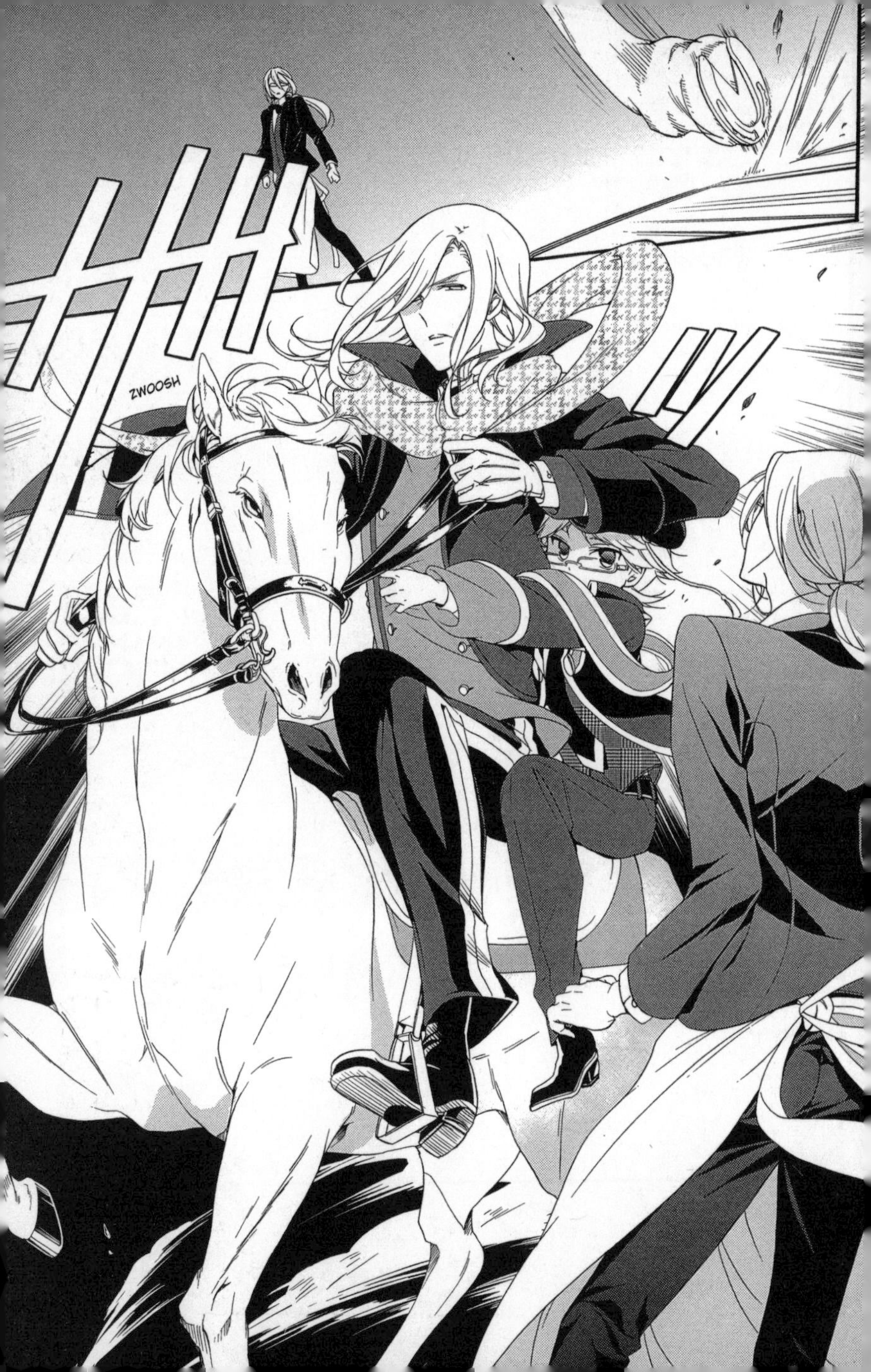
ZWOOSH

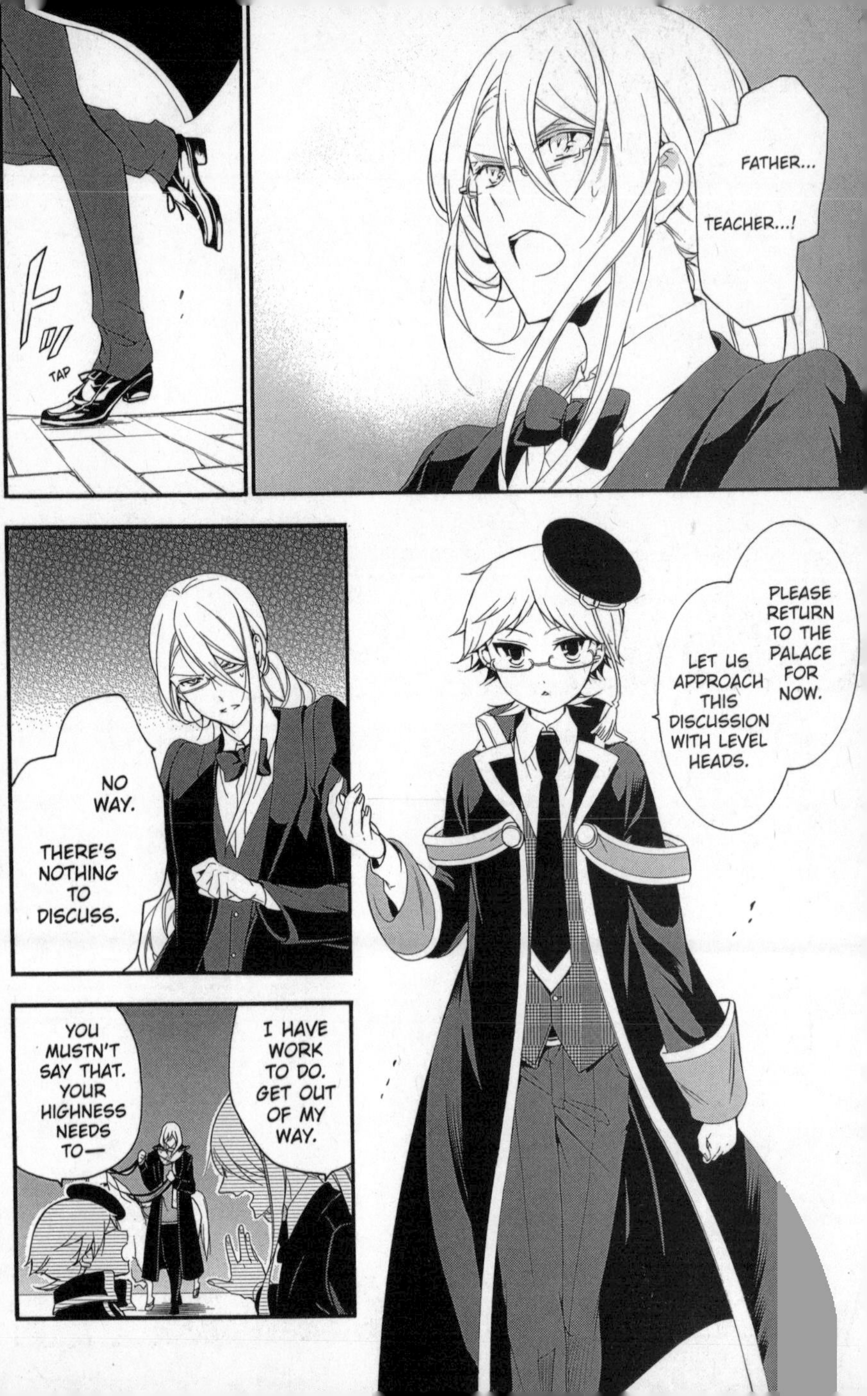
FATHER...
TEACHER...!
TAP
PLEASE RETURN TO THE PALACE FOR NOW.
LET US APPROACH THIS DISCUSSION WITH LEVEL HEADS.
NO WAY.
THERE'S NOTHING TO DISCUSS.
I HAVE WORK TO DO. GET OUT OF MY WAY.
YOU MUSTN'T SAY THAT. YOUR HIGHNESS NEEDS TO—

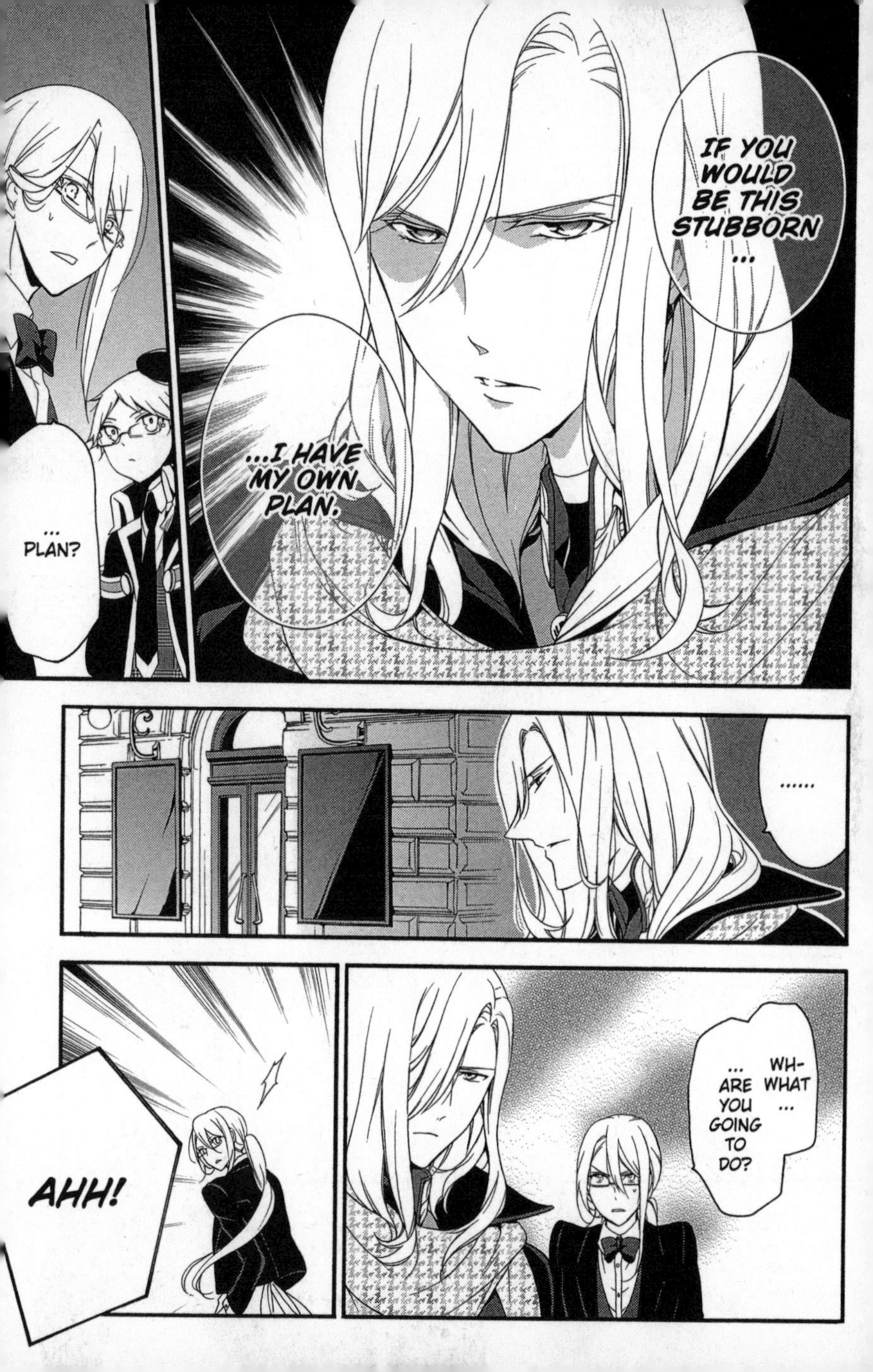
IF YOU WOULD BE THIS STUBBORN ...
...I HAVE MY OWN PLAN.
... PLAN?
......
WH-WHAT ... ... ARE YOU GOING TO DO?
AHH!

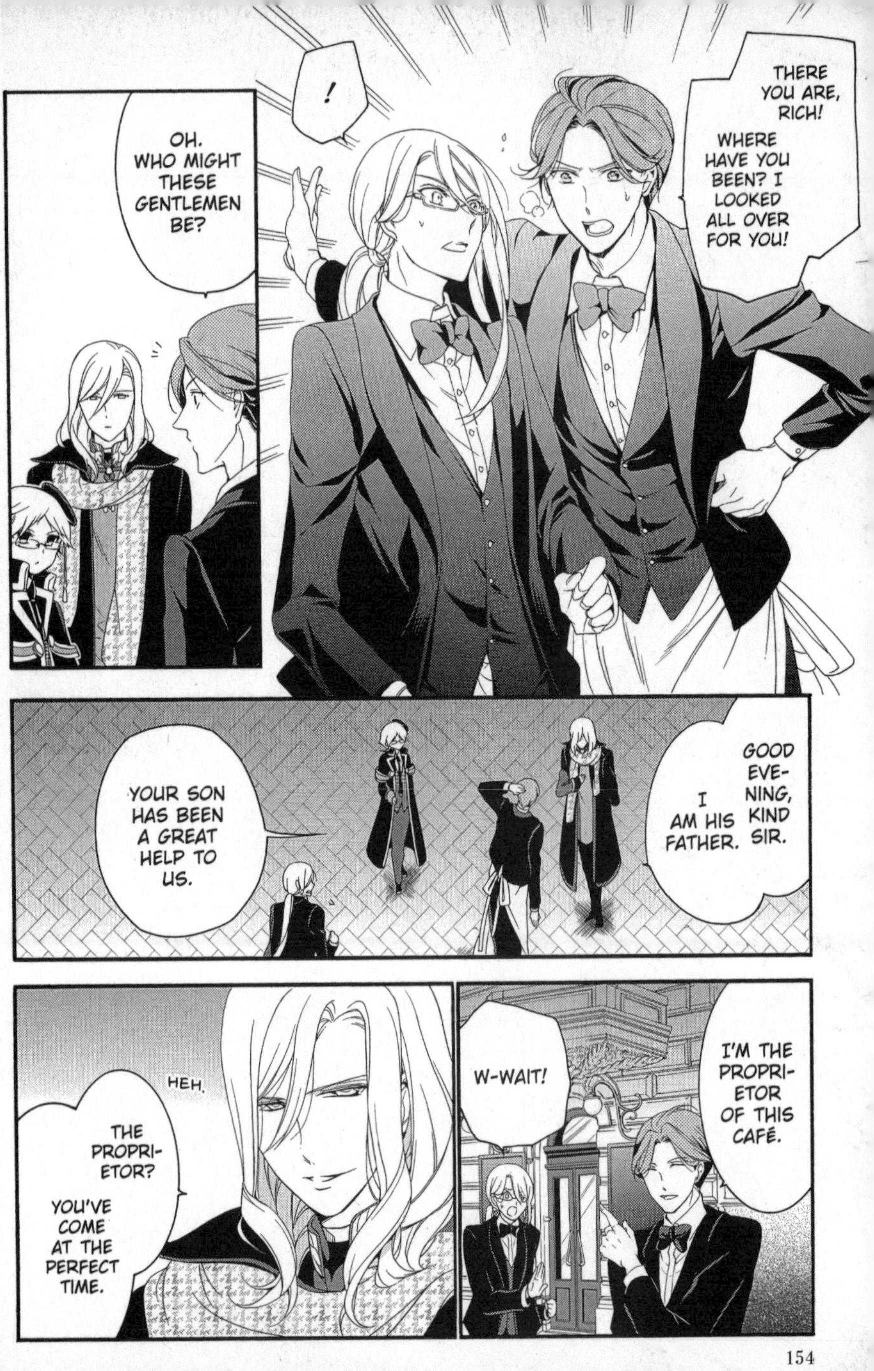
THERE YOU ARE, RICH!
WHERE HAVE YOU BEEN? I LOOKED ALL OVER FOR YOU!
!
OH. WHO MIGHT THESE GENTLEMEN BE?
GOOD EVE-NING, KIND SIR.
I AM HIS FATHER.
YOUR SON HAS BEEN A GREAT HELP TO US.
I'M THE PROPRI-ETOR OF THIS CAFÉ.
W-WAIT!
HEH.
THE PROPRI-ETOR?
YOU'VE COME AT THE PERFECT TIME.

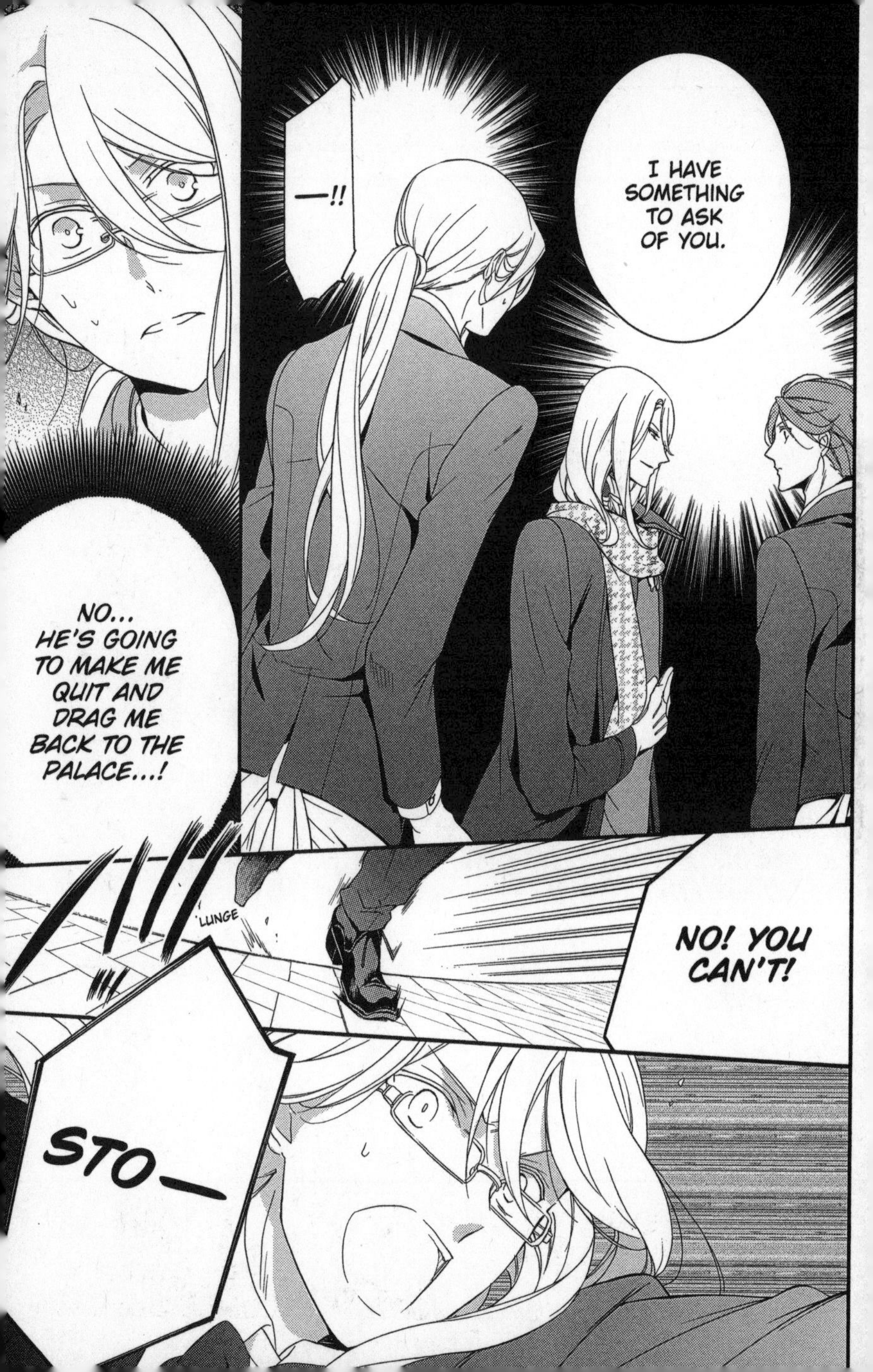
I HAVE SOMETHING TO ASK OF YOU.
—!!
NO... HE'S GOING TO MAKE ME QUIT AND DRAG ME BACK TO THE PALACE...!
NO! YOU CAN'T!
LUNGE
STO—

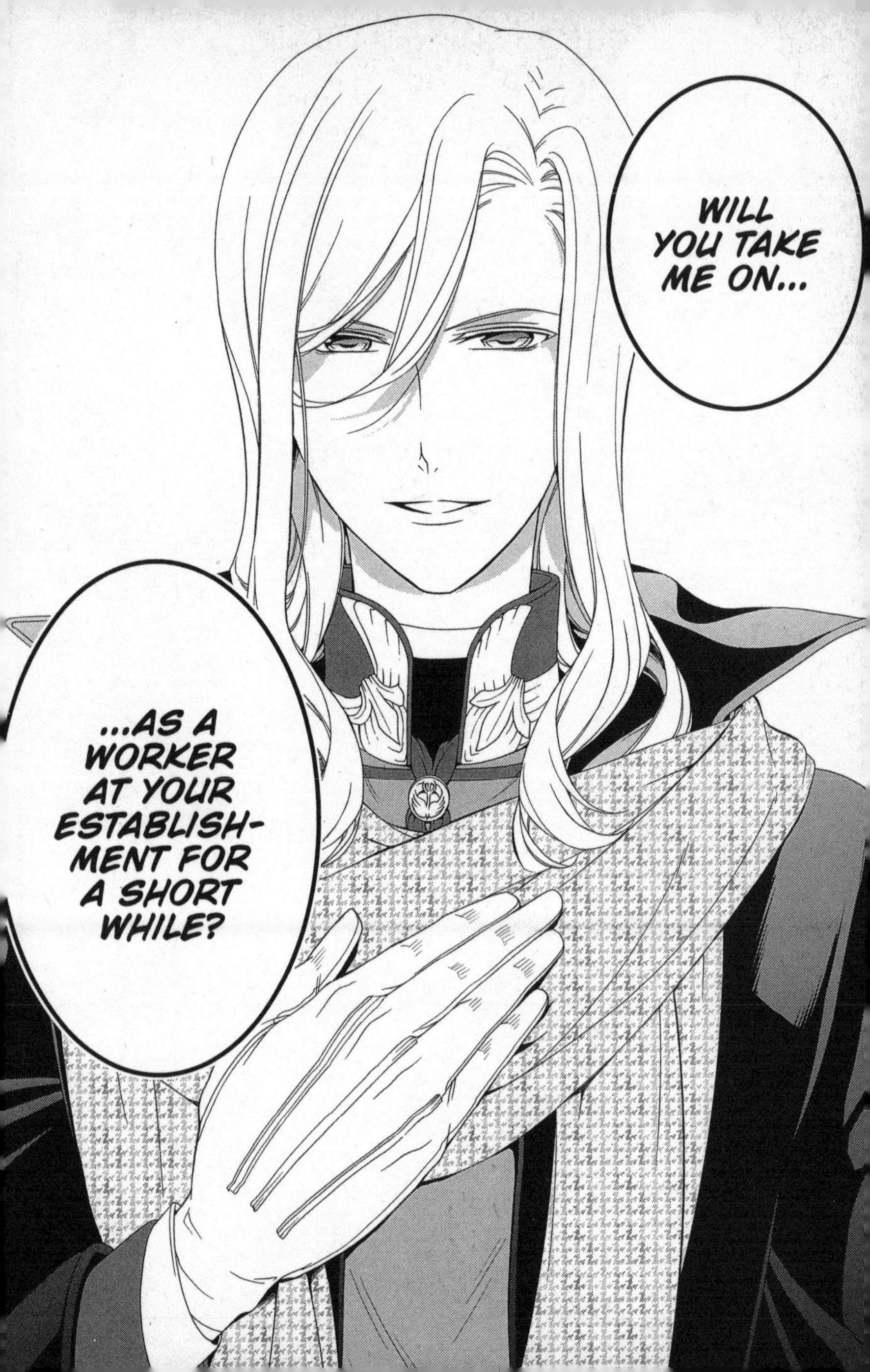
WILL YOU TAKE ME ON...
...AS A WORKER AT YOUR ESTABLISH-MENT FOR A SHORT WHILE?

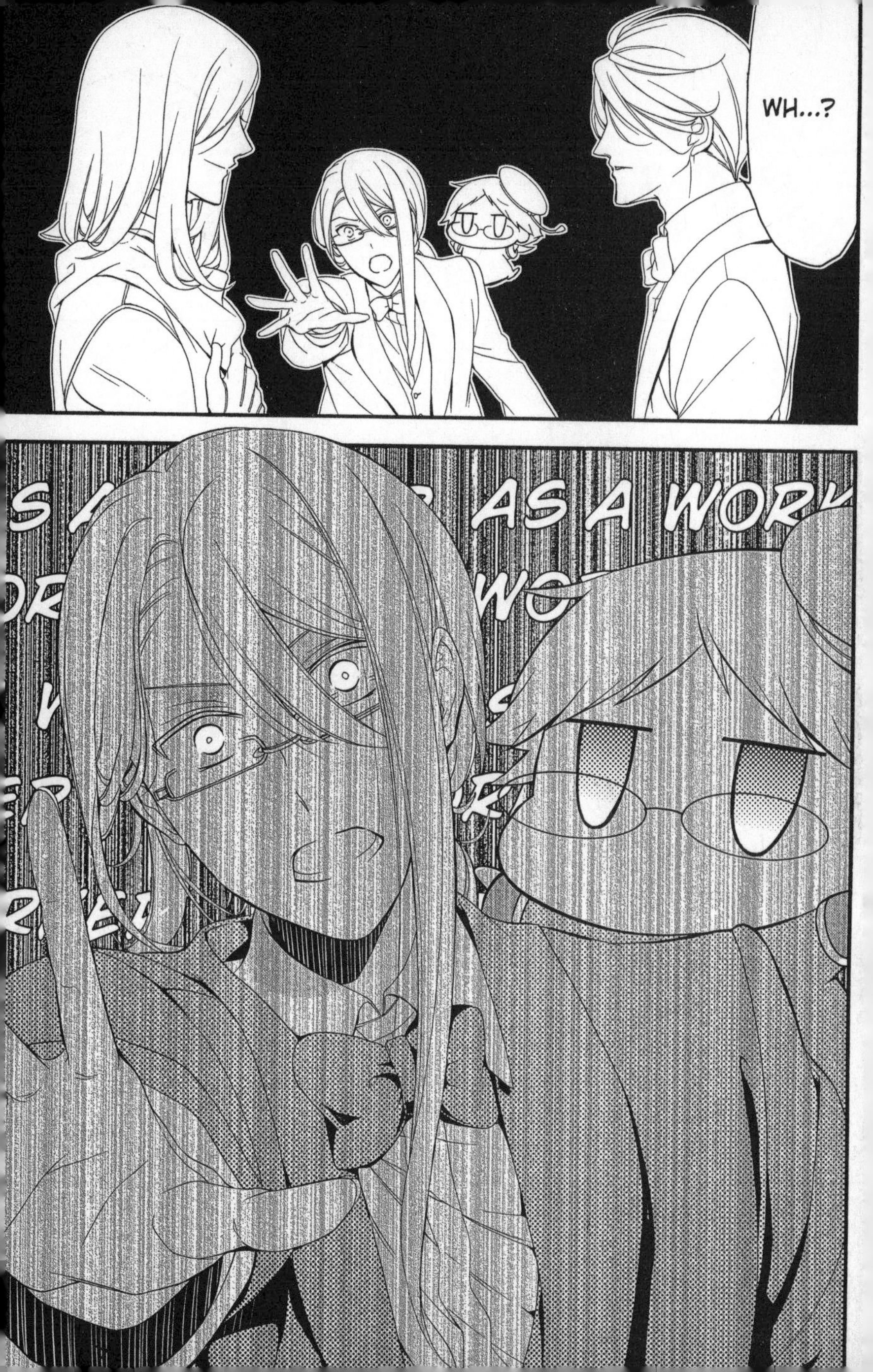
WH...?

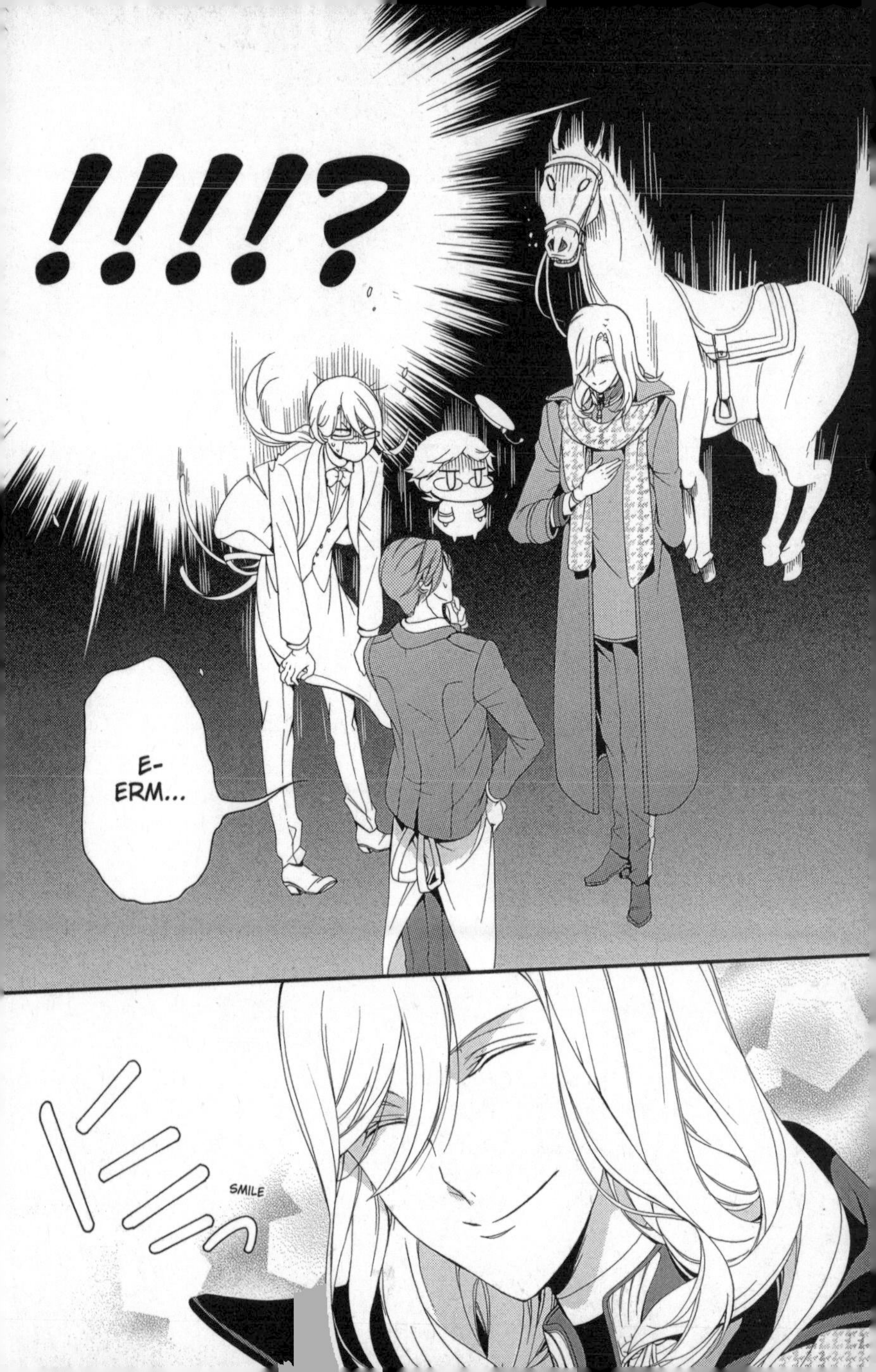
!!!!?
E-ERM...
SMILE

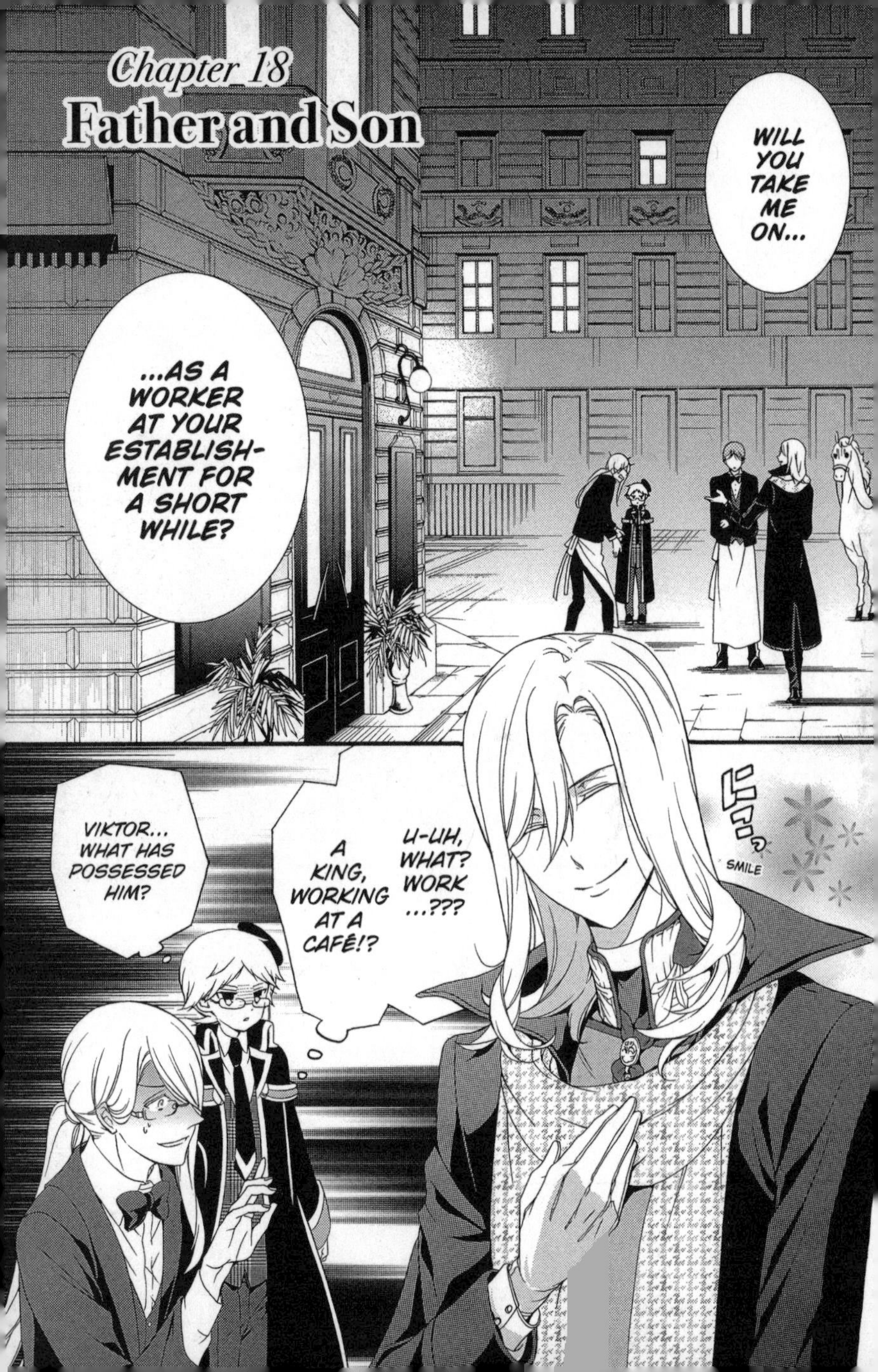
Chapter 18
Father and Son
WILL YOU TAKE ME ON...
...AS A WORKER AT YOUR ESTABLISHMENT FOR A SHORT WHILE?
SMILE
U-UH, WHAT? WORK ...???
A KING, WORKING AT A CAFÉ!?
VIKTOR... WHAT HAS POSSESSED HIM?

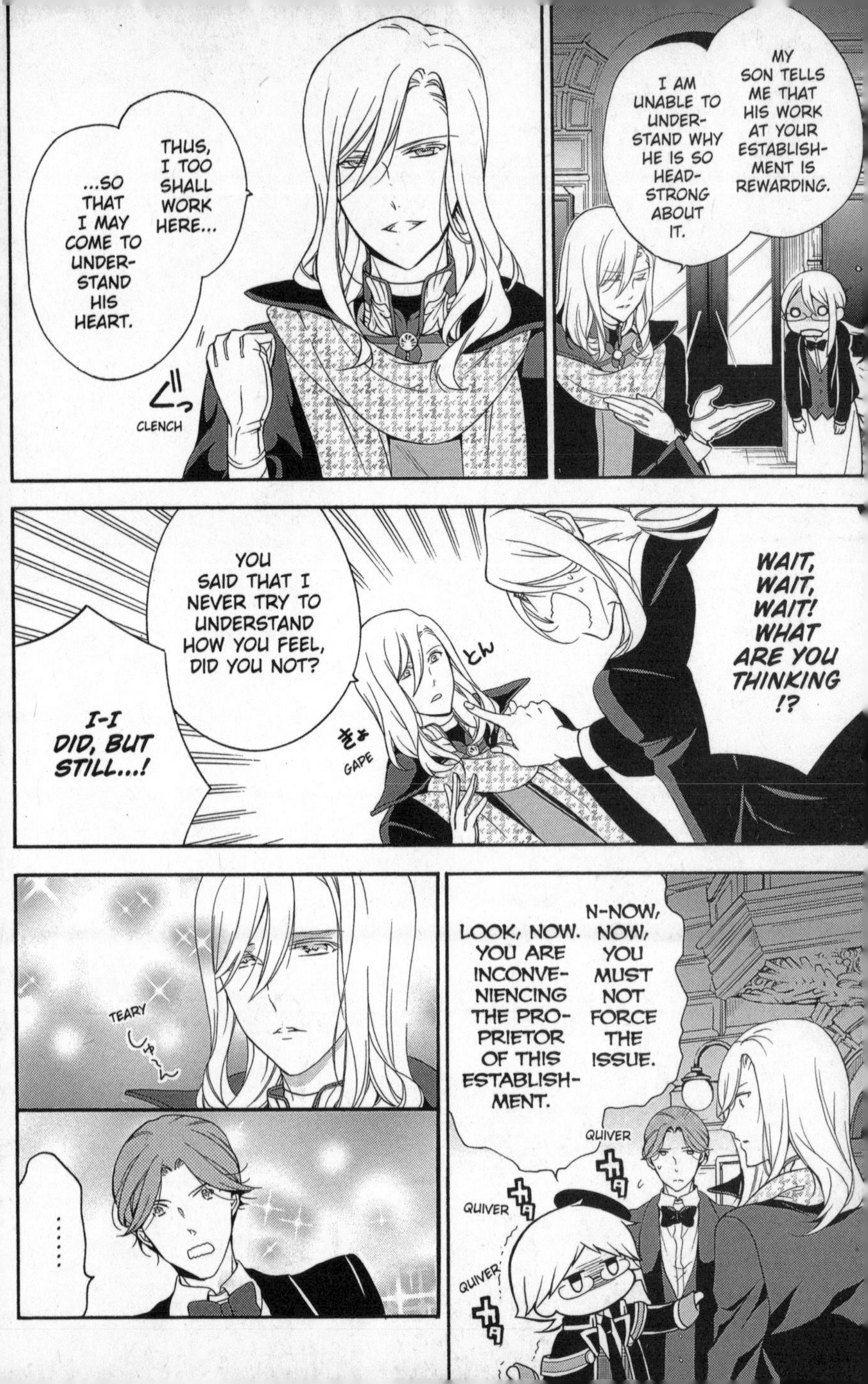
MY SON TELLS ME THAT HIS WORK AT YOUR ESTABLISHMENT IS REWARDING.
I AM UNABLE TO UNDERSTAND WHY HE IS SO HEADSTRONG ABOUT IT.
THUS, I TOO SHALL WORK HERE...
...SO THAT I MAY COME TO UNDERSTAND HIS HEART.
CLENCH
WAIT, WAIT, WAIT! WHAT ARE YOU THINKING!?
YOU SAID THAT I NEVER TRY TO UNDERSTAND HOW YOU FEEL, DID YOU NOT?
GAPE
I-I DID, BUT STILL...!
N-NOW, NOW, YOU MUST NOT FORCE THE ISSUE.
LOOK, NOW. YOU ARE INCONVENIENCING THE PROPRIETOR OF THIS ESTABLISHMENT.
QUIVER
QUIVER
QUIVER
TEARY
......

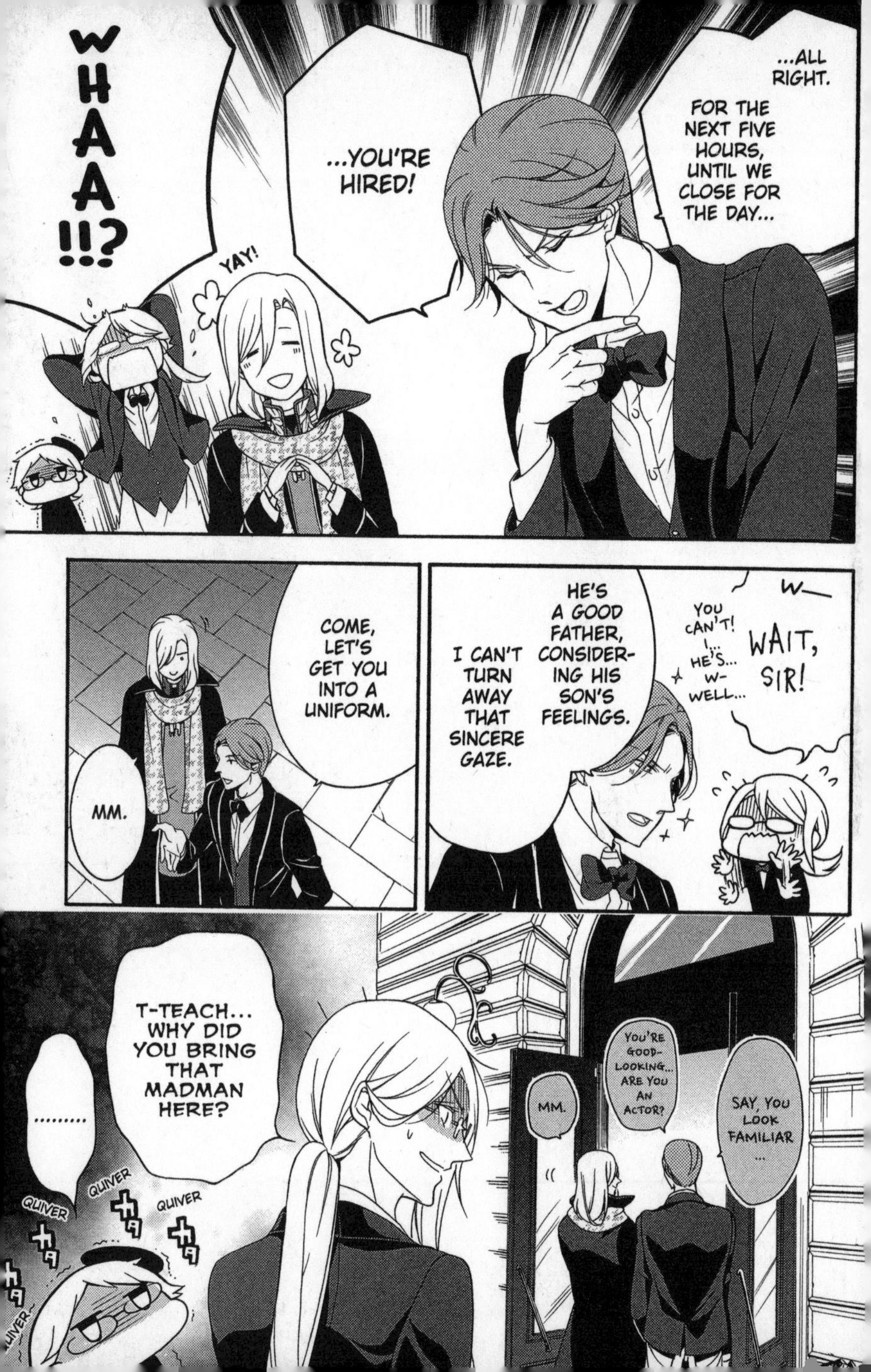
...ALL RIGHT.
FOR THE NEXT FIVE HOURS, UNTIL WE CLOSE FOR THE DAY...
...YOU'RE HIRED!
YAY!
WHAAA!!?
W—
WAIT, SIR!
YOU CAN'T! I... HE'S... W-WELL...
HE'S A GOOD FATHER, CONSIDERING HIS SON'S FEELINGS.
I CAN'T TURN AWAY THAT SINCERE GAZE.
COME, LET'S GET YOU INTO A UNIFORM.
MM.
SAY, YOU LOOK FAMILIAR...
YOU'RE GOOD-LOOKING... ARE YOU AN ACTOR?
MM.
T-TEACH... WHY DID YOU BRING THAT MADMAN HERE?
....
QUIVER
QUIVER
QUIVER

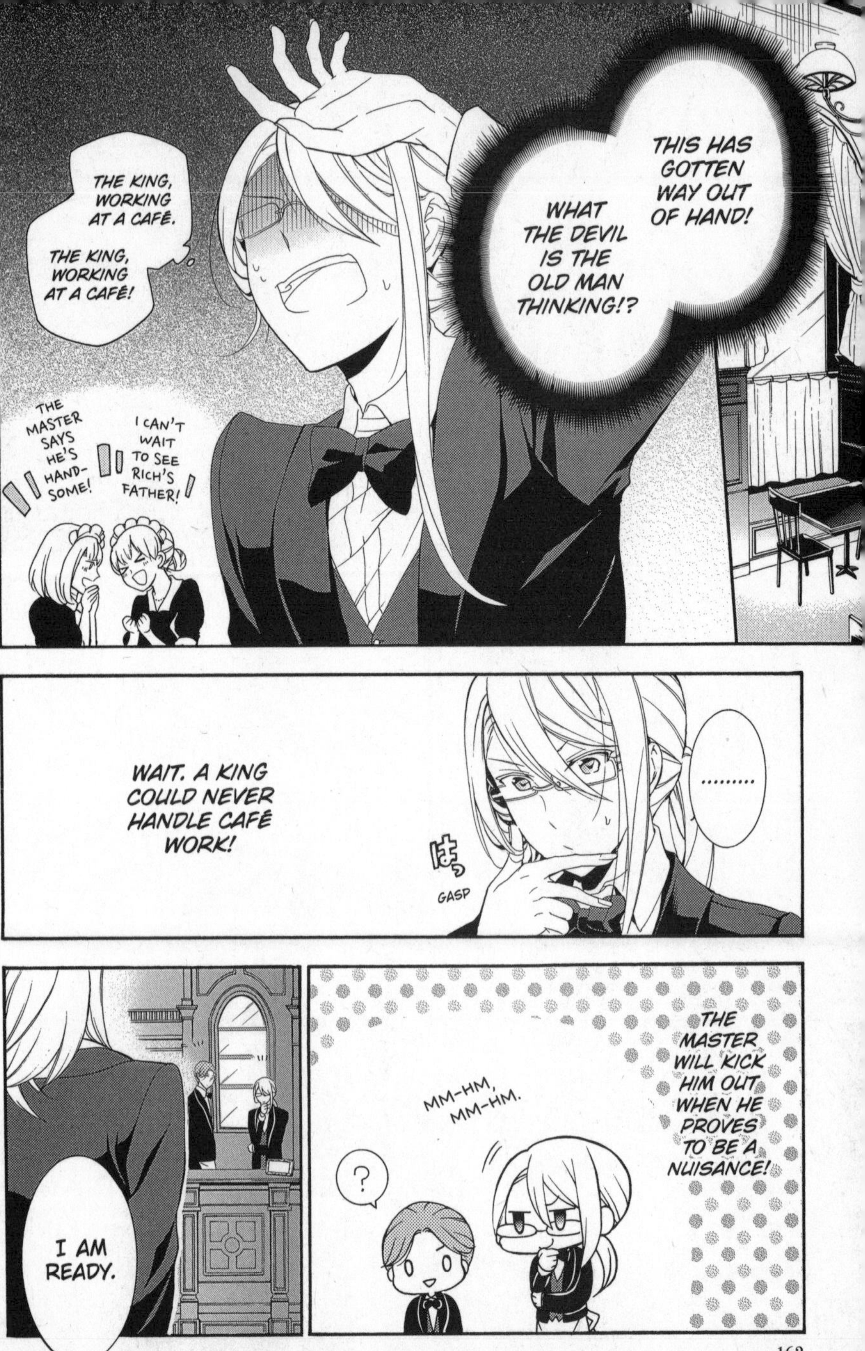
THIS HAS GOTTEN WAY OUT OF HAND!
WHAT THE DEVIL IS THE OLD MAN THINKING!?
THE KING, WORKING AT A CAFÉ.
THE KING, WORKING AT A CAFÉ!
I CAN'T WAIT TO SEE RICH'S FATHER!
THE MASTER SAYS HE'S HAND-SOME!
....
はっ
GASP
WAIT. A KING COULD NEVER HANDLE CAFÉ WORK!
THE MASTER WILL KICK HIM OUT WHEN HE PROVES TO BE A NUISANCE!
MM-HM, MM-HM.
?
I AM READY.

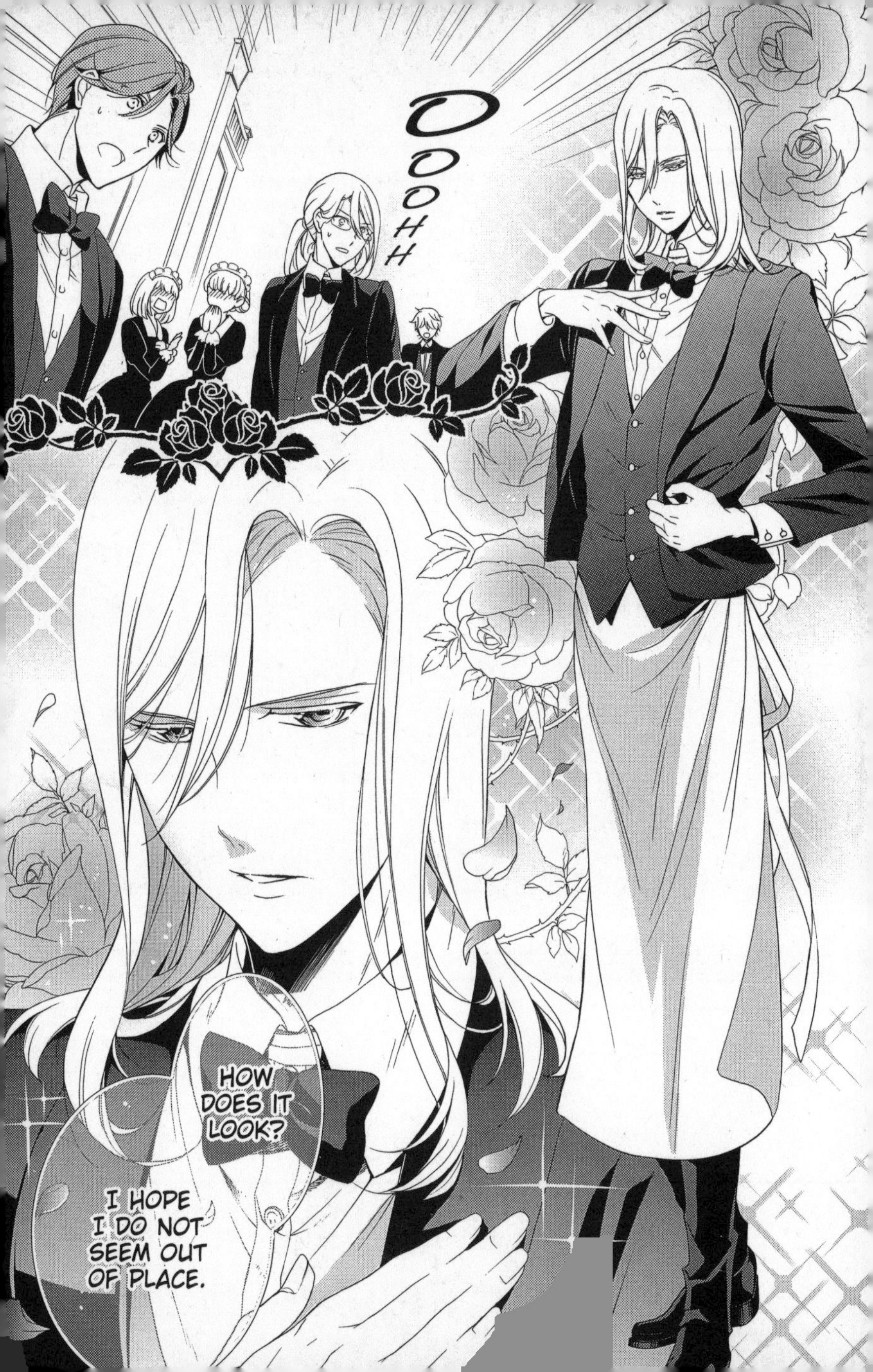
OOOOHH
HOW DOES IT LOOK?
I HOPE I DO NOT SEEM OUT OF PLACE.

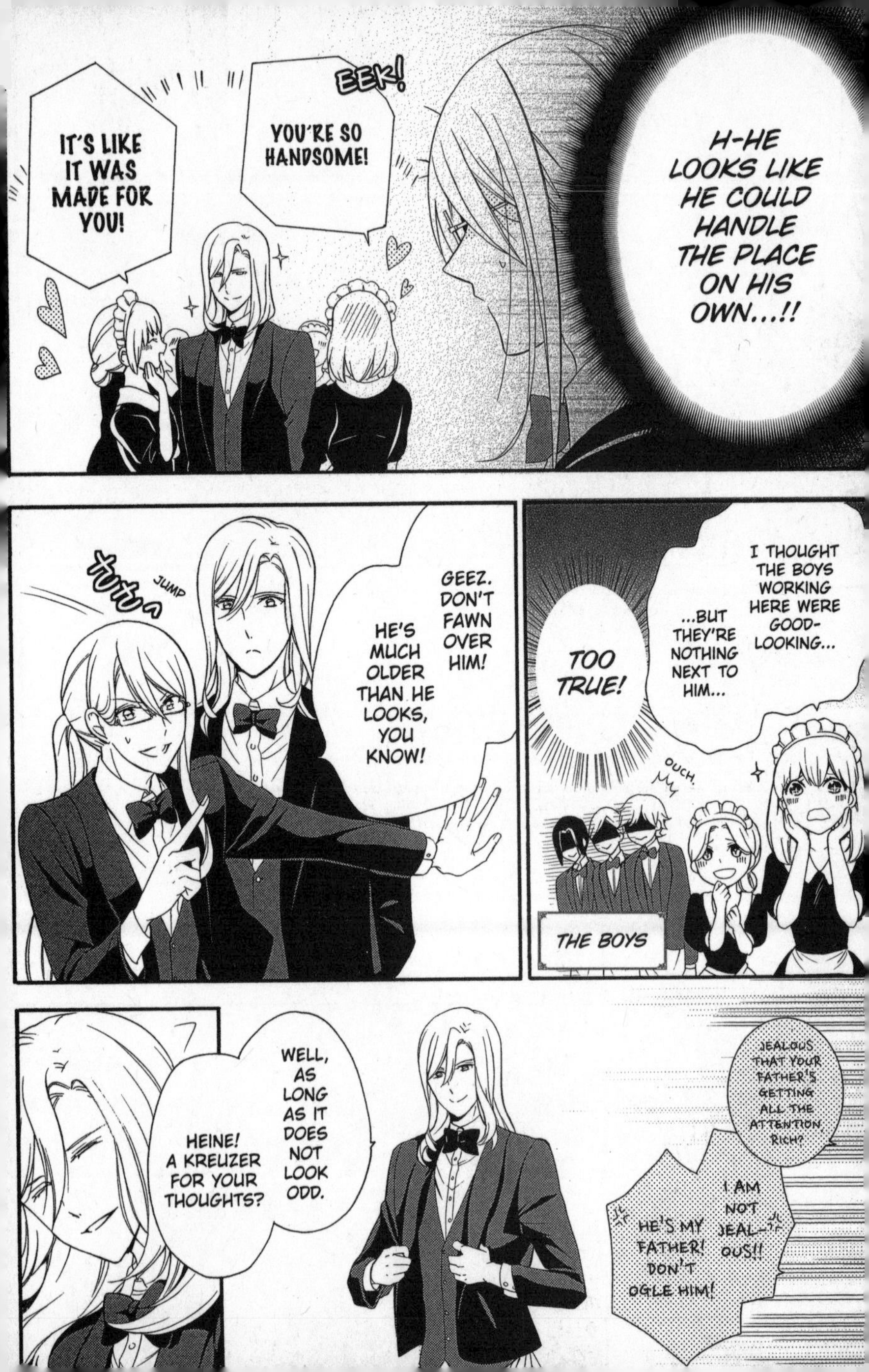
H-HE LOOKS LIKE HE COULD HANDLE THE PLACE ON HIS OWN...!!
EEK!
YOU'RE SO HANDSOME!
IT'S LIKE IT WAS MADE FOR YOU!
I THOUGHT THE BOYS WORKING HERE WERE GOOD-LOOKING...
...BUT THEY'RE NOTHING NEXT TO HIM...
TOO TRUE!
OUCH
THE BOYS
GEEZ. DON'T FAWN OVER HIM!
HE'S MUCH OLDER THAN HE LOOKS, YOU KNOW!
JUMP
JEALOUS THAT YOUR FATHER'S GETTING ALL THE ATTENTION, RICH?
I AM NOT JEALOUS!!
HE'S MY FATHER! DON'T OGLE HIM!
WELL, AS LONG AS IT DOES NOT LOOK ODD.
HEINE! A KREUZER FOR YOUR THOUGHTS?

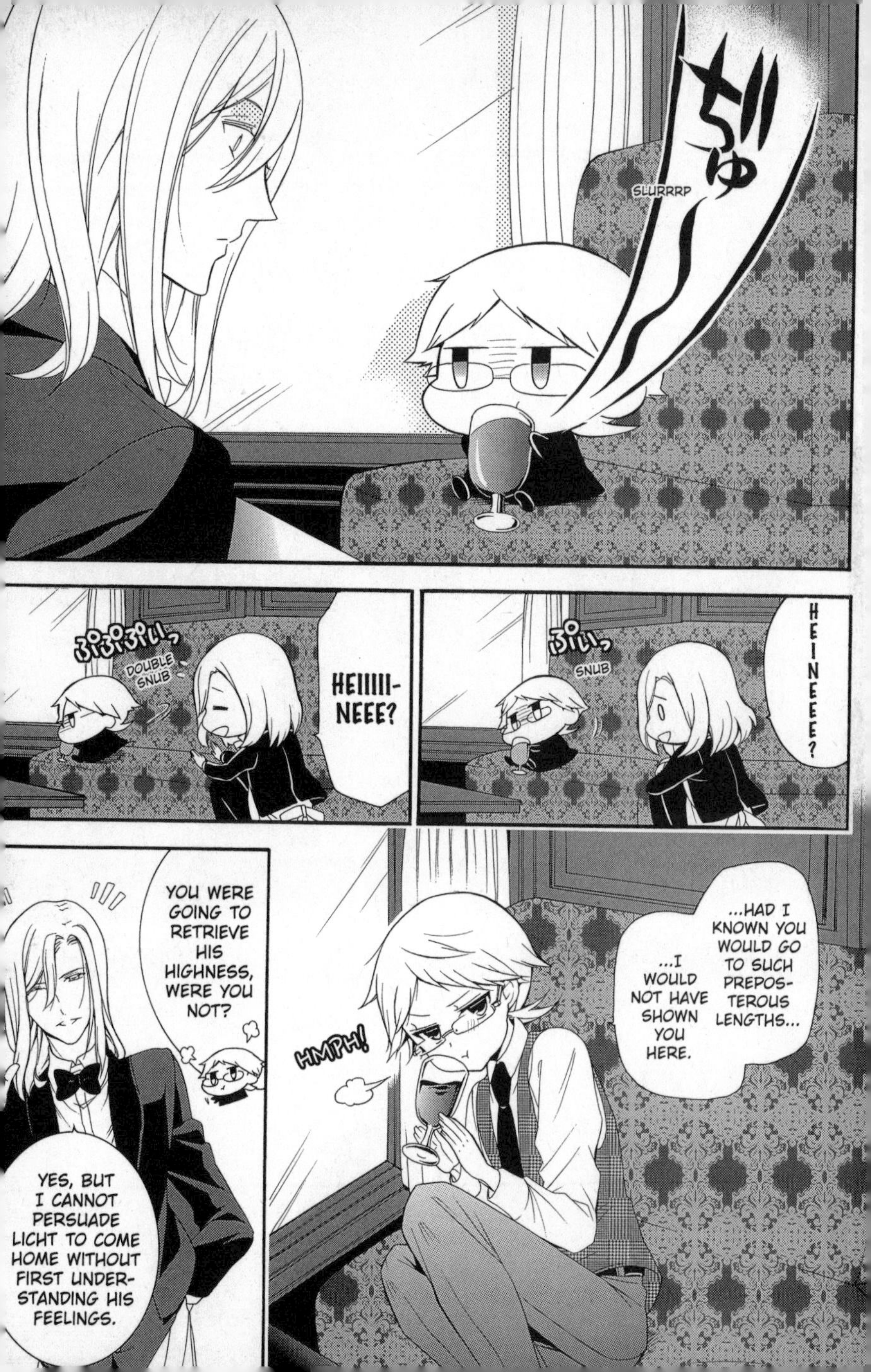
ぢゅー
SLURRRP
HEINEEEE?
ぷいっ
SNUB
HEIIIII-NEEE?
ぷぷぷいっ
DOUBLE SNUB
...HAD I KNOWN YOU WOULD GO TO SUCH PREPOS-TEROUS LENGTHS...
...I WOULD NOT HAVE SHOWN YOU HERE.
HMPH!
YOU WERE GOING TO RETRIEVE HIS HIGHNESS, WERE YOU NOT?
YES, BUT I CANNOT PERSUADE LICHT TO COME HOME WITHOUT FIRST UNDER-STANDING HIS FEELINGS.

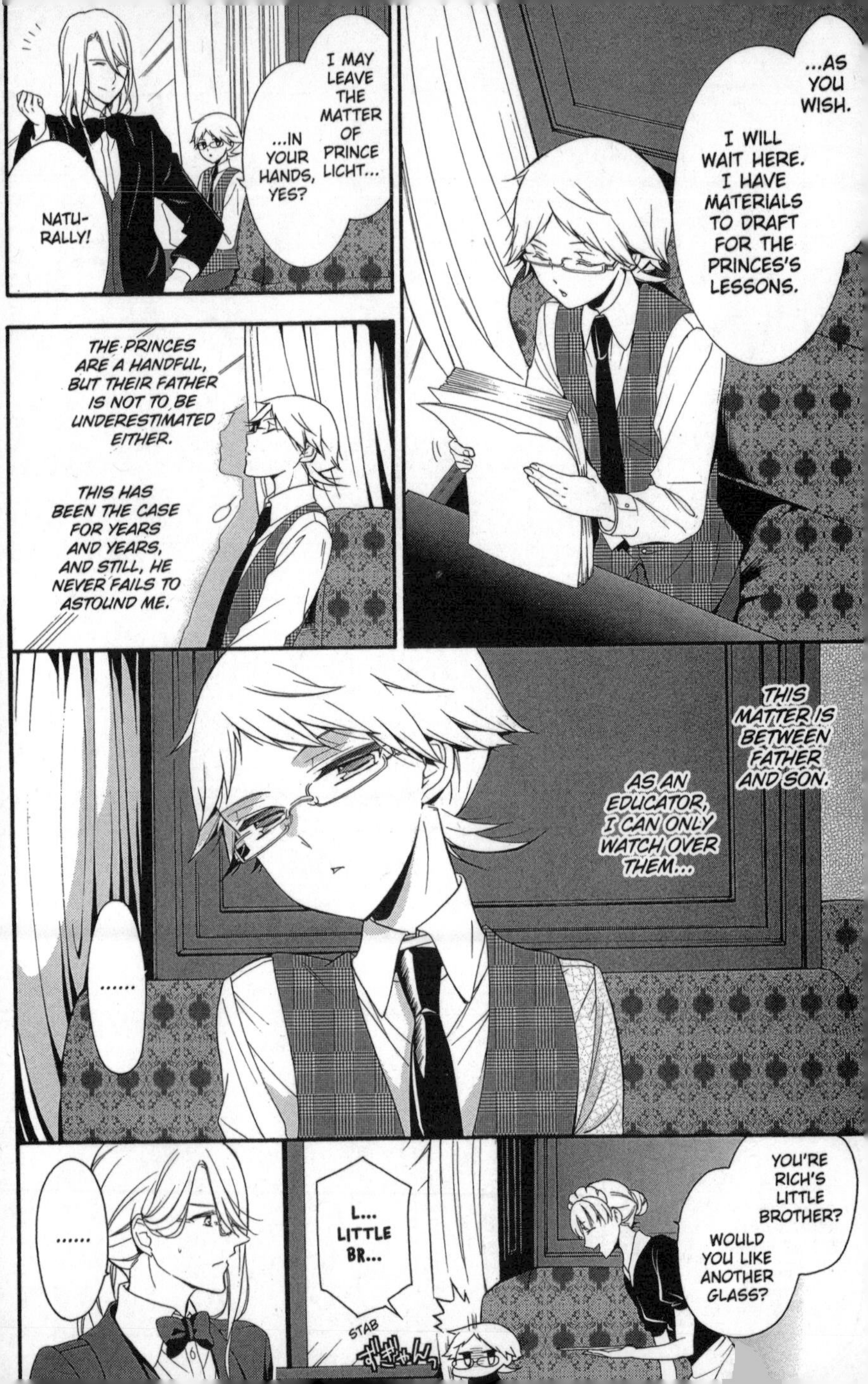

...AS YOU WISH.
I WILL WAIT HERE. I HAVE MATERIALS TO DRAFT FOR THE PRINCES'S LESSONS.
I MAY LEAVE THE MATTER OF PRINCE LICHT...
...IN YOUR HANDS, YES?
NATU-RALLY!
THE PRINCES ARE A HANDFUL, BUT THEIR FATHER IS NOT TO BE UNDERESTIMATED EITHER.
THIS HAS BEEN THE CASE FOR YEARS AND YEARS, AND STILL, HE NEVER FAILS TO ASTOUND ME.
THIS MATTER IS BETWEEN FATHER AND SON.
AS AN EDUCATOR, I CAN ONLY WATCH OVER THEM...
......
YOU'RE RICH'S LITTLE BROTHER?
WOULD YOU LIKE ANOTHER GLASS?
L... LITTLE BR...
STAB
ずぎゃんっ
......

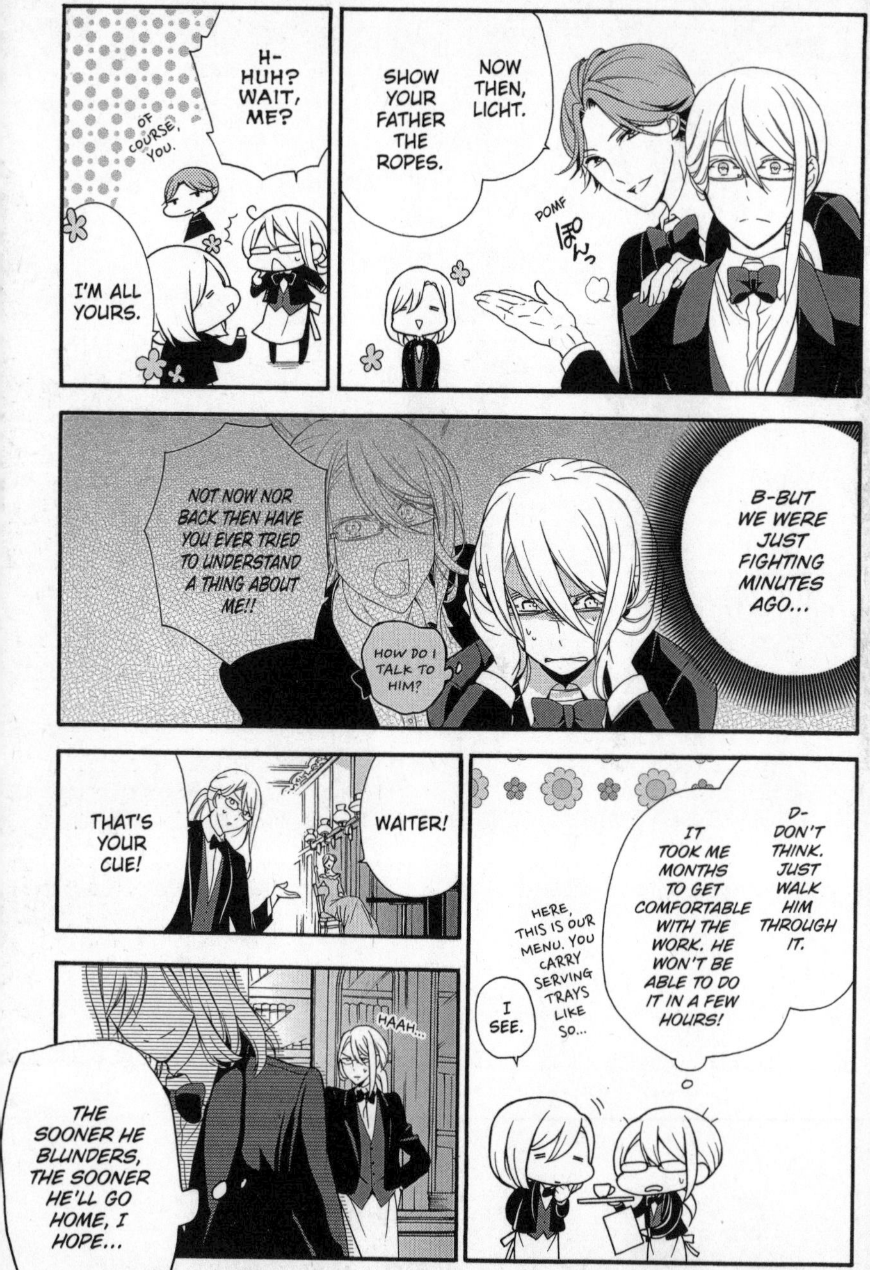
NOW THEN, LICHT.
SHOW YOUR FATHER THE ROPES.
POMF
ぽんっ
H-HUH? WAIT, ME?
OF COURSE, YOU.
I'M ALL YOURS.
B-BUT WE WERE JUST FIGHTING MINUTES AGO...
NOT NOW NOR BACK THEN HAVE YOU EVER TRIED TO UNDERSTAND A THING ABOUT ME!!
HOW DO I TALK TO HIM?
D-DON'T THINK. JUST WALK HIM THROUGH IT.
IT TOOK ME MONTHS TO GET COMFORTABLE WITH THE WORK. HE WON'T BE ABLE TO DO IT IN A FEW HOURS!
HERE, THIS IS OUR MENU. YOU CARRY SERVING TRAYS LIKE SO...
I SEE.
WAITER!
THAT'S YOUR CUE!
HAAH...
THE SOONER HE BLUNDERS, THE SOONER HE'LL GO HOME, I HOPE...

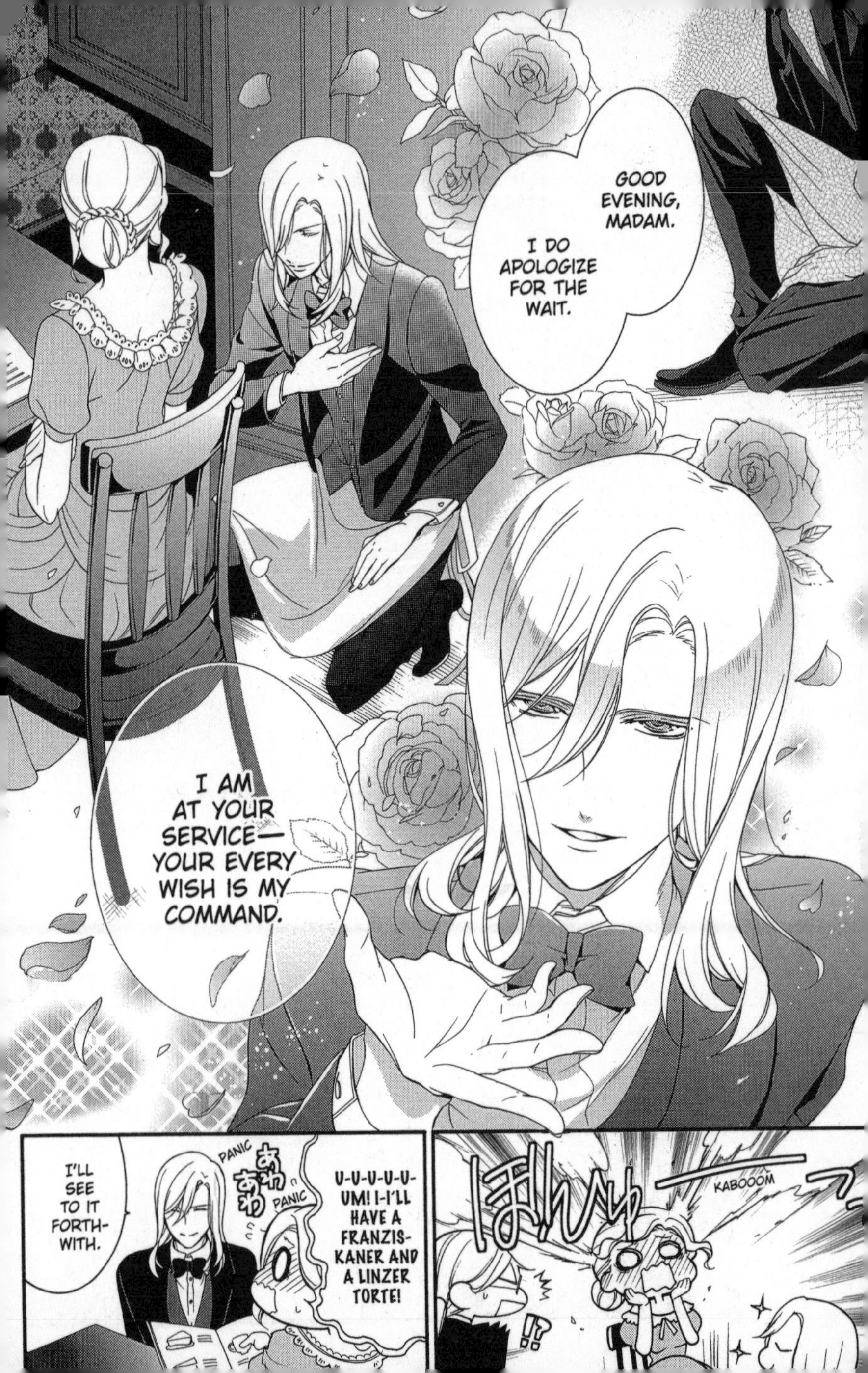
GOOD EVENING, MADAM.
I DO APOLOGIZE FOR THE WAIT.
I AM AT YOUR SERVICE—YOUR EVERY WISH IS MY COMMAND.
KABOOOM
PANIC あわあわ PANIC
U-U-U-U-UM! I-I'LL HAVE A FRANZIS-KANER AND A LINZER TORTE!
I'LL SEE TO IT FORTH-WITH.

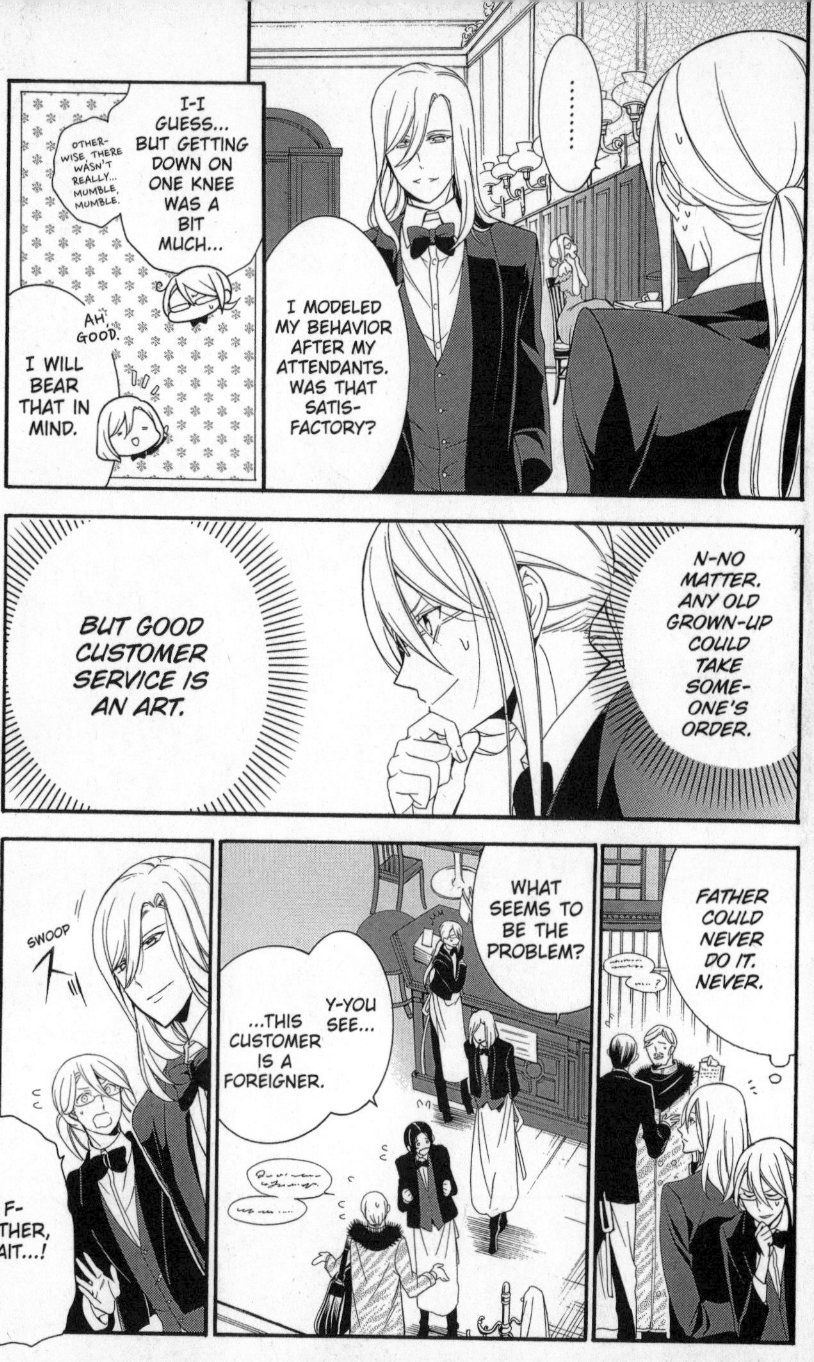
......
I MODELED MY BEHAVIOR AFTER MY ATTENDANTS. WAS THAT SATISFACTORY?
I-I GUESS... BUT GETTING DOWN ON ONE KNEE WAS A BIT MUCH...
OTHERWISE, THERE WASN'T REALLY... MUMBLE, MUMBLE.
AH, GOOD.
I WILL BEAR THAT IN MIND.
N-NO MATTER. ANY OLD GROWN-UP COULD TAKE SOMEONE'S ORDER.
BUT GOOD CUSTOMER SERVICE IS AN ART.
FATHER COULD NEVER DO IT. NEVER.
WHAT SEEMS TO BE THE PROBLEM?
Y-YOU SEE...
...THIS CUSTOMER IS A FOREIGNER.
SWOOP
F-FATHER, WAIT...!

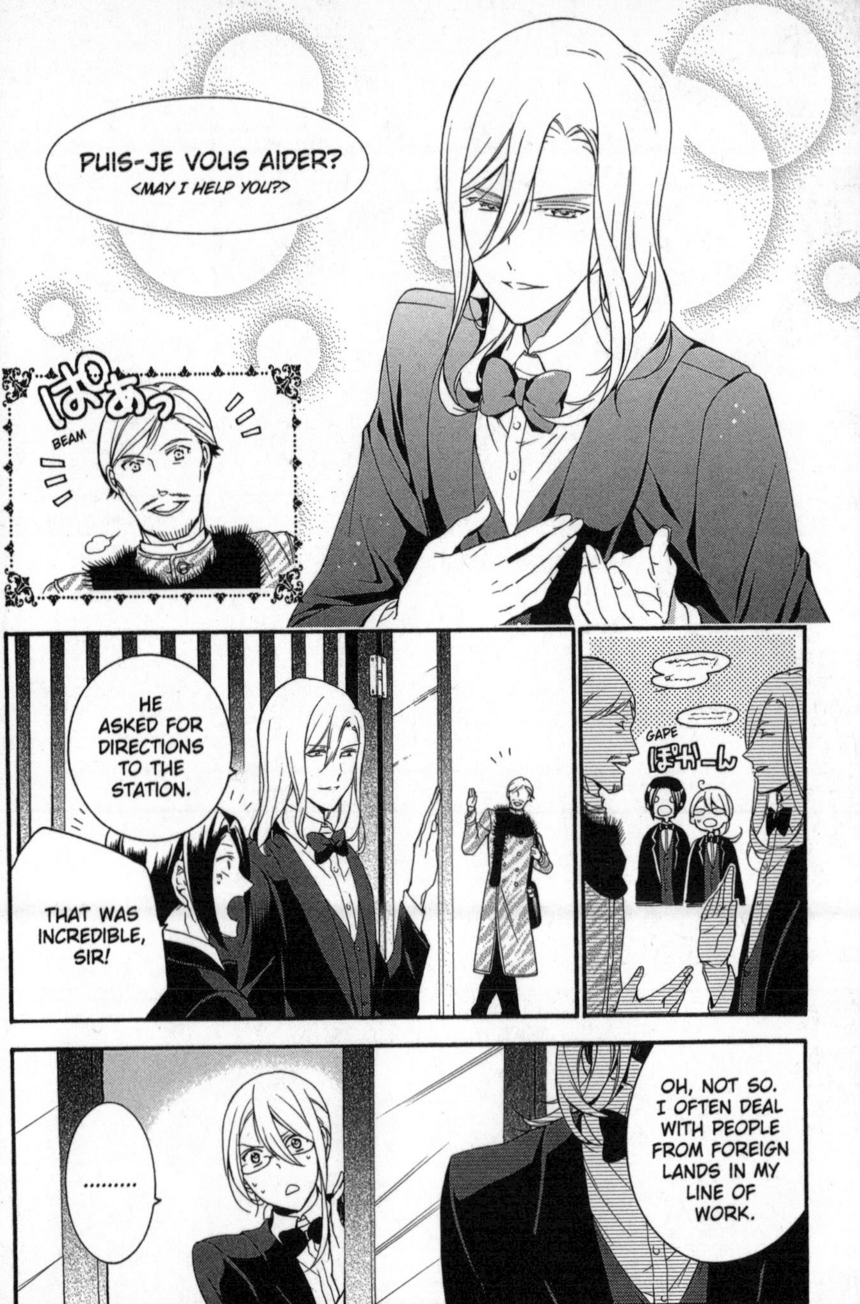
PUIS-JE VOUS AIDER?
<MAY I HELP YOU?>
ぱあっ
BEAM
GAPE
ぽかーん
HE ASKED FOR DIRECTIONS TO THE STATION.
THAT WAS INCREDIBLE, SIR!
OH, NOT SO. I OFTEN DEAL WITH PEOPLE FROM FOREIGN LANDS IN MY LINE OF WORK.
....

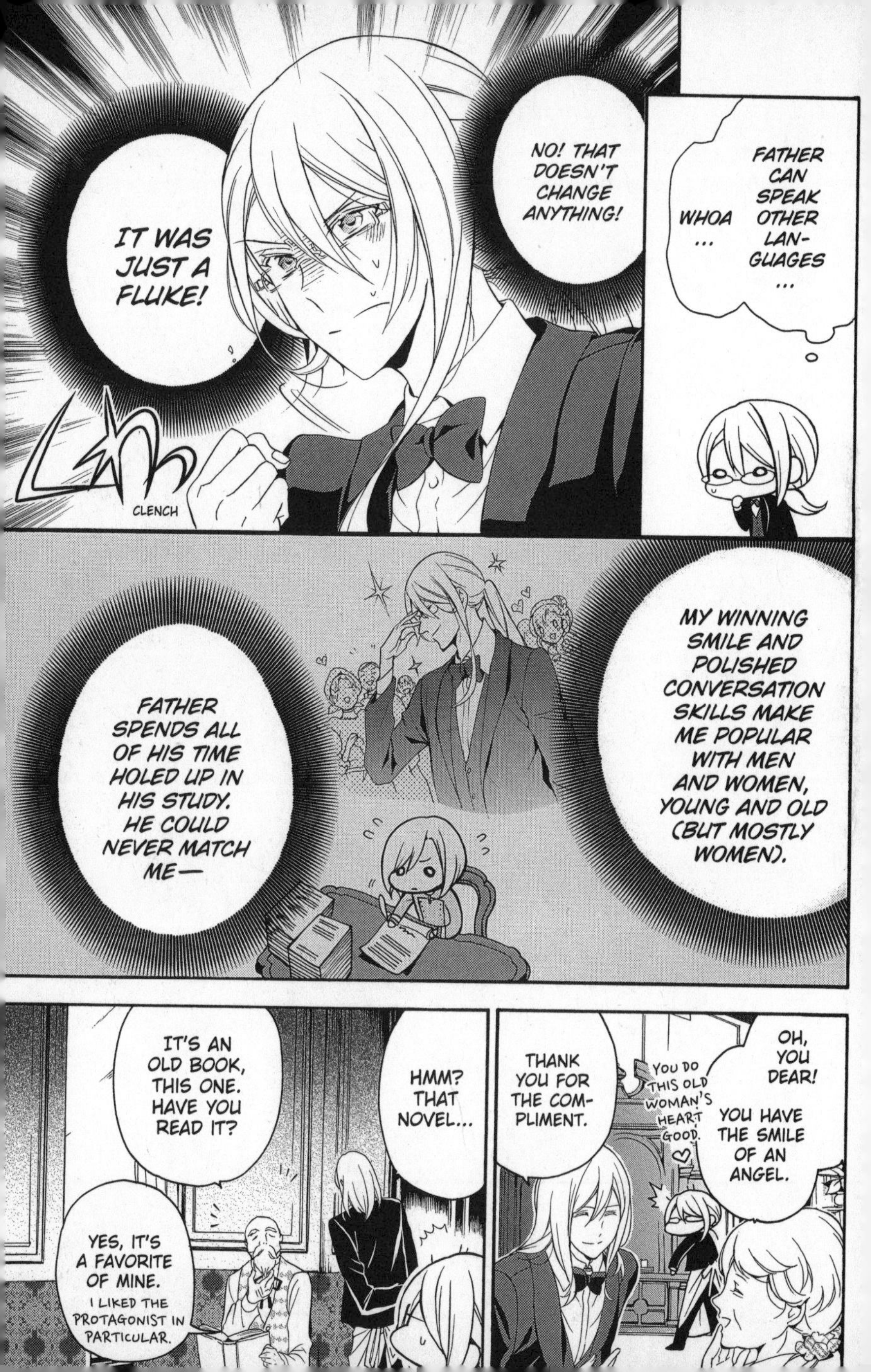
FATHER CAN SPEAK OTHER LAN-GUAGES...
WHOA...
NO! THAT DOESN'T CHANGE ANYTHING!
IT WAS JUST A FLUKE!
CLENCH
MY WINNING SMILE AND POLISHED CONVERSATION SKILLS MAKE ME POPULAR WITH MEN AND WOMEN, YOUNG AND OLD (BUT MOSTLY WOMEN).
FATHER SPENDS ALL OF HIS TIME HOLED UP IN HIS STUDY. HE COULD NEVER MATCH ME—
OH, YOU DEAR!
YOU HAVE THE SMILE OF AN ANGEL.
YOU DO THIS OLD WOMAN'S HEART GOOD.
THANK YOU FOR THE COM-PLIMENT.
HMM? THAT NOVEL...
IT'S AN OLD BOOK, THIS ONE. HAVE YOU READ IT?
YES, IT'S A FAVORITE OF MINE.
I LIKED THE PROTAGONIST IN PARTICULAR.

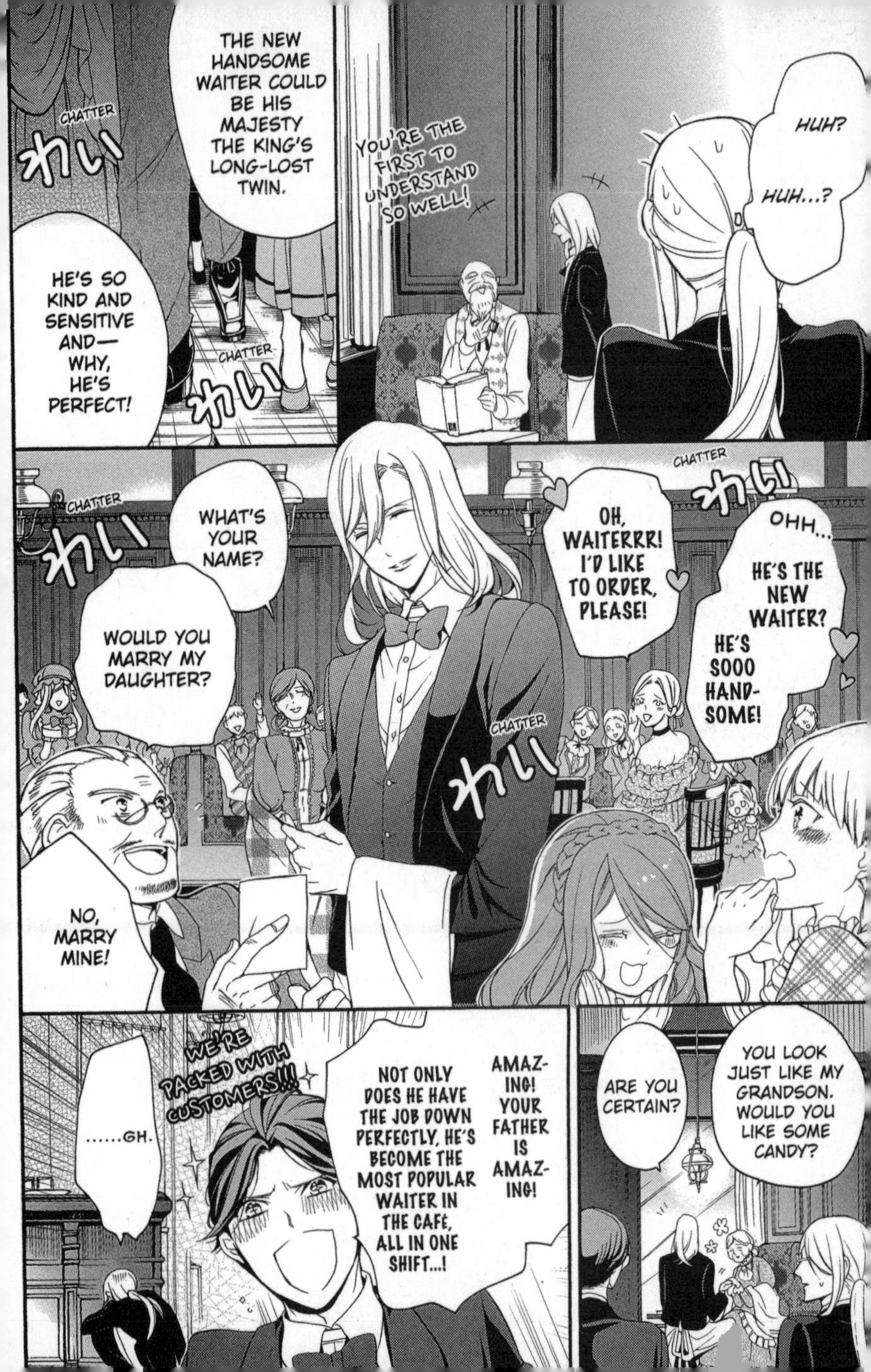
HUH?
HUH...?
YOU'RE THE FIRST TO UNDERSTAND SO WELL!
CHATTER
わい
THE NEW HANDSOME WAITER COULD BE HIS MAJESTY THE KING'S LONG-LOST TWIN.
HE'S SO KIND AND SENSITIVE AND— WHY, HE'S PERFECT!
CHATTER
わい
CHATTER
わい
OHH...
HE'S THE NEW WAITER?
HE'S SOOO HANDSOME!
OH, WAITERRR! I'D LIKE TO ORDER, PLEASE!
WHAT'S YOUR NAME?
CHATTER
わい
WOULD YOU MARRY MY DAUGHTER?
CHATTER
わい
NO, MARRY MINE!
YOU LOOK JUST LIKE MY GRANDSON. WOULD YOU LIKE SOME CANDY?
ARE YOU CERTAIN?
AMAZ-ING! YOUR FATHER IS AMAZ-ING!
NOT ONLY DOES HE HAVE THE JOB DOWN PERFECTLY, HE'S BECOME THE MOST POPULAR WAITER IN THE CAFÉ, ALL IN ONE SHIFT...!
WE'RE PACKED WITH CUSTOMERS!!!
......GH.

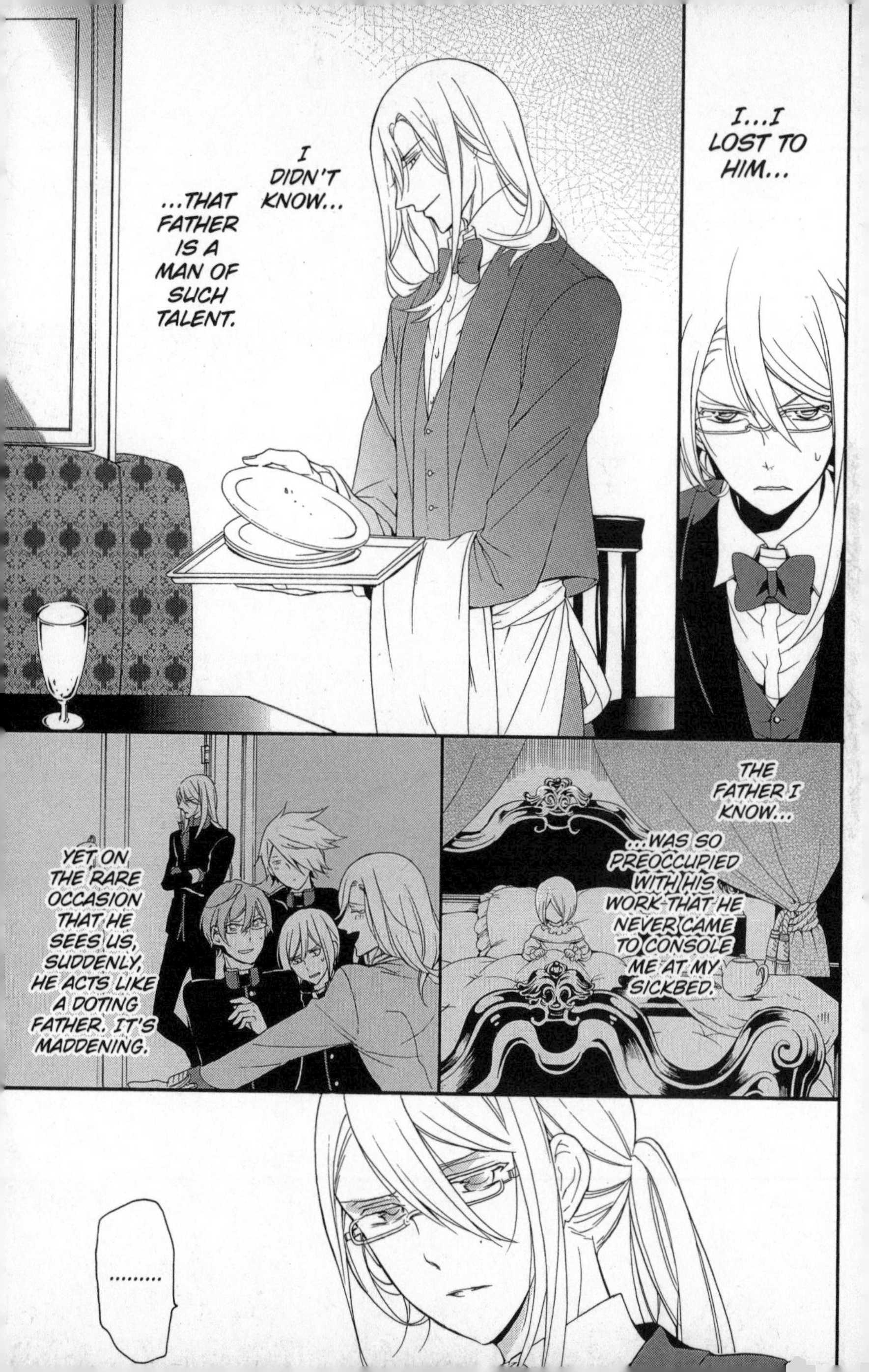
I...I LOST TO HIM...
I DIDN'T KNOW...
...THAT FATHER IS A MAN OF SUCH TALENT.
THE FATHER I KNOW...
...WAS SO PREOCCUPIED WITH HIS WORK THAT HE NEVER CAME TO CONSOLE ME AT MY SICKBED.
YET ON THE RARE OCCASION THAT HE SEES US, SUDDENLY, HE ACTS LIKE A DOTING FATHER. IT'S MADDENING.
....

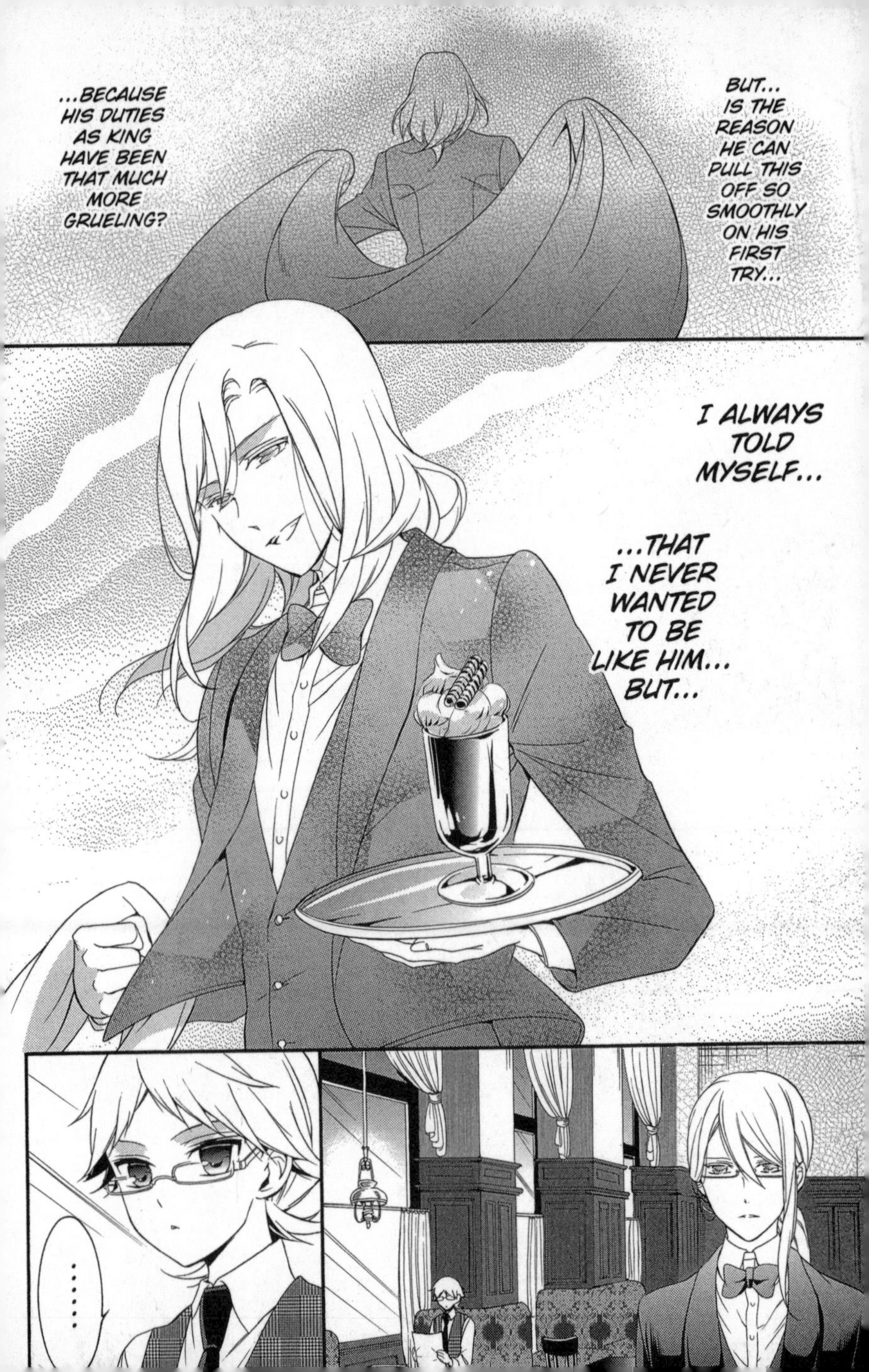
BUT... IS THE REASON HE CAN PULL THIS OFF SO SMOOTHLY ON HIS FIRST TRY...
...BECAUSE HIS DUTIES AS KING HAVE BEEN THAT MUCH MORE GRUELING?
I ALWAYS TOLD MYSELF...
...THAT I NEVER WANTED TO BE LIKE HIM... BUT...
......

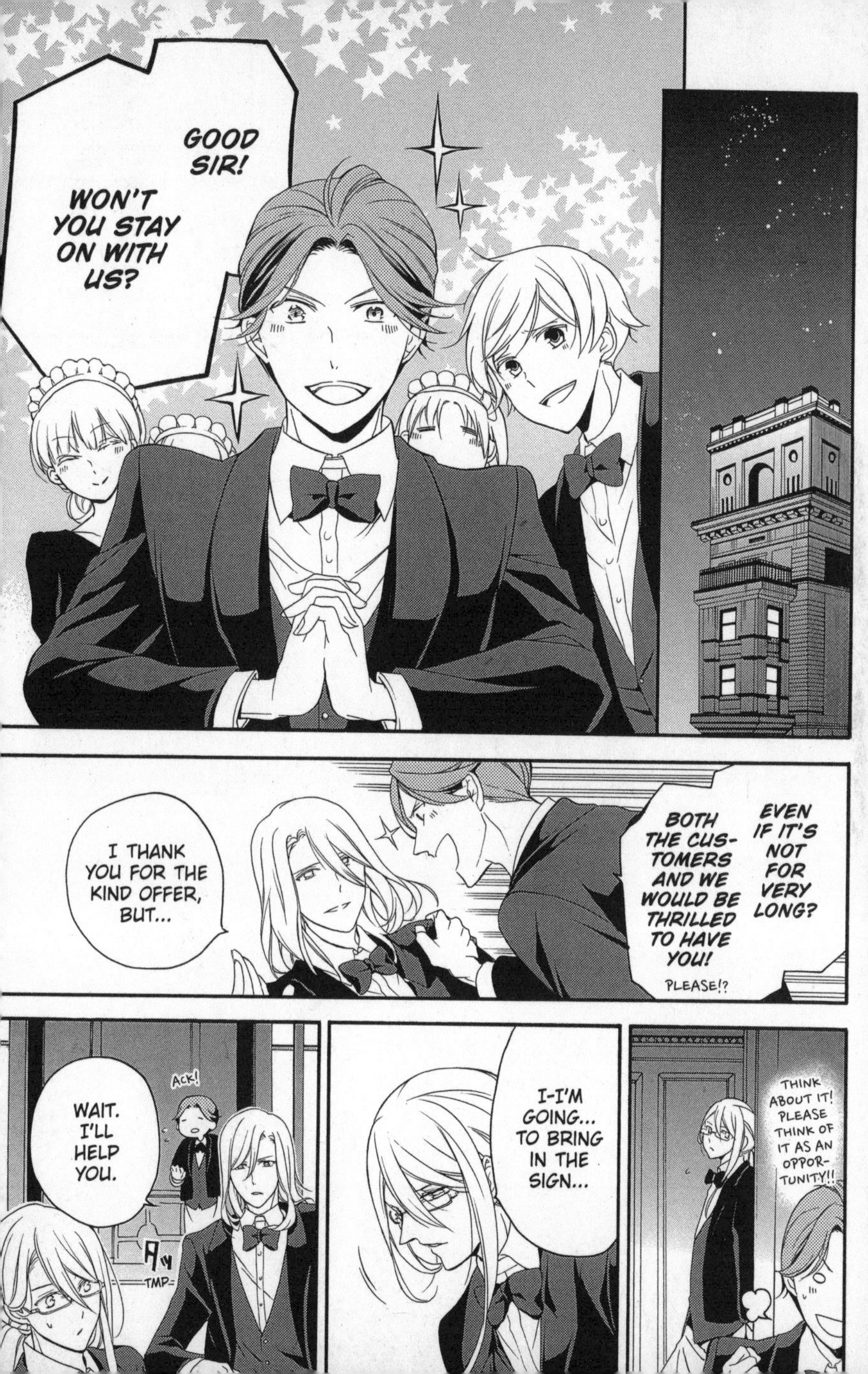
GOOD SIR!
WON'T YOU STAY ON WITH US?
EVEN IF IT'S NOT FOR VERY LONG?
BOTH THE CUSTOMERS AND WE WOULD BE THRILLED TO HAVE YOU!
PLEASE!?
I THANK YOU FOR THE KIND OFFER, BUT...
THINK ABOUT IT! PLEASE THINK OF IT AS AN OPPORTUNITY!!
I-I'M GOING... TO BRING IN THE SIGN...
ACK!
WAIT. I'LL HELP YOU.
TMP

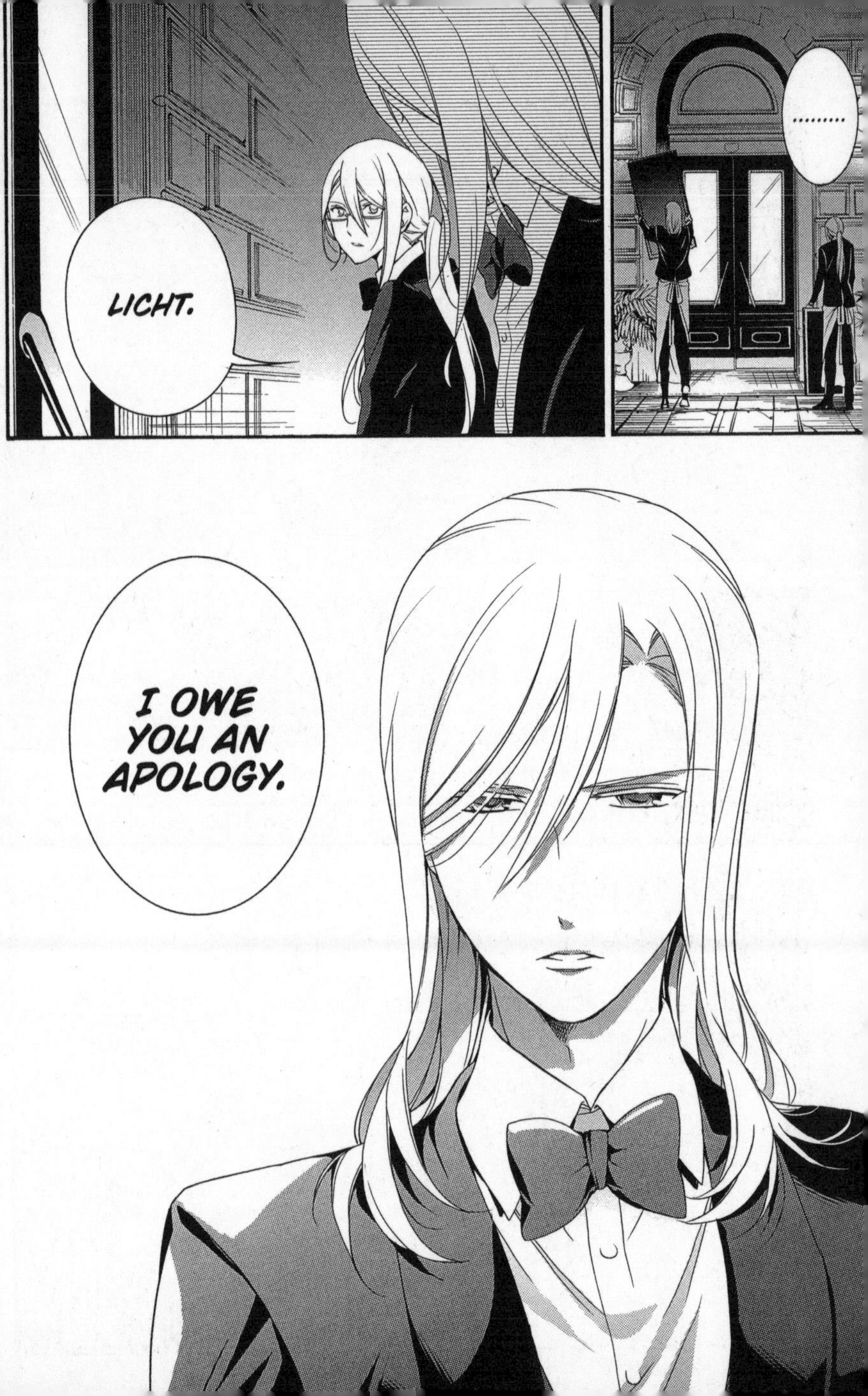
....
LICHT.
I OWE YOU AN APOLOGY.

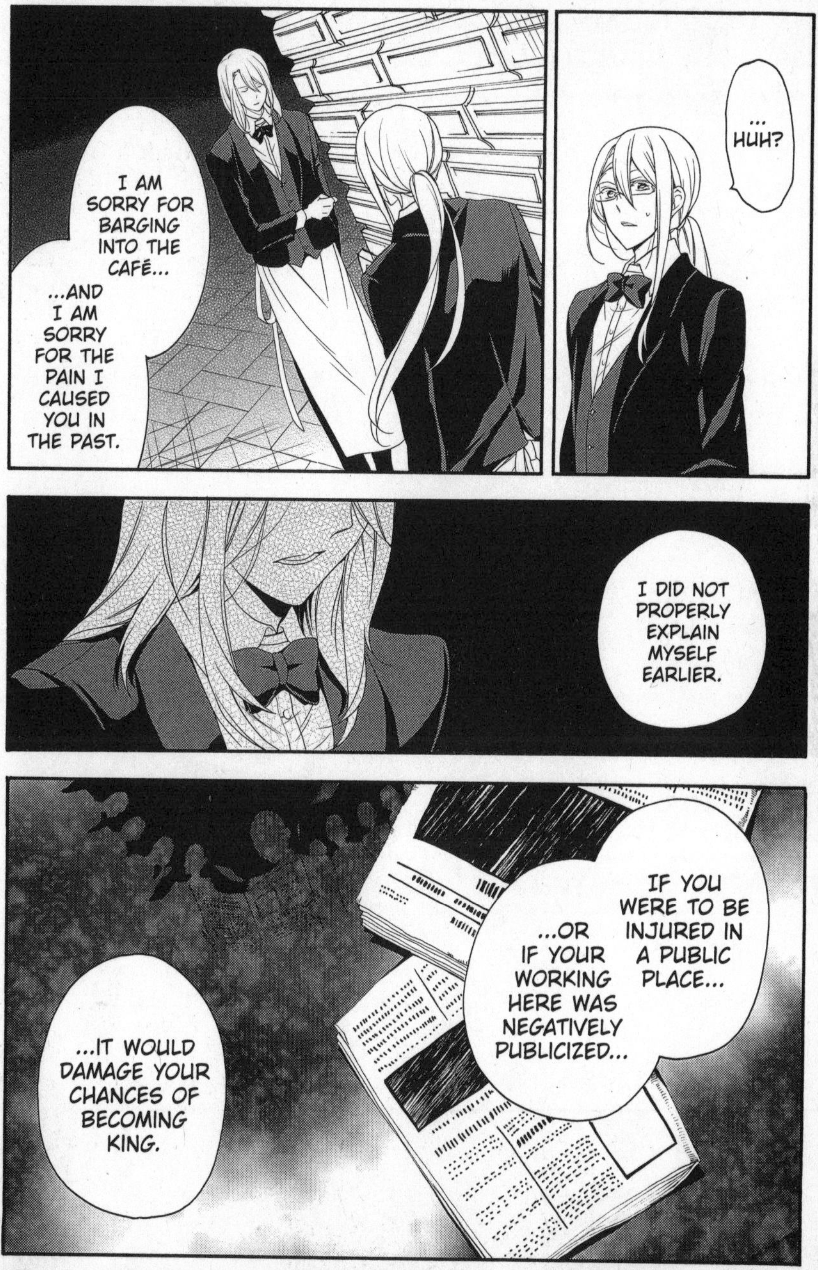
...HUH?
I AM SORRY FOR BARGING INTO THE CAFÉ...
...AND I AM SORRY FOR THE PAIN I CAUSED YOU IN THE PAST.
I DID NOT PROPERLY EXPLAIN MYSELF EARLIER.
IF YOU WERE TO BE INJURED IN A PUBLIC PLACE...
...OR IF YOUR WORKING HERE WAS NEGATIVELY PUBLICIZED...
...IT WOULD DAMAGE YOUR CHANCES OF BECOMING KING.

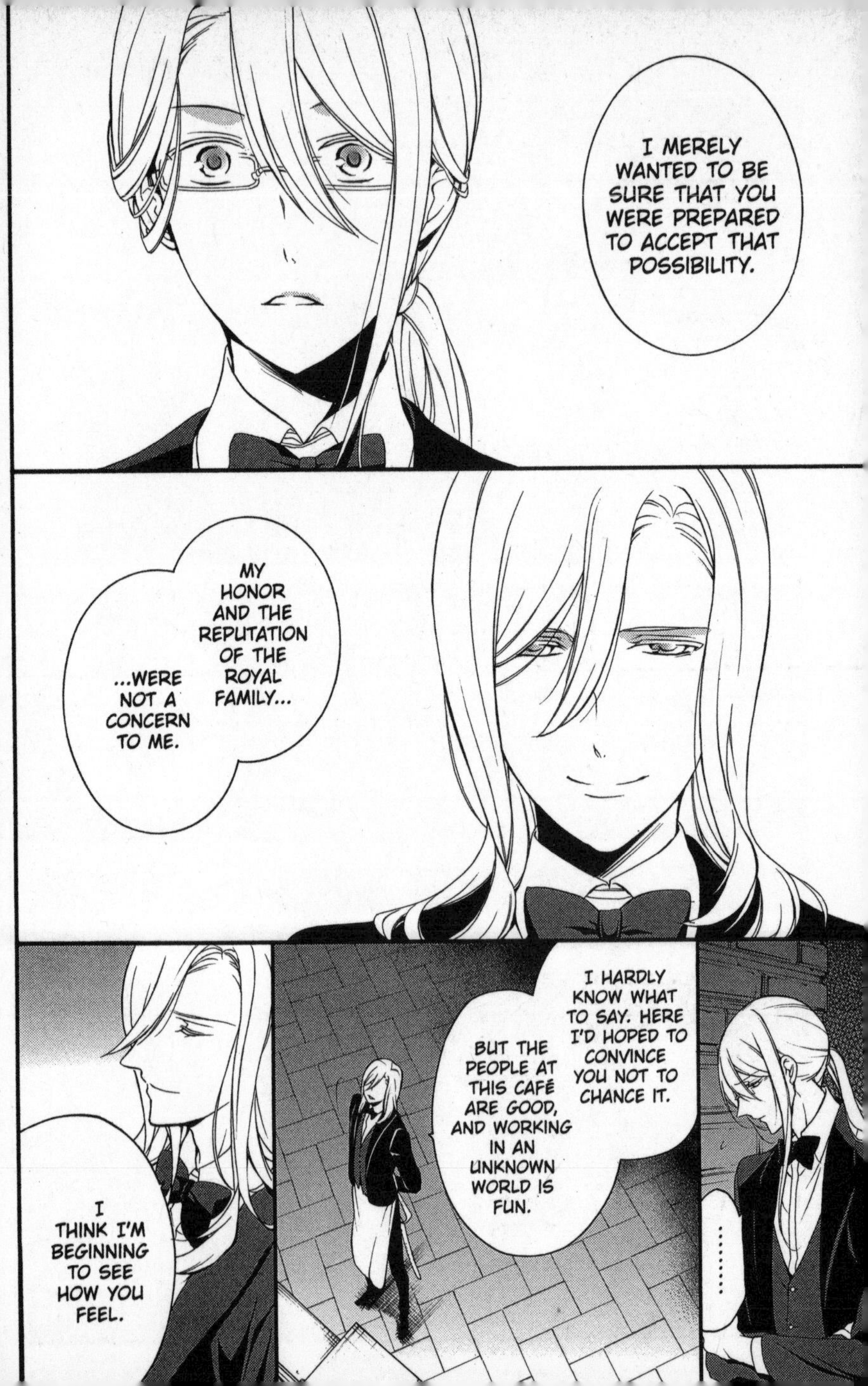
I MERELY WANTED TO BE SURE THAT YOU WERE PREPARED TO ACCEPT THAT POSSIBILITY.
MY HONOR AND THE REPUTATION OF THE ROYAL FAMILY...
...WERE NOT A CONCERN TO ME.
......
I HARDLY KNOW WHAT TO SAY. HERE I'D HOPED TO CONVINCE YOU NOT TO CHANCE IT.
BUT THE PEOPLE AT THIS CAFÉ ARE GOOD, AND WORKING IN AN UNKNOWN WORLD IS FUN.
I THINK I'M BEGINNING TO SEE HOW YOU FEEL.

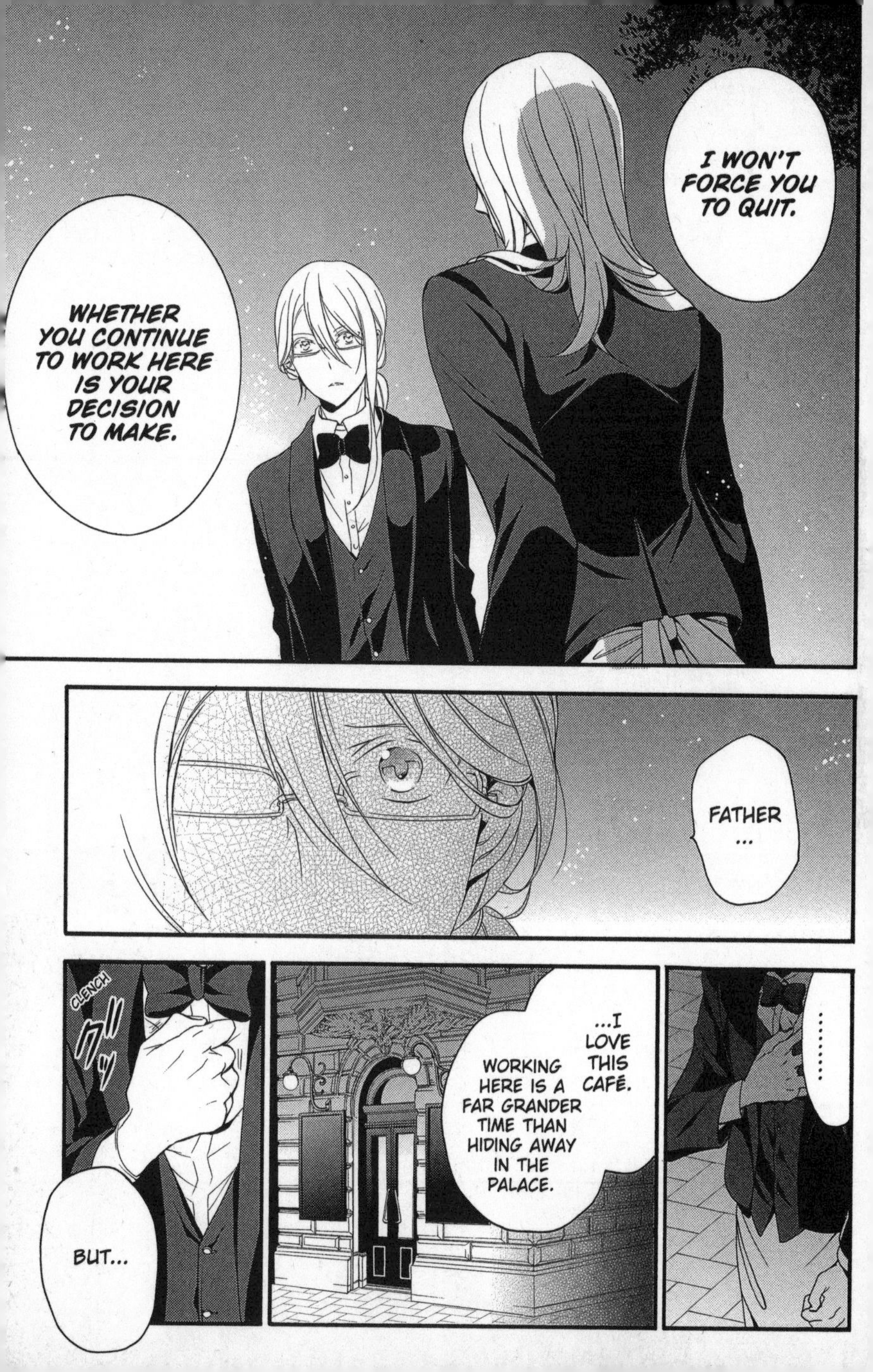
I WON'T FORCE YOU TO QUIT.
WHETHER YOU CONTINUE TO WORK HERE IS YOUR DECISION TO MAKE.
FATHER ...
......
...I LOVE THIS CAFÉ.
WORKING HERE IS A FAR GRANDER TIME THAN HIDING AWAY IN THE PALACE.
CLENCH
グッ
BUT...

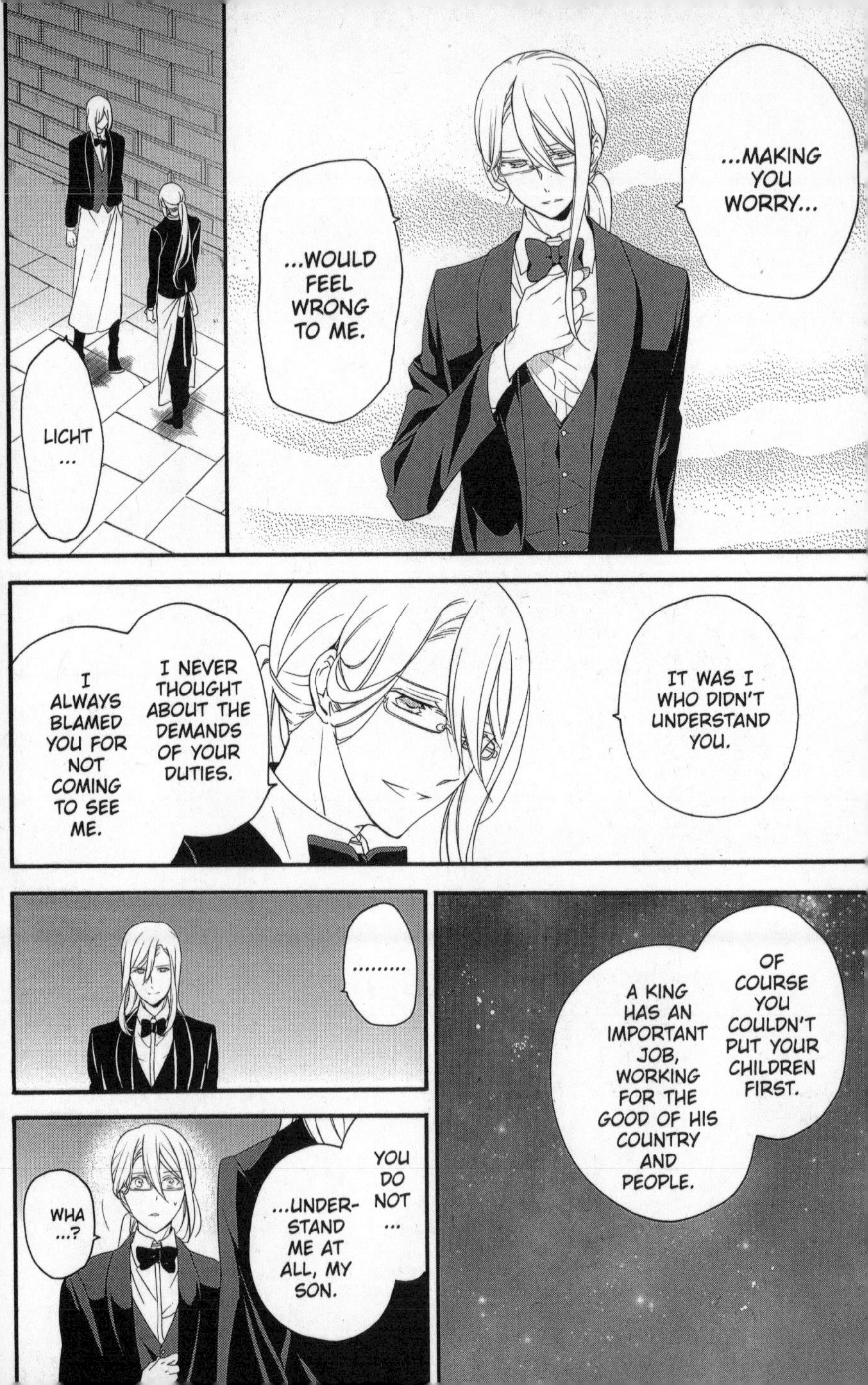
...MAKING YOU WORRY...
...WOULD FEEL WRONG TO ME.
LICHT ...
IT WAS I WHO DIDN'T UNDERSTAND YOU.
I NEVER THOUGHT ABOUT THE DEMANDS OF YOUR DUTIES.
I ALWAYS BLAMED YOU FOR NOT COMING TO SEE ME.
OF COURSE YOU COULDN'T PUT YOUR CHILDREN FIRST.
A KING HAS AN IMPORTANT JOB, WORKING FOR THE GOOD OF HIS COUNTRY AND PEOPLE.
....
YOU DO NOT ...
...UNDER-STAND ME AT ALL, MY SON.
WHA ...?

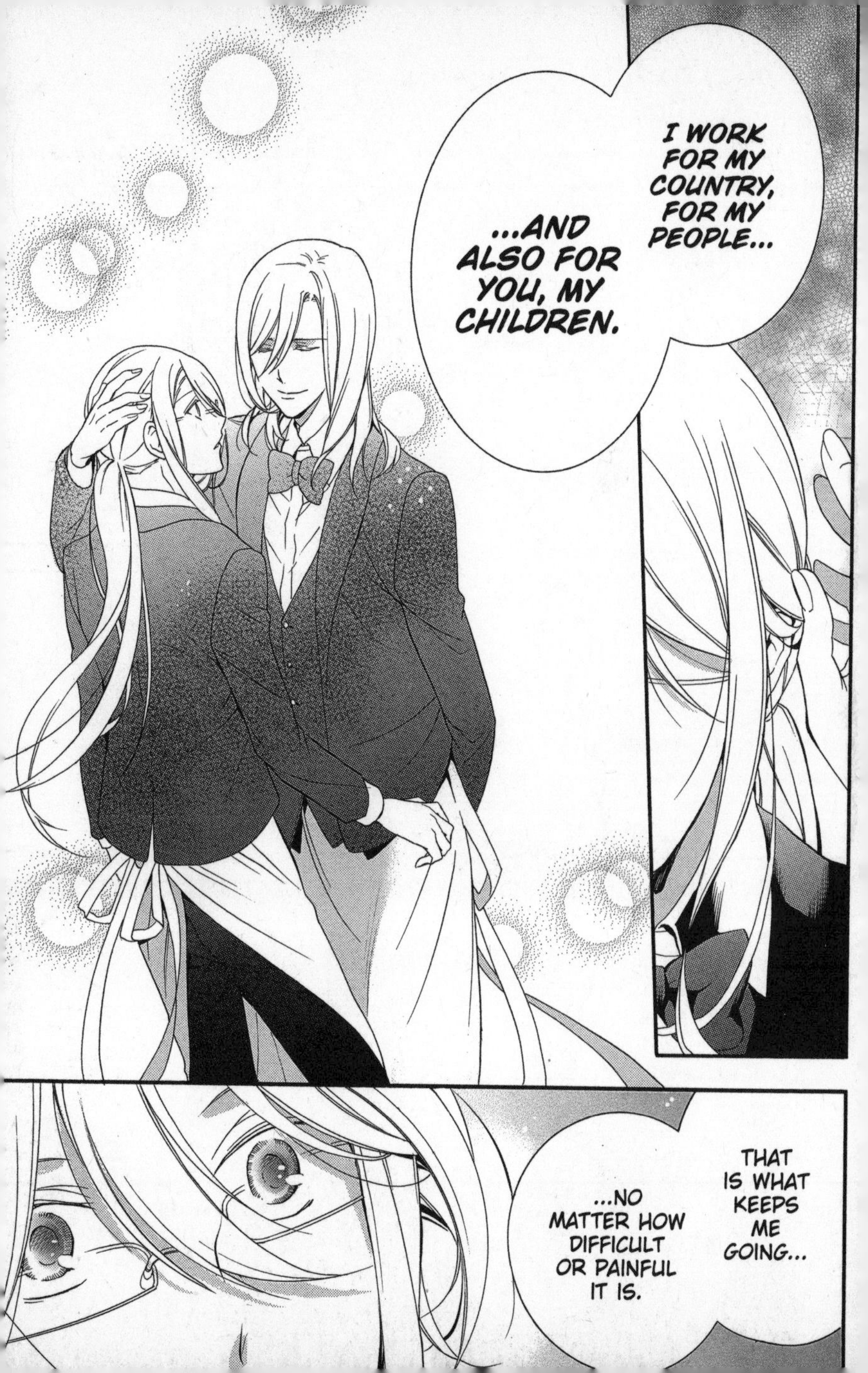
I WORK FOR MY COUNTRY, FOR MY PEOPLE...
...AND ALSO FOR YOU, MY CHILDREN.
THAT IS WHAT KEEPS ME GOING...
...NO MATTER HOW DIFFICULT OR PAINFUL IT IS.

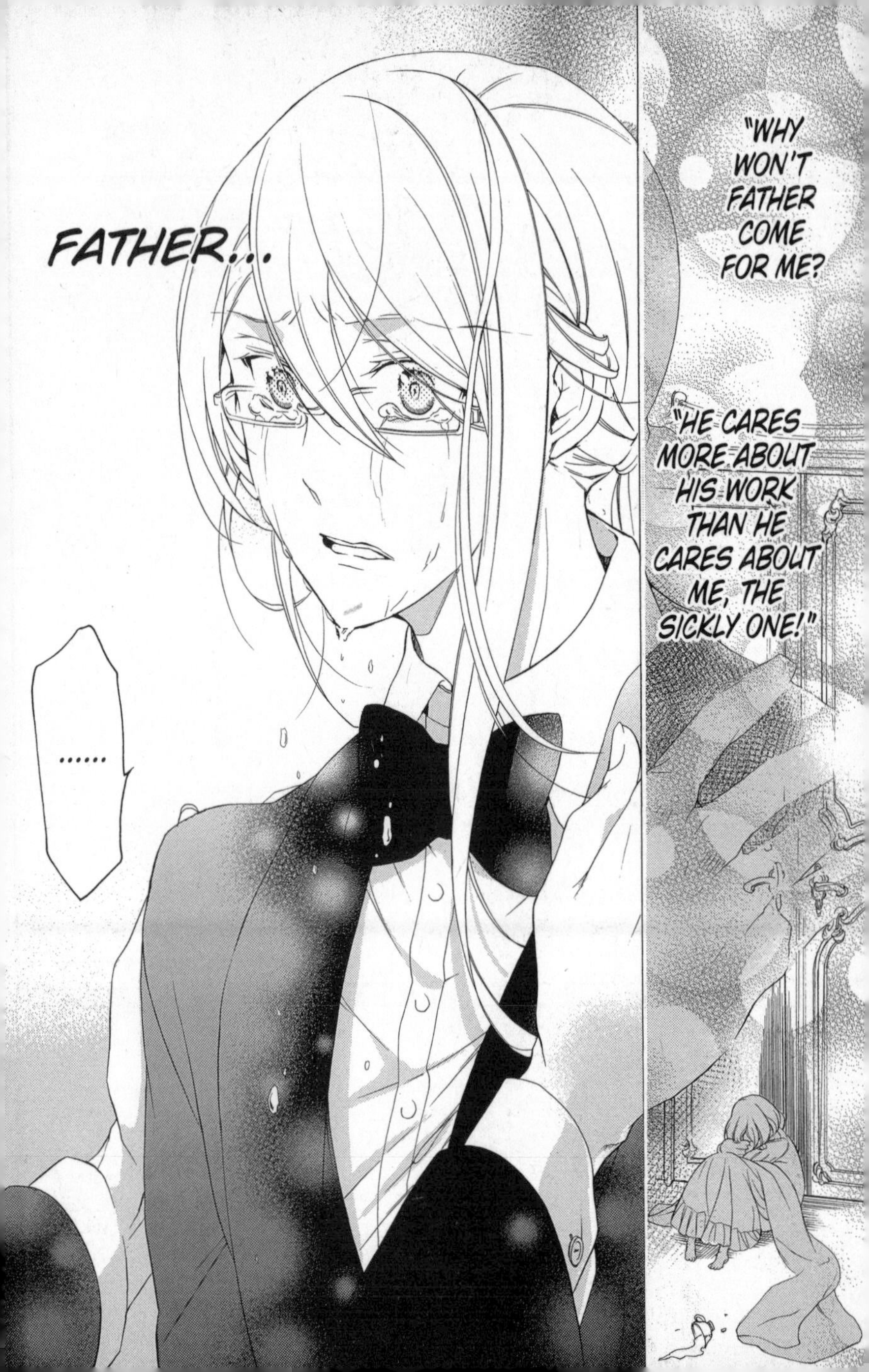
"WHY WON'T FATHER COME FOR ME?
"HE CARES MORE ABOUT HIS WORK THAN HE CARES ABOUT ME, THE SICKLY ONE!"
FATHER...
......

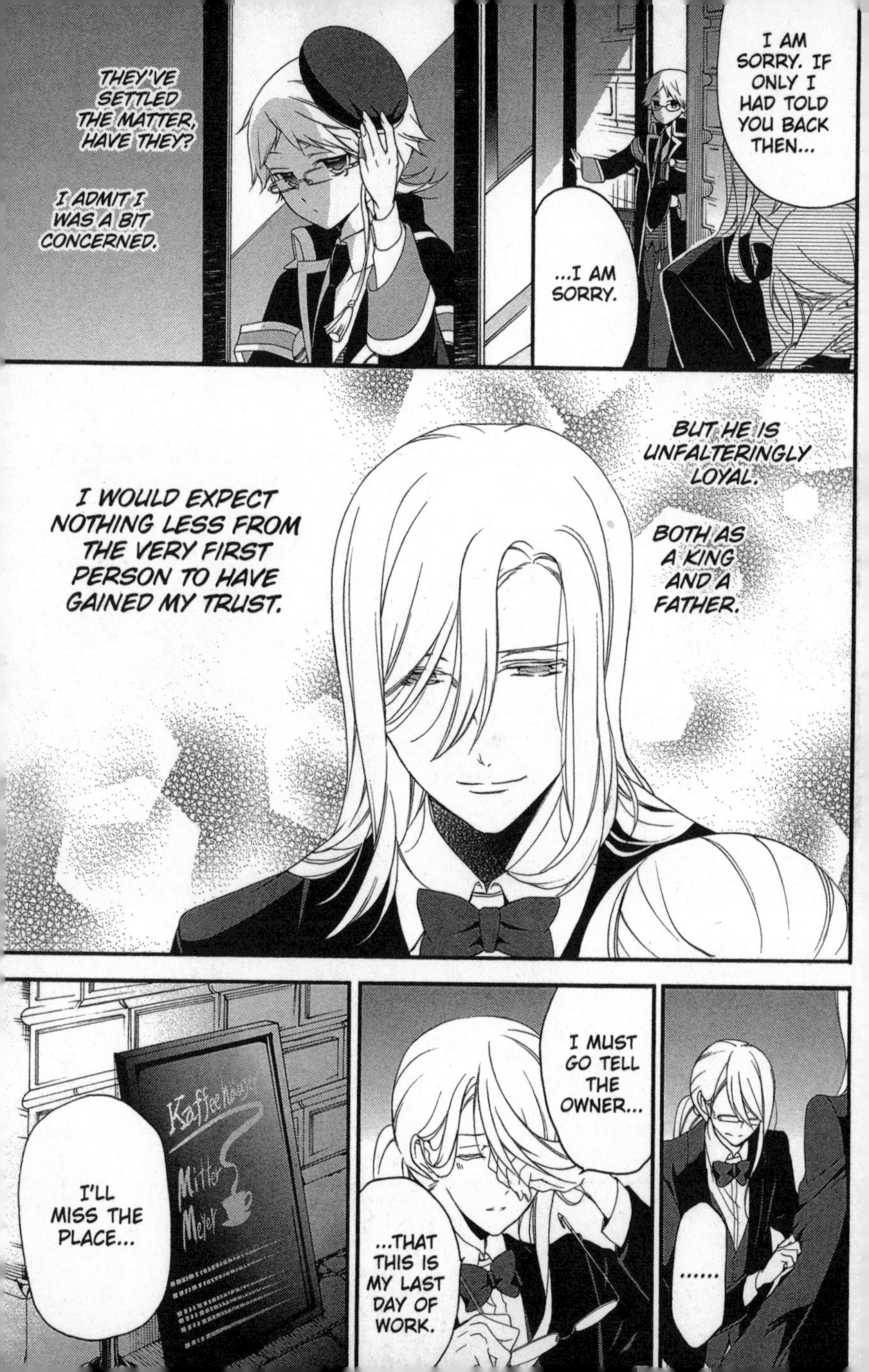
I AM SORRY. IF ONLY I HAD TOLD YOU BACK THEN...
...I AM SORRY.
THEY'VE SETTLED THE MATTER, HAVE THEY?
I ADMIT I WAS A BIT CONCERNED.
BUT HE IS UNFALTERINGLY LOYAL.
BOTH AS A KING AND A FATHER.
I WOULD EXPECT NOTHING LESS FROM THE VERY FIRST PERSON TO HAVE GAINED MY TRUST.
......
I MUST GO TELL THE OWNER...
...THAT THIS IS MY LAST DAY OF WORK.
I'LL MISS THE PLACE...

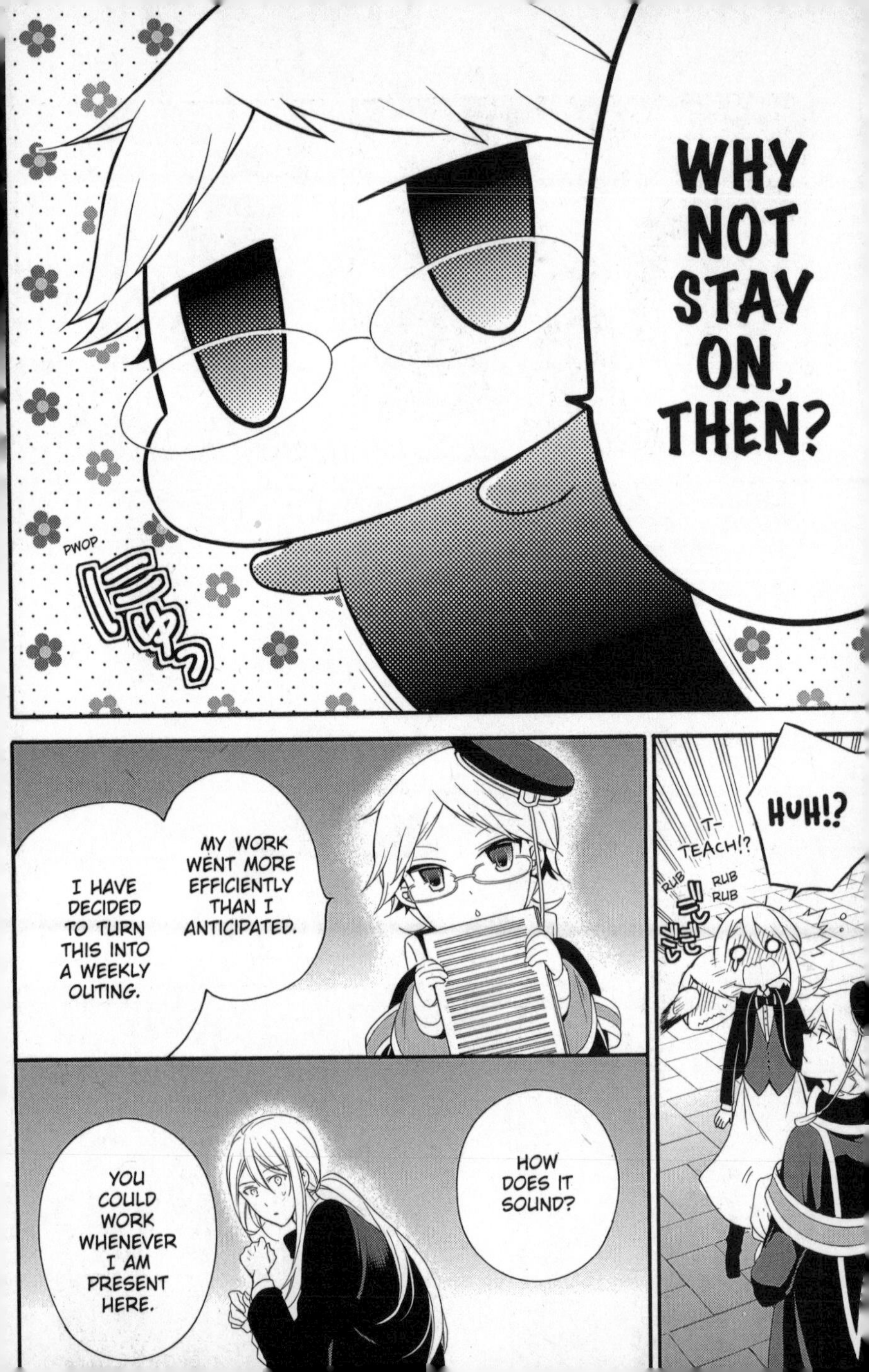
WHY NOT STAY ON, THEN?
PWOP
にゅっ
HUH!?
T-TEACH!?
RUB
RUB RUB
MY WORK WENT MORE EFFICIENTLY THAN I ANTICIPATED.
I HAVE DECIDED TO TURN THIS INTO A WEEKLY OUTING.
HOW DOES IT SOUND?
YOU COULD WORK WHENEVER I AM PRESENT HERE.

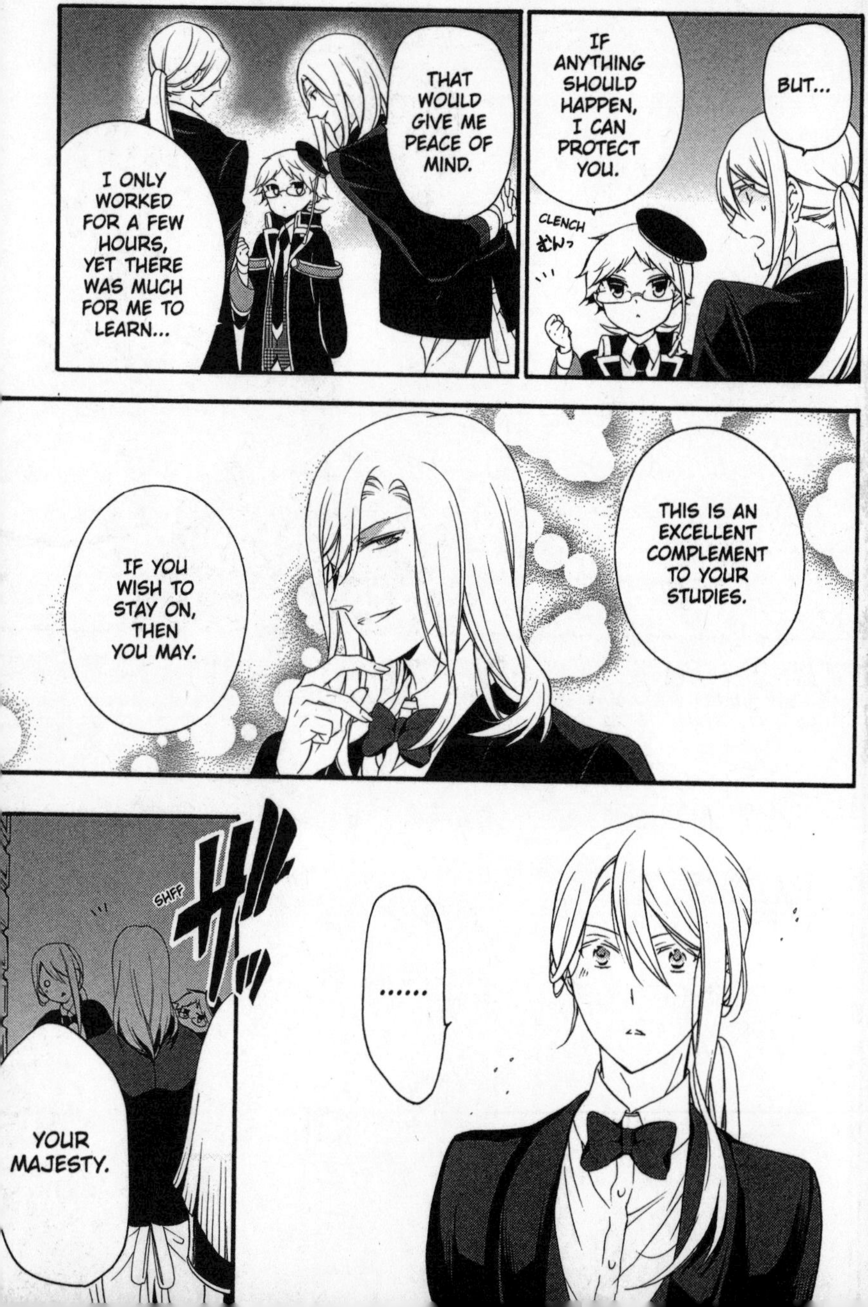
BUT...
IF ANYTHING SHOULD HAPPEN, I CAN PROTECT YOU.
CLENCH
むんっ
THAT WOULD GIVE ME PEACE OF MIND.
I ONLY WORKED FOR A FEW HOURS, YET THERE WAS MUCH FOR ME TO LEARN...
THIS IS AN EXCELLENT COMPLEMENT TO YOUR STUDIES.
IF YOU WISH TO STAY ON, THEN YOU MAY.
......
SHFF
YOUR MAJESTY.

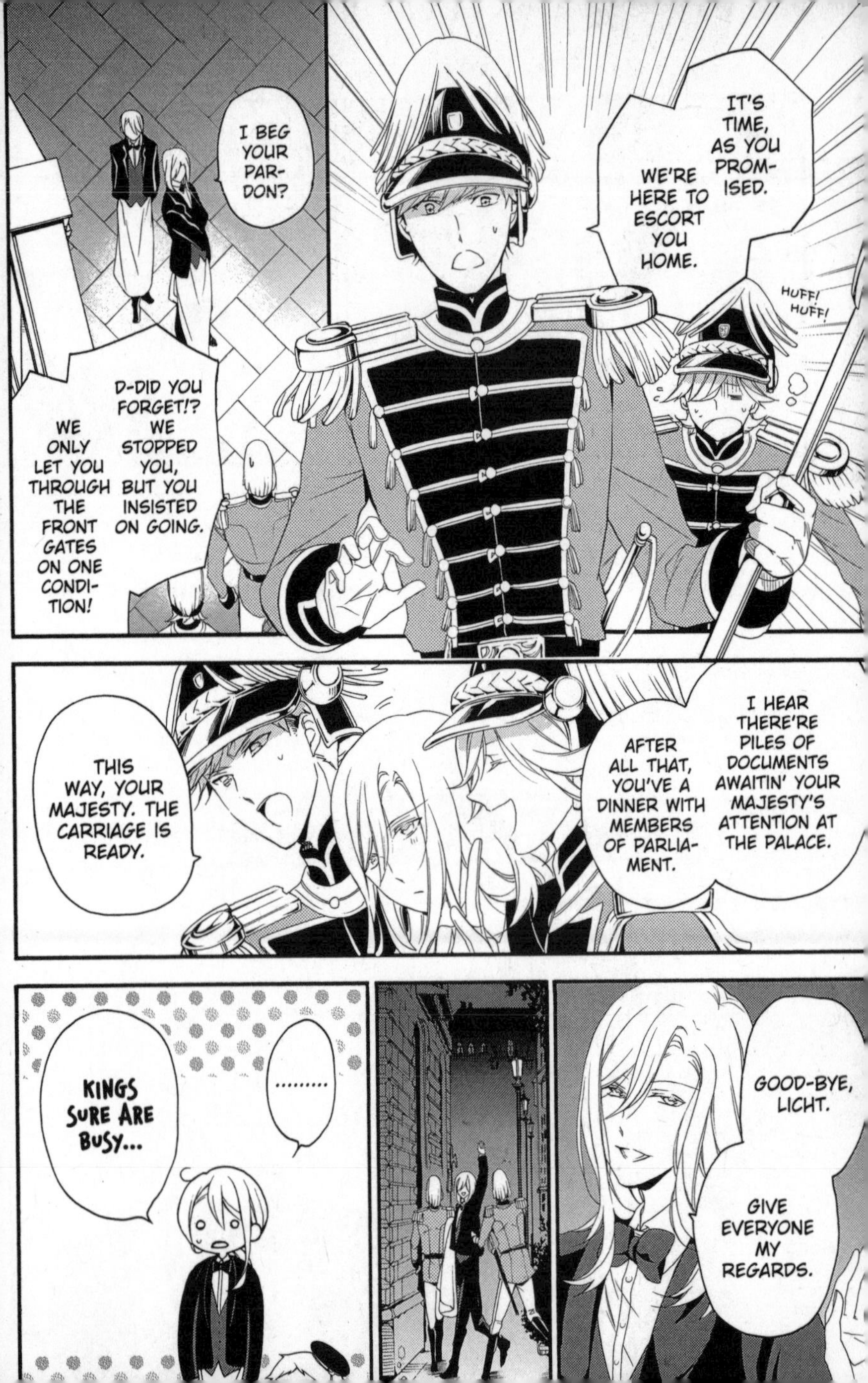
IT'S TIME, AS YOU PROMISED.
WE'RE HERE TO ESCORT YOU HOME.
HUFF! HUFF!
I BEG YOUR PARDON?
D-DID YOU FORGET!? WE STOPPED YOU, BUT YOU INSISTED ON GOING.
WE ONLY LET YOU THROUGH THE FRONT GATES ON ONE CONDITION!
I HEAR THERE'RE PILES OF DOCUMENTS AWAITIN' YOUR MAJESTY'S ATTENTION AT THE PALACE.
AFTER ALL THAT, YOU'VE A DINNER WITH MEMBERS OF PARLIAMENT.
THIS WAY, YOUR MAJESTY. THE CARRIAGE IS READY.
GOOD-BYE, LICHT.
GIVE EVERYONE MY REGARDS.
....
KINGS SURE ARE BUSY...

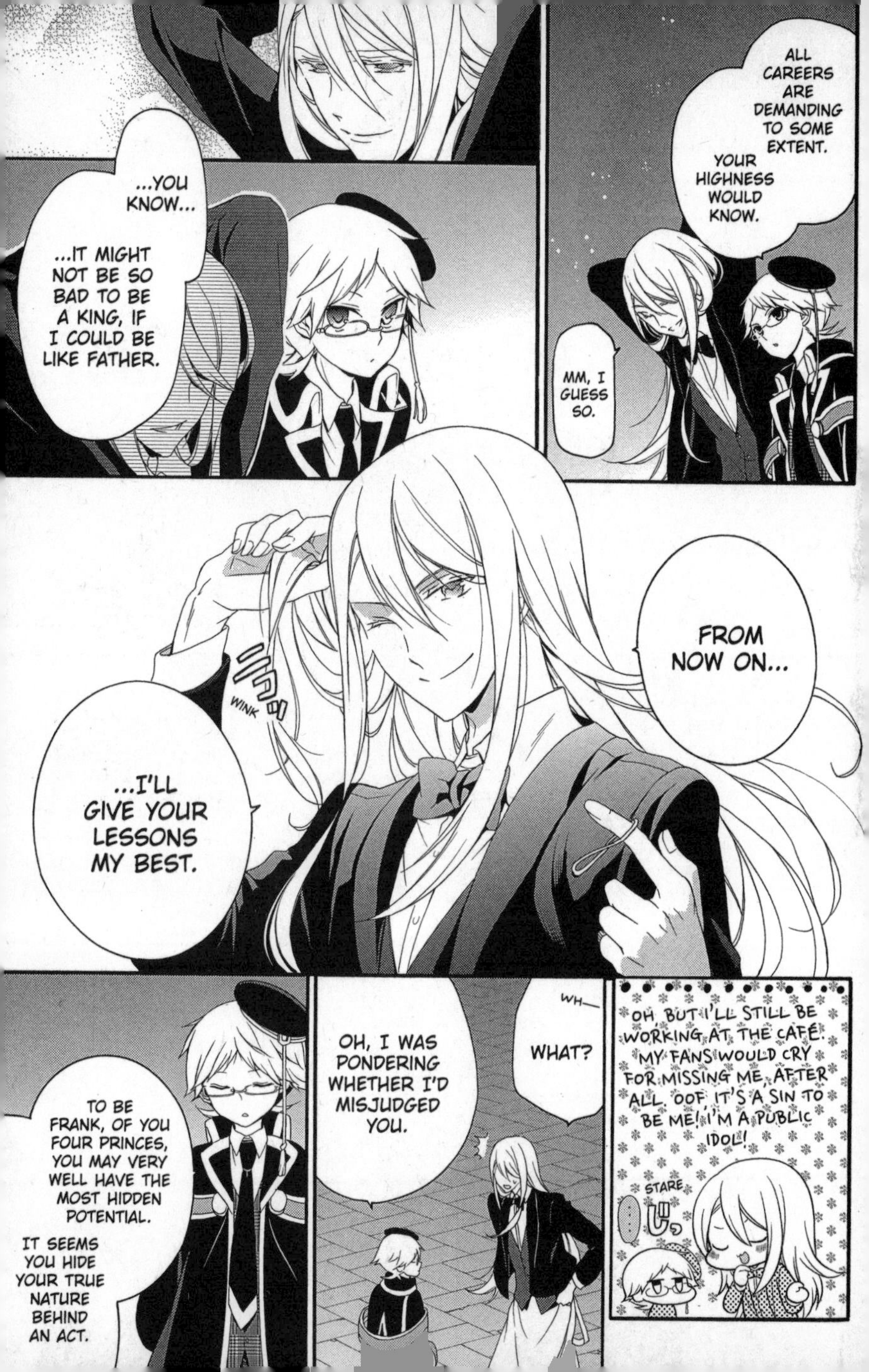
ALL CAREERS ARE DEMANDING TO SOME EXTENT.
YOUR HIGHNESS WOULD KNOW.
MM, I GUESS SO.
...YOU KNOW...
...IT MIGHT NOT BE SO BAD TO BE A KING, IF I COULD BE LIKE FATHER.
FROM NOW ON...
WINK
...I'LL GIVE YOUR LESSONS MY BEST.
OH, BUT I'LL STILL BE WORKING AT THE CAFÉ. MY FANS WOULD CRY FOR MISSING ME, AFTER ALL. OOF, IT'S A SIN TO BE ME! I'M A PUBLIC IDOL!
STARE
...
WH—
WHAT?
OH, I WAS PONDERING WHETHER I'D MISJUDGED YOU.
TO BE FRANK, OF YOU FOUR PRINCES, YOU MAY VERY WELL HAVE THE MOST HIDDEN POTENTIAL.
IT SEEMS YOU HIDE YOUR TRUE NATURE BEHIND AN ACT.

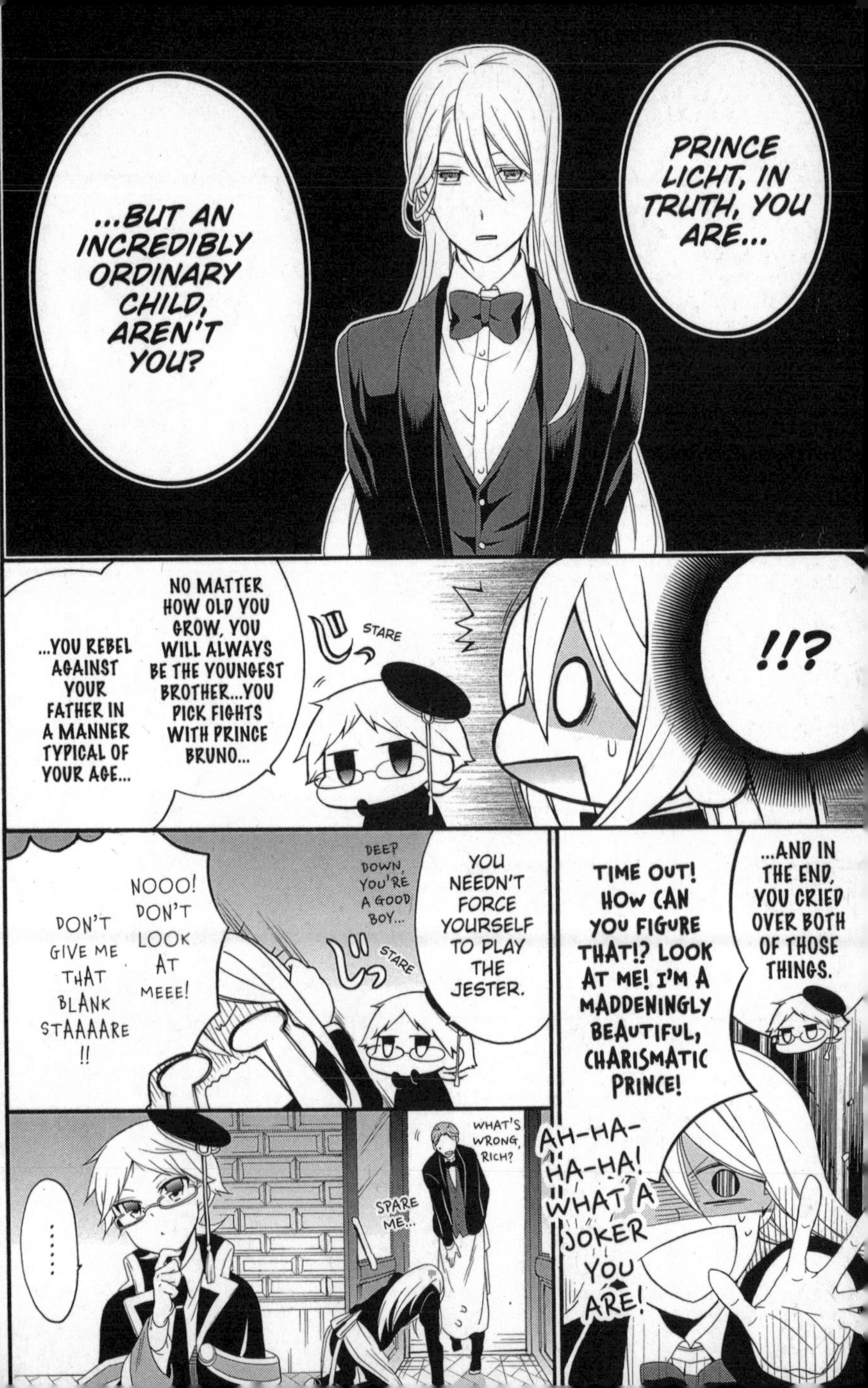

PRINCE LICHT, IN TRUTH, YOU ARE...
...BUT AN INCREDIBLY ORDINARY CHILD, AREN'T YOU?
!!?
STARE
NO MATTER HOW OLD YOU GROW, YOU WILL ALWAYS BE THE YOUNGEST BROTHER...YOU PICK FIGHTS WITH PRINCE BRUNO...
...YOU REBEL AGAINST YOUR FATHER IN A MANNER TYPICAL OF YOUR AGE...
...AND IN THE END, YOU CRIED OVER BOTH OF THOSE THINGS.
TIME OUT! HOW CAN YOU FIGURE THAT!? LOOK AT ME! I'M A MADDENINGLY BEAUTIFUL, CHARISMATIC PRINCE!
AH-HA-HA-HA!! WHAT A JOKER YOU ARE!
YOU NEEDN'T FORCE YOURSELF TO PLAY THE JESTER.
DEEP DOWN, YOU'RE A GOOD BOY...
STARE
NOOO! DON'T LOOK AT MEEE!
DON'T GIVE ME THAT BLANK STAAAARE!!
WHAT'S WRONG, RICH?
SPARE ME...
......

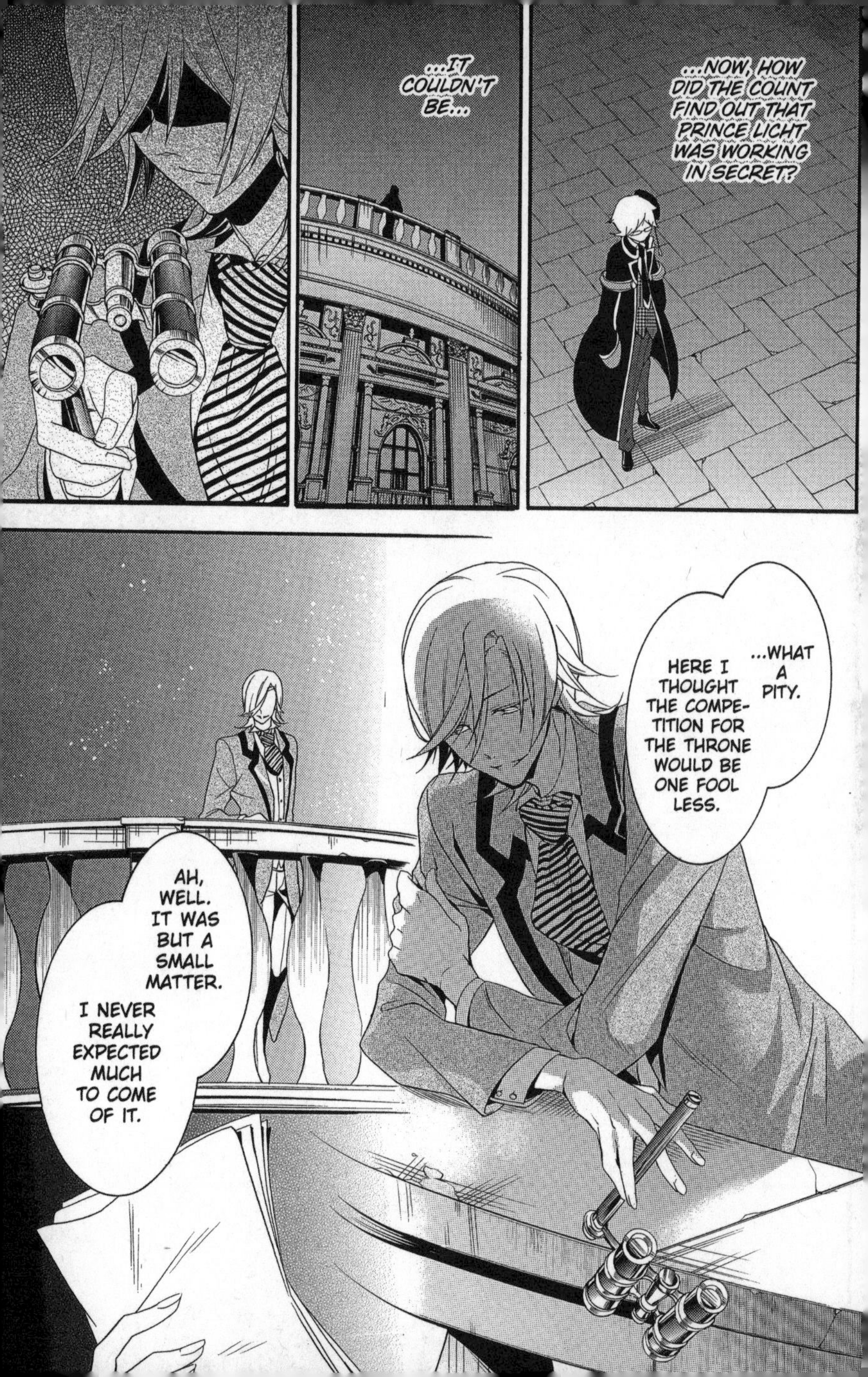
...NOW, HOW DID THE COUNT FIND OUT THAT PRINCE LICHT WAS WORKING IN SECRET?
...IT COULDN'T BE...
...WHAT A PITY.
HERE I THOUGHT THE COMPETITION FOR THE THRONE WOULD BE ONE FOOL LESS.
AH, WELL. IT WAS BUT A SMALL MATTER.
I NEVER REALLY EXPECTED MUCH TO COME OF IT.

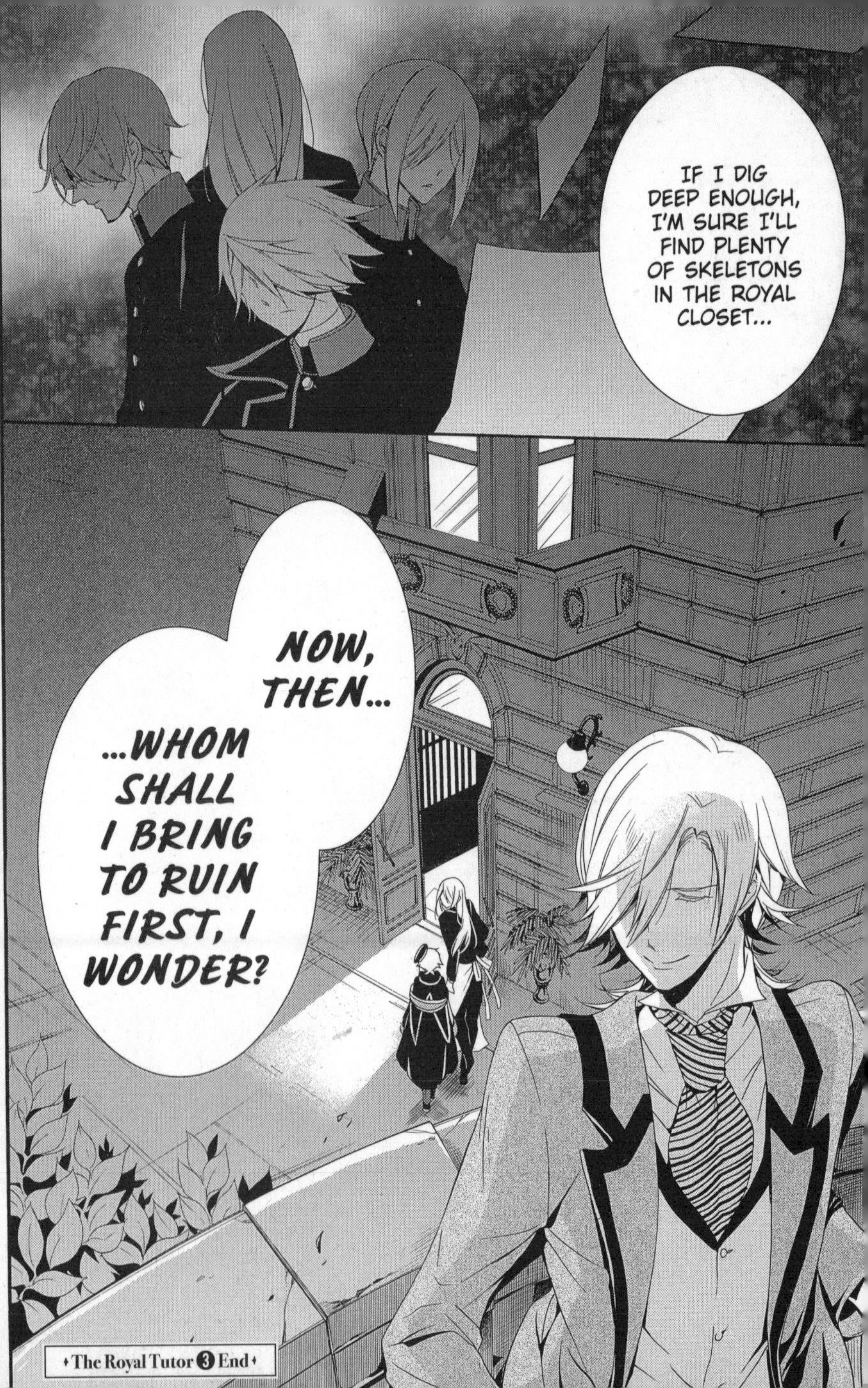
IF I DIG DEEP ENOUGH, I'M SURE I'LL FIND PLENTY OF SKELETONS IN THE ROYAL CLOSET...
NOW, THEN...
...WHOM SHALL I BRING TO RUIN FIRST, I WONDER?
The Royal Tutor 3 End

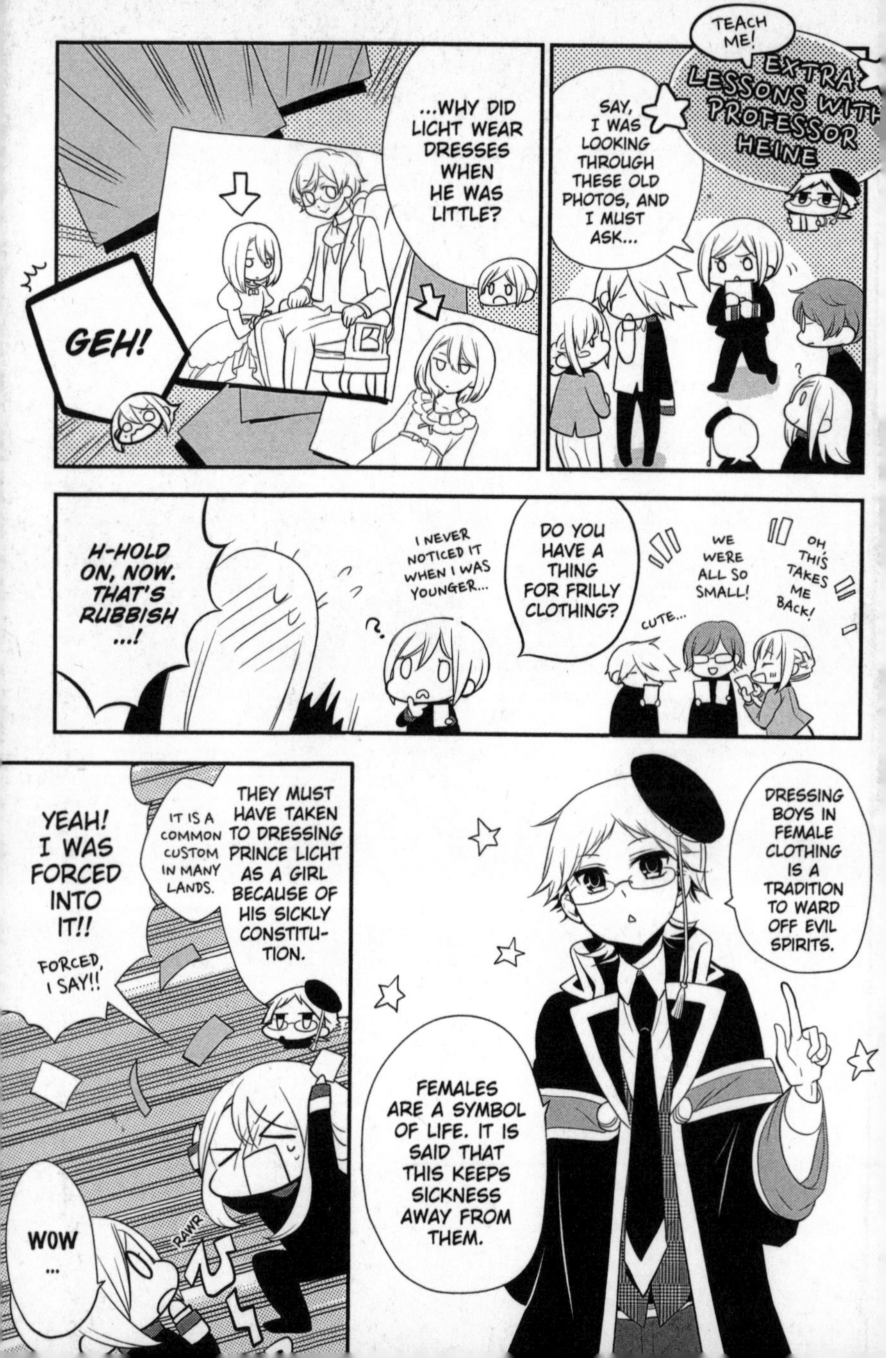
TEACH ME!
EXTRA LESSONS WITH PROFESSOR HEINE
SAY, I WAS LOOKING THROUGH THESE OLD PHOTOS, AND I MUST ASK...
...WHY DID LICHT WEAR DRESSES WHEN HE WAS LITTLE?
GEH!
OH THIS TAKES ME BACK!
WE WERE ALL SO SMALL!
CUTE...
DO YOU HAVE A THING FOR FRILLY CLOTHING?
I NEVER NOTICED IT WHEN I WAS YOUNGER...
H-HOLD ON, NOW. THAT'S RUBBISH...!
DRESSING BOYS IN FEMALE CLOTHING IS A TRADITION TO WARD OFF EVIL SPIRITS.
FEMALES ARE A SYMBOL OF LIFE. IT IS SAID THAT THIS KEEPS SICKNESS AWAY FROM THEM.
THEY MUST HAVE TAKEN TO DRESSING PRINCE LICHT AS A GIRL BECAUSE OF HIS SICKLY CONSTITUTION.
IT IS A COMMON CUSTOM IN MANY LANDS.
YEAH! I WAS FORCED INTO IT!!
FORCED, I SAY!!
RAWR
WOW...

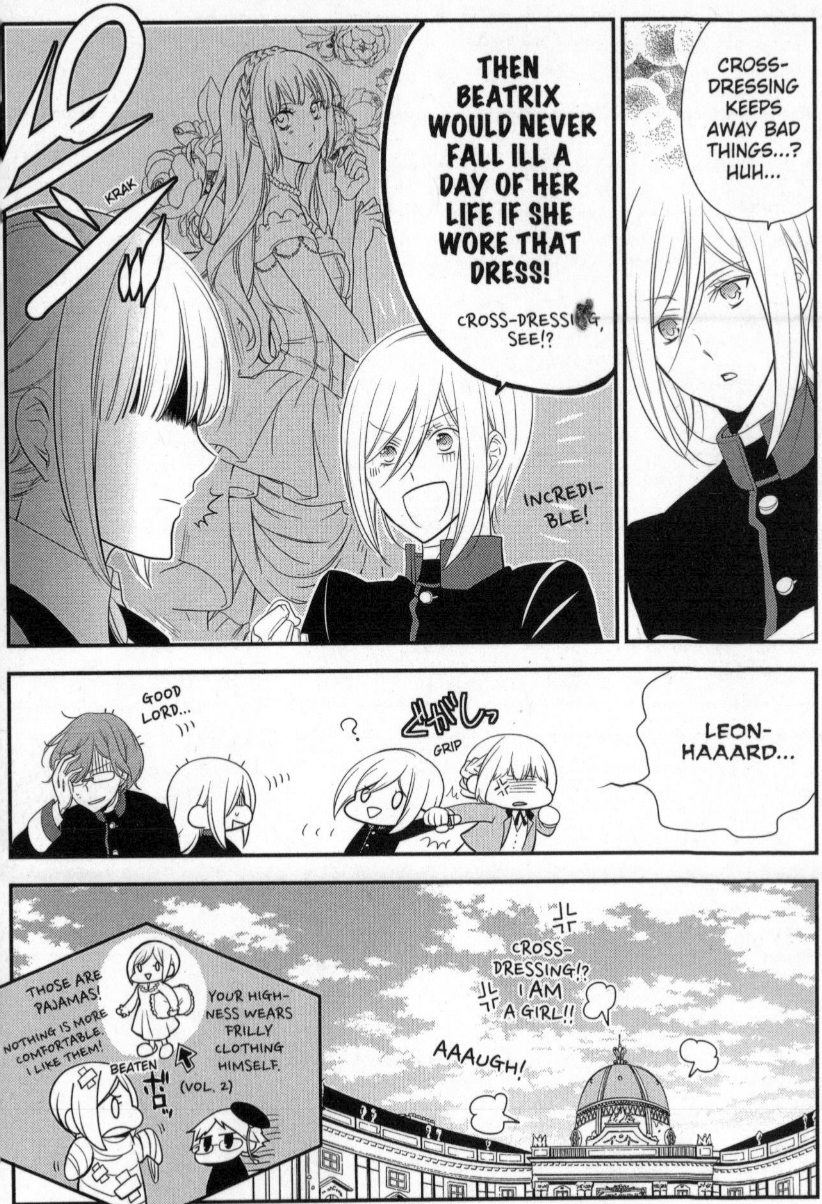
CROSS-DRESSING KEEPS AWAY BAD THINGS...? HUH...
THEN BEATRIX WOULD NEVER FALL ILL A DAY OF HER LIFE IF SHE WORE THAT DRESS!
KRAK
CROSS-DRESSING, SEE!?
INCREDI-BLE!
LEON-HAAARD...
どがしっ
GRIP
?
GOOD LORD...
CROSS-DRESSING!? I AM A GIRL!!
AAAUGH!
YOUR HIGH-NESS WEARS FRILLY CLOTHING HIMSELF.
(VOL. 2)
THOSE ARE PAJAMAS! NOTHING IS MORE COMFORTABLE. I LIKE THEM!
BEATEN

SPECIAL THANKS YOSHI KOUJU-SAN MY EDITOR, AKIYAMA-SAN

Translation Notes

Page 110
Einspänner: A double espresso topped with a dollop of whipped cream and extra sugar.

Kapuziner: As Licht explains, coffee topped with whipped cream.

Sacher torte: A famous Austrian dessert created by Franz Sacher in 1832 for the royal family. It is a chocolate cake with layers separated by apricot jam and is covered on the top and sides with a thick chocolate frosting.

Page 117
Schwarzer: An espresso served black (*schwarz* being the German word for "black").

Franziskaner: A *melange* (espresso mixed with hot foamed milk) topped with whipped cream instead of foamed milk.

Kardinalschnitten: German for "Cardinal Slice." A layered Viennese cake with a coffee-flavored cream filling. When sliced, its strips of white meringue and yellow sponge cake with the common addition of raspberry preserves resemble the robes of officials of the Catholic church, which is where it is thought to have gotten its name.

Germknödel: A yeast dough dumpling with plum jam inside, traditionally served topped with sugar and poppy seeds.

Kaiserschmarren: A pancake, shredded and fried, usually topped with powdered sugar.

Page 123
Fräulein: A form of address for unmarried women, although it has largely fallen out of use among present-day German speakers.

Page 124
Hau ruck: German for "heave-ho."

Page 168
Linzer torte: A short pastry from Linz, Austria, that has a jam filling and a lattice design on top.

The Royal Tutor ❸

Higasa Akai

Translation: Amanda Haley • Lettering: Erin Hickman

THE ROYAL TUTOR Vol. 3 ©2015 Higasa Akai/SQUARE ENIX CO., LTD. First published in Japan in 2015 by SQUARE ENIX CO., LTD. English translation rights arranged with SQUARE ENIX CO., LTD. and Yen Press, LLC through Tuttle-Mori Agency, Inc., Tokyo.

English translation ©2015 by SQUARE ENIX CO., LTD.

Yen Press
1290 Avenue of the Americas
New York, NY 10104

Visit us at yenpress.com
facebook.com/yenpress
twitter.com/yenpress
yenpress.tumblr.com
instagram.com/yenpress

First Yen Press Print Edition: September 2017
Originally published as an eBook in September 2015 by Yen Press.

Yen Press is an imprint of Yen Press, LLC.
The Yen Press name and logo are trademarks of Yen Press, LLC.

The publisher is not responsible for websites (or their content) that are not owned by the publisher.

Library of Congress Control Number: 2017938422

ISBN: 978-0-316-44100-1 (paperback)

10 9 8 7 6 5 4 3 2 1

BVG

Printed in the United States of America